THE LONG BALL

*The Summer of '75 —
Spaceman, Catfish, Charlie Hustle, and
the Greatest World Series Ever Played*

Tom Adelman

Little, Brown and Company

BOSTON   NEW YORK   LONDON

First Edition

The quotation that appears as the epigraph is from
Crash: The Life and Times of Dick Allen by Dick Allen and Tim Whitaker.
Copyright © 1989 by Richard Allen and Timothy Whitaker.
Used by kind permission of Tim Whitaker. All rights reserved.

Library of Congress Cataloging-in-Publication Data

Adelman, Tom.
    The long ball : the summer of '75 — Spaceman, Catfish, Charlie Hustle, and the greatest World Series ever played / Tom Adelman. — 1st ed.
        p. cm.
    Includes index.
    ISBN 0-316-06899-3
        1. World Series (Baseball) (1975) 2. Boston Red Sox (Baseball team) 3. Cincinnati Reds (Baseball team) I. Title.
    GV878.4 .A32 2003
    796.357'646 — dc21   2002031281

10 9 8 7 6 5 4 3 2 1

Q-FF

Book design by Robert G. Lowe

Printed in the United States of America

For my dad, Jack Adelman, who taught me
to watch the game until the very end

And for Hannah

The freer you make baseball in every respect, the better the game's going to be. We saw that with Jackie Robinson. Jackie liberated the game. He was free. Free to steal home. Free to turn a single into a double. Free to play his game with a sense of danger and urgency. That same sense of freedom should apply to free agency. If baseball owners would concentrate on making their franchises exciting and happy places, instead of work camps where guys punch in and out, ballplayers would fight to stay.

— Dick Allen

CONTENTS

Part One — THE PRESEASON   1

Part Two — THE SEASON'S FIRST HALF   57

Part Three — THE ALL-STAR BREAK   113

Part Four — THE SEASON'S SECOND HALF   125

Part Five — THE POSTSEASON   167

CONCLUSION   340

NOTES   345

SELECTED BIBLIOGRAPHY   355

ACKNOWLEDGMENTS   359

INDEX   361

PART ONE

THE PRESEASON

ONE

AT EIGHTEEN MONTHS of age, Carl Yastrzemski drags a tiny baseball bat with him everywhere he goes. A battered Philco floor-cabinet radio blares in the background, broadcasting battles between Allies and Axis, between Red Sox and Yankees, between Ted Williams and Joe DiMaggio.

Sometimes announcers talk to Williams after a game, and in an impatient, authoritative tone, he discusses batting against Lefty Gómez or Rip Sewell. Ted has been advised by two-time Triple Crown–winner Rogers Hornsby, "Get a good ball to hit." Concise yet full of intriguing implications, this nugget is all that passes at the time for strategy in the bigs. Williams studies the snap of his wrists, the flex of his shoulders, his stance and pivot. At the plate, his cleats seek balance in the batter's box as his mind weighs every factor, from the wind and light to the particular tree from which his bat was hewed.

Carl is eight when Ted Williams wins a second Triple Crown. By now, Carl is hitting tennis balls in the backyard while his father pitches. Scouts from the majors start to watch him catch Little League games. The Milwaukee Braves offer him a pitching contract.

Carl refuses. He signs instead with the Boston Red Sox as a short-stop. They make him a second baseman.

When he is twenty, he meets, at last, Williams, his hero. Ted shares what he has learned in a career spent repeating and revising Hornsby's homily. He works vigilantly to articulate the best ways in which a stick-bearing body might move in order to ricochet a pro-pelled ball any prescribed distance. He has this idea of hitting as a kind of science. From Williams, Carl receives four succinct funda-mentals: "Number one, close your stance and back away. Number two, watch the ball. Number three, hit the ball through the middle. Number four, be quick."

Williams has played one side of Boston's Fenway Park outfield since before Carl was born. Carl is strengthened, stabilized, encour-aged by Tom Yawkey, the unassuming millionaire who owns the ball club and ardently adores this big-nosed Polish kid. In 1961 some-one will have to replace the retiring Williams, and Yawkey thinks Carl is the one. It goes okay. Years pass. Boston managers come and go like magazines, one a month, but the fatherly Yawkey remains and his unwavering faith in his left fielder holds constant.

Meanwhile, the Red Sox sign other local ethnic boys with overly syllabic names. The ever-dwindling fans at Fenway shorten the names to paint them on placards, to fit them in their mouths and make them familiar. Yastrzemski becomes "Yaz." Tony Conigliaro, a brash and beautiful Boston boy who homers in his first game at Fen-way — Opening Day 1964 — is promptly dubbed "Tony C." (the last initial becomes necessary to distinguish him from hockey's Tony Esposito, or "Tony O.").

There's also the silent Americo Petrocelli, a shortstop with deli-cate features. To fans he's just "Rico" (to teammates he's "Petro"). When he arrives, he's nothing but a melancholy benchwarmer, too shook-up to be very reliable, until Dick Williams is named Boston's manager. He senses that all Petro needs is confidence, and Williams supplies it.

The year is 1967. Carl glances up and around the field. It dawns on him: this is a new ball club. Something has happened. Nobody from his rookie season remains, though his teammates still dress in the same flannels, the button-front jerseys and belt-loop trousers, the cap with the fancy red B on the bill, their chests saying BOSTON in plain block capital letters just as they had when Ted Williams was a rookie. The view from the Fenway grass and bleachers is the same — indeed, the same as it's been since the stadium was built in 1912. But this is a new ball club, and with a spectacularly invigorated Rico batting behind Tony C., who in turn is batting behind Yaz, the dependably droopy, dreary Red Sox engineer a dramatic turnaround. In 1966 they ended the season twenty-six games out, in ninth place. Now, with Dick Williams at the helm, they beat up the league for the first time in decades. The cheering of baseball in Boston is heard once more. Old fans flock back; new fans descend.

During the pennant stretch, Ted Williams happens to catch a game on TV. He professes deep concern about the way Tony C. hugs the plate. He gets a message through to Conigliaro — *Back off, you're gonna get beaned*. Charming, gorgeous, popular, healthy, strong, and young, Tony laughs off Ted's advice. Instead, on a Friday evening in Boston, August 18, he leans way in. He's watching for a slider on the outside corner. He doesn't see the high, inside fastball. (You rarely see the pitch that comes at your head.) At the last second, Tony flinches. His half-shell batting helmet flips off. Carl, standing on the top step of the dugout, hears "a deafening sound, a sickening sound." Tony feels the baseball penetrate his skull. He imagines it coming out the other side. Rico runs over from the on-deck circle. Tony flails in the dirt beside home plate, barely conscious and bleeding from the ears, nose, and mouth. "It's going to be all right," Rico cries desperately. Tony's jaw is visibly dislocated, the cheek smashed. Immediate hemorrhaging inflates his left eye into a black balloon. "You're going to be fine." Conigliaro is rushed to the hospital. In his stead, a pinch runner is put on first. Rico triples the man home and the Red Sox win, but everyone's thinking of Conigliaro and wondering if he'll live through the night.[1]

Tony does survive, to the surprise and relief of physicians and fans alike, but takes time to recover from his near-death experience on the playing field. He's ravaged by terrible headaches. Boston's 1967 Impossible Dream season drifts on without him. Carl becomes the only Boston player besides Williams to win the Triple Crown. The Red Sox claim the American League pennant in baseball's closest race and tightest finish ever. But with Conigliaro's bad depth perception, Boston must play the World Series without a cleanup hitter. Even so, seven games are required before the richly talented St. Louis Cardinals can claim superiority.

New England prays for Tony C.'s return. He is not just the hometown hero, the local high school star living out big-league dreams. Fenway's close wall in left perfectly complements Tony's punishing, right-handed swing. He is Boston's most natural source of power; but as hard as it is for Tony C. to step back into a batter's box, it's harder still for him to see and hit the ball. Blind spots cloud his vision. He guesses a lot on location and speed. He studies pitchers, learns to read their tendencies. He manages occasionally to get lucky (he clouts sixty round-trippers from 1969–71), but far more often he swings at a pitch and misses by a foot. He makes no excuses, reveals no weakness, claims perfect vision. He's too proud to tell the truth. All he's ever wanted to do is play baseball, but he can't judge fly balls in right field, he can no longer gauge the rotation on a major-league pitch. After endless frustrations and setbacks, in 1971, at age twenty-six, the former golden boy announces his retirement.

He tries this and that, he sings at bars, he travels, he opens a nightclub on the Atlantic shore. He's at loose ends. In 1972 and again in 1974, his old team seems about to win a pennant, but without Conigliaro's clutch hitting, the Red Sox fall short.

He fidgets restlessly, haunted by mirrors, viewing in them the reflection of a ruined romance, shattered dreams, a man destined until recently to be one of the all-time greats. Whenever he thinks about baseball, it makes him sick. His look changes. The smile is more tentative, the hair shaggier, the sideburns long and wide. The boyish features harden. The chocolate-brown eyes develop dark bags. Crags and furrows appear. In October of 1974, he snaps on the television and there's the Dodgers' ace Andy Messersmith pitching in the World Series. Tony can't shake the feeling that he could hit this guy.[2] His body screams for a second chance, but Tony worries he's too old; he's been away too long. He doesn't want to look undignified, a child who won't grow up. He's thirty now. A friend reminds him that Ruth hit two-thirds of his home runs after turning thirty, and Ted Williams — well, he went away for the duration of World War II and came back fine.

Tony decides to attempt another comeback. His eye seems improved. His vision is nearly normal. Once more he doggedly pursues the lost love of his life. He's pure guts. His drive is relentless. He swings bats for months, heavy lead bats or weighted wooden ones, in basements, in batting cages, against pitching machines or indulgent hurlers.[3]

The pitcher Tony saw, Andy Messersmith, is indeed great. Messersmith's twenty victories and six losses gave him the best won-lost percentage this year in the majors. And yet nobody in 1974, not Messersmith, not anybody, throws a baseball better than James Augustus Hunter, a droll, country bumpkin with rock-star clothes, lengthy brown hair, and the nickname of "Catfish." Nearly all of Hunter's victories are complete games; a considerable number are shutouts. He gives up fewer earned runs than anyone else in his league. He isn't overpowering; he just wins a lot. He never seems to wear out. For almost ten years, he's been throwing strikes on the corner of the plate without altering his motion, and when his overhand curve works right, it breaks twice — with the action of both a curve and a slider.

Hunter and his team, the Athletics, are owned by a consummate skinflint and showman named Charles O. Finley. When Finley first saw Hunter, he saw a hayseed in need of a handle. Immediately, Finley conjured up this name — "Catfish" — as well as a back story to lend it hick credibility. He convinced Hunter to play along. Hunter's mother was saddened. She preferred "Jim." Still, she was philosophical about the change. "He could have gotten a worse nickname," she conceded, after some reflection. "If Mr. Finley had known that Jim loves bass fishing, he might have named him 'Big Mouth' instead."[4]

The Athletics hate their owner. They regard Finley as unapologetically exploitative. All of them loathe the distraction of his marketing pranks: the fireworks after home runs, the team mascot, the cabdrivers bringing pitchers in from the bull pen, the use of Miss USA as a batgirl, the miniature zoo beyond the fence in left, the sheep grazing in right, the mechanical rabbit named Harvey who pops up behind home plate with baseballs for the umpire. Through it all, Finley cheats and manipulates and stabs his boys in the back. He assures the players he'll keep the club in the Midwest, encourages them to buy homes and settle down nearby, then abruptly moves the whole operation to Oakland. All over the Bay Area, sports attendance is down — but even that doesn't account for just how few bother to come out to the Athletics' cold and colorless Coliseum (which the team itself calls the "Mausoleum," complaining how the heavy air of despondency hurts their bodies and dispirits their swings). When, despite all of the owner's petty cruelties, the team manages to succeed, Finley hogs every bit of the credit.

After Hunter wins the 1974 Cy Young Award, he receives even better news. An arbitration panel has determined that Finley sought a tax advantage by delaying payments that were due to the pitcher. Hunter's contract with Oakland is declared invalid and Catfish is named baseball's first free agent. "I feel like I got out of jail," Hunter sighs happily.

Of course, no one in baseball is surprised that it is Finley, the bushy-browed bungler, whose shiftiness at contract time led to this. The other owners despise his incessant two-bit hustling, his reckless and rude micromanaging. Finley badgered them into using a designated hitter in the American League, got them to schedule the all-star and World Series games at night. He always wants more action, bigger payoffs. Fed up with the slow pace of the game, Finley suggests using orange baseballs so that sluggers can see them more easily. He recommends that batters earn a walk after three balls. He argues that his purchase of a world-class sprinter as a "designated runner" should win Oakland fifteen more games each season.

Charles Finley strikes even Tom Yawkey as a man with no class, and Yawkey is hardly a snob. Finley simply belongs to no tradition. He is no gentleman. Of all the owners, perhaps only George Steinbrenner of the New York Yankees impresses Tom Yawkey as more crude than Finley — and thankfully, Steinbrenner shouldn't even be around much this year. The Yankee owner has pleaded guilty to a federal felony, having misled law enforcement officials who were investigating his furtive contributions to Nixon's reelection campaign. This scandal recently caused Commissioner Bowie Kuhn to ban him from acting as owner of the Yankees for two seasons. (Kuhn will later reduce Steinbrenner's suspension to just 1975.)

Yawkey knows this pitcher, Jimmy Hunter, very well. He likes him a lot. Though Yawkey is forty-four years older, he and Hunter are in truth very similar — two Carolina boys who like to hunt and fish. He badly wants Hunter to join his ball club and steady his pitching staff.

Yawkey is notorious for his open billfold. He's been the sole owner of the Red Sox since he was Catfish's age. When he bought the club, the press dubbed the team the "Gold Sox." Yawkey's salaries were high and bonuses large. He gave the St. Louis Browns $50,000 for a catcher and a southpaw. He gave the Yankees $100,000 for a pitcher and an infielder. He gave the Athletics $125,000 for Rube Walberg and Max Bishop . . . $150,000 for Jimmie Foxx and Footsie Marcum . . . $75,000 for Doc Cramer and Boob McNair. He bought another pitcher and an outfielder from the Indians, a second infielder from the Yankees, a southpaw from the Cardinals. For a quarter-million, the Washington Senators' Clark Griffith even sold Yawkey his manager/shortstop/son-in-law, Joe Cronin (who had married Mildred Robertson, Griffith's adopted daughter).

And this is the way, to Yawkey's mind, it still should be. If you don't possess enough talent, you deal with another gentleman owner. Perhaps it's quaint, but the seventy-two-year-old Yawkey prefers it that way. Having legal arbitrators invalidate a baseball contract feels wrong; this has never happened before, it sullies the game, and the sudden availability of a Cy Young Award winner (which initially delights Yawkey) comes to trigger an altogether new breed of baseball transaction, far beyond Yawkey's ken, in which no other team will be compensated. It will be, in no way, an exchange of athletes.

It'll be an auction.

There will be no gentlemen involved.

The news of Catfish's release drifts across the major-league landscape and smokes a series of wealthy white men out of their offices in the city.[5] They arrive, as if by migratory instinct, at a seldom-used airport in northeastern North Carolina, where they rent black sedans with leather interiors and drive to the offices of Hunter's attorneys. It's the middle of winter.

These visitors are the proud keepers of baseball's ledgers. They are neither glamorous nor, in any way, memorable. Most of these round-bellied men never played the game, and the negligible careers of those who have — such as Sully (the treasurer of the Boston Red Sox, Haywood Sullivan) or Smoky (the manager of the Los Angeles Dodgers, Walter Alston) — left no lasting impression. The rest are vice presidents or general managers or chairmen of the board or executives in charge of player personnel — deskbound, clean shaven, and infrequently photographed. All of them wear dark suits of a conservative cut and neckties. They squint at the day like rodents brought out into the sun. Their hair is trimmed short in back, parted low on the side, and slickly combed over. Their eyes light up only when drunk.

Each receives an appointment to meet with Hunter's attorneys. As this may be a slow process, the club representatives reserve beds at the town's sole motel, the rustic Tomahawk. At night, they lie on lumpy mattresses in the coarsely furnished rooms, the ice machine purring in the hall as they wrestle with how much to pay for a first-place finish.

For the last three seasons, Hunter has steered a stormy, and at times rudderless, Oakland team to a world championship. Catfish not only has made the A's great but has kept them great for a long time. A baseball dynasty of such prolonged excellence is almost unprecedented. In a century of organized ball, only the Yankees have accomplished such a feat: first under Joe McCarthy, then under Casey Stengel. The Orioles of Earl Weaver have not done it; nor have the Athletics of Connie Mack; nor the Giants of John McGraw or Leo Durocher; nor the Yankees of Ruth, Gehrig, and Lazzeri; nor the Cubs of Tinker, Evers, and Chance; nor the Cards of Musial; nor the Dodgers of Koufax. It is hard to do. Slumps and injuries are inevitable. Three straight times in the seventies, the National League sent strong, deep teams — the Reds, Mets, and Dodgers — and all, playing their hardest, ultimately lost a World Series to Oakland.

The economics are simple. Tickets cost little, players make little, and few noncontenders turn a profit. Whoever signs Hunter receives the guarantee of twenty victories. Only the Astros, Angels, and Padres missed first by more than twenty games last year.

Over the next few weeks, each delegation is welcomed, separately, into a small, drab room in the back of the lawyers' offices and seated at a brown table. Cups of stale coffee are served from an unplugged percolator. A secretary is taking notes. Hunter is there, mustache thick, hair down to the collar of his flower-print shirt, a plug of Red Man in his cheek. His chewing keeps the room smelling of baseball.

The Yankees offer $1.5 million for five years, the Mets raise it to $2 million, the Padres to $3 million.

Hunter and his attorneys struggle to keep their jaws from dropping. The sums under discussion confound them. They had no idea that a simple ballplayer could earn so much. Players were making, on the average, $43,000 a year. To ask for a million was incomprehensible. After all, it's still the same game as Little League — yes, the ball travels faster, the gloves are bigger, the bats are heavier, but it is still about hitting the cutoff man, avoiding the double play, moving the man over, stealing the signs, knowing when to bunt; grass, dirt, afternoon. The speed and scope of play may have increased since elementary school, but the fundamentals are the same.

The Rangers propose a huge farm annuity, $150,000 a year for three years, plus $30,000 a year for fifteen years.

The Royals submit a bid of $825,000 for six years, a farm-equipment purchase option, $5,000 per year per child for college, plus $50,000 a year for life.

With features carefully arranged to hide their astonishment, Hunter's attorneys jot down the offers on legal pads and take notes. Catfish intently studies each visitor, chewing and saying little. As he watches these lifeless men, his poker face occasionally dissolves. He chuckles behind his mustache to hear how each of the sixteen teams with whom he is meeting is very near to winning a championship — at least, according to each club's executives. Poor showings in the past have been remedied, every need has been addressed, the champagne is on ice, and the World Series rings are being sized.

Catfish shakes them off, but he has no sooner thrown out the last pitch than a new club steps in: the Red Sox, their delegation led by the pasty, balding executive vice president, Dick O'Connell.

O'Connell and Hunter shake hands, take each other's measurements. An overhead light buzzes. Catfish's features suddenly soften. A goofy grin breaks through his mustache. He bursts into Li'l Abner–speak, regales the room with country-flavored praise for Tom Yawkey. In 1966 the Red Sox owner regularly visited Hunter after his emergency appendectomy in Boston. "A good man," drawls Catfish. "*Real* good man."

Although Hunter seems slow and unsophisticated, O'Connell knows that he is not, for that is the mistaken assumption shared by most major-league batters. They allow themselves to be set up by Catfish's easy motion, by the way he conceals the ball behind his glove and left knee, his long stride, his three-quarter delivery. His is the very definition of a crafty manner.

O'Connell looks calmly at Catfish. "Mr. Yawkey is not like any other owner out there." He addresses the beguiling pitcher in earnest, direct language. "Mr. Yawkey is not in baseball to make a buck. He is not in baseball to feed his ego. The reason he is in baseball is: he loves the game. When he was younger, you know, and even up until a few years ago, he used to work out with the team, take batting practice with the boys before the game. He still closes down the park some days, puts on spikes, he puts on baseball pants and a sweatshirt, and he gets Vince Orlando — you know Vince? — to pitch so he can hit line drives off the wall in left.[6] You should talk to the guys on the club, Cat. They will swear by him."

One of Hunter's lawyers coughs and holds high an assemblage of stapled notes. "Well, we did receive a telegram from Ted Williams. An affidavit of sorts."

"Yes. He's been notified of Mr. Yawkey's desire to have Catfish join our squad. I hope that's all right."

"Of course. It's quite a ringing endorsement. 'Mr. Yawkey has the most humility of any person I've ever known.'"

"Ah, that's . . . that's Ted."

"Although here . . ." The lawyer shuffles between pages. He chuckles. "Well, it's a bit amusing. On this here, it says, 'Mr. Yawkey is soft as a grapefruit.' And on this over here, it says, 'He has a heart the size of a watermelon.'"

O'Connell grins.

The older lawyer knits his brow, volunteers an opinion. "That man certainly has great respect for fruit."

"Ted Williams," says O'Connell, "can do no wrong in the eyes of Mr. Tom Yawkey. I remember — do you remember? — when the ASPCA made a big stink because Ted was shooting at the starlings that roosted on the left-field fence. Mr. Yawkey defended him."

From above the Styrofoam rim of his improvised spittoon, Hunter's eyes twinkle mischievously. "What gauge was the man usin'?" Catfish asks. "Can y'recall?"

"Uh, no. Unfortunately. But my point is, Mr. Yawkey never criticizes his players. And if he has one credo, well, it is a demand for loyalty, because he is always so ready to give it. There is no telling how much money he spends aiding players or former players in time of illness or financial distress. His good deeds are done without fanfare. When a veteran player is released, Mr. Yawkey adds him to the Red Sox payroll in some other capacity. And it will always be that way. The managers arrive and depart, the clubhouse men, the public relations directors, even, I dare say, the general managers, but the owner is always the same."

The air in the room grows stale, so the executive vice president rises. The others in his delegation follow suit. They head to the door. On the way out, O'Connell unexpectedly whirls around. "You pitch well in Fenway," he reminds Hunter. "The mound suits you. You're someone who needs good execution behind you and we've got ourselves a fine set of fielders. Rooster. Rico."

"A pitcher gives up lotsa home runs in y'park."

"A fair amount, yes. Not a lot. Far fewer than in Detroit. Fewer than in Cleveland. In fact, more home runs are hit in Yankee Stadium every year than at Fenway."

"That a fact?"

"Indeed."

Yet, Hunter thinks, *with all that money, Yawkey ain't been able to buy no championship* — in two World Series, Boston failed to defeat St. Louis by one game. Are his Red Sox *too* pampered, like a well-fed dog that won't hunt?

As Christmas passes in North Carolina and temperatures drop, the bids continue to rise. Hunter's lawyers are most delighted by the offer presented by the Dodgers: $3,000,000 for two years, divided up in whatever way they like.

In private, Hunter shakes his head. "I don't care to go to the Dodgers," he tells his representatives. He picked up a divisive vibe from the team during the World Series two months ago, more than the usual glimpse of cliques and factions, the hippies like Messersmith, the wusses like first baseman Steve Garvey, a sour chemistry behind all that talk of bleeding Dodger blue.[7] "But," Catfish finally reveals, after weeks of pondering options, "I'd really like to play for the Yankees. If I can get near or the same amount of money as the other clubs, that's who I want to sign with." Exasperated by the abrupt change of direction, Hunter's attorneys roll their eyes. He smiles. "See what you can work out."

So it is, on a late-December day lightly dusted with snow, that Hunter comes to terms with New York, despite deep reservations about working for Steinbrenner ("Couldn't be any worse than working for Finley," a friend points out), and despite the fact that the Yankees haven't won a World Series since firing Casey Stengel in 1960. This is nonetheless a promising team that plays in a pitcher's park, against hitters Catfish already knows. They have a heritage of cunning hurlers (Lefty Gómez, Whitey Ford, Waite Hoyt), the best catcher in the American League (Thurman Munson), two nineteen-game winners (Pat Dobson and Doc Medich), and a bull-pen ace, Sparky Lyle, with a hundred saves in three seasons. Their second-place finish in 1974 was the closest the Yankees had come to a pennant in ten years, but the frustration of not winning everything apparently sent them to the trading post. They came back with Bobby Bonds, fledgling superstar, to be positioned in the outfield with Elliott Maddox, Roy White, and Lou Piniella while Chris Chambliss at first and Graig Nettles at third would anchor the infield.

Dick O'Connell places a telephone call to Tom Yawkey on the last day of the year.

"Sir, I wanted you to know that the Yankees have a press conference scheduled for eight fifteen tonight."

Yawkey grunts in acknowledgment.

"It's to be held at their offices in New York."

Another grunt.

"I think you know what this is about."

"Jimmy Hunter."

"His deal will be one hundred thousand a year for five years, half of it deferred."

Yawkey is not the least bit startled by the figures. "That all?"

"No. Fifty-three thousand, four hundred sixty-two dollars and sixty-seven cents a year in insurance annuities for ten years; a one-hundred-thousand-dollar signing bonus; fifteen years at one hundred thousand per year until nineteen ninety-four; twenty-five-thousand-dollar college endowments for his children; two hundred thousand in attorney fees; plus a brand new Buick every year for five years."

"All right."

"Are you okay, Mr. Yawkey?"

"Sure, Dick. Fine, fine. Well, at least he didn't sign with the hamburger king." Yawkey had been worried about Ray Kroc, founder of McDonald's and owner of the San Diego Padres.

"That's right."

"Well. You still say that Tony C. is gonna come back to us?"

"He asked if he could attend training camp with us this spring and I told him 'of course.'"

"Yes . . ." There is a pause on Yawkey's end. "Ah, damn."

"Yes, sir." Something tells O'Connell that the owner is still thinking about Hunter. "I'm truly sorry we didn't get Catfish for you, sir."

"Oh . . . I know, Dick. You tried, you tried. You know, I don't know whether I want to stay in baseball much longer, Dick. I'm disturbed at what's going on. That players' strike made me stop and . . . and think what the future holds for this game . . ."

"I know, sir."

"That Marvin Miller keeps saying all owners are SOBs and that really bothers me. I don't think my players feel that way about me."

"Of course they don't, sir."

"At least, they never said so to my face."

"I think your players have great fondness for you, sir."

"Thank you, Dick."

"Have a good afternoon, sir."

That evening at his forty-thousand-acre game preserve, Tom Yawkey is down in the kitchen with his press steward, Tommy McCarthy, and his colored help. It's New Year's Eve. They've popped open cans of beer and gathered around the transistor radio, which is set up on the shelf above the cutting board. The radio provides them with live coverage of a press conference in Manhattan.

"I always wanted to be a Yankee," Jimmy Hunter is responding cheerily to a reporter's question at the press conference. "I remember I used to get chills just walking into Yankee Stadium. Now there's going to be a new Yankee Stadium. With a natural grass surface I'll be proud to be a part of it. All that great tradition."

Yawkey spins angrily. His chest hurts. Why, of all teams, did Jimmy choose the Yankees? Here Yawkey thought he'd created a place that would attract guys like Jimmy: guys who drive Ford pickups with a dog pen in the back — Tarheels.

Yawkey stalks out through the servants' entrance. His blue eyes burn like sapphires and then cool into something more sorrowful. He smokes a cigarette and grievously studies the night. Where did he go wrong? Shouldn't a fellow like Jimmy Hunter feel he belongs? Certainly it wasn't the money. Yawkey had okayed a bid for four million with the treasurer, Harrington.

Only twice during Yawkey's generous span of ownership have the Red Sox managed to win the American League championship. In 1948 his boys tied for the AL pennant, lost it in a single play-off game; in 1949 they lost first place on the last day of the season; in 1972 they lost the division by half a game; and then this last year, 1974, the seven-game lead on August 23 just vanished and they finished the season in third. . . .

Time is running out. His boys will never win him a world championship. Why aren't today's great players welcoming a chance to play for Boston? Yawkey aches to blame it on the president of the players' union, Marvin Miller. . . .

Everybody knows that Yawkey has 200 million bucks.

Nobody yet knows he has leukemia.

TWO

BASEBALL LIMPS INTO 1975, obviously hurting. Revenue is down, bickering is up. In Pittsburgh and Oakland, where the teams are outstanding, the fans prefer football. The patrons in Detroit boycott Tiger Stadium, still feeling betrayed at the abrupt manner in which Billy Martin, their club's excitable and highly successful manager, was fired two seasons earlier. The Giants and Expos and Twins have scant attendance; the Astros and White Sox and Braves simply have no money. Washington, D.C., and Seattle possess many baseball enthusiasts but no team; each has lost a franchise to Minnesota. Baltimore is a famously great baseball town, but now even the owner of the Orioles wants out.

Crowds will still turn out to watch contenders in New York, Boston, Cleveland, and Milwaukee, but their division, the American League East, has become stagnant and weak, without many winners, while the AL West's Oakland, despite its lousy attendance figures, dominates the game.

The times everywhere are cool and groovy while the purveyors of the national pastime remain square and clueless. The sportswriters can't understand the athletes, their personalities and flamboyant styles, their desire for money.

Controversial innovations are rampant. The American League owners, desperate to revive the offensive allure of the sport, are now allowing a player to bat in place of the pitcher while the National League owners, wanting to quicken the game's pace, increasingly cover their fields with synthetic grass. The dramatic introductions of AstroTurf and the designated hitter share one goal: to bring back the fan. These changes, however, are not enough. Baseball has grown stale, having not experienced a revolution since the late forties, when — against the wishes of the majority of owners — Jackie Robinson brought the style and spectators of the Negro Leagues into the ballparks of the major leagues. Another revolution is imminent. Again, it will go against the wishes of the majority of owners. It begins January 1, 1975, with Catfish Hunter's signing, and culminates late the same year, when pitchers Andy Messersmith and Dave McNally ask the neutral arbitrator on baseball's grievance board to review their contracts.

To Bowie Kuhn, this revolution means the death of his beloved sport. Kuhn compares 1975 to 1860, the last year in which slavery was legal in the United States. The neutral arbitrator in the Messersmith-McNally case, Peter Seitz, sides with the players' union, ruling that baseball's standard language is insufficient to keep players perpetually reserved by their teams. As a consequence, ballplayers are afforded a right already held by every other American laborer: the ability to negotiate for a competitive wage by accepting bids from a range of employers. Although Seitz pointedly stresses that he is not Lincoln freeing the slaves, Kuhn feels otherwise. "As the Civil War doomed the Old South," Kuhn will lament in his memoirs, pressing the analogy, "the Messersmith-McNally decision and the coming of free agency doomed the old . . . ownerships of baseball."

Kuhn sympathizes with the slave owners, who were blindsided, then bankrupted, by this new concept of liberty. These are the elder club owners in whose historic company he revels — Tom Yawkey,

Chicago's Phil Wrigley, San Francisco's Horace Stoneham — men who've run the game for almost half a century. Kuhn imagines himself to be an activist in their presence, a consensus-building moderate within the rebel camp; he acknowledges that free agency has to come, but he wants it to spread gradually, preserving the traditional players in the game, and preventing a "new game" of "high-stakes poker, a game most were not prepared to play." His vision of casual reformation is frustrated by Messersmith and McNally. After 1975, Kuhn feels, the best part of baseball is gone.

In truth, the game has been slipping from Bowie Kuhn's grasp the entire time he's been commissioner. His tenure began in 1969, the same year the St. Louis Cardinals tried to send Curt Flood and three other players to Philadelphia in exchange for Dick Allen and three Phillies. Flood was the best outfielder in the game, a perennial .300 hitter. He didn't want to go. Flood feared Philadelphia, which he called "that northernmost southern city," a city that behaved despicably toward Allen, its greatest ballplayer, pelting him on the field with garbage, taunts, and racial epithets — for Allen, like Flood, was black. And Flood dearly loved St. Louis, where most of his friends and family lived, and where he ran a successful business in portrait painting on the side. He'd been a Cardinal since 1958. If he was forced to wear another uniform, Flood believed that at least the colors should be of his choosing.

Flood refused the trade. "I do not feel that I am a piece of property," he wrote the commissioner. Kuhn read this, sighing, and shrugged. *What does that have to do with anything?* The two men went to court. Flood wanted baseball's longtime immunity from antitrust legislation to be struck down so that a player might be freed from helpless fealty to his team, a fealty spelled out in the contract of every major-league player as a series of provisions collectively termed "the reserve clause." Kuhn countered that this reserve system maintained honesty between clubs and players, and that without it, the game had no integrity.

In the early seventies, *Flood* v. *Kuhn* sprinted through the district court, the appellate court, and the Supreme Court. Each time Curt Flood lost and Bowie Kuhn won. Flood, a proud and sensitive man who had twice won the World Series with St. Louis, could not stand it. He fled. He was spotted in 1974 on the Spanish island of Majorca, running a bar for American sailors. He disappeared from the island soon after, hauling along his trophies and his clippings and a substantial debt — and his girlfriend, and her teenage son. The three of them slipped clandestinely into Andorra. Flood went unrecognized. Through 1975 they rented a room above a pizzeria owned by a British subject. Because of Flood's skin color, Andorran authorities refused to grant him a work permit. He could only take menial jobs. He frequently voiced regret over taking a stand against baseball. He was liked by the people of Andorra, although everyone remarked on his extreme alcoholism. A snapshot of Curt got taped up behind the bar of Nelson's Tavern in Andorra, with a caption that read "Super Hermit."[1]

And what of Dick Allen, the other big name in the Flood trade? Allen obediently reported to the Cardinals, delighted to be going from one of baseball's worst organizations to one of the best. In St. Louis, he found a new kind of fan: learned, watchful, appreciative. He loved being a Cardinal. The feeling was not mutual. He was traded after only one year. For reasons that escaped him, Allen kept getting called "difficult." He next became property of the Dodgers. This also seemed a happy prospect. Growing up, he'd been a Dodger fan. He got goose bumps "just putting on the Jackie Robinson blue-and-white threads." But the general manager declared Allen's "personality" to be "a travesty to the spirit of the Dodgers," so again, after a single season, without being told why, he was sent packing. This was 1972. Now he was in the American League, playing for the Chicago White Sox. He hit .308 and led the league in home runs, walks, runs batted in, and slugging percentage. He was named the AL's Most Valuable Player, but he was still being branded a badass, too independent and hard to handle, and so, after the 1974 season, he was again traded, this time to Atlanta.

At last, like Flood, Dick Allen said no. He would not go down south. He had already served his time there, as a frightened teenager playing in the Phillies' new triple-A franchise in Little Rock, the first black to play professional baseball in the state of Arkansas. He'd been received then with placards: NIGGER GO HOME. Threatening notes had been taped to the clubhouse door, left on the windshield of his car, sent in the mail. DON'T COME BACK AGAIN NIGGER.

Allen refused to accept the trade.

At the time, few skilled players were ever traded. A veteran was as valuable a local institution as the ballpark itself. He lived year-round in the town where he worked, exerting a quiet pull on the community. Willie Stargell had been in Pittsburgh since 1962, and his resolute dignity helped better not just the Pirate organization but the whole city; so too with Boston's Carl Yastrzemski and Cincinnati's Pete Rose. To see them in a different uniform would be to barely recognize them. To lose them to another team was inconceivable. Only half-talents changed teams, or men branded as troublemakers — men such as Dick Allen.

After 1975, all will be different. The game will be saved, the wealth more equitably distributed, and the meaning of the uniform changed forever.

THREE

ONE AFTERNOON IN 1955, in the town of Fort Worth, George Anderson (a so-so fielder with no bat to speak of and an exceedingly short fuse) charges yet another umpire. "The sparks are flying tonight!" exclaims the radio broadcaster, who's a bit exasperated and quite parched. "Count on this, uh —" and here the perspiring announcer wilts for an instant before audibly gulping a beverage — "this *Sparky* fella to argue any call on behalf of his teammates!"

The name sticks, and Sparky Anderson takes his new tag seriously, growing a mite proud of his way with spit and vinegar. Initially, he seems almost in pursuit of Casey Stengel's early record for being thrown out of the most professional baseball games, but then he mellows, becomes instead a great manager, a salesman of the game. By his midthirties, Sparky is an old-fashioned, voluble personality. He even starts to resemble the eighty-year-old Stengel.

The ejection record stays on Casey's mind. He recalls it in 1967, while dedicating Stengel Field in Glendale, California. Casey tells the crowd, "I feel greatly honored to have a ballpark named after me, especially since I've been throwed out of so many."

Casey's old friend from the 1935 Dodgers, Rod Dedeaux — who runs the USC baseball program but also, when school's out, manages a semipro team — commences to use Stengel Field as his home park in the summer. Casey, who lives close by, likes to attend their games. Rod frequently introduces Stengel to his young players, who grow tongue-tied as the great man rumbles at them to always keep their eyes on a fly ball, never to look where they're running, because they got groundskeepers to see that there's no ditches in this park. Invariably, the solemn youths nod at the sage advice. Casey winks broadly at Dedeaux behind their backs.

One evening, Dedeaux brings over a sixteen-year-old with dark-brown hair. Casey is seated in the wooden bleachers, intently leaning his chin atop his walking cane, as a child does with a baseball bat. Dedeaux introduces Fred Lynn to Stengel as "my left-handed pitching star." He has a lively fastball, a good change-up, a good curve, fine control, a good pick-off move, he runs fast and hits well. Stengel casts his blue eyes upon this graceful figure and doesn't say a word. He merely bows his head in deep respect, and shakes Lynn's hand; this time Casey knows better than to wink at Dedeaux.

By 1975 Casey Stengel no longer sleeps through the night.[1] If a game can be found, he might listen, perhaps while drowsing against a memorabilia-crammed cabinet in the study. Perhaps there is a wooden milking stool. He may sit on that, or sprawl upon a divan; regardless, if Stengel is awake, he is talking. Increasingly, he ducks down the densely populated corridors of his mind to reminisce with past friends, mostly dead.

My guy, I tell ya, there ain't nothing he don't think he can do; my guy makes the pivot, he executes good, the Oakland guy, the skinny fella, it's the infielder I mean, my holler guy, he's been such a soldier, good soldiering for me, this fella with the nose.

The current subject is Billy Martin. Perhaps this is initiated by hearing on the nightly news that Martin has re-upped to skipper the Texas Rangers; perhaps it is the telephone call Stengel receives from a researcher at *Sports Illustrated*, who is in the process of fact checking their Billy Martin cover story. Whatever the source, whoever has roused him, Casey is alone now, but the recollections still topple out in a torrent.

Martin was in the military service during 1954, when Stengel's Yankees lost their first pennant. *My guy commences to in fact be a soldier when that year I drop my first one and I'm without a holler guy so I have less surprise maybe than most.*

Casey and his mangled syntax have been stuck in the public ear since he was twenty-three. Wherever baseball sent him, Stengel won over the fans and the newspapers — first as a clutch hitter for Wilbert Robinson's Dodgers and then for John McGraw's Giants, later as manager of the Toledo Mud Hens, the Brooklyn Dodgers, the Boston Bees, the Oakland Oaks, the Milwaukee Millers, the unbeatable Yankees, and the hapless Mets.

Now, our Mr. Weiss — George Weiss, general manager, New York Yankees, 1947–60 — *he wants me to tell my guy he's got himself traded, which is a fact at this very minute, but oh . . .*

His hair a-fright, his house a-shambles, Stengel is preoccupied with employing baseball's order to straighten out his mind. The game is mathematically precise. It is counted in threes: three strikes, three outs, three bases, three outfielders, three-times-three innings, three thirty-foot steps between each base. When he looks back on his life, what does he see? Splintered bats, missed signs, force-outs, blurred chalk, smeared lines, and mushy baseballs, black with licorice-spit and tobacco. "I used to chase the balls Babe Ruth hit" is how he summarizes it at his Hall of Fame induction.

He is forgetting things. This weighs heavily on him. Still, he remembers the contributions of Billy Martin with gratitude and reverence. *When Brooklyn had the bases loaded in the end of the championships, when I put in the relief pitcher, which the relief for me was left-handed and the Dodger Stadium at Ebbets Field with that short left field, I tell ya, this raised eyebrows.*

In the 1952 World Series, Casey gambled — with game seven

on the line — by bringing in little-used lefty Bob Kuzava to retire Duke Snider and Jackie Robinson.

The sun was no good all over the right side of the infield, the glare, and the wind — oh, the wind was gutsy. He means *gusty. Oh. Oh! But my left-hander makes Duke pop the ball up like he did, and then Robi'son . . .*

With two outs, Jackie Robinson drove a ball high against the wind. *When my guy alone tracks Robi'son's hit, none of them other road apples can even make out the ball.* Billy Martin was positioned deep at short. *He runs all the way, it's tremendous, he's out on the outfield grass, he comes in, and in, running — when you see the motion pictures, really, the jaw drops — my guy passes the mound, keeps running, and he's almost to home plate when he catches it down around here.* Casey motions to indicate knee level.

Saves the game. This was Casey's fourth straight world championship.

The hardest thing Stengel ever had to do was let go of Billy Martin, his best soldier. Weiss felt the hard-drinking, light-hitting Martin was a bad influence on his stars, particularly Whitey Ford and Mickey Mantle. In 1957, despite a preponderance of eyewitness testimony to the contrary, the GM scapegoated Billy for a brawl at New York's highly visible Copacabana Club. Weiss forced Stengel to send Martin away to the small venue of Kansas City, which ironically was Casey's hometown (and the source of his nickname, for he was first called "K. C. Stengel"). The GM gloated, but the manager and the player both wept, and Billy never forgave Casey for siding with Weiss against him.

Like Tom Yawkey, after a life in baseball, Casey Stengel has no sons. Yawkey comforts himself with surrogates — Ted Williams, Carl Yastrzemski. Casey has Billy Martin and Mickey Mantle . . . or he had them, once.

Just now, Billy Martin is at a spring training camp in Pompano Beach, Florida, drilling his Texas Rangers in fundamentals. He coordinates a regimented practice over two fields. Each man takes a turn at the plate and sees nine pitches. The first pitch represents a hit-and-run situation. The batter has to hit the ball to right field. On the second pitch, the batter moves the runner over to third. He hits a sacrifice fly on the third pitch. The fourth pitch is a suicide squeeze, and on the fifth pitch, the catcher calls for a pitchout so that the players can practice their appropriate positions. The batter swings away on the next four pitches and then becomes a runner.

Elsewhere, bunting is practiced. Fielders work on relays, run-downs, pickoffs. Over and over, grounders get hit to the first base-man, and the pitcher runs to cover the bag.

Billy watches it with impatience, seething, wishing occasionally that these dainty boys might break into some cold-blooded game from when he was a kid, like Elephant. Few in his neighborhood could afford baseball gloves. Instead, a team of ten guys lined up, locked arms, and ran hard at another team of ten guys. If anyone broke the line, or fell down, the other team won and got to jump on you repeat-edly. Black eyes, broken bones, bruises — that was Elephant.

Billy grew up essentially on a city playground, with no father, mostly broke. It was a neighborhood on the edge of Oakland, and the children were poor and always bored, so they picked fights with one another or with the Navy recruits who came around looking for trouble. Billy never started a fight, but he never backed down, and he never lost. He didn't have a knife or a chain; no one did, because those things cost money. Billy just had his fists. He could hit like a truck. He never went down.

But then someone gave him a mitt, and he fell head over heels in love with baseball.

While Martin glares at his Rangers, back in Oakland's Bushrod Park — where Billy used to play and where both Frank Robinson and Curt Flood later played — a remarkable teenager named Rickey Henderson is found.[2] Like Billy Martin, Rickey is a little guy who works hard, and he's growing up like Billy Martin did, without a dad or much in the way of comfort, and always getting in a lotta trouble, but madly loving his momma, Bobbie, all the while.

Bobbie raises Rickey alongside six other children. A big-boned kid, Rickey's got a lot of Bobbie in his face, his complexion, his thinking, his strength. He has tremendous energy.

Every time Rickey Henderson accomplishes something on the ball field, a nice woman from school, Mrs. Tommie Wilkerson, gives him a quarter. One day, he gets five hits and steals five bases and walks away with $2.50, enough to buy hamburgers for a week. Rickey is in heaven. He's good at everything he tries, including dice. ("If you didn't get nothing else from your father," Bobbie tells him, "you got his gambling habit.") Rickey's best buddy is Louis Burrell. The two of them often shoot dice at Bushrod while Louis's brother Stanley tags along, singing, dancing, carrying a radio, listening to music.

Whenever there's an event at the Oakland Coliseum, this little Burrell, Stanley, goes off and performs in the parking lot. He imitates James Brown's dance moves. People toss him bills.

Before some meaningless preseason matchup, the owner of the Oakland A's, Charles Finley, happens to catch Stanley's act. Finley appreciates it. He invites Stanley inside and seats him in the owner's private box. Very quickly, in just a matter of weeks, Stanley becomes the owner's trusted assistant. Finley has Stanley keep an eye on the clubhouse. Stanley is just a youngster, but the owner gives him more and more responsibilities. The Oakland players adopt Stanley. They think he resembles Henry Aaron, so they start calling him "Hammer."

Finley is cheap. The owner and Stanley essentially compose the team's entire front-office staff because Finley is disinclined from expanding the payroll. This has a curious side effect. His players fight among themselves, as twenty-five strong men are apt to do when spending eight months a year locked together in close quarters, but lacking the requisite media managers and press go-betweens, the A's find that word of their battles leaks out. Though no more contentious than other teams, they become known as "The Swinging, Brawling A's."

Stanley rarely sees Finley in person. The owner travels. He phones from wherever he is, always telling Stanley to make manager Alvin Dark *do things.* If there's been a miscue on the field, Finley tells Stanley to have the player removed. If Finley hears that his pinch runners are not being deployed enough, he asks Stanley to get them played. Stanley sits in the owner's private box, where the phone rings constantly with Finley barking orders. Dark feels helpless to refuse, and so must implement a game strategy that he can neither defend nor predict. This intrusiveness creates a void. The team often fails to understand the objective.

Their emotional captain, third baseman Sal Bando, opportunely fills this gap in leadership. On the field, Bando is keenly aware of the levels on which baseball is played. He studies the opposition. He looks after the team. He alerts fielders to the hitters' tendencies, visits the mound and suggests ways to work the situation. He serves as an example. He is steady at the plate, doing his job in quiet ways; he sacrifices the man over, and he gives himself up so the team advances. He carries the respect of his teammates. He is, undeniably, the heart of the Oakland A's and the cause of their success, but this cannot be meaningfully represented by statistics, and so, year after year, Charlie Finley points out his low batting average and gets away with paying Bando as little as possible.

Stanley Burrell generally enjoys a rapport with Mr. Finley. Stanley loves the players and their nickname for him. Later, he will outgrow the job, but he'll never outgrow the nickname. In the years to come, when Stanley Burrell launches a musical career, he'll be known as "MC Hammer."

FOUR

On their first date, Johnny Bench takes Vickie Chesser to Las Vegas.[1] It's New Year's Eve, absolute madness. At the MGM Grand, everything's flashing, glistening, whirring, clattering — noisemakers and shiny hats, chimes and bells, yells and sequins. Among it all, Bench and Vickie calmly play twenty-one at a gaming table. Though young, Bench is nearly bald and oddly proportioned in person. His hands are gigantic and his head resembles that of Charlie Brown. Vickie is seated on a stool beside him, her deep green eyes radiant. Her silky hair is shoulder length, feathered, wavy, and blond. She applies lip gloss to her pink, smooth lips with a finger. She is often recognized for starring in a toothpaste commercial, by people who identify her as the "Ultra Brite smile."

It's an odd first date, but things are on a fast track. They've been talking marriage since the first phone call, a few days earlier, when a friend gave John the phone number. "Give her a call, old boy," the friend recommended. "Vickie Chesser, lives in Manhattan, a swinging lady."

Who is this woman? Bench telephoned business friends in Dayton, who informed him Ms. Chesser was represented by the prestigious Wilhelmina Agency and that each year she earned, as a model, in the neighborhood of $100,000. Bench was shown Vickie's head shot in *Fashion 70* — a twenty-five-year-old honey blonde; a heritage of Swedish, Irish, and Cherokee Indian; a face of flawless beauty. She had been queen of her home state's tercentennial and Miss South Carolina in 1970, as well as first runner-up in the Miss USA pageant.

Bench dialed the number, introduced himself, then matter-of-factly asked Vickie to join him in Las Vegas for New Year's Eve.

"You're bananas!" she said. She recognized the name, she realized that Bench was a famous athlete, but she didn't know anything else about him. "We haven't even met. It might be a drag."

"Look, you'll have your plane ticket and your room, and if we don't hit it off, you go your way and I'll go mine. What do you have to lose?"

"Nope."

Come to Cincinnati in a few days, Bench next compromised, for the wedding of Bill and Mercedes — Bill being the program director of a radio station and a friend of Bench's. John's will was strong. "If you like it, we'll go on to Las Vegas for New Year's."

Vickie relented. "I guess I'm as crazy as you are," she sighed. "Okay."

"Now, the airport. I'll pick you up there. It's in Kentucky, but don't you worry. It's still the Cincinnati airport."

"How will I recognize you?"

"I look a lot like Johnny Bench."

"And what does Johnny Bench look like?"

"Never seen me?"

"Nope."

"Not even a picture?"

"Nope."

"I'm, uh . . . more like a football player than a baseball player, but . . . don't you worry, I'll recognize you."

She hung up, oddly put off by his self-assuredness. *I have always made my own decisions,* she thought, *and here is somebody who can make them for me. Is that something I want?*

Vickie asked about Bench. Friends identified him as the prized prince of baseball; they saw him a lot on television shows — rich, solid, famous, single, six foot one, a bit bland. At this point, none of Vickie's friends thought to point out the ominous dark cloud that hovered over John: the bus crash he barely survived in high school, the near-cancer he developed in 1972, the family in frail health — a mother in the hospital for fourteen weeks, his father before that, his brother and sister quite ill.

She threw some things into a suitcase with no idea that this trip would change her life. She flew off, met this Johnny Bench, and immediately liked him. He was interested in so many more things than most men — and they had so much in common! They were earthy, just a couple of old local yokels, and both Southern Baptists (all of Vickie's other men had been Jewish or Catholic). In the car, leaving the airport, Bench sang a country-and-western song. "There's not one thing in this world worth a single dime," he crooned, " 'cept old dogs, children, and watermelon wine." Then he gave Vickie a peck on the cheek and showed her Cincinnati. Afterward, naturally, they continued on to Las Vegas with Bill and Mercedes, John's parents, and other friends from the wedding.

They kiss for the first time, really, in Las Vegas.

Vickie has never been in love before. "I've never even been in *like*," she admits. "My mother always tells me not to look so hard that I won't find him, but I always tell her I'm not going to settle for second best."

Calmly and quietly, Bench talks to Vickie of his difficulty in maintaining a wholesome image. He confesses that he has a girl in every port and that people call him a "playboy," the "all-time conqueror of women." He wishes he had shown a little more moderation, but he's been around. He has a lavish triplex condominium in the hills of Cincinnati, with three floors of window walls, but he has no one with whom to share the lovely river views. Sensitive to his reputation, Bench considers settling down. It's a feeling he has. His parents are infirm. Most of his coworkers are married. Maybe he's ready for a family.

After a few days in Vegas, Bench travels to Houston on business. Vickie comes along.

Vickie calls her parents. "There's a boy," she tells them. Eileen, her mother, squeals. Her father, Clyde, comes unhinged once he hears the name "Johnny Bench." Clyde is a welder in a shipyard and a big fan of baseball. He is not usually an excitable person, but now he bubbles with chat. He tells his daughter that Bench is not only a former Rookie of the Year but a perennial all-star and Gold Glover who has revolutionized his position by catching one-handed. His strong arm and quick release make him impossible to steal against. Pitchers trust the way he thinks. He gives them a wide target, which makes him look a lot closer. Although a big man, Bench can play his position very near to the ground and can get his glove four to six inches lower than most catchers, making him adept at handling drop pitches. He has tremendous agility. He fields balls like an infielder and does things with his bat that catchers almost never do. He leads the league in home runs and RBIs. He was the youngest MVP in baseball history, is one of only a handful of people to win the award twice, and knowledgeable people — such as Casey Stengel, who has studied all the greats behind the plate: Bill Dickey, Gabby Hartnett, Yogi Berra, Roy Campanella — feel that Bench is the best ever, period.

In another part of the country, Johnny Bench is telephoning his manager. "There's a girl," he tells Sparky Anderson. "I'm comfortable around her. I know it's right."[2]

Sparky gives his blessing but reminds Bench he has to be in Tampa by February 21 for spring training.

"What if I'm late?"

"How late?"

"A day late."

"A day late for your wedding, John, the club can overlook that. Don't stretch it more than that, though."

"Right, Skip."

"You sure about this girl?"

"Hell yeah. And 'sides, it's the only way I can get my apartment cleaned up."

Sparky chuckles, sets the phone in the cradle, returns to listening to a sports broadcast on his radio. He stands at the picture window behind his desk, gazing out at the wild steep hills, the prickly pear cactus blooms, the desert sprouts and rejuvenated scrub. His hands are clasped behind his back. He's cursing at the window in a blue streak.

Living as he does in southern California, in enemy territory, Sparky has been exposed to a lot of "dynasty" talk about the Dodgers. The TV sports programs and the radio talk shows are full of this shit. Sparky's fed up. *So LA won the NL pennant in 1974, big deal, they still couldn't get past Oakland.*

His wife, Carol, enters. Sparky spins about, leans across his desk, and snaps off the radio. "Carol," he says, "I'm sick to death of this." He gestures toward the radio. "The Dodgers ain't no dynasty."

"Yes, George."

"They're a onetime deal; you mark my word." Agitated, Sparky opens and closes his hands. "There ain't *no damn way* all them guys who had good years, great years, *exceptional* years, no way are they gonna repeat."

"Okay, George."

"Some'll have great years," Sparky allows, rubbing his eyes wearily. "Yeah. But not all of 'em. I mean, they beat us, yeah, but we won *ninety-eight times* without playing real good."

"All right."

"Next time they're gonna have to win a hundred games, but if they do, we're gonna win a hundred and one." Sparky blows out a breath. "I ain't gonna tolerate all this crap they're putting out, and neither is Rose or Morgan or Johnny Bench. None of my guys are gonna stand for it."[3]

Driving to his parents' duplex in the middle of January, Johnny Bench calls Vickie Chesser in New York and proposes marriage. "Yes!" she shouts into the phone. "Yes! Yes!" They agree to be wed on February 21, seeing as how they played so much blackjack on their first date.

"It's just like a fairy tale," sighs Vickie.

The sudden announcement shocks their friends. Their engagement follows a courtship of three weeks and three days. John's doctor friend calls from Florida to see if Bench is ill. John does acknowledge he'll miss the carefree life, with nothing to worry about except ol' numero uno, but says he is looking forward to the sharing. Everyone asks him the same thing: *Who is this woman?* "She's, uh, shapely," explains Bench, "of course. She's a model. She's about five-six and I'd say sorta blond."

"Are you sure, are you sure?" Vickie's sister keeps asking. "Can't you wait a while?"

"Why should we wait?" demands Vickie. "We've both been around, *really* around, and we know what we want. I love John soooo. I feel I've known him all my life."

Vickie worries to John about getting a proper write-up in the Cincinnati papers. She wants a really super description of her "fab" Halston wedding dress on the society page. Bench laughs at her. "Honey," he says, "never mind about the society page. You're going to be on the *front* page." And Bench is right, for Cincinnati immediately embraces the couple as royalty. The locals want a world championship, but a wedding will do. They need a chance to sing about all the city's recent improvements, the redesigned downtown, the elevated walkways, the renovated public spaces, and the construction of a new ballpark for Johnny Bench, which would replace rickety old Crosley Field. What arose from the riverbank was a 44-million-dollar, multipurpose sports stadium, ringed with metal halide lamps and thirteen thousand volts, the crown jewel of the Queen City. The stadium floor was covered with husky nylon filament fibers, dyed green to resemble grass, and thus accommodated all weather. Completed in 1970, it came to be called Riverfront Stadium.

As soon as Johnny Bench arrives back in Cincinnati, he goes to Riverfront Stadium and meets behind closed doors with the management of the Reds.

Every year, a ballplayer receives a new contract. Left fielder Pete Rose has already signed, being forced to accept a cut in pay because, although he drew a career-high 106 walks in 1974 and led the league in doubles and runs scored, his batting average fell below .300 for the first time in ten years. First baseman Tony Perez has already signed, after enduring the miserable humiliation of being trade bait all winter, and second baseman Joe Morgan has signed. Shrewdly, Bench waits to sign until the management can't help but notice how the local media now adore him. He's all over the papers, all over the television. His pending marriage endears him to the city as never before. It's a timely romance, as judged by any gimlet-eyed accountant. Bench signs at last for $175,000 a year, the largest contract in Reds history.

The wedding date hurtles toward them, hastened by an avalanche of presents. The MGM Grand, site of their first date, gifts the couple with a huge sculpture of a man and woman embracing. "Magnificent," says Bench. On the appointed day, at Christ Episcopal Church, Clyde Chesser gives away his daughter, and Rev. Victor Frederiksen betroths her to a pretty celebrity in a powder-blue tuxedo. The bride and groom mutter smart-aleck barbs on the altar, more from nerves than anything else, then trade rings and kiss. They lead their guests up a wide, red-carpeted staircase in the Netherlands Hilton Hotel to a reception at the Hall of Mirrors. Through the window, Fountain Square can be seen below, the great public space seeming to encircle a dazzling fire of light. In the midst of the long, chandeliered baroque room are two three-hundred-pound ice blocks sculptured into vases for flowers. Noted vocalist Gwen Connelly sings "Ave Maria" and "I Can't Last a Day Without You." Five thousand cocktails are mixed and twelve hundred egg rolls served. Six off-duty policemen mill about to thwart the gate-crashing efforts of eight hundred teenagers attending a junior achievement dinner dance one floor above. Hundreds of pounds of shrimp, ham, and roast beef are set out. Surrounded by cameramen, Mr. and Mrs. Johnny Bench dine, they dance, they sidle over to the cake, a five-tiered creation containing thirty-five pounds of flour and fourteen dozen eggs. It was prepared by Marvin Barton. He once baked a five-hundred-pound cake for presidential candidate Barry Goldwater.

Once they've been well photographed cutting the cake, the newly-weds are urged by guests to go.

"Why leave?" John asks.

"You *know*."

"But this is our party!"

Somewhere in the ensuing festivities, Vickie loses her husband. John goes off with a buddy from Oklahoma to play Ping-Pong.[4] He returns very late, just in time to pack, and then it's the next morning, and they are off to spring training.

Bench had been Cincinnati's second draft pick in 1965. The first was a Detroit hothead named Bernie Carbo. Both were seventeen years old, but Bench matured faster and was promoted to the big leagues while Carbo floundered around the instructional league. Bernie grew famous for throwing tantrums, smashing dugout faucets, getting thrown out of games, being threatened with suspension. His teammates called him "The Idiot." By the time Sparky was Carbo's manager — in South Carolina, 1968 — "The Idiot" had become "The Clown." Sparky saw Bernie fielding from his knees in the outfield. He heard the guys on the bench applaud whenever Carbo made a catch. He saw a fantastic talent being squandered. The rehabilitation of Carbo became Sparky's project (just as Stengel had worked on Mantle). Sparky held him in batting practice until Carbo's hands bled.[5] He kept him shagging fly balls alone every day for hours. He rode him mercilessly about the length of his sideburns, or his hair, or his hippie sandals and blue jeans.[6] He fined him whenever he argued a call. Carbo responded in 1969 by leading the minors with a .359 average, helping his team win the Southern League championship. Both he and Sparky advanced to Cincinnati in 1970. The rookie manager platooned the rookie Carbo with another rookie, right-handed Hal McRae, and Sparky won seventy of his first one hundred games, not to mention the National League pennant. Carbo was a runner-up for Rookie of the Year.

In 1971 he stumbles. Carbo begins to drink; he takes drugs: Dexedrine, Benzedrine, Darvon, Darvocet, codeine, cocaine.[7] Sparky grows distraught. *What can I do?* Sadly, he realizes that Bernie needs a change. Thinking that if Carbo doesn't go somewhere else, he'll be all through, Sparky ships him off to the Cardinals. When Bernie finds out he's been traded, he's beside himself. He curses Sparky as he would his own haughty and malevolent father, had he the nerve.[8] He plays the 1973 season in St. Louis, then is sent along with Rick Wise to Boston in exchange for Reggie Smith. In 1974 Smith hits .309, Carbo hits .249, and Wise wins just three games.

Despite his terrible 1974 performance, Bernie Carbo requests a raise from the Red Sox. He's already earning $45,000, more than most ballplayers of the time. He becomes the first player in Boston's history to take deep-pocketed Tom Yawkey to salary arbitration.

Carbo loses.

Fires are kindled indoors as blizzards hit the northeast. Aggravated seas pound the coast of Maine. Winds howl through the Connecticut River Valley. Snow piles high against New Hampshire barns.

As always, the mood is both grim and hopeful. Last year the Red Sox, perennial near-champs, again acted like contenders. Yet again the team's fans loyally fell for it, and once more their baseball season closed with heartbreak. It's an old, tragic ritual, perfectly suited to a hardworking yet romantic immigrant city such as Boston. Like the Irish themselves, the Red Sox have been trying to win since 1919, in pursuit of an ever-approaching instant of respect that never completely arrives.

It's front-page news all over New England as Tony Conigliaro flies to Florida to try out for the Boston Red Sox. Fathers sit hearthside, faces lit by flickering flame, eyes shining bright, and they recount the legend of Tony C. Children pull their blankets to their chins. An alliance wholly primitive is exchanged, a tribal affiliation, deep as blood. Seeing their elders charged with such unusual vigor, kids listen, spellbound by the tale of the youngest American Leaguer ever to hit a hundred home runs, a teen slugger unprecedented in Red Sox history.

Winter eventually retreats: temperatures rise, snowdrifts thaw. Disappointments are forgiven. Expectations run rampant that Conigliaro's long-overdue return will spark the Red Sox to new levels of excellence.

Ironically, in Pittsburgh and Oakland, where baseball is reliably better played and the clubs are postseason shoo-ins, fathers and sons are less caught up in the arrival of spring training. They're still excited about their magnificent football teams, the Steelers and the Raiders, who play in the baseball stadiums during the winter and sell out every game. The two teams are rivals. In Pittsburgh's first professional football play-off game, in 1972, Franco Harris defeated Oakland in the final minute with his famous "Immaculate Reception." In the 1973 play-offs, the Raiders beat Pittsburgh; in the 1974 play-offs, the Steelers beat Oakland.

Neither city enjoys good economic health. Pittsburgh, the Iron City, is suffering a decline in steel demand and an increase in foreign competition. Many of its mills are closing. Oakland has one of the country's largest black populations, most of whom are poor. Fans in both cities can afford to follow only one sport, and increasingly baseball seems a luxury while football requires less of an investment: less time, money, sweat, and tears.

It's quite the opposite in Cincinnati, where buds feather the branches of the trees, and the willows that hang over the Ohio River seem laced with faint green hair. Any economic hardship just adds to the Queen City's eagerness for spring and its hunger for baseball. The city's newspapers, having extra room in their pages now that Johnny and Vickie's nuptials are past, dwell at length on the imminent exhibition games that — like a gathering mirage, like something out of Greek mythology — will be played between the brightest athletes in some loftier location, where it's warm. *Warm* — the heart shivers in hearing these accounts — *as it will be here, very soon.* There is less sleep, for in the distance a club that represents this region will soon reconvene for spring training.

Seventeen of the twenty-four major-league clubs train in Florida. Six go to Arizona, and the Angels are in Palm Springs, California.

As they practice down south, the Red Sox and Pirates confront a knotty dilemma while the A's grapple with the same problem in the west. Each lacks room in its outfield for its most promising slugger. (Presently, the Reds recognize that they have this difficulty too.) The clubs arrive at identical solutions. A senior outfielder is sent to play the infield. Thus Carl Yastrzemski, Willie Stargell, and Joe Rudi — three of the finest veteran outfielders in the game — move to the gateway position, first base, so that youngsters Jim Rice, Dave Parker, and Claudell Washington can play every day.

At twenty years old, Washington is the youngest of the three. He is being rushed into the starting lineup not only because of his hitting ability but because he is a famous local boy, a homegrown Oakland talent, and Finley hopes that his daily presence will increase the draw at the gate. Unfortunately, because of his lack of seasoning, Washington is prone to mental mistakes on the field. This would be less remarkable if he was replacing anybody but Joe Rudi, a Gold Glove winner in 1974. To his peers, Rudi is the least-recognized great player of his age. He is quiet and fair haired. He resembles an overwhelmed deputy in a Western. Teams regularly offer packages of players in exchange for him, and Finley seems to take delight in turning them down before resigning Rudi for a pittance.

During the winter of 1974, speculation was rampant that Finley might, at last, trade Rudi in a deal with Boston for pitcher Bill

"Spaceman" Lee. "If the Red Sox turn it down," said Lee, "they're crazy. He's the best everyday player." Crazy perhaps, or blessed with vision and foresight, Dick O'Connell spurned Finley's offer. Boston had no need for more outfielders, and the left-handed Spaceman added a valuable balance to the staff.

Tom Yawkey comes upon Bernie Carbo in the locker room at training camp. Bernie is near tears. He explains that he needs $10,000: he's got a child and a pregnant wife; he has to make a down payment on a house. Yawkey slips him the money. It's a gift. No one knows. And just like that, Bernie feels like Yawkey's son. He falls in love with baseball all over again. *For the first time in my life,* he tells everyone, *I'm playing for the uniform.* At the initial Red Sox team meeting of 1975, he tells his teammates they should stop complaining so much. "Just try and remember," he exhorts them, "how lucky we all are to be here."

For the better part of four seasons now, Tom Yawkey's Red Sox have started strong and then, at the drop of a hat, looked junior league.

"I've got a *sister* who can pitch better than you," snarls Boston's indignant catcher Carlton "Pudge" Fisk during a visit to the mound. The inning is going against the pitcher. "If you don't feel like doing the job, we'll find someone who does. I'm *busting my hump* back there, and you should be too."

Alas, this bad-luck team is something of a tragic burden for intense, young Pudge Fisk. He carries it around like an ailing relative on those broad, local-boy shoulders of his. As long as Pudge stays healthy — and Carl Yastrzemski and pitcher Luis Tiant, for that matter — there is no better group of players. But Carl and Tiant are grizzled, and late in the season their backs frequently ache while Fisk, over and over, has freak accidents.

Nineteen seventy-four starts typically. In an early exhibition game, Bill Lee is on the mound, Cardinal first baseman Joe Torre at the plate. As he delivers a pitch, Lee happens to notice one of Fisk's testicles hanging out, pinched between his thigh and his cup. He thinks about saying something, but before he can, Torre strokes wildly at Lee's slider, driving the pitch foul, straight back, and directly into the catcher's crotch. It nails Fisk's testicle. Pudge falls to the ground. Both dugouts wince.

Fisk goes on the disabled list, returns in May, plays fifty games, hits .299. Covering home in Cleveland one night, with the score tied and two outs in the bottom of the ninth, Pudge is hit by a sliding Leron Lee. The catcher's knee is torn apart. Surgeons operate, but they've never seen an injury this bad. They say Fisk's career is over. He'll be lucky if he can even just limp for the rest of his life. He ignores their prognosis. He creates a rehabilitation program: a two and a half–mile run each morning, paddleball, an hour with weights, time in the sauna, fifteen laps in the pool at the YMCA in Manchester, New Hampshire, sixty deep knee bends, and ten miles on an Exercycle at home.

He returns in spring training, 1975. He catches one game and he's exhausted, but he's also determined. Batting the next day, he refuses to bail out when the pitcher drops down to throw sidearm. The pitch is inside. Fisk holds his ground. The ball breaks in on him. Pudge puts up his hands. He is struck, and the distal end of his ulna is fractured. His right arm goes into a fiberglass cast for two months.

Vickie's husband's team takes on the Fiskless Red Sox in an exhibition of the preseason Grapefruit League. It's the first time Vickie Bench has ever been to Florida, the first time she's ever watched a baseball game. (For that matter, it's the first time she's ever been "Vickie Bench.") During the national anthem, John catches Vickie's eye and winks, and then a squad of men in red-trimmed outfits engage in polite competition.

Vickie believes that her husband looks cute with his baseball cap on backward, and she expresses this with great insistence. Otherwise, the point of this contest baffles her. Her dad gave her an awful lot, but he didn't lend her an appreciation of baseball, so — like most daughters — she never learned how to share her father's love for the game. It's like watching weather form, he might have said. Two fronts collide and feel each other out. There is a distant rumble, an accumulating uncertainty, tension. Abruptly the silence is broken — a crack of electricity. You don't always know where to look. Everything is in motion, in flux, changing, and then more thunder, and again an eerie stillness. Leads evaporate. The whole experience is ethereal. When you see the sport in person, or you listen to it on the radio, it seems to be composed partly of air, but this aspect never really comes through on the television. . . .

Without her father's guidance, Vickie merely observes the game. Perhaps she thinks, *This is like watching weather.* By this she means, *Boring.* She remains unaware that both these teams played extremely well for two-thirds of the previous season, and if not for the Reds' delayed maturation and the Sox's early demise, they (instead of Los Angeles and Oakland) would have met in the 1974 World Series. "How do you know when they're doing good?" Vickie finally asks John's boss, Sparky Anderson.

"I'll tell you as we go along," Sparky assures the emerald-eyed woman.

Meanwhile, in the press box, the reasons why the Red Sox failed to gain last year's division title are being debated hotly. Rick Wise was supposed to win fifteen or twenty games; he won three. Fisk was great for about two months, and so was Carbo, and so was the pitcher Reggie Cleveland. Rico and Carl both started strong but faded. At season's end, two minor-league hotshots named Jim Rice and Fred Lynn saw sporadic use, but while Lynn hit .419 in fifteen games, Rice was undependable: he had sixty-seven at bats and couldn't get focused. Fisk says cliques formed and no one respected DJ — manager Darrell Johnson — who'd been a backup catcher in the fifties and a good talent scout in the sixties, but who, as a manager, was predictable and uninspiring. Johnson admits his politics were poor, that he lost control of the team. Dick O'Connell suspects that the dugout held too many aging horses, the field was too full of venerated statues, and plainly no one cared; there was too little speed, too little passion.

The reporters ask Boston pitcher Bill Lee about it, and he blames his new child.

On the evening of August 24, Boston was in first by seven and a half games. Lee was facing Catfish Hunter and the Oakland A's at Fenway. His very pregnant wife, Mary Lou (a former Miss Alaska), was sitting right down in front, in back of the screen. She went into labor, but Spaceman stayed in the game. He finally left in the eighth inning, with the score tied at one run apiece, with a blister on his thumb, with his wife's contractions coming every three minutes. She gave birth to Andrew Lee while Boston's Diego Segui relieved and lost the game. The Red Sox went on to lose eight straight, eleven out of their next thirteen, eighteen of their next twenty-five, while Baltimore won twenty-eight of thirty-four. Lee's thumb stayed bad. All the plants in his house died. Three weeks later, Boston was well in back of the Orioles and Yankees. Runs were scarce or inopportune. The team as a whole wasn't hitting.

"It had to be the kid's fault," Spaceman dryly admits. "Someday he is going to find out and will be mad as hell."

In the course of losing to Cincinnati this afternoon, Boston tries out two catchers, two first basemen, two second basemen, two third basemen, and three pitchers. They've got too many in the outfield, no infield, and now — with Fisk hurt again — no one to link the old men with the upstarts, no glue.

Amid it all is Bernie Carbo, fighting as always, working hard to secure a starting position in the Red Sox outfield over Lynn, Rice, Conigliaro, and the rest. The Reds manager studies his former pupil. Sparky can see that Bernie's still a firebrand, and the skipper probably wouldn't mind having him back on the Cincinnati squad, except that Carbo now hardly speaks to his old mentor, refuses to acknowledge him, can't look him in the eye. Sparky doesn't grasp the extent of Carbo's continued drug consumption. When this information later comes out, Sparky will be shocked, not because a man would willingly do that to his body, nor because a ballplayer would ravage his talent that way, but because Sparky continues to regard Bernie as part of his family. Sparky's two sons, Albert and

Lee, were the batboys in South Carolina when Bernie played for him. Bernie gave Lee a baseball glove. That was a big thing. Sparky's wife thinks the world of Bernie. Carol calls him "Bernardo Carbo," which sounds like some sort of heavenly pasta dish, and often she tenderly replays Carbo's kindnesses of 1969, a big year for both her boys and her husband. Bernie himself would be surprised to hear how much, thanks to Carol, thanks to Albert and Lee, he remains a hero in Sparky's household.[9]

It becomes apparent, as spring training rolls along, that Boston is young and spotty. At first, Carl and Rico are the only ones left from the roster of their last championship series, but then Tony C. has a couple good games at the plate and makes the team as a designated hitter, and the old, classic trio is back together again.[10]

Despite the fact that the American League East division has become more competitive, Boston's most newsworthy change remains Tony C.'s addition. The other teams have been plugging holes like crazy. Baltimore has added first baseman Lee May, switch-hitting right fielder Ken Singleton, pitcher Mike Torrez. Cleveland has installed designated hitter Frank Robinson as their new player/manager (baseball's first black manager) and added first baseman Boog Powell. And New York has right fielder Bobby Bonds and pitcher Catfish Hunter.

Through March, while the other Florida teams solidify their line-ups, the Red Sox proceed with a growing lack of definition. Beetle-browed Dwight "Dewey" Evans is in right and "The Rooster," Rick Burleson, is at short. Each is twenty-four, a fine fielder, a .280 hitter. Rico is at third, with the unremarkable Doug Griffin at second. The powerful right-handed starters Wise and Reggie Cleveland, neither of whom threw particularly well in 1974, say they're now healthy. Lynn — the kid from Casey Stengel Park in Glendale — lays claim to center field. He's still an unknown, but he hits all kinds of pitches, has all kinds of speed, fields alertly, throws superbly. Of course Fisk is hurt, so the team has no cleanup hitter. Much is expected of taciturn rookie slugger Rice, who has outhit everybody in the minors for years, but Rice grows so immersed in bettering his outfield glove skills that he pays scant attention to his lack of contact at the plate. The roster in spring training fluctuates between two hard-hitting first basemen in Yastrzemski and Cecil Cooper, two poor-hitting designated hitters in the distracted Rice and the ailing Tony C., and a host of spotty outfielders in Rick Miller, Juan Beniquez, and Bernie Carbo. They drop twenty of thirty-one Grapefruit League contests.

Yastrzemski, the thirty-five-year-old veteran who repeatedly shook off the mantle of team leader, can no longer hold his tongue. He calls a player meeting and rips into his cohorts, says they have the worst attitude coming out of spring training of any team he's ever been on. "If we play the season the way we did the spring," he tells them bluntly, "we'll end up in last place. We sat back all spring and waited to get beat. It was a disgrace." He recalls one game when Burleson hit a ball to the right side, giving himself up to advance a runner, and no one said a thing when he got back to the bench; no one patted him on the back. "If we're going to be in this pennant race, we're going to have to execute, hustle, and run. We've got to start as a unit and finish as a unit. We're not going to overpower anyone. We'll have to play together."

Except for the Red Sox, each team breaks from spring training in positive spirits. Any number of things seems possible. The talent runs deep and wide. The batting champions play for Minnesota and Chicago. The best pitchers are with San Diego and Baltimore. Philadelphia, Oakland, and Milwaukee have the strongest sluggers; California and Kansas City the swiftest runners; Los Angeles and St. Louis the most overpowering relievers.

The Cardinals, Phillies, and Pirates are picked to top the NL East. The Dodgers and Reds are given equal odds to lead the NL West. The Athletics are still the best team in the AL West, and the Yankees — with last year's surprisingly strong second-place finish, plus their addition of two bona fide superstars in Bonds and Catfish — are expected to take the AL East over the Orioles, who dominate the division seemingly every season.

Reporters don't believe in these Red Sox, and pick them to finish no higher than third. New England's fans, however, have faith from the start, and they will pack the stadium for the entire season. In the end, they will see Yastrzemski's challenge ("execute, hustle, and run") more than met by the remarkable rookie duo of Lynn and Rice. The two young men will be called the "Gold Dust Twins," for though they look nothing alike, their value will be immense. They will dance the Red Sox into the postseason, a long ball culminating in a World Series some will call the greatest ever played.

FIVE

A BRISK AFTERNOON in southern California finds Jack
Brett and his youngest son out in the backyard with a ball, two
mitts, and a wooden bat. A rusty pitch back is set up, and a
wadded-up T-shirt thrown on the lawn as home plate.

Jack's youngest, George, is twenty-one, blond, exuberant, rug-
gedly built. Last May, when George became the everyday third baseman of the Kansas City Royals, the task proved almost too much
for him. He was overmatched by big-league pitchers. A Royals coach
named Charlie Lau offered help. George accepted, gratefully. George,
Hal McRae, and a few other diligent teammates worked long hours
with Lau before every game, taking batting practice, gathering
insight, gaining wisdom, hitting and listening, and then hitting some
more. Lau is a complex, weathered stump of a guy, gruff yet compas-
sionate, warm and intensely loyal. As the players grow to trust him,
their batting averages invariably climb.

Jack Brett frequently scowls. He is jealous of Charlie Lau.
"What happened to your big, handsome stance?" he barks in the

backyard, as George takes some practice cuts. His son used to hold the bat nice and high and take those long strokes.

"Charlie Lau said I had a floppy swing; I had to make it more compact."

"Floppy?" Jack Brett makes a fist. He always liked George's swing. It was the swing of Carl Yastrzemski, *the* Carl Yastrzemski. As in the last man to win the Triple Crown of batting. That sort of swing gives George power, and he'll need that if he's ever going to be an MVP. He motions George toward the T-shirt, encourages him to step in. "The old man's gonna toss you a few, I want to see your swing."

Ignoring him, George bends and touches the full length of his bat to the ground.

"What's that?" asks Jack.

"I'm getting rid of tension."

A neighbor's mongrel barks as jet planes appear out of the impossibly blue sky and drift toward LAX. Lofty, cumulous clouds roil over Jack's head, tricking the eye such that he appears, in fact, to be receding from his son.

George rocks slightly on his feet. This is also new, something Charlie Lau has been stressing about the necessity of a rhythmic weight shift. Lau says that George tries to pull too much, that he has no discipline at the plate, no organization, and terrible mechanics.

Jack Brett pulls off his baseball cap, rubs a trembling hand through his hair, muttering to himself. *I say what's good enough for Yaz is good enough for Jack Brett's boy.* . . . Jack raises his hands at his sides in a gesture at once loving but confrontational, tells his son to get up to the plate.

George checks his position. "I'm good." He's standing before the pitch back, beside the T-shirt. "Charlie Lau moved me away from the plate."

"Oh God. Well, at least raise up your bat a little. Who are you, Pete Rose?"

"Charlie Lau wants me to keep the bat parallel to the ground."

Jack hurls his glove down, spins, and chucks the baseball in the direction of his neighbor's howling dog. "Fuck Charlie Lau!"

His son's mouth opens and closes a few times without making a sound. His eyes harden. His lips tighten. "Well," George says finally, with a sharp expulsion of breath, "fuck you, Dad!"[1]

Elsewhere, it's no easier.[2] Bobby Bonds watches his eldest child vomiting over the side of the motorboat and feels that familiar twinge of hopelessness, the sensation of something stoppered up. *How to help?* He can't always relate to this boy of his. Bonds nibbles off the top of an Oreo and absently scrapes his teeth against the frosting center. "Feeling better, Son?" he asks, with all the tenderness he can muster.

The boy raises his chin, runs the sleeve of his shirt across his mouth, and glares. "I *hate* this."

"Right," sighs Bonds. A couple of dreary clouds drift near the boat. Bonds jiggles his fishing pole and squints into the sea. "Fish ain't biting," he says softly.

He thinks of this boy at age eight months, his left hand grabbing for the bottle — a plaintive gesture that ten years later still infuriates the father. "No, Barry," Bonds tried correcting the infant. "Grab with the *right* hand." Being a lefty would limit the positions his son could play; nearly all infielders are right-handed because, in pegging the ball to first base, a left-handed player throws away from his body. Barry refused to heed his dad's advice. Ignoring him, the son insisted on becoming left-handed. *Already he was beyond his father's reach, even at eight months.*

"Why do we always have to go fishing when you're home?" whines Barry. "Nobody else goes fishing."

"You think I care about everybody else, what everybody else does?"

"We never catch anything!"

Bonds grits his teeth and keeps quiet. His feeling is that Barry should thank his lucky stars for what he does have. When he was Barry's age, he would've killed for a chance to go fishing in the

Pacific Ocean. At times his family was so poor that he couldn't get diddly. He'd have holes in his shoes, and both soles would be flapping. He and his sister and his brothers would go play in an open field in back of the home, sometimes they'd bat rocks. Or they'd wad up an old sock, wrap a string around it, and bat that. Or they'd throw those little red berries off the bushes. As long as you hit the berry back, you kept batting. One miss, and you were out.[3]

A bigmouthed seabird sweeps low over the sea, crooks its gray wings, and settles in their proximity. It seems drawn to the former contents of Barry's stomach, which float now atop the sea, disgustingly close. After a certain noble deliberation, the bird dips its long beak, shrieks in disapproval, flaps, and leaves.

"Barry, um . . . There's never anything better than two parents who love you. You know? That's worth everything."

"Yeah, yeah," grumbles Barry.

"It's important that we have time together. Because . . . you know I'm going away."

"You *always* go away."

"You're right," Bonds admits. His presence in Barry's life is no more substantial than a wisp of smoke. His wife does everything: she writes "from Dad" on the Christmas presents, she takes Barry to baseball or football practice, she goes to all of the school events. "Well, you heard I got traded."

Oh, Barry knows *all* about the trade: Bobby Murcer for Bobby Bonds, the new Mickey Mantle for the new Willie Mays. "I can *read*, Dad." The newspaper calls it the biggest one-for-one exchange in baseball history, the first time one six-figure player has been traded for another. (The paper also says his dad uses dope and drinks too much.)[4] "You might not like New York," Barry says, repeating something he read.

"Oh, I'll like New York."[5] Bonds catches a startled look from his son and smoothly covers. "I mean, I'll miss you. I'll miss my family, of course, but New York . . . I mean, the Yankees . . . The center of the infield is a little soft — Mason, Sandy Alomar . . . still it's gonna be a romp. I mean, I'm just worried, you know, all I'm worried about is the pitchers. I got that great big swing and I'll be facing those American League guys for the first time, and how are they gonna pitch me? That's what's got me worried."[6] He digs another Oreo out of the package, screws off the top. "I'll like New York, though."

"Willie sure didn't like getting traded to New York."

"Well, yeah." Willie, okay, now *that* is something Bobby and Barry share — their idol, Willie Mays.[7] Willie is so charismatic that it gives them goose bumps just watching him put on a coat. As a teenager, Bobby quite willingly accepted less money to sign with San Francisco so he could play near Willie. And it's true that Mays didn't appreciate being traded to New York. Still, he went, accepting the tradition that baseball's greats eventually must go back home. Willie returned to New York just as Rogers Hornsby returned to St. Louis and Babe Ruth returned to Boston.

Bobby Bonds looks off where sea meets sky in a line of silver mercury. There is the sound of distant applause as a flock of shiny birds lifts off toward the horizon, a scattering of tinfoil.

His son splashes seawater on his face, cleans up. He doesn't feel so nauseous anymore. He peers out, takes a measure of the ocean. *There ain't no fish out here.*

At long last, they turn back and head home.

George Foster awakes in the room of his boyhood, smiling.[8] He feels like a giant in this little bed. *Wishful thinking.* When he played for San Francisco, he liked being a Giant. "We're Giants!" he and Bobby Bonds would regularly enthuse, clapping one another on the back at their good fortune. They shared hotel rooms and ballpark outfields. "We're Giants!" They were appropriately magical words, for it was something out of a fable to be on a team with Mays and McCovey, and with Bobby there too, treating Foster like a family member.

Foster scratches his head, frowning. They aren't Giants anymore, he realizes. Desperate for money, San Francisco traded those three just as, years ago, they traded him.

The children begin to gather outside his mother's old wooden house. They call for Foster, treating the twenty-four-year-old athlete like a star when he isn't even a starter. They sing his name, voices ringing with innocence and cinnamon, and when Foster emerges onto the paint-peeled porch, rubbing the sleep from his narrow eyes with the heel of a hand, they yell "Hooray!" and their young coiled bodies spring nimbly into the air. They look up to him. Between Foster's broad nose and knobby, prominent chin, his crease of a mouth widens shyly into a smile. Foster puts his head down and goes inside. No one ever played ball with him when he was small. He returns a minute later, wearing a big equipment bag over one shoulder. The children shriek. As together they walk the few blocks to a nearby field, all the kids work to touch him. Those who cannot manage to get near enough to hold on to his arm instead grasp at the elastic waist of his sweatshirt or hang off the belt loops of his Levi's. Foster possesses immense strength; Pete Rose says that Foster could hunt bears with switches. Perhaps, perhaps not, but he could, if he wanted, haul all these children atop his broad shoulders.

The Giants sent Foster to the Reds, who seemed not to need him. They already had Gold Glovers in their outfield and a long string of brute sluggers. He arrived in Cincinnati while they were clinching their second pennant in three years. They employed Foster as if he were a bit of putty, something to shove in to fill up the unseemly cracks. There was nothing steady or fun about it, and then, at season's end, they optioned him to their triple-A farm club in Indianapolis. "Exceptionally decent," Sparky called him. "Extremely sensitive." Foster became despondent at being sent down, and his gaze grew cloudy. He frequently winced for no reason. He felt lost and full of hate. At someone's suggestion, he visited a hypnotist. (Ballplayers had secretly been seeing hypnotists for ages.) Closing his eyes, Foster relaxed into a trance.

The cruel babble in his head finally ceased. It was a liberating sensation. After he awoke, he recalled the religion with which he'd been raised. He returned to the Bible. This helped. He roomed in Indianapolis with right fielder Ken Griffey, a kind family man who reminded him of his old pal Bonds. This also helped. He played the outfield alongside Griffey and Ed Armbrister. All three had excellent speed, good range, fine arms. They made every catch look easy. Foster started to like baseball again. Once more, he was dispatched to Cincinnati.

Foster and the children arrive at the field. He removes his wristwatch and hands it to a short, heavyset boy with blond wavy hair and sparkling eyes. *Why keep track of time?* Baseball doesn't go by the clock. It's about history, contemplation, remembrance.

There is the loud clatter of bats and balls as Foster dumps the equipment bag. The older children move in to grab gear and then, with a holler, sprint toward the corner backstop in order to figure out what to use for bases and get a game going.

The younger children do not move. They stand uncertainly outside the heap of equipment. Foster scrutinizes them. At last, he smiles.

He takes up a ball and rolls it until each has become confident of his catches. Gradually, over the next hour, he starts to bounce it. By now, a few have wandered off to sit in the tall weeds and cheer the older children in their game. Others remain determined to learn. Foster begins throwing it to them underhand, and then overhand. Their little faces fill with laughter and light.

"The main point of this game," he instructs the small ones, so softly they have to strain to hear him, "is to have fun." They nod with grave sincerity.

Foster walks over to observe the older kids. Baseball is a kind sport. There's room for many different body types and levels of coordination. It's democratic in its distances. Kids who are small can't hit the ball real far but can move quickly between the bases while the sluggers usually can't run. On the playground, everybody has a chance.

Foster feels that a few of the older kids should level their swings. He tells others to hit in front of the plate. They have to use a bat that's comfortable, and they shouldn't grip it too tightly — just enough so the ball won't knock it out of their hands.

"Most of all," he encourages them, "practice and patience."

The game has halted and the children draw close. They ask how good he was at their age. They're sure he was the very, very best player . . . but they want to know just how much better he was. Foster assures them that he wasn't the best. He hit five home runs during his strongest summer, but another boy in the same league, a boy named Dave Kingman, had twenty home runs. A few of the older children recognize that name.

Kingman's with the Mets. He plays every day, unlike Foster, who's still a utility player. Sparky brings in Foster to pinch-hit or pinch-run, or occasionally to play if a left-hander pitches. Although this continues to frustrate Foster, he tells himself to be patient. Sparky may think that he's in charge; Foster knows better. *The Lord has a plan.* Foster trusts that it will be revealed soon.

PART TWO

THE SEASON'S FIRST HALF

SIX

TRADITION DICTATES that the first contest in the National League be played where the broad Ohio River rises, then twists south — for it was there, in 1869, that the Cincinnati club inaugurated the national pastime and there, in 1937, that they played the first night game in the big leagues; so it is there, in 1975, that the season begins, with the Reds against the Dodgers, two teams that have been barking and growling at each other in the western division for years now. This is the tenth consecutive sellout match between these two rivals. Each has speed and fine fielders, but otherwise a very different character.

The Dodgers are young, their talent mostly homegrown. They have the more consistent pitching: two curly-haired aces in Don Sutton and Messersmith and, in the bull pen, rotund, arrogant, and mustachioed Mike Marshall, who last season became the first reliever to win the Cy Young Award.

The Reds have experience and a richer offense. Cincinnati usually wins the division, but only after overcoming a ten-game deficit and dramatically wresting the lead away from LA at season's end.

Last year, this annual charge of theirs came too late, allowing the Dodgers to capture their first pennant since the Koufax era.

One of the smallest cities to have a major-league team, Cincinnati is in many ways both southern and midwestern, easygoing but hardworking. Its love for baseball is rivaled only by its dedication to church and family. Many of its earliest white settlers were of German descent, a heritage that has established the city's reputation for fine craftsmanship, as well as for beer and sausage. It was not a city of high renown until the 1970s, when it leaped into the national consciousness as the home of Sparky's Reds — of Pete Rose, Johnny Bench, and Tony Perez.

By the time Joe Morgan joins in the winter of 1971, they are already being called the "Big Red Machine," the ball team for whom victories are automatic. The phrase captures not just the team's relentless efficiency but also the impersonal, robotic nature of their power and roster. The front office caters to the conservative taste of the region, regulating the team's look and behavior to ensure wholesome family fun. Facial hair is prohibited and players are instructed to mind their posture. In order to project an image of cleanliness, the team shoulders a larger laundry bill than any other in the majors. Each player is supplied with at least eight spare uniforms and is encouraged to step inside and wash up in the middle of the game.

This region-savvy marketing of the team has clearly succeeded, for the Opening Day crowd is the largest in Cincinnati history. They watch in fascination as the two rivals fight to a standstill. Sutton throws for seven innings. Marshall throws for five. A total of seven pitchers are used. The score remains tied at one apiece. In the bottom of the fourteenth, Sparky watches a Red get nailed in a rundown between third and home. *Two away.* Now he has a man at third with his pitcher due up. A small sound of frustration escapes from deep in his throat. The situation demands a pinch hitter, but Sparky's out of substitute options. He scratches at one ear. He's already sent up the left-handed Terry Crowley, he's used Merv Rettenmund. His eyes probe the lineup card, assessing. He squares his shoulders, faces the bench. Foster has been sitting down at the far end of the dugout for three and a half hours, all the while squeezing a small rubber ball à la Ted Williams. Foster's a slow starter; he doesn't always pay attention, but Sparky is desperate. He orders Foster to grab one of his hickory-stained bats and get out there.

Foster rushes to the plate, believing his career rides on this at bat.[1] Fifty-two thousand, five hundred twenty-six spectators and innumerable radio listeners share the feeling. He tries to loosen up in the batter's box. He swivels his hips and rocks his elbows. He studies a few pitches, takes a mighty cut. The abrupt descent of the pitch surprises him. His black bat grazes the very top of the ball. It weakly dribbles into fair territory. Foster flushes with shame. He catches sight of his teammate breaking for home.

Foster spins and starts toward first. His legs are cramped. He can't seem to get moving. The base retreats along the chalk and scampers nimbly away. He chases it into right, out the stadium. He pursues it to Indianapolis, running past his old minor-league park and down the street of his mother's house, where the heavyset boy with blond hair to whom Foster handed his wristwatch is listening with his family to a broadcast of the proceedings.

Meanwhile, something about Foster's slow roller confounds his opponents. The Dodgers take what seems like many hours to locate it. When finally Foster's foot hits the bag, Garvey is only just receiving the ball. Two thuds sound simultaneously.

An exact tie. Which goes to the runner.

The radio exults in Cincinnati's first victory of the year.

One day later in Cleveland, the Indians and Yankees are dressing for the season opener.

Boog Powell, now with the Indians, is aghast at the home uniform. Other players agree that Cleveland's radically redesigned outfits seem too red. Their player/manager, Frank Robinson, snorts and rolls his eyes. The beefy Powell is particularly distraught that

Robinson, his former companion in the proud black-and-orange-trimmed suits of Baltimore, appears so unsympathetic. Boog gazes at himself in the mirror. "I feel like a massive blood clot," he says glumly.

In the opposing clubhouse, Bobby Bonds grapples with a similar anxiety. "I look funny," he declares after putting on his first Yankee uniform. "I don't look like a Yankee at all. Some people look like Yankees. Some don't." He glances around the locker room. "Elston Howard over there does. Even Alex Johnson does. But Walt Williams looks like a Chicago White Sock and I still look like a San Francisco Giant." Bonds sits, struggling with his new team identity. "I know Willie Mays never looked like a Met," he says softly to reassure himself, but then he catches sight of his reflection and grimaces. "This uniform looks funny on me."

Meanwhile, the new Giant, Bobby Murcer, the man for whom Bonds was traded, is getting dressed in San Diego. Murcer's also frustrated, but it has nothing to do with his work clothes. It's the weather. San Francisco's Opening Day game against the Padres has been twice delayed due to rain. Murcer is beside himself. "All those years I was with the Yankees, I used to think how nice it would be to open a season in southern California." He gestures toward the bulky blue tarpaulin that is spread across the field of San Diego's Jack Murphy Stadium. "I finally get my wish, and this."[2]

Eventually, the game gets under way. The curly-haired southpaw sinker baller Randy Jones has been picked, somewhat arbitrarily, to start for San Diego. Last season, Jones was the losingest pitcher in the majors. He's been working lately to improve his conditioning, his pitching mechanics. He's nervous.[3] He surrenders a hit to Murcer and three other Giants, but none of them score. San Diego's defense is sharp. Randy throws nine shutout innings. Unfortunately, the offense is no better than before, and the Padres are also blanked. Randy is lifted: pitching coach Tom Morgan doesn't want him exhausted by his first outing. Murcer immediately doubles off the reliever. Gary Matthews follows with another double. The Padres lose in ten innings.

The next day, the Cincinnati Reds arrive. Fred Norman starts against his old team. Norman is still recovering from a rib cage injury. His hair has begun to go gray and his high cheekbones look weathered. He needs command of at least two of his five pitches to succeed. But as he pitches in San Diego this evening, only his change of pace is working. The leadoff man immediately hammers him for a double, and next Bobby Tolan digs in. Sparky sees no threat. Then Tolan squares around to bunt, a prospect for which none of Anderson's men are prepared. Tolan beats out the bunt, the center fielder singles, and then Dave Winfield doubles. Three runs, no outs, top of the first. The Padres win the game, five runs to two. In the next game, the Padres face Gary Nolan, who is making his first major-league start in two years. Early in his career, Nolan had been a devastating fastballer who, with Bench, formed the youngest and perhaps most promising battery in baseball history. But in 1972 he fielded a grounder, threw off balance to first, and his arm died. By 1973 he couldn't win a game. Though tonight he is uncomfortable and erratic, there are glimmers of genius. The Reds lose, three to two, but pitching coach Larry Shepard remains philosophical. "We lost a game —" he shrugs — "but won a pitcher."

And it continues this way, a miserable series, cold and long. Sparky keeps coming back to that astonishing bunt. As he drives north to see his family, he remains knotted up about the utter surprise of Tolan's at bat — the galling fact that a longhair could ever outthink him — and when Sparky arrives in Thousand Oaks and sees no change in the lengthy hair of his seventeen-year-old son Lee, all hell breaks loose.[4] All of Sparky's pent-up emotions come out. They have a knock-down-drag-out fight — purely verbal, nothing physical, but nothing nice.

In retrospect, Sparky will be ashamed. "If anyone ever handled a family crisis poorly, it was me," Sparky Anderson will eventually admit. "I failed miserably. Me, the guy who was getting credit everywhere for running the happiest baseball family in the country — the team that had no cliques — the short-haired club that was being written up everywhere for its togetherness. I failed with my own son."

In 1974 Sparky tried eight different men at third base, none worked out, and the Dodgers grabbed the pennant. To silence LA's dynasty blather and avoid what befell his boys that year, Sparky regards as imperative the establishment of a quick jump in the standings, an early, strong lead. To accomplish that, he needs a third baseman; he has five outfielders and no one to man the hot corner. The Reds deal with the Brewers for John Vukovich, a classic "no-hit, good-glove" infielder. Sparky figures that, with three of the last five league MVPs in his lineup, the team can carry Vukey's weak bat. Two weeks into the season, with his team in sixth place and below .500, Sparky realizes he's wrong.

Sparky's got the highest salaried infield in baseball (earning collectively $650,000 a year). He's got all-stars up the middle — catcher Johnny Bench, second baseman Joe Morgan, shortstop Dave Concepcion, and center fielder Cesar Geronimo. On the mound he can count on Don Gullett, a shy youngster Sparky feels is fated for three hundred career victories, as well as on the versatility of workhorse Clay "Hawk" Carroll, the fourth most active pitcher in major-league history. His gloves are strong in the corners of the diamond and along the outfield flanks, with Pete Rose in left, rookie Ken Griffey in right, Tony Perez at first, and Vukovich, the redheaded newcomer, at third.

Gary Nolan makes three more strong starts, gets no decisions. In the Reds' initial eighteen games, the first three men in the batting order — Rose, Concepcion, and Morgan — board base ninety times but come around to score only twenty-eight runs. Morgan leads the league in hitting with a .405 average and an on-base percentage of .557. But Sparky performs some calculations and realizes that with the team's inability to consistently get men home, Morgan will have to get on base sixteen hundred times this season to score one hundred runs. On the average, Sparky's batters strand nine men a game. Three regulars — Perez, Bench, and Vukovich — keep failing clutch situations, squandering at bats. Morgan can only do so much. "If Joe keeps up his present pace," Sparky concludes with a glum shake of his head, "he'll be dead in another month."

Sparky knows that Perez will eventually snap out of his slump. And aside from that, Sparky needs him in the lineup in order to comfort the younger Latins — Concepcion and Geronimo. There is no Cincinnati player more popular, inside or outside the Reds' clubhouse, than Perez. He learned baseball by playing for a sugar-cane factory team in his native Cuba. His signing bonus was $2.50, the cost of a U.S. visa. His debut major-league home run was a grand slam. He was the first player to reach Riverfront's red seats, with a four-hundred-eighty-foot blast. He is one of the most prolific run producers in baseball history. He averages ninety-six RBIs every season, he has no ego, he adores his teammates, he jokes about anything, he talks to everyone. He lubricates the Big Red Machine, keeps it humming. Fans alertly recognize his value. Pete Rose is their gap-toothed Prince Valiant; Johnny Bench is the smartest catcher; Joe Morgan is the greatest all-around talent; but no one is more beloved by Cincinnati than the clutch-hitting Tony. They call him the "Mayor of Riverfront." He is the one player on the roster who is never booed.

So Sparky isn't worried about Perez — he's no rally killer — and the manager trusts that his all-star catcher also will soon start to hit, and besides, Bench is needed to hold the pitching staff together.

But still, something has to change, and Vukovich is his only option. So, as Cincinnati is being humiliated in Los Angeles, about to be swept in four straight, Sparky calls Vukey back to the dugout. The bases are full and the manager isn't about to miss this chance. He announces Dan Driessen as the pinch hitter.

Vukovich goes numb. The color drains from his gaunt face. He is in verifiable shock. *It's the second inning!* he sputters. He's never heard of such an insult, replaced before the first at bat of the evening.

Driessen goes to the plate in his stead and lofts an easy pop-up that Steve Garvey squeezes for an out.

Vukey is livid.[5] He was removed *for that!* He bellows in fury, and as he retreats beneath Dodger Stadium, down the tunnel of concrete to the showers, he punches out lightbulbs and calls his manager all kinds of nasty names.

Sparky gives Vukey a day to cool off and then calls him into the office. He closes the door, steps behind the desk, and fixes the kid with an icy glare. "There's one thing you'd better get straight, kid, and I mean *get it straight right away*," he snarls. "I run this ball club! I'll pinch-hit for *anyone* any time I think it can help me win a ball game." Sparky scowls at the stat sheet on his desk. Vukey's career batting average is sixty points below even Sparky's own miserable mark. "According to my sheet," Sparky spits with distaste, "you don't happen to be a *star* in this league yet."

"You won't give a guy a chance to prove anything," snivels Vukovich. "You kill a guy's confidence."

"I'm not here to build your confidence! Jesus Christ, *I'm here to win a baseball game* and if I think I can win by pinch-hitting in the first inning, then, shit, I'll pinch-hit for you even in the first. You just play your position. Let me worry about running the club!"

Late in May, Sparky sends Vukovich to the minors and calls up an unknown relief pitcher, Rawlins "Rawly" Jackson Eastwick III. It's a quiet move, but its effect is enormous. Nobody in the league will have more saves this season than Eastwick.

Vukovich will end up with the Phillies. During the next five years, he will hit safely just fourteen times. He will retire in 1981, with a career batting average of .161.

SEVEN

MAJOR-LEAGUE STANDINGS ON MAY 1, 1975

NATIONAL LEAGUE

East Division

	W	L	Pct	GB
Chicago	12	5	.706	–
New York	9	7	.563	2½
Pittsburgh	9	7	.563	2½
Philadelphia	8	10	.444	4½
St. Louis	7	10	.412	5
Montreal	5	11	.313	6½

West Division

	W	L	Pct	GB
Los Angeles	15	8	.652	–
San Diego	11	10	.524	2½
Cincinnati	12	11	.522	3
Atlanta	12	12	.500	3½
San Francisco	10	11	.476	3½
Houston	8	16	.333	7

AMERICAN LEAGUE

East Division

	W	L	Pct	GB
Detroit	10	6	.625	–
Milwaukee	9	7	.563	1
New York	9	10	.474	$2\frac{1}{2}$
Cleveland	7	8	.467	$2\frac{1}{2}$
Baltimore	7	9	.438	3
Boston	7	9	.438	3

West Division

	W	L	Pct	GB
California	12	8	.600	–
Oakland	12	8	.600	–
Kansas City	11	9	.550	1
Texas	9	9	.500	2
Minnesota	6	10	.375	4
Chicago	7	13	.350	5

Casey Stengel finds himself at his big house in Glendale, and maybe now April is over, but once again he's reading in the newspaper about Opening Day at Fenway Park. They shoveled snow out of the grandstand. Stengel seems to recall that they have done this before. Maybe every year. Maybe never. His memories feel unfamiliar, and several times Stengel looks up from reading about Opening Day at Fenway Park and sometimes it's night outside and sometimes it's daytime — he's still working to finish the article, or just starting it.

He sees as how Boston began its season by playing Milwaukee and that quiet Hank Aaron was there, making his American League debut, and cocky Tony Conigliaro was there, making his official comeback, it was some kinda madhouse, and Aaron went oh for four while Tony C. singled in the first and led the Red Sox to victory, but there is something wrong with Casey's eyes, for behind every figure in the lineup he sees a long series of ghostly shadows, with more ghosts and shadows lined up behind them — all the generations that led these young men to where they are today, playing in the major leagues.

Many things have changed dramatically in Casey's lifetime, but the essential continuity of baseball remains. This comforts him, as it comforts every one of the game's enthusiasts. Of course, he understands why there are shadows of fathers all over the place. It's the most normal way to see baseball. After all, it's a game which magically tweaks time, inching along while the lessons of the past hover and the mistakes of the future loom. The son will grow up to take his father's place. Naturally, when yesterday is superimposed atop tomorrow, the present dances a little, becoming blurry.

Casey Stengel keeps reading about Opening Day at Fenway Park, when he notices that the doorbell has been chiming and realizes that he has to answer it.

Early on the Red Sox are swept by the Tigers. Bill Lee loses a ten-inning, three-two heartbreaker on a misplayed bad-hop grounder. Spaceman sits alone in the locker room afterward, methodically shredding his uniform.

Boston's Rick Wise also loses to Detroit by a single run, and so does Luis Tiant. Tiant's game is a one-to-nothing masterpiece. After retiring the first fourteen batters in a row, all of whom are waving harmlessly at his deliveries, he tosses a change-up to rookie Danny Meyer and the young Tiger swats it into the chummy right-field seats. With Mickey Lolich on target, sitting down the final fifteen Boston batters, the one run is sufficient to offset Tiant's two-hitter.

"I never saw anything like him before," Meyer later says. "So I just went up there swinging, hoping to get my bat on the ball."

This quote runs in the *Los Angeles Times*. Stengel reads it, grasping Meyer's meaning without any particular difficulty, but confusion sets in when he sees Luis Tiant's name in the box score, for Casey pictures not the son but the eponymous father, not the rotund, ill-shaven righty of the Boston Red Sox but the rail-thin southpaw of the New York Cubans. He remembers watching Tiant Sr. defeat Babe Ruth's all-stars. He can see it still, one of the most dominating performances he's ever witnessed. He especially admired Tiant's phenomenal pick-off move. The batters grew so bewildered that they were never sure when he was coming home; occasionally, they would swing when Tiant threw to first. Casey wanted this pitcher for his own squad, but he knew it was impossible. This was before integration of the game, which was why the dark-skinned Tiant played in the Negro Leagues and could oppose the legendary Anglo players of the day only in meaningless exhibitions.

Jackie Robinson came to the Brooklyn Dodgers the same year that Tiant Sr. retired from baseball, returning home to Cuba in frail health with his wife and their little boy, his namesake. In Havana, the family listened avidly to ball games, until a doctor warned Tiant Sr. that he was becoming too excited for his own good, and ordered him to stop.

The son grew up; the son went away. Tiant Sr. never got used to the absence. Every minute of every day his heart was heavy. He longed just to touch the son, to clutch him in an embrace, but the revolutionary government would not allow this.

Tiant Sr. took a job as a pump jockey in a dilapidated service station. He worked there every day.

He's still there, in 1975, at age seventy. In his spare time, he plays dominoes and dreams about his son in America.

Newspapers slap doorsteps and porch stoops around the country at May's start, bearing only bad news. Karen Anne Quinlan is dying; Patty Hearst is on trial. Jimmy Hoffa will soon go missing. Many presidential aides still await sentencing. Unemployment is climbing, inflation is looming, and South Vietnam is falling to the Communists. A huge military transport plane loaded with escaping Vietnamese orphans crashes immediately after takeoff in the worst U.S. air disaster in history.

Someone asks Boston pitcher Bill Lee how he justifies his particular profession during these dark ages. "No one wants reality and bad news all the time," Lee explains. "I'm out there to help people escape from the doldrums of life, to help them find a little pleasure. I feel beautiful doing that."

Unfortunately, the doldrums bleed through to the sports section. Discounting the play of last year's World Series contestants, Oakland and Los Angeles, there's nothing but bad baseball all over the place. None of the noteworthy off-season acquisitions are doing well. In New York, Catfish Hunter is one and three and Bobby Bonds is hitting .247. Billy Williams (Athletics) bats .210, Henry Aaron (Brewers) .218, Harmon Killebrew (Royals) .219, and Lee May (Orioles) .183.

In the AL East, only two teams are even at .500, and the juvenile Detroit Tigers lead the division with ten measly victories. Despite having four men in the top ten in batting (Thurman Munson, Roy White, Elliott Maddox, Chris Chambliss), the Yankees' record is nine and ten. Baltimore and Boston are both seven and nine. Carl Yastrzemski's batting average is .215. Bill Lee is one and three. Luis Tiant is two and three. The Red Sox have still not shaken free of the malaise which befell them in late August of the previous year.

In cafeterias and luncheonettes, men speak sports without much enthusiasm. It feels like a long time since any major-league team outside California has played the game well. It's been a month of depressing baseball, plus now the Viet Cong flag flies atop the Presidential Palace in Saigon.

Senator George McGovern flies to Cuba, by way of Mexico City, for an unofficial meeting with Fidel Castro.[1] McGovern reasons that, since the United States now has relations with Moscow and Peking, it's time to open doors to Havana. He meets Castro very late in the evening. McGovern is struck by the magnetism of the Cuban president — an impression of great physical strength. They recline in worn leather armchairs, comfortable with cognac and cigars. Sweeping through the open window is the sound of music and the clang of lanyards from the harbor. The air smells of gardenia. There is a fire in the fireplace and a bullet-riddled flag in a glass case on the wall.

The men are alone but for the translator, who is unnecessary because Castro, though speaking quietly, always makes himself understood. They converse casually about the senator's war record and the 1972 presidential election, which McGovern lost to Richard Nixon by one of the biggest margins in history. "If I lived in your country," Castro tells him, sincere if preoccupied, "I would have voted for you." The senator extends his thanks, but again noticing Castro's distractedness, he inquires whether everything is okay.

A bit rueful, perhaps even embarrassed, Castro acknowledges that he has just come from a baseball game. The team from Oriente, his home province and the birthplace of his revolution, competed against Havana in a game for the national championship. His team lost. Castro removes the cigar from his mouth and frowns at it. Oriente's defeat has shaken him. He's finding it difficult to absorb.

The American senator reaches out sympathetically to pat the Cuban president's arm. It's late; they're both tired. They will have time later this week for more serious meetings. McGovern recognizes the desire to maintain an informal chat, but he senses this moment may be propitious for one item on his agenda.

"Mister President," McGovern asks respectfully, "you know of Luis Tiant?"

"The father, or the son?"

"Ah, well. Interestingly, Luis Tiant the son has named his own son Luis Tiant, so there is actually a father, a son, and a grandson."

"Three Luis Tiants." Castro strokes his beard. "Interesting." He knows about the two pitchers named Luis Tiant, of course. Both are cunning, nervy hurlers, with a wide assortment of pitches and a sporadic fastball used to fine effect. Castro himself was a pitcher with a fairly good breaking ball, before he overthrew Fulgencio Batista. Secretly, Castro still follows American baseball. He can recite Tiant's statistics with Boston; he knows them so well that he's even been heard to argue how the shape of last year's Red Sox season provides the clearest model for the imperial destiny of the United States: the early brilliance, the promising middle, and the inevitable decline — this is how 1974 went for the Red Sox, and this is what one sees already occurring in the United States, the decline in agriculture and trade, the rotting urban centers, the crime, the poverty, the hunger, the smog, the student uprisings, the race riots, the class warfare. The loss of Vietnam will travel back home and soon the empire itself will be lost in revolution.

"I have a letter here," Senator McGovern says. He hands across an envelope.

Castro glances at the return address. It comes from Edward W. Brooke, the junior senator from Massachusetts. Castro opens it, quickly scanning the letter.

". . . writing . . . matter of deep concern to myself and one of my constituents, Mr. Luis Tiant . . . impossible to predict how much longer he will be able to pitch . . . hopeful that his parents will be able to visit . . . to see their son perform . . . not had the chance to spend any significant time with them for many years . . . such a reunion would be a significant indication that better understanding between our peoples is achievable. . . ."

Castro studies it pensively. He folds the letter with care, returns it to the envelope, and places it in his breast pocket. *Good news is so infrequent*, he thinks, *and they have so little to look forward to, these desperate Americans.* He feels a keen pity for the followers of the Boston Red Sox. "Well," Castro responds after a time, "let me check on it."

The next afternoon, by way of opening their first major policy discussion, Castro announces that the request made by Senator Brooke will be granted. Tiant's parents may go to Boston and stay as long as they wish. He hopes the gesture will bring a little pleasure. And McGovern has given a thank-you to the people of Massachusetts, the only state he won in 1972. Maybe this will help turn things around.

In the Riverfront clubhouse, on the night before the Kentucky Derby, Reds are congregating to lay odds on tomorrow's ponies, when the sporting goods guy comes to give Pete Rose a first baseman's mitt to break in for Pete's daughter, Fawn. Rose is touched, even though he has certainly made no secret of the fact that he cannot stand Fawn. The sporting goods guy asks whether Rose might get him in to see Sparky, but the player points out the office door is closed. Sparky huddles inside with scouts and advisers and pours over charts and statistics that detail how, as of May 1, George Foster is hitting .320; every five trips to the plate, he knocks in a run, and they still can't fit him in their goddamn batting order.

A short time later, Sparky emerges to take a stomp around the field. Rose is scooping up grounders off the mat at first and thinking to himself how great it would be to play the infield, up near the good-looking folk and out of range of the bleacher fuckheads who have been lobbing bottles and cherry bombs and shit at him. Plus Pete's been lonely out in left, where there's no one to talk to. Playing the infield, he could chat with the other team's coach, the base runner, the umpire. He could even run over to speak with the pitcher now and then.

Sparky approaches briskly. "What's all this about?"

"I'm breakin' in this mitt for Fawn," Pete replies, a man duty bound.

Sparky stops to admire him for a while. He's impressed how much Peter Edward gives of himself in this (essentially meaningless) task. Even as he breaks in a glove, he's Charlie Hustle.

And watching, an idea forms in Sparky's mind, a deliriously happy thought. A year after Rose made the all-star team at second base, he was asked, publicly, to move to third base. Rose grudgingly tried it a few games in the spring, announced that he didn't like third, and demanded his old position back. A later compromise moved Rose to left field, which Riverfront's customers now call the Rose Garden. All of this maneuvering, however, went on before Sparky's time.

"You look pretty good around this bag," the manager mutters with pretend indifference. He shoves a wad of bubble gum and tobacco into his face, folds his arms, and nods laconically across the diamond. "How do you think you'd do at the other corner?"

"Are you serious?"

"I am."

Silently, they both imagine what that might accomplish, and how much Foster's bat could contribute if he were to play daily.

"Well —" Pete gives a shrug. "I'll do anything to help the ball club."

"Awright. Don't say anything about this to anybody, but you're my third baseman tomorrow."

"Swell."

"Promise to tell me if you feel uncomfortable so I can get you the hell out of there."

"I won't be comfortable. But that can't affect my play."

The next day, against the Braves at Riverfront, Rose starts at third with Foster in the outfield. This proves to be one of the most important personnel moves in Cincinnati history. Foster doubles in the fifth to ignite a rally, and homers in the sixth. Joe Morgan notes that there are no longer any outs in the lineup. Gary Nolan pitches the whole game. He allows only five hits and gains his first victory since October 3, 1972.

In the sixties, Philadelphia's Dick Allen had to play the field in a batting helmet in order to protect himself from all the junk heaved at him by the hometown fans. It was a habit of protection he continued to maintain as he was shuttled about, team to team, St. Louis to Los Angeles to Chicago. Six weeks into the 1975 season, the thirty-three-year-old slugger still hasn't reported to the Braves, so Atlanta trades him to, of all teams, the Phillies. He's come full circle. Allen goes to work hauling his legendary forty-one-ounce bat and a worn-out, patched-up first baseman's mitt. The owner greets him in the clubhouse with a warm handshake. "Welcome home, Son." Allen is as sensitive as he is strong, and he's very strong. Tears well up in his eyes. He's only been away for five seasons, but everything is different. The team has moved to South Philadelphia. The stadium is big and modern. It has artificial turf. The fans sit further away. His uniform is of a new fabric, design, and color, which seems especially appropriate since the connotation it carries, the meaning of being a Phillie, is totally new. Allen still wears his batting helmet on the field, but these days it's unnecessary. Philadelphia, whose racism once scared Curt Flood right out of baseball, now embraces Dick Allen.

He debuts on a hot, humid night in mid-May. Instead of taunts he receives only standing ovations. In his first at bat, he singles off Cincinnati's Pat Darcy. The Phillies win. The Reds, in the middle of a five-game losing streak, accept Allen's return graciously. Johnny Bench even applauds the Phillies for making a smart move. "Our team would have never taken him," admits the Reds' catcher. "They worry about what has happened in someone's past. We have no long hair, no mustaches on this team. That's our style, and the fans in Cincinnati seem to like it. But the Phillies, they're a very loose team."[2]

Easy distinctions of this sort are valid for the last time in 1975. Soon the players will become free, and the identity of a team — the particular uniqueness of any baseball organization — will become smudged by free agency, by frantic trades and frequent transactions. By 1980 Dick Allen will be long retired, and Philadelphia will be led to its first world championship by, of all people, the flower of Cincinnati, the transplanted Pete Rose.

Five and a half games behind the Dodgers, the Reds fly north to Montreal. They lose that game too, plus now there's blood all over the place. After Morgan is spiked in a collision at second base, a doctor sews fourteen stitches into Joe's shin. The next day, he is limping around the small, filthy shed they call the "visitors' clubhouse" in Parc Jarry's right field. He's in obvious pain. *He'll have to go on the disabled list,* Sparky thinks.

The last time Morgan went on the disabled list, late in the 1974 season, he watched from the bench and realized, for the first time, the many things he could do to help his team win. He began to work with the pitching coach to strengthen his arm so he could turn more double plays. He started the 1975 season at a run: in the first inning of the Reds' first game, he drew a walk, he stole second, he stole third. In his next at bats, he singled and doubled. In the next game, he stole another base and hit three singles. By June he led the league in walks, hits, stolen bases, and batting average, but his team was still not winning enough, so, despite standing just five foot seven and weighing only 155 pounds, Morgan promptly began to hit for distance, smashing home runs, piling up RBIs. He bristles when they call him the strongest little man in baseball, a prestige player, a superstar. All he wants to be is the complete teammate.

Sparky wonders who in the world can possibly replace this guy. He is considering his options, debating the lineup card, when Little Joe limps up. "I want to play today," Morgan says with quiet urgency. He is determined to make Cincinnati get the pennant this year, and nothing will stop him.

Sparky can't believe he's serious. The manager is so moved that he calls a clubhouse meeting. "If Joe can play," he yells, "you all can play!"

The game is nationally televised. Expo errors give the Reds three unearned runs in the fifth frame, but Montreal comes back to tie the score. Shortstop Tim Foli singles and scores on right fielder Gary Carter's double in the fifth, second baseman Pete Mackanin hits his first major-league homer in the sixth, and first baseman Jose Morales slams a pinch-hit homer in the seventh. Griffey leads off the tenth inning with a homer to snap a three-three tie. Bench follows with another homer one out later.

Their six-game losing streak is over.

The next afternoon, Gary Nolan faces a reportedly hurt Dave McNally. Hurt or not, McNally doesn't have much on his pitches, and he displays none of the command he had against Sparky's boys in the 1970 World Series — in that awful third game, when McLucky not only went the route but punched a grand slam as well. *A grand slam!*

In the top of the second, Foster starts a rally. In the sixth, he homers. Nolan shuts down the Expos. McNally loses his fifth in a row.

"Tonight," says Johnny Bench, "Gary Nolan turned around our season. It indicated to everyone that he was going to be a big winner.

Guys on the club started saying to themselves, 'Hey I'm not gonna have to do this alone.'"

A new confidence sweeps through the Cincinnati staff. "When you watch Gary, you know you are watching a master," says reliever Will McEnaney. "He used to just rear back and throw the fastball. Now it's a game of mind and body. I enjoy watching him. He concentrates so deep."

In the season's second month, the Boston Red Sox win six in a row, then drop six of seven. They now host the Oakland Athletics for three games. In the first contest, a weak Luis Tiant surrenders eleven hits but goes the distance to beat a wild Blue Moon Odom, ten to five. The next night, an unseasonably sultry May 20, Bill Lee throws a two-hit, seventy-eight-pitch shutout, hitting spots all night, facing twenty-five batters through eight innings and perversely striking out only one, Bert "Campy" Campaneris — the last man he faces — in the bottom of the ninth, with two men on.

Vida Blue absorbs the loss, giving up four home runs, including a wallop by Tony C. that sails over the wall, over the screen, and across Lansdowne Street. It's Conigliaro's eighty-seventh home run at Fenway Park, and, though nobody knows it yet, his last.[3]

In the series closer, Rico homers off Ken Holtzman, and Yastrzemski hits a grand slam. Having thus swept the defending world champions, the Red Sox shift positions in the American League East division. Milwaukee stays in first, but now Boston is second, followed by Detroit, Baltimore, New York, and Cleveland. Each club is separated in the standings by one game. With growing confidence, Boston now sets its sights on another California team, the Angels. Bill Lee has become unhittable, winning four of his last five with devastating command. Opponents are batting just .122 against him. Two weeks earlier, on May 11, he pitched against the Angels in Anaheim. Spaceman beat them easily but refused the credit. These, after all, were the same weak-hitting Angels who, according to Texas manager Billy Martin, could take batting practice in a hotel lobby without breaking anything. Spaceman went so far as to steal

Billy's put-down, telling reporters, "The Angels could take batting practice in the lobby of the Grand Hotel and not bother a chandelier."[4] Lee will forever get credit for the line.

Now it's Saturday afternoon, May 24, and the Angels play the Red Sox at Fenway. The game is nationally broadcast. No doubt Stengel is watching from his home in Glendale. It's a battle of lefties: Andy Hassler against Lee. Casey must be happy to see Spaceman pitch. Stengel knows him as another outstanding USC graduate, a student of his friend Dedeaux. Lee pitched alongside Tom Seaver on one of Dedeaux's championship teams.

These two wisecracking baseball enthusiasts, Bill Lee and Casey Stengel, are related — not by blood, but behavior. Like Stengel, Spaceman exudes the vibe of a mad genius, an errant charisma. His manner confuses the baseball men who came alive in the age of another Boston pitcher named Bill Lee. (Not a relation, he was right-handed and called "Big Bill" — even though Spaceman is just as tall and is actually heavier — because back in Big Bill's playing days that *was* big. He pitched mostly with the Cubs and Phillies, and won ten for the Red Sox in 1946.) When asked about a pitching performance, Spaceman answers in riddle, musing over pseudoscientific explanations, quoting Eastern philosophy, frantically jumping subjects. He is irreverent. He enjoys baseball brawls. He follows strange habits. He jogs from his house to Fenway for each home game. He boasts a repertoire of fifty-five pitches. Once, while his team awaited its flight, Bill Lee blasted a tape of the "William Tell Overture" in the airport lobby. He was wearing a pith helmet. He pretended to be conducting. Nobody much noticed; it didn't seem exceptional. Another time, Lee popped out of the airport luggage chute, wearing a red wig. Often he curses Pudge for visiting the mound. Once, after the southpaw gave up a game-losing home run, the catcher approached in the locker room. "That sure was a chickenshit pitch you threw," Fisk grumbled.

"Sure was," Spaceman agreed impishly. "And you called it."[5]

Stengel could just as easily have earned the nickname "Spaceman." Instead, the media dubbed him a clown.

The clock chimes. A housefly buzzes. A timer sounds. A kettle whistles. The doorbell rings. When he watches a game, Casey ignores them all. Doubtless he's eager to observe this new blooper ball of Bill Lee's, this "eephus" that Lee calls a "sludge curve." He worked on it all spring and debuted it against the Yankees a month ago, with tremendous success.

Lee doesn't attempt the trick pitch in the early innings, because he's feeling too wound up from the longevity tea he drinks before every game. But as the game progresses, Lee grows a bit more mellow. Both Petrocelli and Burleson drive Andy Hassler pitches into the left-field screen. Lee leads by six runs in the fifth, with an oh-and-one count on center fielder Mickey Rivers. He brings the ball high over his head and flips it. The ball, though quickly rotating, travels with paradoxical slowness. It goes up; it goes down. Its leisurely arrival mocks the tension of the circumstance. Tripping forward, the ball floats in for a strike. Rivers is frozen. He looks slowly at the umpire and shakes his head.

Certainly Stengel is amused by the pitch, though a bit disappointed to note that it is really just a slow curve with an extraordinary arc. It can hardly be compared with the pitch introduced by the Pirates' Rip Sewell in 1943. Sewell's toss to the plate would sometimes soar twenty-five feet off the ground. He called it his "eephus," a name he got from a teammate. The name, like the pitch, was nonsense.

Lee remains well ahead in the eighth inning, but he senses that the Angels are conspiring to exhaust him. They keep taking pitches, extending the count, forcing him to work. Again Rivers comes to bat. Whenever Lee sets himself to throw, Rivers steps out of the box. Lee grows furious. He can feel his tea wearing off. Rivers sees his fourth ball and receives a walk, but the whole time he jogs down the base path to first, Bill curses him horribly. The umpire dashes out from behind the plate. He warns the pitcher, but lets him remain in the game. Lee doesn't look that sharp, but he's making the big pitches. He keeps Rivers from scoring, and in the ninth, with the bases loaded, he gets catcher Bob Allietta to ground into a game-ending double play. This completes Lee's second shutout in a row. He has now thrown twenty-one straight scoreless innings. The win lifts the Red Sox into first place, a half game in front of Milwaukee, who lost to the Twins, three to two, and five games ahead of New York, who beat the Rangers, nine to five, because Bonds cracked a three-run home run and stole two bases.

Boston is thrilled, but less so are two ballplayers, namely Bernie Carbo and Fred Lynn. Both Carbo and Lynn were benched against the southpaw Andy Hassler in favor of right-handers Jim Rice (in left) and Juan Beniquez (in center). Naturally, neither Carbo nor Lynn was happy to sit. Carbo remains stung by how Darrell Johnson gave up on him in midseason last year and is fighting to see more playing time. Lynn has homered in each of the last two games, but there is a rumor, unfounded, that he bails out against lefties. After the game — with steely determination — Lynn insists to himself that no fair-fielding Juan Beniquez will ever seize his rightful position. The next afternoon, Lynn gets one of only three hits off California's undefeated, short-arm thrower, Ed Figueroa. The next day, Lynn singles in a run. He is walked in the eighth. He scores on a home run by Dewey Evans. He goes one for four in the next game, two for four in the game after that, and three for four in the next. Laying the bat on the ball with a slight uppercut, sometimes catching the pitch on the tip end of the stick with alacrity, the rookie drives everything hard to all fields. His hitting streak deepens, lengthens, broadens. He soon ranks among the league leaders in every offensive category. He draws walks, steals bases, and scores runs. He advances runners. He slugs in clutch situations. He hits in the day and at night, against lefties and righties, on the road and at home. He pounds knuckleballs in Illinois, sliders in Texas, fastballs in Minnesota. It frustrates Darrell Johnson because he likes to uncover a player's tendencies and then employ them accordingly. But Lynn doesn't reveal tendencies; he just hits. Opposing managers see him as an old-fashioned, all-around, natural talent, comparing him to Stan Musial and Roger Maris, not realizing that Lynn honed these instincts through years with Dedeaux at USC, where every day was spent drilling fundamentals, and practices had all the pressure of a championship game. Evans, the young man in right, has been considered Boston's best outfielder and strongest arm, but now he and whoever is stationed in left — Rick Miller, Carbo, Rice, Beniquez — race to keep up, inspired by the daring way their rookie center fielder plays his position. Without ever looking, Lynn can see the whole field. He always positions himself to back up infielders, he hits the right cutoff men, he cuts down runners at the plate. He ranges about center — alert, intense, and confident. His spectacular diving catches grow commonplace. The glow in his soul erupts and bursts, shining over the entire outfield. Fenway scarcely needs its lights for night games. Boston travels to play the Royals on their home AstroTurf. That weekend, in Kansas City, Lynn gets six hits and drives in eight runs, and Boston takes three of four from the Royals. Lynn has now hit safely in twenty consecutive games.

The streak ends in Detroit, but as soon as it does Lynn sets out to start a new one. He arrives early at the ballpark to take extra batting practice. The rhythm of his swing is off. It bothers him. He goes one for four that day, drives in a run, and scores, and his team wins the sixth of their last eight, but something in his at bats doesn't feel right. He wonders if he's overstriding.

Or maybe he's just distracted.

In the newspapers, Fred keeps finding himself compared to Carl Yastrzemski, because both are left-handed, both are named for their fathers, both have the middle name of Michael, and both stand an inch over six feet and weigh around one hundred eighty-five pounds, have similar haircuts, and hit line drives with short, compact swings. The comparisons embarrass Fred, whereas they remind Yastrzemski of being a rookie, when he was constantly compared to Ted Williams. Carl's first two months in the majors were his worst in baseball: he hit just .210, dropped fly balls, and always got booed at home. His first good game occurred against the Tigers, when he got a couple hits, including a long home run into the right-center stands. A warm, June night in Detroit — this was the first time Carl felt like he truly belonged in a big-league uniform.

And now, fourteen seasons later, in Detroit, in June, Fred Lynn lies anxiously awake in bed.[6] This is Detroit's first year since 1954 without the great Al Kaline in right. There's something to envy about the veteran's retirement. It was Kaline who talked about wishing to hide when you leave the ballpark, about how you begin to lose your concentration on the field because of what happens off of it, and about how you have to conquer the game of baseball or it will conquer you. Fred is shy, has always been shy. He was the last one in his school to wear flares, and he still hasn't really learned how to curse. He looks at the ground a lot. His mouth has the tendency to hang open. He likes to disappear in a crowd. He is surprised by how much it takes to play in the majors. It looks so easy; it isn't. A pundit describes Lynn's soft features as "a visage of Velveeta," then asks Fred how he's enjoying his splendid year. "One doesn't really stay aware," he answers, and even Fred's grammar is detached. "You go day to day."

At last, around 3:30 A.M., Fred Lynn gives up on sleep, throws off the sheets, shrugs into some clothes, and walks from the Pontchartrain Hotel with no destination in mind. He just walks. His impressions are vague — a hydrant, an airplane, a building. Youths in hooded jackets. A siren passes. Pigeons erupt from a construction site. It's hardly safe or smart, but Fred goes about Detroit without paying attention to where he walks or who he passes, his brain fogged and restless and telling itself not to speculate, thinking that he mustn't think but simply go, and feeling the air, and seeing the dawn.

He arrives at the park in a daze, too tired to think. He has sleep in his eyes. In the first inning, with one man on, he hits a high curve into the upper deck in right field for a home run. In the second inning, with two men on, he hits a low forkball off the facade of the roof for another home run. In the third inning, with two men on, he hits a low slider off the left-center fence. It misses being a home run by two feet. Fred settles for a triple. In the eighth inning, he beats out an infield tapper for a single. In the ninth inning, with two men on, he hits another high breaking ball into the right-field bleachers for his third home run of the game, his fourteenth of the season. "You never dream a rookie can do what he has done," laughs Darrell Johnson. Lynn has faced four different Detroit pitchers in one day, hit them all hard, and become only the ninth player in major-league history to drive in ten or more runs in one game (Reggie Jackson did it last, at Fenway Park). His sixteen total bases tie the American League mark set by Ty Cobb in 1925. "In all of my years in the game," Boston third-base coach Don Zimmer testifies, "I've never seen anyone do everything — hit, hit for power, field, throw — like this kid. He's been just unbelievable."

After Lynn's power display, hundreds of reporters seek out the modest boy for still more comments. "When I'm tired," Fred patiently explains, "I seem to hit better." The reporters learn that he was raised by his father alone; few inquire whether his parents were divorced. Many articles, as well as a hardback biography later published for children, mistakenly assume that Fred's mother is dead.

His father is quoted as saying how, once, in the backyard, he tossed a hardball against little Fred's head in order to teach him that he couldn't get hurt, that he shouldn't shy away, that there was never anything to fear when playing baseball.

Fred sees this in the *Boston Globe*. A peculiar tingling sensation goes off inside. It's creepy. He cannot remember his father ever doing this. *Did it really happen?* Fred is too overwhelmed and exhausted to be sure of his own memories. It takes his every faculty now just to focus on each game, each opponent, each at bat, each pitch. He thinks he can remember finding his swing in Little League, a smooth cut with his hands clear down on the end of the bat, and then remembers arguing with his father, who said that Fred should choke the bat for more controlled hitting, but he isn't sure if that happened either. All he knows for certain is that he uses that swing now, it came to him some time ago, and it still feels good.

The ball, the bases, the walls of Fenway: all clearer and clearer. The rest: blurred by the roar of the crowd, by the glare of a million flashbulbs.

Despite the grandeur of Fred Lynn's performance, the Red Sox still have a problem. They are getting beat by left-handed pitching. They need another righty in the lineup if they ever expect to get around the likes of Frank Tanana, Ken Holtzman, or Jim Kaat. Their second baseman, the right-handed Doug Griffin, appears particularly vulnerable to southpaw pitching.

Meanwhile, in the league's western division, veteran Denny Doyle has been crowded out of California's infield by hotshot rookie Jerry Remy. In mid-June the Red Sox obtain Doyle's contract from the Angels in exchange for cash and a player to be named later. To make room on the roster for him, the Red Sox send their weakest hitter down to the minors. He's batting just .123. He's displaying poor bat speed and a complete lack of coordination. His name, unfortunately, is Tony Conigliaro.

With the plug pulled on the Tony C. experiment, with Doyle added, and with Fisk soon to return, the Red Sox can field two pretty good squads, a veteran squad of Pudge, Carl, Doyle, Rico, and Carbo, or a slightly less-potent, younger squad of Tim Blackwell, Cooper, Griffin, Beniquez, and Miller. Both squads need Burleson, Lynn, and Evans; these are the three least replaceable gloves on the 1975 Red Sox.

On those occasions when the veteran squad plays, and neither Tiant nor Rogelio Moret pitches, the Red Sox become the only team in the majors still to field an entirely white team. This goes unnoticed by the majority of Red Sox fans. A large segment of Boston's population — the predominately Irish-Catholic and white working class — remains acutely uncomfortable around those of African descent. They appreciate the reluctance of Tom Yawkey's integration. The tale is often told of Jackie Robinson trying out in 1945 at Fenway, with a few other Negro Leaguers, before Branch Rickey had seen him; the black ballplayers all performed impressively, but were rushed out after Yawkey shouted, "Get those niggers off the field!" Some Yawkey loyalists dispute the story's veracity; most don't bother. True or not, the anecdote inspired the NAACP to picket Fenway in the late 1950s and demand that Yawkey sign a player of color. Twelve years after Robinson and Rickey broke baseball's color barrier, once every other major-league club had an integrated roster, Yawkey finally relented, signing infielder Pumpsie Green in 1961. Later, a few other blacks were added, notably George Scott and Reggie Smith, and then traded.

Observers who continued to complain about this slow pace of desegregation were derided as Cambridge radicals. The NAACP now stayed out of it, having become embroiled in a broader battle with the school committee of the city of Boston to end de facto segregation of local public schools. Black neighborhoods had overcrowded classrooms, poor physical facilities, inadequate and outdated materials, more limited curricula offerings in the secondary schools, and a large number of inexperienced teachers. Responsibility for these inequities fell on the Boston school committee, which managed and operated the city's public schools. The school committee, chaired at the time by Louise Day Hicks and supported by vocal antibusing advocates such as City Councillor Albert "Dapper" O'Neil, denied that this was racism. Racists, they said, were people like George Wallace, or Lester Maddox, or Bull Connor — people who used picturesque tactics on television, wielded billy clubs and tear gas, they kept the poor from voting, they lynched people. Racists lived in the South.

The Boston chapter of the NAACP begged to differ. Throughout the 1960s, they staged one-day boycotts and marches to highlight their demands that the school committee end "racial imbalance." These accomplished little. In 1972 the NAACP had a group of black parents file in federal district court, contending that the school committee had denied black children equal protection of the laws by maintaining a racially segregated school system. In June 1974, U.S. District Court Judge W. Arthur Garrity Jr. found in favor of the parent plaintiffs and ordered new school assignment plans making use of the busing of students. Minutes after he delivered the decision, Garrity was burned in effigy throughout Boston.

So when the white Tony C. pulls a hamstring, and then injures his groin and hits under .150, he's still the popular pick to be the designated hitter over the dark-skinned rookie who hits .300. And when Tony C. is finally sent down, there is no warm welcome for Rice, the team's first-round draft pick, the man who won the Triple Crown in double A in 1973 and again in triple A in 1974, and was named the *Sporting News'* Minor League Player of the Year. Rice is the African elephant no one will acknowledge — young, strong, and black in Boston at the worst possible time. And yet, as a player, Rice is exactly what the Red Sox need. Bill Lee describes him as "one solid piece of muscle," and his threatening presence in the batting order helps Lynn receive better pitches, as Conigliaro once did for Yastrzemski.[7] Lynn is the more consistent (like Carl) while Rice is the more powerful (like Tony). Both Lynn and Rice were gridiron stars, and now they attack their lofty baseball positions with the snarling footballer's primitive concentration. They are both private people, but they like each other, they enjoy being companion rookies; they live in the same apartment complex in North Quincy, each with a young wife, and they usually drive to work together, and go golfing on their off days. Lynn receives the newspaper headlines, with his easy smile, his effortless swing, the photogenic blonde he married out of high school; in contrast, Rice and his wife, Jeannie, appear morose and moody. Already most Boston fans treat this silent black slugger, with his murderous strength, as some sort of impending troublemaker, their Dick Allen.

And here again, 1975 resembles a lost world, a small world, full of unfair prejudice and hateful mischaracterizations, but a time too of strong community pride, when neighbors display a fierce allegiance to one another, like teammates on a ball club. By court order, South Boston's self-imposed isolation must come to an end. No ideas can supersede those of justice and equality for all, not even pleas for the stability of bygone eras, when loyalty was the order of the day. In baseball, as in South Boston, togetherness soon will be discredited.

Suspicion will mount. Although it would be wrong to glorify this small world's lack of mobility and mistrust of freedom, it's wrong also to deny the identity that will subsequently be lost.

In the Astrodome, late in May, Montreal pitcher Dave McNally singles home a run. It's the second inning. Now he leads by five runs. It might be enough, just maybe. He hasn't won a game all month; he hasn't felt good all season, not on the mound, not anywhere. The miserable weather, the crummy defense, the lack of power. The team made him commitments that they haven't kept. It was supposed to be all settled. They said he'd get a tax shelter, a big raise; now they're quibbling. McNally only agreed to be an Expo because the club president, John McHale, promised moving expenses, that sort of item. But none of this has materialized.[8] McNally's living in a motel in Canada. His family is down in Maryland. The season's already two months under way and McNally doesn't even have a contract. Instead, he's playing under the automatic renewal clause from last year's contract. He hates these distractions. He wants to go out and pitch, go out and win. He stands on first, glaring at the scoreboard.

"I know what you're doing," says a voice. McNally turns. It's Houston's kindly first baseman Bob Watson. He's been pondering McNally's apparent lack of command.

"What's that?" asks McNally.

"You're a cagey old left-hander. You're sitting back, throwing that soft stuff, to set us up for your fastball."[9]

McNally answers with a small, mysterious smile. In fact, he's throwing as hard as he can.

Houston comes back as McNally's velocity and location diminish. After eight singles, four walks, and three doubles, McNally is out of the game. In his next start, he blows another lead, and now the former Baltimore ace — who once won seventeen straight decisions — has gone seven consecutive games without a victory. Montreal's meager attendance plummets still further. The fans are all over the manager, but the front office is realistic. "Sometimes," says a team

spokesman, "you have to sit and bleed until you stop bleeding."
McNally's next start comes June 8 against the Padres. Again, he loses.
Watching the game from his box, the Expos' owner dismisses the loss
and blames it on two bad pitches. McNally will not be consoled. It's
insulting to be beaten by the Padres and the Astros, two teams with
terrible records and, not coincidentally, the world's ugliest uniforms.
His arm doesn't hurt; he just stinks. His ERA is 5.26 and his record is
three and six. He can't stand it. When he leaves the clubhouse that
day, he leaves the game. He flies home and announces his retirement
from baseball. He says he'll be moving with his family to Billings,
Montana, where he will join his brother in an automobile agency.[10]
The Expos are stunned. At first, McHale challenges him to a fistfight,
and then the Expo president declares his intention to coax the pitcher
out of retirement, but his plans are interrupted when, on June 17,
McNally begins to hiccup and cannot stop.[11] After three days, he is
checked into the hospital, still hiccuping. The doctors cannot explain
it.[12] The switchboard is swamped with people calling from all over
the country with home remedies.[13] Nothing helps. For twelve days
the hiccuping goes on and on, and then finally, on June 29, it stops as
abruptly as it began. McHale has, in the meantime, placed McNally
on the disqualified list, making him ineligible to play with any other
club. The pitcher is said to be in violation of his contract, though the
contract in question is from 1974 and was signed with Baltimore.
McNally still has never officially signed with Montreal. It seems
unimportant. Presently, the significance of all this will come clear,
but by then it will be too late for the owners.

The Yankees, like the Red Sox, take time getting started. They're
uninspired, playing home games out of Shea while Yankee Stadium
is being renovated. They're mired in last place until the middle of
May, when the complexion of everything abruptly changes, Catfish
wins, Bonds hits, and their team wins sixteen of its next twenty. By
June New York is only one game back of first-place Boston.

The Yankees travel to Chicago for a night game. Bonds, looking
every bit the surefire MVP, snaps his wonderful quick wrists and

connects for the thirtieth leadoff home run of his career. He homers again in the fifth. The White Sox answer with a rally. The Yankees' narrow lead is threatened, and the contest hangs in the balance late in the game when second baseman Jorge Orta slams a two-out line drive into right. Bonds strides in intent pursuit, dives like an Olympic gymnast, and makes a spectacular catch to preserve the victory. Bonds now leads the league in home runs (fifteen) and RBIs (forty-five) — but unfortunately, at that moment, having dramatically snagged Orta's smash, Bonds cannot even get up off the grass. He has mangled his right knee.

Bonds rests for a week, then tests out the knee when Chicago visits New York. He bats third and plays right field. His son Barry flies out for the weekend. Bonds really wants to do well.

Barry attends the game on Saturday afternoon and utterly captivates the children of the other Yankee players with his brooding presence, despite the apparent fact that none of the kids care in the least for Barry's gimpy dad, who has a stiff swing and goes hitless that day. Nonetheless, there's a command implicit in Barry's every movement, so the children admire him, and they seek to imitate his nonchalant way of swaggering about the clubhouse, greeting superstars with an exotic handshake and a soulful wink of recognition.

The next day, Bonds is indefinitely benched, but his son has a great day. It's Bat Day at the home park, so Barry and 53,561 others receive full-size major-league bats. Catfish hurls a shutout. Munson drives in some runs. That's okay, but it gets boring after a while. The children grow restless, and gladly follow Barry down underneath the stands with their bats. They find things to hit, wadded-up napkins, cast-off weenies. Soon, they realize that they have to choke up on the bats or else they will fall down after each swing. It's a turning point in the development of Barry Bonds — who several decades later will go on to hit more home runs in a single season than any player in baseball history — the moment he first chokes up and grasps the true meaning of bat control.

*   *   *

On Monday, June 23, the Indians come to Fenway. The Red Sox are a game and a half ahead of the Yankees. Pudge Fisk appears on the field for the first time since catching against Cleveland on June 28, 1974, and now here's Cleveland again, the first team he will face in his comeback. *Does it take guts?* He isn't sure. *Possibly.* Initially, the crowd is kind. They give Fisk a one-minute standing ovation. *It's just like getting married. You plan for it; you know it's coming. And when the day arrives, you're still nervous.* His team immediately responds with three leadoff errors. Left-handed pitcher Jim Burton, a twenty-five-year-old rookie making his major-league debut, abandons the game with two outs in the first inning, having given up four runs. Pudge himself leaves after five innings, hitless in two at bats. The Indians score two more runs in the sixth, two more in the seventh. The score is now nine to one.

The home crowd grows restless. They never get to see their team play well; the Red Sox are only a game over .500 at home, but they're nineteen and ten on the road. If they lose tonight, they'll be just a half game in first, and it's beginning to seem inarguable that — with their lack of speed, lack of pitching, plague of injuries, and dependence on inexperienced rookies — they haven't a prayer of holding out against their more formidable opponents. Assuming they can somehow dodge the Yanks, they'll also have to deal with the Brewers, who, of all teams, are on a devastating tear. It's not like the Indians or the Orioles are going away, either.

And so 19,591 Fenway fans scatter boos into the night, and when Yastrzemski strikes out in the eighth, they're all over him like he just lost the pennant. Carl slams his bat into the bat rack so hard that he bruises his left hand. He's immediately embarrassed, because he's keenly aware that Al Kaline broke his hand behaving this way in 1967, which helped Boston clinch the league championship. Cecil Cooper also can't believe how stupid it was of Carl. Coop refuses to replace him in the field afterward, so Darrell Johnson positions backup catcher Bob Montgomery at first. Cleveland adds two more runs in the ninth to win by a score of eleven to three.

In the clubhouse after the game, the Red Sox feel terrible. The press are everywhere, predicting failure. Carl ducks into the trainer's room to avoid them. Determined to create a diversion on his behalf, Bill Lee picks up a trash can and heaves it across the locker room. "Boston is a horseshit city!" he yells. "A racist city with horseshit fans and horseshit writers! The fans boo Yaz when he's playing his heart out, and they boo Fisk, who always gives his all. They are all afraid we're going to lose their precious little pennant! This place doesn't deserve us. After we win the World Series, I'm going to get the hell out of here and ride into the western sunset. If the writers and fans want to quit on us, fine. Then they're quitters. But what can you expect? The only guy with guts in this town is Judge Garrity!"[14]

Although Lee does believe that Judge Garrity is doing the right thing, he knows with Stengelese certainty that by making an issue out of it at this moment, he'll goad most of the writers into forgetting about Carl so they can criticize him instead. They do, and as the Red Sox go on to be swept by Cleveland and fall from first place, Bill Lee is deluged with sackfuls of hate mail. His favorite letter comes from Dapper O'Neil, one of the aforementioned leaders of the antibusing movement. It arrives on the city councillor's official letterhead. Lee nearly busts a gut reading it. The type runs all over the page and the punctuation marks are misplaced. Everything is misspelled. The letter accuses Lee of being ignorant. It casts severe doubts on his pitching abilities and questions his manhood. "I wonder now," Dapper coyly concludes in a postscript, "if you've the guts to write me a reply?"

Lee immediately grabs a pen and a piece of paper. "Dear Mr. O'Neil," his response begins, "I think you should know that some moron has stolen your stationery and is writing me letters on it."[15]

The Yankees visit Fenway next, a game and a half in front of Boston. Fisk hits his first homer in more than a year, and Lynn drives in three runs with a triple and a single. Luis Tiant gives a vintage performance, striking out eight New Yorkers with a full array of twists, spins, and pirouettes that leave the visitors wide-eyed. Bill Lee is asked how he feels when observing such artistic perfection from Tiant. "It's like going to a concert or listening to the opera. The orchestra comes out and everything starts banging and it shakes the place. Then it comes to the middle part of the symphony and things get very calm and sweet, and you want to kind of fall asleep. Then, all of a sudden, you sense that the end is coming. Everyone starts getting noisy again. The whole gang is letting out with all the instruments. Then, boom! The whole show is over. That's Tiant! Hard at the start, a little sweet, slow stuff in the middle, and then the big explosion at the end."

Tiant wins easily, six to one, his eighth win in his last ten decisions, his seventh consecutive victory over the Yankees in Fenway. The next night, Rick Wise throws eight and two-thirds' innings of shutout ball. With two outs in the ninth, Bobby Bonds hits his seventeenth home run of the season. Boston wins, nine to one, before a season-high crowd of 35,489, and retakes first place.

On Saturday, June 28, Bill Lee starts against Doc Medich. The game is nationally televised. Each starter gives up six runs. Neither is involved in the decision. The tie holds until the eighth, when Walt "No Neck" Williams lines a screamer past Rico to score Bobby Bonds from first. Now New York has the division lead.

Thurman Munson is particularly satisfied by the day's results; batting fifth in the lineup, he went two for three and knocked in three runs while Carlton Fisk went hitless in the number-eight spot. Munson regards Pudge as an inferior, and he delights in every statistic that confirms this.[16] Gruff Thurman knows that the cheerleader Fisk will always be more popular, no matter how many injuries he suffers, no matter how many runners he strands, no matter how many throws he muffs, because Thurman is uglier and has a flabby butt, a grouchy reputation, and a messy mustache while Pudge always carries himself with dignity and smiles beautifully. *But the numbers . . .*

Munson's glee is short-lived. The next day, with the TV cameras turned away and looking elsewhere, Thurman goes oh for three while Fisk doubles off Catfish Hunter, drives in a run, and carries the Red Sox back into first place.

Late that night, a car driven by Red Sox starting pitcher Reggie Cleveland hits a puddle in a Boston tunnel and flips over. The pitcher is pinned, unconscious, beneath the car. Pulled from the wreckage, Cleveland receives fifteen stitches around the right ear and eight in his mouth.

The next night, in the ninth inning, another promising, big, young Boston pitcher, Dick Pole, is finishing up his sixth good start in seven outings. He tries a low fastball on Baltimore's Tony Muser. Muser catches it squarely on the meat of his bat. He drives it right back into Pole's face. Rico fears the pitcher may've swallowed his tongue. He sprints over from third base and, as he did with the fallen Conigliaro so many years before, assures Pole that he'll be all right. He's rushed to the emergency room, taken into surgery. His cheekbone is demolished. Doctors can't say when his eyesight will normalize.

Their pitching staff thus quickly cut down, they lose two of three to Baltimore while Milwaukee takes two from New York. The Yankees and Brewers are now tied, each a game back of Boston, with the Orioles closing in. As in April, the American League East has fought itself to a standstill. But the fans, who once scoffed at the inability of any team to distinguish itself, grow impressed by the intensity of the contests. They realize that every victor's uncertainty is due not to a lack of divisional talent but a surplus of it. This is simply a stronger AL East than it has been for many years.

Boston arrives in Milwaukee on the heels of both a Pink Floyd concert and a thunderstorm. The County Stadium outfield is a trampled, rutted quagmire. In the first game, Rick Wise has a no-hitter going with two outs in the ninth when he gives up a game-winning home run to designated hitter Boomer Scott. In the second game, the Sox lose, four to three. In the third game, in the tenth inning, with the score tied at two apiece, Brewers first baseman Kurt Bevacqua hits a single to center. Slipping about in the center-field slop, Lynn tries for a quick pickup so that he can throw out the runner. He misjudges the ball. Shortstop Robin Yount races around to score from first on the error, and the Brewers move into a virtual tie for first place, just two percentage points behind Boston.

Bill Lee blames Pink Floyd. Others, noting Lynn's appearance this week on the covers of both *Sports Illustrated* and the *Sporting News*, suggest a double whammy of misfortune. Lynn shrugs when informed that he's the latest victim of *SI*'s famous curse. "I guess it is a jinx," he agrees laconically.

Meanwhile, Jim Colburn of the Brewers is asked whether anything can stop his supercharged team. "Yes," he says. "If someone plants a bomb in the middle of the clubhouse and wipes out about fifteen guys."

Though appreciative of Colburn's suggestion, Boston General Manager Dick O'Connell chooses to disregard it. Instead, O'Connell goes shopping for long relief. He returns with right-hander Jim Willoughby, a former Giant, a former Cardinal, a thrower of good fastballs and low curves, the winner of eleven major-league games in four years, the loser of fourteen.

For the third time in four years, Tom Yawkey starts thinking pennant.

EIGHT

MAJOR-LEAGUE STANDINGS ON JUNE 30, 1975

NATIONAL LEAGUE

East Division

	W	L	Pct	GB
Pittsburgh	44	29	.603	–
Philadelphia	42	33	.560	3
New York	36	34	.514	$6\frac{1}{2}$
St. Louis	35	37	.486	$8\frac{1}{2}$
Chicago	36	39	.480	9
Montreal	31	38	.449	11

West Division

	W	L	Pct	GB
Cincinnati	48	28	.632	–
Los Angeles	42	36	.538	7
San Francisco	37	39	.487	11
San Diego	36	40	.474	12
Atlanta	32	43	.427	$15\frac{1}{2}$
Houston	28	51	.354	$21\frac{1}{2}$

AMERICAN LEAGUE

East Division

	W	L	Pct	GB
Boston	40	30	.571	–
New York	41	32	.563	$\frac{1}{2}$
Milwaukee	39	34	.534	$2\frac{1}{2}$
Baltimore	33	38	.465	$7\frac{1}{2}$
Cleveland	30	41	.423	$10\frac{1}{2}$
Detroit	27	43	.386	13

West Division

	W	L	Pct	GB
Oakland	48	26	.649	–
Kansas City	41	34	.547	$7\frac{1}{2}$
Texas	36	39	.480	$12\frac{1}{2}$
Chicago	34	38	.472	13
Minnesota	33	38	.465	$13\frac{1}{2}$
California	34	43	.442	$15\frac{1}{2}$

The New York Mets host their fourteenth annual Old-Timers' Day. Shea Stadium's tiny locker room is stuffed with current players and old-timers getting ready. Don Newcombe jostles Joe Torre. Jerry Grote attempts to change but keeps rubbing up against Carl Hubbell. Joe DiMaggio plants a leg in Dave Kingman's uniform, and Willie Mays hogs the mirror.

The Mets have arranged for heroes to make special entrances. Stengel enters in a Roman chariot, waving a Ben-Hur–style whip. Fans hold up signs saying ALL HAIL CASEY! He wears his old uniform with the familiar thirty-seven across the back. He looks weathered, haggard.

Stengel is on very good terms with the Mets' current manager, Yogi Berra. By catching most of Stengel's championship games, not to mention playing in more World Series games than any other player in history, Berra has had the opportunity to be schooled by the game's most subtle strategist. In observing Stengel so long, Berra picked up not just Casey's on-field craft but his skillful ease with the media.

Each is a long-eared clown with a comically inelegant body. And while Casey created Stengelese, Yogi coined its first aphorisms. "You can observe a lot by watching!" Berra yelled at the '64 Yankees. His favorite coaching tip was "Ninety percent of the game is half mental."

"If you can't imitate him," Berra told Ron Swoboda, after hearing him say he was determined to hit like Frank Robinson, "don't copy him." Reminiscing with Nolan Ryan one day about the 1969 Mets, Yogi observed, "We were overwhelming underdogs." When a reporter reminded the manager that his Mets were still nine games out of first in July of 1973, Yogi retorted, "It ain't over 'til it's over." As Johnny Bench gets closer to breaking Berra's record for most home runs by a catcher, Yogi repeatedly congratulates Bench with "I know my record will stand until it's broken."

At the party in the clubhouse after the old-timers' game, Yogi has no new funny lines, so the newsmen turn eagerly to Stengel. They inquire about his flight. "Don't ask about my trip," he replies. "Ask about my body." His famous vaudeville shrug is locked into a permanent hunch. The blue eyes are milky and distant. His broad wink is gone. He doesn't seem a man as much as a tree or a crippled hawk.

The reporters ask about Edna, his wife of fifty-one years.

"She's no good from here up," he says, motioning from the neck. Edna has been confined to a nursing home ever since the stroke. "I miss her and why wouldn't ya after your whole life?"

Casey goes to the podium that's set on a stage. There's a microphone. He addresses the gathering. Immediately, he's babbling. People want to laugh, but it's not clear if Stengel is getting his own jokes. The heat upon his face and hands must be tremendous, just unbelievable. The tone of his speech is distressing; he sounds suspicious, then jubilant, then guarded. He feels himself melting beneath the lights. The cameras just keep taking pictures. His voice rises, turns shrill. Someone moves toward the microphone. A piano player begins to play "For He's a Jolly Good Fellow." Everyone sings. Finally, they drown out Stengel. He gestures defiantly. He droops, defeated, into a chair at a vacant table, at last silent. He stares glumly at a stack of used coffee cups. The singing continues.

"In retrospect," one guest admits, "I should have punched the piano player right in the mouth."

There is, in the meantime, an insufferably warm night in Cincinnati in which the Reds lead the Braves in the top of the ninth. Atlanta's number-eight hitter, shortstop Larvell "Sugar Bear" Blanks, steps in against Don Gullett. Night has borne no relief to Riverfront. The air hangs damp with fever. Gullett's long, narrow face is flushed and his eyebrows lifted, like always, in an expression of total perplexity. The pitcher is one out away from his fourth straight complete game. He is the key. Sparky trusts him. Gullett alone is allowed to finish what he starts, because his stuff gets somehow meaner late in the game.

Gullett blows out a breath, winds up, and delivers a fastball through the electric haze of the AstroTurf evening. Sugar Bear catches it low on his bat and ricochets a smash up the middle. Gullett leaps in the way. He drops to his knees. He fumbles around with both hands to find the ball. Sugar Bear is safe at first. A sudden agony roils through Gullett, more pain than he has ever experienced. Time is called. Sparky sprints from the dugout, joined by the trainer and the pitching coach. Observers realize then that Gullett stopped the line drive with his pitching hand. His left thumb, from the base to the tip, is etched deeply with the baseball's stitch marks. Gullett goes off in an ambulance, Pedro Borbon comes in, retires the pinch hitter for Knucksie Niekro, and the game's saved.

Everyone showers, dresses, and goes home. As for Sparky, he returns to the hotel room he'll inhabit until his California family comes to Ohio for the summer, after the kids get out of school. The next morning, a ringing telephone awakens him. It's the team's publicity man, calling to inform the skipper that Gullett's thumb is badly fractured. The pitcher will be out from eight to ten weeks.

Sparky rides down to the coffee shop, runs into the young guy who manages the hotel.[1] They chat about Gullett for a time, his swiftness, his astonishing control. An extraordinary athlete from just south of Cincinnati, Gullett once scored eleven touchdowns and kicked six extra points in a single high school football game. The Reds' number-one draft choice, less than a year out of high school, the modest Gullett was being hailed by Sparky as another Lefty Grove. Walter Alston regarded him as the next Sandy Koufax. Even Willie Stargell was awed; Stargell, who once compared hitting Koufax to drinking coffee with a fork, described Gullett's hard one as "wall-to-wall heat."

Sparky is forty-five years of age, but this morning, in the eyes of the hotel manager, he appears twice that old. His bull pen has been employed in every game for the past week, his best pitcher's out for two months, and his team is just a couple games ahead of the Dodgers with ninety-eight still to play. "What can you do now?" the hotel manager asks softly.

Sparky considers it and suddenly smiles. "Well, my boy —" He chuckles. "I'll tell you. Now you're going to see genius at work."

In the half second required for a baseball to travel from the hand of a major-league pitcher to home plate, the batter must predict how the ball will bend and decide, accordingly, where to place his bat. A few of the game's very best hitters can glimpse the rotation of the thread on a curveball as a small spot of red. This gives them an edge. Ted Williams saw the red spot, and so does Pete Rose. This is why, on average, Rose gets one to two base hits in every game, every year. It's also why, at the plate, Pete can do almost anything — anything, that is, but hit San Diego's Randy Jones. Randy's drowsy pitches behave like quaaludes while amphetamines are more Pete's style. "Throw harder," Rose orders Randy from the batter's box. Irritated, Pete pushes some dirt around. This is the National League, the league of the slugger, the league of the fastball. "Throw hard, dammit!"[2] The southpaw Jones is one of only two pitchers against whom Pete never switch-hits and, in Rose's long career, the third all-time most difficult pitcher for him to hit. The fourth hardest, according to Pete, was Randy's childhood hero, Sandy Koufax.

Randy loses his first game in May, then proceeds to win five in a row. He beats the Dodgers in Los Angeles and shuts out the Reds in Cincinnati. He one-hits the Cardinals for ten innings until his team finally gets him a run. (It seems that every game is a pitching duel. No matter who the Padres face, they can't hit him.) In his next start, Randy defeats the mighty Pirates in an hour and forty-one minutes. He employs only sixty-eight pitches (forty-nine strikes, nineteen balls). He occasionally comes inside with his fastball, just to keep right-handed batters honest, but mostly he throws his sinker ball, placing it consistently between the top and the bottom of the batter's kneecap. To Pittsburgh's power hitters — Willie Stargell, Dave Parker, Manny Sanguillen, and Al Oliver — it's thoroughly exasperating. Control of this sort stretches the definition of big-league pitching. They can see the ball, but they can't achieve solid contact. His pitches straddle the line; they're too good to take, not good enough to hit. Stargell feels mocked.

During the first two weeks of June, Randy Jones twice starts opposite Philadelphia's Wayne Twitchell and New York's Jerry Koosman. The pitching rotations remain synchronized like some low-budget movie that recycles the cast — or, as Koosman's manager Yogi Berra once put it, it's déjà vu all over again. Both times, once on each coast, Randy defeats Koosman. He splits the games against Twitchell: he loses the road game and wins the home game. Already, by June 14, Randy has piled up more victories than he did all of last year.

Thus on June 29, Rose nearly falls down, dumbfounded, aghast, appalled, when Foster, his own teammate, homers against Jones. "Jesus-mutha-God!" exclaims Pete. "Keerist!" Now, granted, Foster is on a tear; he hits a home run every week, hit one the night before, and will hit four more before the all-star break. Still, by Rose's reasoning, hitting a long ball off Jones is like going all the way with the wife of the president: it can't be done by mere mortals. Just to lift Randy's sinker ball into the air requires a batter to swing practically from the ground. Pete can conceive of a midget, albeit an extremely coordinated one, being able to get beneath one of Randy's pitches and deposit enough wood on it for a legitimate hit. Even then, Jones throws so softly — dipsy-doodle pitches, they're called — that this imaginary and unnaturally coordinated midget would need to provide every bit of power if he desired to drive it any distance at all. It's in watching him loft the long home run off Jones that Rose finally recognizes the brute strength of Foster.

And in this, Pete stands corrected. Initially, when Sparky brought the whole triple-A outfield — Griffey, Foster, and Ed Armbrister — up from Indianapolis, it struck Pete as too much. Sparky labeled Griffey another Lou Brock and, for once, this was not overblown hyperbole on the manager's part. Griffey was a talent, Rose wouldn't deny that. He was fast on the bases, patient at the plate, solid in the field. But Foster was elusive, unreliable, too quiet, too wide-eyed, while Armbrister was not serious enough. Indeed, Armbrister was always exploding with song. Singing in the dugout! By God, it bothered the fuck out of Rose. *Lighthearted*, Pete figured, *means light-headed*, but in this too he turned out to be wrong. Work means something different in the Bahamas, where Armbrister's from. Work means long hours for low pay. There are no baseball coaches. There are no playgrounds or ball fields. Using tree limbs as bats, Ed and his friends played baseball games wherever they were allowed to trespass — in dead-end streets, on vacant lots. For a time, they played the game in the cemetery, but they knocked over too many grave markers and got in trouble. To be paid to play a child's game — Armbrister cannot help but giggle.

By now, Foster is outhitting Rose, Claudell Washington is outhitting Joe Rudi, and Jim Rice is outhitting Carl Yastrzemski. But of all the youthful sluggers this season who will force a veteran outfielder to the infield, the biggest success story may be the large, wide, and swift Pirate named Dave Parker. Parker is a natural leader, which gives Willie Stargell a much-needed break. Stargell is having an off year, hampered by injuries and troubled greatly by the publication of a candid biography he disavows. Though Stargell is destined to grow into one of baseball's most inspiring team captains, in 1975 he seems intent on delaying this fate for as long as possible, dodging interviews, rarely addressing the club. Parker, an agile speedster with a powerful throwing arm, steps into the void, playing brilliantly and inspiring his teammates not only with his strength but with his quick and deadly intelligence. They call him "Cobra" and pity the pitcher who must retire him.

Every time the "Gunner," longtime Pirate broadcaster Bob Prince, looks up from his score sheet in the booth, Cobra is on second base, or sliding into third. Pittsburgh may be blasé about the game this year, but they're still crazy for their colorful, infectious Prince. The Gunner is an institution, a highly partisan Mr. Baseball, and soon he has the city swooning over Parker, who in turn carries the Pirates for most of the season: him, and a cobbled-together pitching staff. Cobra is twenty-four years old. Along with second baseman Rennie Stennett (who's Rod Carew crossed with Bill Mazeroski), Parker represents to Prince the future of the Pirates and appears poised to assume the mantle of leadership from Stargell and aging catcher Manny Sanguillen, and eventually take his place among Pittsburgh's cherished Hall of Famers — Clemente, Arky, Pie, the Big and Little Poisons — an unbroken litany that extends all the way back to the great Honus Wagner, large and comically bowlegged, German, a child of the coal mines, modest and gentlemanly, the only man Ty Cobb could not scare. . . .

It's a dream, that's all it is. Tomorrow such things won't matter. Prince will be the first to go, then Sanguillen, Stennett, Stargell, and Parker.

In the future, no star will shine in just one city for long.

On the third of July, the two comeback kids, Randy Jones and Gary Nolan, square off against each other in San Diego. Nolan surrenders two hits before leaving for a pinch hitter in the ninth. Jones is even better. He retires twenty-one Cincinnati players in a row. His perfect game ends in the eighth, when Tony Perez hits a routine grounder to Padre third baseman Hector Torres and Torres nervously flings the ball away. Jones still has the no-hitter, but one out later, he gets careless. He throws a high sinker. Cincinnati's backup catcher Bill Plummer wallops the mistake for a double. Perez comes around to score the tying run. Fortunately, San Diego rallies in the ninth, scores a run on a single, a double, and an error. The one-hitter gives Randy his eleventh victory in sixteen decisions. After the game, Randy learns that Walter Alston has chosen him for the all-star squad. The honor is so special, so unexpected, and Randy himself is so unassuming, that it rattles his concentration. For the next couple of weeks, until he travels to Milwaukee for the midsummer classic, Randy is no better than he was a year ago. His ERA steadily climbs. He doesn't win a game.

The Reds hold first place, though the Dodgers keep threatening to overtake them. Los Angeles begins the month winning five of seven, but Cincinnati wins six of seven and stays ahead.

The question remains: how can Sparky win without a pitching ace?

The answer is in his bull pen.

Until Sparky was plucked from obscurity and tossed the reins of the best team in baseball, polite society rarely broached the scandalous topic of relief pitching. Some baseball prudes might grudgingly confirm that a team, to be successful, did indeed need a man who could enter late in the game and reliably hold a lead, but any further discussion was frowned upon as decidedly vulgar. After all, a single pitcher was supposed to throw for the whole length of the grand old game; that was how Doubleday designed it. To think otherwise was hateful, for it implied not just an un-Christian lack of faith in the starting pitcher but a disrespect for the quintessential American fairness of the contest. Relievers were permitted, yes . . . but only as the game's dirty little secret, a late-inning indulgence, like pep pills or the occasional "illegal pitch."

But Sparky's sole concern is winning. He does try to involve his starters long enough for them to gain credit for the victory, but otherwise he cares nothing about fattening their stats, about helping them accrue innings or complete games. He discounts the traditional respect for a pitcher's ability to transcend a tough situation or gather a second wind. He wants wins. "For five innings it's the pitcher's game," he declares flatly. "After that, it's mine."

Sparky noticed, upon arriving in Cincinnati, how the unspoken shame about relievers had led to a peculiar lack of consensus among major-league management on how best to organize a relief corps. The sole operating principle seemed to be *Use one until he breaks, then find another.* Mike Marshall could be cited as evidence of such near-sightedness. Marshall was a rude, tubby pitcher who apparently never tired. The muttonchops on his jowls hearkened back to the dark ages of organized baseball, but his right arm looked to be a modern miracle. Throwing for Montreal in 1973, Marshall became the league's best reliever. In the process, his narcissism outraged proud Canadian baseball fans. Expos' management feared the acrimony could "burst into open warfare," so they shipped him in a trade to Los Angeles, five thousand miles away. Smugly, Marshall shrugged. He bragged that his knowledge of body mechanics rendered him a vastly superior specimen. He claimed that he could pitch daily, so his new manager, kindly Alston, indulged him. Alston was of the opinion that pitchers should not be coddled but gone through, rather like firewood (thus did he burn up Koufax at the green age of thirty-one).

In his first season as a Dodger, Marshall pitched 208 innings, more than most of Alston's starters, while appearing in a record 106 games. Recklessly, as if training a dog, Alston tested the proud man's endurance beyond what medical experts recommended as safe. Marshall was called upon to retire approximately twenty-eight major-league batters a week, from April 5 to October 17. At one point in the middle of the season, he was used in thirteen successive games. Alston put in the bullish Marshall regardless of the situation, sometimes for the final out, sometimes for five innings.

At the start of 1975, the physical strain caught up to Marshall. He was lost to the disabled list for ten weeks. For all of his schooling in the science of kinesiology, his heart and mind still belonged to his body.

After Gullett's injury, Sparky aspires to something nobler than Alston's ethic of *drain, then discard.* Ten arms remain available to him. One belongs to Gary Nolan, who is doing great but is still spurty — of concern — without nine innings' worth of stuff. Two tall and fair-haired righties are ex-Astros, the uninhibited youth Pat Darcy and the journeyman Jack Billingham, while another two — Clay Kirby and Fredie Norman — used to be Padres. A pair of unlikely but longtime teammates, hulking hick Clay "Hawk"

Carroll and scowling, half-crazed Dominican Pedro Borbon, provide veteran resilience. Twenty-three-year-old Will McEnaney and
twenty-four-year-old Rawly Eastwick are the eccentric rookie
flamethrowers. Lastly, Sparky's got a strong kid from Indianapolis,
Tom Carroll, who's got stamina, but he doesn't figure to do much.

Pitching coach Larry Shepard corners Eastwick. Rawly has this
good fastball and sinker, but he's aiming altogether too much; he's
getting into trouble. He's given up sixteen runs in just twenty-four
innings. Shep lays into him, scolding, warning that if this continues
he will be sent down. Shep tells him to rear back, dammit, and
throw, without thinking. "Otherwise, who do you think will go to
Indianapolis once Gullett is ready to pitch again?" Rawly shoots
Shep a look of terror, then promises to buckle down.

A muggy blur of twi-night games begins. At the hint of any scoring threat, out comes Sparky and out goes the pitcher. Some call it a
lack of affection. "My mother, I love her," Sparky is heard to say,
"but she don't pitch for me." Sparky's relationship with his battery
men turns sour. The fans side with the frustrated hurlers; they label
Sparky "Captain Hook" and boo as soon as his white head pops from
the dugout. Sparky is undeterred by foulmouthed curses or denunci-
atory banners. In Philadelphia, the muscular Darcy might cast dirty
looks and sputter angrily when Sparky arrives at the mound to yank
him; in Atlanta, Darcy may raise a hefty foot against the rosin bag as
if it were his manager's head. It doesn't seem to affect their dugout
commander, the tactless tactician. Nor is it any easier for the older
guys — for Nolan, Kirby, Norman, or even laid-back Billingham —
to adjust to such fussiness, such impatience. On the mound, their
chagrin is evident. They are reluctant to hand over the ball. They
don't appreciate being interrupted at work. Some flick their arms
about in exasperation; some stiffen at the spin, jaws tightening. Cocky
Clay Kirby looks off into the Wrigley Field twilight with scarcely con-
cealed contempt. The diminutive southpaw Norman fidgets, nostrils flaring like a tuckered pack mule. (His skin looks sickly and
green, but this is somewhat common for a night game at Shea.)

Each game is a tightly played symphony, with Sparky as conductor, the bull pen his orchestra, and percussion provided in the dugout, where pulled pitchers throw equipment and topple watercoolers.

Sparky removes a pitcher one night and finds out later he was booed by even his daughter, Shirlee.

"Why would you boo your father?" he asks her in dismay.

"I didn't want them to know you were my father," she candidly admits.

Anderson shakes his head. "One of these days they are going to have Spear Day at Riverfront," he predicts, "and the fan coming closest to my heart when I yank a pitcher will win a Buick."

One night Eastwick pitches in front of his home folks. Rawly grew up ten miles from Philadelphia's Connie Mack Stadium, and now, at Veterans Stadium, he calmly comes to the mound in the bottom of the eighth. Two outs, and the bases are loaded. Rawly is Sparky's fourth pitcher of the inning. Dick Allen, the childhood hero whose intensity and power first inspired Rawly's desire for baseball, stands on third, representing the tying run. The batter is Mike Schmidt, an intense young slugger whom Allen calls "the baddest white boy I've ever seen play the game."

Throwing nothing but fastballs, Eastwick rapidly strikes out Schmidt, then pitches a scoreless ninth and picks up the first of his twenty-two saves this season.

"You really gave them a show," Anderson congratulates him.

Near the end of July, Pat Darcy's slider will begin to work. The big right-hander will no longer be bothered by blisters on his pitching hand. One night, Sparky will amaze everyone by letting Darcy pitch nine innings against San Francisco. It'll be the first complete game thrown by a Cincinnati pitcher in a record forty-five consecutive games, and afterward two weeks go by before Billingham will throw the next. By then, the Reds will have won eighty-two games, more than any team in history has won up to that week in the season.

The Dodgers will be seventeen and a half games back, in second place.

NINE

MAJOR-LEAGUE STANDINGS ON JULY 4, 1975

NATIONAL LEAGUE

East Division

	W	L	Pct	GB
Pittsburgh	47	29	.618	–
Philadelphia	44	35	.557	4½
New York	39	35	.527	7
St. Louis	37	39	.487	10
Chicago	37	42	.468	11½
Montreal	31	41	.431	14

West Division

	W	L	Pct	GB
Cincinnati	51	29	.638	–
Los Angeles	45	37	.549	7
San Francisco	38	41	.481	12½
San Diego	38	42	.475	13
Atlanta	33	44	.429	16½
Houston	28	54	.341	24

AMERICAN LEAGUE

East Division

	W	L	Pct	GB
Boston	42	34	.553	–
Milwaukee	43	35	.551	–
New York	41	36	.532	1½
Baltimore	36	40	.474	6
Cleveland	34	42	.447	8
Detroit	29	46	.387	12½

West Division

	W	L	Pct	GB
Oakland	49	29	.628	–
Kansas City	43	35	.551	6
Chicago	37	39	.487	11
Texas	37	41	.474	12
Minnesota	35	41	.461	13
California	37	45	.451	14

Billy Martin is the best manager in baseball and he knows it. His teams leave the others looking spiritless, unresolved, and gullible. "I managed in Minnesota, and I won the division there, and I managed in Detroit, and I won the division there. And then I took over the Texas Rangers, which at the time was one of the worst teams in baseball, and in one year I had them to within an eyelash of the pennant."

He stands apart from other managers, resembles a kid in a motorcycle movie, a slickhair with a fresh mouth. He refuses to regard the owner as his boss and is often fired after an explosive confrontation of some sort. He fumes, even in victory, fueled by the insult of his playing days, because all he'd ever wanted was to spend his life playing for Casey Stengel and the Yankees of beautiful New York, and all he'd ever done for them was win the World Series by catching a most impossible pop-up, and all he ever got was traded into exile because of what happened at that midnight at the Copa, which sure as hell wasn't his fault.

Martin hates batting averages. "Baseball's got a heart and a stomach and a brain, and averages don't reflect any of those things." He enjoys suicide squeezes and seeing fielders knocked down in the course of a double play. He feels that any player, no matter how slow, should be ready to steal home. "Watch the third baseman in order to get a big enough lead . . . when the pitcher starts to move his hands, you break for the plate . . . the pitcher, being a creature of habit, will go right through his windup so that by the time the ball reaches, you're already there." He preaches the same fundamentals as every other manager of the time, but for some reason his intense style consistently ignites teams. Players know he means it, and they play almost in fear of him. He is part Stengel — Stengel crossed with some feral rodent. "He doesn't talk about anything else," Stengel's wife, Edna, once said. "He doesn't think about anything else. He has only one life, and that's base-ball." So too Martin. "My whole childhood," Billy says, "baseball was all I did. Girls weren't the name of the game. Baseball was."

Billy Martin brags, in 1975, that his Rangers are the team to beat. He thinks his tall, right-handed pitcher Ferguson Jenkins will win twenty-five games again, right fielder Jeff Burroughs will per-form at MVP quality again. Billy assumes he can get by with a sparse bull pen dominated by right-handers. Naturally, none of this comes to pass. In the first week of the season, the Rangers lose four of five. Jenkins twice loses badly. Burroughs swings at everything, destined to lead the league in clutch strikeouts. Agonizing weeks pass, and the Rangers bounce from second place to fifth, to fourth, then back to second. Billy loses fifteen pounds. His players lose their poise. "Errors, pitchers getting the ball stuck in the webbing of their gloves, balks, everything is happening," moans Martin, a paranoid pencil of a man. "A guy couldn't stay at home at night and try to dream up more ways to get beat." Billy blames the umpires and begins wearing a microphone on the field to incrimi-nate them.[1] He gives the ball to twenty-year-old David Clyde who, two years before, was their phenom; Clyde pitches seven innings, misplays a bunt, takes the loss, and is gone for the season. Martin shouts expletives at his center fielder, then kicks the sportswriters out of the dressing room for "snooping around."

When the Kansas City Royals come to Arlington Stadium in early July, Billy Martin has a strategy, of course. He focuses on keeping the ball away from Brett and McRae, whether on the field or at the plate; they're the only two Royals who concern him. They play the game with spit and hustle — they do it right. He can see that. They learn the pitchers. They focus on mechanics. They practice spray hitting. They lower their heads and go. They dirty their uniforms. Martin admires them as worthy adversaries, in particular the self-deprecating blond kid, Brett, who's got the mitt of Brooks Robinson and the bat of Rod Carew, and who gets on base, without fuss or fanfare, time and again to score the unseen runs.

Arlington Stadium is horribly hot that night. Billy's strategy seems effective: keep McRae (one for four) and Brett (oh for four) off the bases and the Royals can't win. In the fourth, John Mayberry launches a home run into the darkness beyond the right-field wall. He does it again in the seventh, and again in the ninth, when Harmon Killebrew also homers. Each, however, is a solo shot while the Rangers, thanks to alert baserunning, score five and win the game. But Martin has awakened a sleeping giant. Mayberry, with only nine home runs on the season and a .243 batting average, homers in the next three games. When the White Sox meet them next in Kansas City, Chicago assumes the spaciousness of Royals Stadium will help to contain Mayberry's drives. It doesn't. He homers three times in the next three games. His slugging percentage for the week is 1.250. Mayberry sends balls splashing into the right-field water spectacular. He dents the bull-pen car with one home run, and blasts another into the concession stand far behind the right-field general-admission seats. Increasingly, to the annoyance of clout ball fans, Mayberry is walked intentionally. Pitchers treat him as a left-handed version of Milwaukee's Boomer Scott, a man who'll rip twenty-five to thirty home runs and knock in a hundred runs a year. Right on cue, as if to enhance the comparison, Boomer brings down his Brewers to meet

Big John's Royals. Both teams are rallying, second in their respective divisions. Three games are played, and Mayberry and Scott walk at least once each game. They both hit home runs. The Brewers take the first game; the Royals take the second.

That night, someone asks Dick Williams which current player he would take if he could have anyone, and the Angels manager answers "Yount." George Brett is sure to hear about this from his father.[2] Jack has long tried to induce a rivalry between his youngest son and Robin Yount.[3] They were both drafted out of LA-area high schools as star teenage infielders, but Robin went almost immediately to the bigs while Brett was made to play three years of minor-league ball. Both are the youngest players on their teams; both are contact hitters batting in the shadows of the game's aging home-run heroes. But Yount has been chosen for the 1975 all-star team while Brett will head home during the break for some much-needed rest.

The next day, in the swing game of Kansas City's series with Milwaukee, Brett takes off for second. Yount moves to cover the base. Two-hundred-pound George unhesitatingly drops his shoulder. He doesn't slide but instead roll blocks the 165-pound shortstop into the outfield. Brett is out on the play. Yount is nearly out of the game. The Royals go on to lose anyway, dropping the series two to one, but Brett goes into the all-star break feeling okay. At this point, he is thinking only of making his father proud. He has no idea that one day he'll have sons of his own and name the littlest one "Robin," after Yount.

PART THREE

THE ALL-STAR BREAK

TEN

IN THE MIDFIFTIES, baseball's biggest fans in the country resided in Milwaukee. They adored their winning Braves and their hammerin' young Hank. Happily, they hosted the 1955 all-star game. Mickey Mantle stepped up in the first with two men on, for some reason positioning himself unusually far from the plate. Robin Roberts, the great Phillies right-hander, was on the mound. Roberts suspected he could slip one through on the outside corner. He was wrong. Mantle's consequent 430-foot blast landed in the trees that used to grow beyond the center-field fence. The National Leaguers rallied in the late innings (just as Milwaukee's Braves often did) and tied the score. The game went on and on, into extra innings. Stan Musial walked to the plate in the twelfth. He turned to Yogi Berra, the catcher. "You know," Musial admitted, "I'm getting kinda tired." Berra nodded, and the pitch came, a fastball. Musial swung, and sent it over the old wire fence in right field to win the game for the Nationals.

Twenty years later, owner Bud Selig brings baseball, Aaron, and the all-star game all back to Milwaukee.[1]

Selig's Brewers have been performing wonderfully. The first week of July, they were tied for first in the AL East. Boston then enjoyed a streak of seven victories, a fluke really, while the Brewers split the next six games. But while Milwaukee enters the all-star break four and a half games out, none of the Brewers are worried. "There's no way Boston can keep playing the way they've been playing," assures Boomer Scott, infused with Milwaukee's newfound confidence.

Tuesday, July 15, arrives. The sun sets. The weather is perfect for baseball, a warm summer evening. Fifty-one thousand, four hundred eighty people arrive, the largest crowd ever to attend a baseball game in County Stadium. Their allegiances have changed since last they hosted an all-star game; they used to be a National League city, now they're American. The Hammer's name in the pregame introductions brings down the house. He played his first all-star game there in 1955. He has played in every one since. Of course, Aaron has switched sides too. Tonight he performs in his twenty-fourth all-star game, tying Musial's record — but, for the first time, Aaron is on the Americans' side.

The American League has lost eleven of the last twelve of these annual matchups. Their one victory in recent memory occurred in Detroit, 1971. Vida Blue started that game for the American League. Initially, when the National League named Pittsburgh's Dock Ellis to oppose him, Dock refused the assignment. "I will not start against another soul brother," Dock declared. He relented, eventually, and lost to Blue, who was then in the middle of one of the finest years any pitcher has ever experienced, in which he would strike out 301 batters and collect a 1.82 ERA, a Cy Young, and the AL MVP. It was his first full season in the major leagues. He was twenty-one years old.

Now Vida Blue starts his second all-star game. He figures he'll win. The only guy who hit him hard in the 1971 game was Henry Aaron, and now Aaron has joined him in the AL dugout.

Musial and Mantle are both there, chosen as honorary captains to commemorate the anniversary of their all-star home runs. Stan the Man is his usual jovial self, but the Mick strikes many as morbid. Mantle can't stop wishing aloud that he could do it all over again. He hovers about, telling the players to appreciate their moment in the sun.

To initiate the proceedings, Mantle is sent out to present the starting lineup card to the umpires. The AL starts five A's, three Yankees, and a Twin — not a single Red Sox player, despite their being in first.

AMERICANS

Bobby Bonds, *center field*
Rod Carew, *second base*
Thurman Munson, *catcher*
Reggie Jackson, *right field*
Joe Rudi, *left field*
Graig Nettles, *third base*
Gene Tenace, *first base*
Bert Campaneris, *shortstop*
Vida Blue, *pitcher*

Musial emerges from the other dugout, carrying the NL's lineup: four Reds, three Dodgers, one Cardinal. Dock Ellis's teammate Jerry Reuss has been picked as the opening pitcher.

NATIONALS

Pete Rose, *right field*
Lou Brock, *left field*
Joe Morgan, *second base*
Johnny Bench, *catcher*
Steve Garvey, *first base*
Jim Wynn, *center field*
Ron Cey, *third base*
Dave Concepcion, *shortstop*
Jerry Reuss, *pitcher*

Blue delivers a scoreless first, as does Reuss, but in the second, Blue falls swiftly behind. He throws back-to-back home run pitches to LA's Garvey and Wynn.

The Americans are down by two in the bottom of the second,

with two outs and two on, when a pinch hitter steps in for Vida Blue. The crowd goes crazy. It's Henry Aaron. He represents the go-ahead run at the plate. Unimpressed, Reuss tries a slider inside. It saws Aaron off. The Hammer's bat splinters over the playing field. The ball flops through the air like a wounded bird. Shortstop Dave Concepcion gloves it easily, three away.

The Nationals' Lou Brock leads off the third with a single to left center. Young Steve Busby is on the mound in place of Blue. On first base is a man who stole 114 bases last year, more than any other baseball player in history. At the plate is Joe Morgan, the man most responsible for the Cincinnati Reds' winning forty-one of their last fifty games. In the National League dugout, the all-stars are making noise. "Go! Go! Go!" they shout at Brock. "Go! Go! Go!" Busby comes unglued. He balks. Brock advances. He retires Morgan, but then Johnny Bench steps in. Brock steals third. Bench singles to left. Brock scores.

Fred Lynn watches from the bench in awe. Lynn has been en-joying the all-star break — he's been visiting with various relatives he has in the area — but when he got to the locker room tonight and looked around, he became terribly nervous. These are players he watched as a kid, and now here he is, beside and against them. He wasn't on the ballot this year; instead he was a write-in, just like Garvey last year, a clean-cut, polite surprise.[2]

In the fifth, the National League switches around its outfield, with Bobby Murcer going to right. Pete Rose, the Nationals' start-ing right fielder, moves to left. Bobby Bonds steps in against Don Sutton, who relieved Reuss. Bonds immediately tests Rose's range with a flare to left, which Pete pursues through the lumpy grass and, tumbling dramatically, catches for an out.

Lynn stands in for Campy Campaneris in the bottom of the sixth. There's two on and one out. The score is still three to nothing in favor of the Nationals. Tom Seaver now pitches in place of Sut-ton, and Chicago's Bill Madlock plays third base. Lynn skies one to right. Murcer positions himself under it for the catch. Billy Martin, the AL's base coach at first, displays uncharacteristic restraint and keeps both runners at their bases.

Two away, and now Lynn's teammate Carl Yastrzemski bats for Jim Kaat.

Carl is annoyed by all-star games.[3] It's a lot of travel, inconvenience, and hassle smack in the middle of the season, right when his body is beginning to tire. Carl would rather have the time off, three days' vacation in mid-July, to relax his aching muscles. Every year he begs Tom Yawkey to lie, to tell the press that Carl has injured himself and sadly won't be able to play in the all-star game. Every year Tom Yawkey says no, and every year Carl comes and performs stupendously.

Seaver starts him off with a heater. Expecting this, Carl sharply swivels and snaps his wrists. He connects. The ball soars over right center and lands in the bull pen for a three-run homer. Americans three, Nationals three.

The tie holds until the top of the ninth. Catfish Hunter is on the mound. Consecutive misplays by Oakland left fielder Claudell Washington have put two Nationals aboard. No outs. Hunter leaves. Rookie Rich Gossage comes in to pitch. He throws hard. He's tough to squeeze on.

Gossage hits the first batter to load the bases.

Still no outs.

The next batter is Madlock. He's hurting from a recent back injury. He's taped, beneath his uniform, from his shoulders to his waist. He wants to put the ball in the air, to score a run with a sacrifice fly. He fouls off two fastballs. The count climbs to two and two.

Madlock is a freak for baseball. He enthusiastically follows several clubs besides his own, looking for clues, routines, secrets. He watches the White Sox on television almost every day that the Cubs aren't on the road, and as a consequence, he's familiar with Gossage. Madlock knows the guy's pattern, knows that after three fastballs and a slider, he'll be trying a breaking ball.

Instead, Gossage delivers inside with a change-up, but it's close enough to what Madlock is looking for. Madlock pulls it down the third-base line for a single. Two runs score, and another scores on a sacrifice fly from Pete Rose. Nationals six, Americans three.

Walter Alston, the National League's manager, looks down at his bull pen.

Jon Matlack has already completed two innings for Alston, striking out Rod Carew, Bucky Dent, Gene Tenace, and Fred Lynn. Now Alston needs a reliever. He has his choice of four veterans, or Randy Jones.

The phone rings in the bull pen. Andy Messersmith grabs it.

"Warm up that little curly-haired left hander who gets everybody out," Alston tells him.

"All right," says Messersmith. He hangs up and jerks his head at Randy Jones. "Go to it," he says encouragingly.[4]

Jones hasn't pitched well for a while. He's been unable to keep his tosses low, and his control has been less than outstanding. His record has ballooned to eleven and six, with his ERA a bloated 2.25.

Randy faces Hal McRae, who taps a two-oh pitch back to the mound. Randy throws easily to Tony Perez at first, one away.

Boomer Scott walks to the plate. The home crowd momentarily revives. Jones throws a strike, a ball, a strike, and a strike. Boomer sits down, two away.

Rod Carew is next. He flies out on a two-strike pitch, and Jones jogs in, having thrown a perfect ninth to preserve Matlack's victory. Catfish Hunter is tagged with the six-to-three loss.

The American League has now lost twelve of the past thirteen all-star games.

The next day, the twenty-four owners of major-league baseball meet behind closed doors for a summit. They talk garrulously about money, about the lack of it, and about how, despite the enduring financial success of outfits such as the Dodgers, the enterprise of baseball, when taken as a whole, is barely breaking even.

Walter O'Malley, the wisecracking, cigar-smoking owner of the Dodgers, refuses to worry. Alarmists have been predicting the death of baseball ever since the incorporation of national basketball and football leagues, but baseball survives. Baseball is in a momentary slump, O'Malley will admit. He privately blames Charles Finley, whose moving of the A's to Oakland fractured the fragile fan base of the San Francisco Giants such that occasionally only a few hundred might attend a game in Candlestick while Finley's Mausoleum sells out only on promotion nights.

And then there is Oakland itself. Finley has assembled one of baseball's all-time greatest teams, but he has them playing their home games off in nowheresville. A dynasty from Oakland, believes O'Malley, just isn't good for the commercial health of the national pastime. O'Malley, who once decided Brooklyn was too small a stage, looks at Oakland and growls.

Finley, of course, points the finger of fault elsewhere. The flamboyant showman blames Bowie Kuhn, who is a particularly dull steward of the game, an organization man in countercultural times. Ever since Kuhn came aboard as commissioner in 1969, he and Finley have never seen eye to eye. Repeatedly, Finley attests, Kuhn has overstepped his authority, meddling in "personal business dealings." The commissioner has even dared to penalize the owner.

Kuhn will be up for reelection in a year. O'Malley trusts the competent and obsequious Kuhn, who has served him well by fighting off the players' union and preserving the reserve clause, so O'Malley seeks to use the occasion of this meeting at the Milwaukee club to preemptively renew Kuhn's contract for another seven years.

But Finley has arrived in Wisconsin with his own agenda. It requires the agreement of one-sixth of baseball's management to kick out the commissioner — that's only four people. Finley probes secretly and learns of three other men who hate Kuhn almost as much as he does: Jerold Hoffberger of the Orioles, Steinbrenner of the Yankees, and Brad Corbett of the Rangers. Together they (or their surrogates) stand in Milwaukee and announce that Kuhn must go and a new commissioner must be elected.

Their announcement stuns the room.

Finley breaks the silence by demanding a vote.

The other owners put him off.

Kuhn departs to his hotel room. He frankly hurts. He sits with the *Milwaukee Sentinel*, studying the jobs offered in the classifieds. "One of the curses of the commissioner's role in baseball is sitting in suites waiting out league meetings," he writes. "Matters of great importance are resolved while the commissioner stares helplessly into parking lots."

O'Malley the puppeteer quickly immerses himself in fixing this mess, in restoring order, in shoving the owners back in line. Other items on the regular agenda are taken up and dealt with, as meanwhile O'Malley's operatives furtively work the corridors, pulling various executives aside for cryptic exchanges, seeking a way to undermine the ousters before the four owners succeed in calling a formal vote.

Billy Martin and Mickey Mantle are downstairs getting drunk in the hotel bar.[5] They are still as close as ever. Mickey lives in Texas and likes to go to Arlington Stadium to watch Billy's Rangers play.

Rumors now reach the lounge. The two ex-Yankees — one feisty, the other stupid, and both intoxicated — learn that Commissioner Kuhn is getting dumped. They hear next the gossip that Bob Short might be behind it.

Bob Short is Billy Martin's best friend.

Bob Short owned the Washington Senators. The Senators were Kuhn's hometown team, his childhood favorites. Short decided to pick up and move them, which Kuhn sought to prevent. Short won. The capital lost its team. Kuhn made Short's life miserable as a result. He no longer owns a ball club, but Short still hates Kuhn, and the scuttlebutt speculates now that this vengeance is his doing.

All of which sounds marvelous to Mickey and Billy, so the ex-Yanks slip out of the bar and begin knocking on doors, cornering passersby, urging everyone they see to vote against Kuhn.

In this rare instance, the Dodgers beat the Yankees, as O'Malley's influence and powers of persuasion triumph yet again, and the anti-Kuhn bloc disintegrates. Ultimately, after a long and suspenseful night, Kuhn is reelected. Only Finley and Hoffberger vote against.

Kuhn is fetched from his suite and escorted downstairs to the meeting room. He enters to a standing ovation. He smiles "Thank you, gentlemen," he says, "especially those who voted *for* me. It's too bad it took so long." He looks angrily at Finley. "But it's not surprising, considering the quality of the opposition."

"What a joke!" Finley bellows.

Next Kuhn holds a press conference. Finley is in the back of the room, trying to give reporters his own version of the proceedings.

Kuhn is in no mood to tolerate this.

"Charlie," Kuhn says into the microphone, as cameras click and tapes roll, "you may leave my room."

"Thank you, Commissioner," Finley answers, visibly seething, "that just shows more class," and he storms out. "I've never seen so many damned idiots as the owners in this sport," Finley will tell *Time* a few months later. "Baseball's headed for extinction if we don't do something."

The next year, Finley will attempt to sell Rollie Fingers and Joe Rudi to the Red Sox and Vida Blue to the Yankees before the three players have a chance to become free agents. Kuhn will veto the transaction for failing to be in "the best interests of baseball." A court battle will ensue, ultimately affirming Kuhn and thereby enhancing his power as commissioner.

Throwing up his hands, Finley will abandon baseball.

Kuhn will again be reelected and will serve until the end of the 1984 season. His fifteen-year tenure as commissioner will be second in longevity only to that of Kenesaw Mountain Landis.

PART FOUR

THE SEASON'S
SECOND HALF

ELEVEN

MAJOR-LEAGUE STANDINGS ON JULY 21, 1975

NATIONAL LEAGUE

East Division

	W	L	Pct	GB
Pittsburgh	58	35	.624	–
Philadelphia	53	40	.570	5
New York	46	43	.517	10
St. Louis	45	46	.495	12
Chicago	43	51	.457	$15\frac{1}{2}$
Montreal	38	50	.432	$17\frac{1}{2}$

West Division

	W	L	Pct	GB
Cincinnati	62	32	.660	–
Los Angeles	51	44	.537	$11\frac{1}{2}$
San Francisco	44	49	.473	$17\frac{1}{2}$
San Diego	43	52	.453	$19\frac{1}{2}$
Atlanta	41	52	.441	$20\frac{1}{2}$
Houston	33	63	.344	30

AMERICAN LEAGUE

East Division

	W	L	Pct	GB
Boston	54	38	.587	–
New York	48	44	.522	6
Milwaukee	47	46	.505	7½
Baltimore	45	45	.500	8
Detroit	42	49	.462	11½
Cleveland	41	50	.451	12½

West Division

	W	L	Pct	GB
Oakland	58	34	.630	–
Kansas City	47	45	.511	11
Chicago	45	46	.495	12½
Texas	44	51	.463	15½
California	43	53	.448	17
Minnesota	40	53	.430	18½

A week after the all-star game, Billy Martin is fired. So too is Jack McKeon of the Royals, who is dismissed via telephone at 3:00 A.M. on a team flight. Both men had been counted on to pilot AL West contenders. The A's, without Catfish Hunter, were thought to be vulnerable. Instead, at the all-star break, Oakland is in first, with Kansas City eight and a half back, and Texas is in fourth. Oakland manager Alvin Dark sees in the standings the hand of the Lord, for only a miracle could explain why his team continues to possess such a commanding lead.

Billy Martin is replaced, for the moment, by his third-base coach, Frank Lucchesi, while McKeon's successor is, of all people, Martin's predecessor in Texas, Whitey Herzog. Before the year is out, ten more managers are replaced. Fully half the teams in baseball lose their skippers in 1975, an unprecedented manifestation of pennant anguish.

*   *   *

In the last weekend of July, Boston comes to New York for a show-down.

Luis Tiant starts on Friday. The Yankees, determined to get back in the pennant race, take advantage of Tiant's sore shoulder. He is hit hard by Bonds, Munson, and first baseman Chris Chambliss, but right fielder Lou Piniella does the worst damage, tripling in the third, singling in the seventh, and driving in four runs. Tiant takes the loss, his tenth on the season. He's truly hurting.

The next day, the score is tied in the ninth, and Boston has the bases loaded, when Fisk singles. Carl and Lynn score. Boston starter Reggie Cleveland gets two outs in the bottom of the inning before giving up a walk, a wild pitch, and a single. Boston's lead falters. Darrell Johnson brings in Jim Willoughby. Rick Burleson stabs a line drive behind second base to give Willoughby his fifth save.

Sunday's doubleheader climax draws 53,631 customers, the biggest crowd ever to attend a Yankee game at Shea Stadium (where the Yankees are still playing until the refurbishment of Yankee Stadium is complete). Having split the first two games, the Yankees tell reporters that they'll have to sweep in order to maintain their legitimacy.

The opening game is a suspenseful pitching duel between Lee and Hunter. Lee gives up six hits, but a string of defensive gems by Rick Miller, Denny Doyle, and Rico Petrocelli keeps the Yankees from scoring. The game remains scoreless in the ninth, when Lynn gets to first on an error. Rice strikes out swinging, but Lynn steals second. With two outs, the next batter singles to left center and Lynn comes around to score.

The drama continues through the bottom of the ninth, when the Yanks' Graig Nettles slashes a long, twisting drive close to the warning track in left center. The crowd cheers. They see Lynn playing Nettles in right center. Lynn pivots and crosses the expansive Shea outfield in long strides, telling himself that the ball has to be caught. He dives at the last minute, bounces three times, rolls over, and holds up the ball.

In the second game, Jim Rice gets four hits and Carl homers.

In the eighth, the Yankees bring in a seldom-used rookie left-hander from Louisiana named Ron Guidry. He gets three strikeouts and pitches two shutout innings, but the Yankees lose, six to nothing.

From his club box alongside the dugout, George Steinbrenner watched his Yankees as they were held scoreless in both games. His mood blackened. Only rarely did his team hit the ball hard, and when they did, Boston's suddenly superb defense neutralized the threat. The Red Sox appeared to have positioned Gold Gloves all over the field, turning doubles into singles, turning singles into outs. His team had the bases loaded, with nobody out, and they couldn't score even once.

Manager Bill Virdon calls a team meeting immediately after the second game.[1] They congregate, without having showered, still wearing the stains of Shea's grass upon their knees.

The manager stands before pitcher Rudy May's locker, holding a small tape recorder.

"What's that?" asks Sparky Lyle.

"Shut up!" says pitching coach Whitey Ford.

"Gather 'round and listen," Virdon simply says.

"Will this be inspirational music?" cracks Lyle.

"Shut up!" Whitey repeats.

Virdon presses play. From the tinny speaker erupts the unmistakable voice of their team owner, exiled in body but not in speech.

"I'll be a son of a bitch," Steinbrenner exclaims, "if I'm going to sit up here and sign these paychecks and watch us get our asses kicked by a bunch of rummies."

Someone starts to giggle. It spreads rapidly.

"Shut up!" cries Ford, to no avail.

Steinbrenner continues to squawk away furiously, the players laughing now more openly.

Virdon isn't amused. He looks morose, says nothing.

"Now goddammit!" barks Steinbrenner's disembodied voice. "Like they say down on the docks, *You have to have balls.*"

The players maintain this as a private joke. For days afterward, at all the wrong times, a Yankee grabs his crotch and solemnly tells another, "You have to have balls."

When Steinbrenner learns that the Rangers have let go of the best manager in baseball, he telephones Texas to get Billy Martin's number, but Billy is not at home, and no one knows where he's gone. George imperiously summons a Yankee scout and orders him to track down Martin. Steinbrenner strikes a match, lights his cigar. *After all, he's a scout, that's his job, finding people.*

Soon enough, Billy is discovered trout fishing outside Denver. He's relaxing with his family.

Billy is unmoved to hear that the Yankees need him; when *he* needed *them*, where were they? After all these years of banishment, he's supposed to forgive them, forgive Casey Stengel for sending him away?

The Yankees' GM appears in Denver. He proposes an annual salary of $72,000, but Billy doesn't appreciate the terms, doesn't trust the contract, doesn't know this George Steinbrenner, and doesn't feel like jumping right back into the circus. He'd like a few months to recover, but next the phone rings and it's Steinbrenner imploring him to climb aboard, reminding Billy that this is his big chance to manage his old team, something he's always wanted to do, and warning him that this offer will never be made again. Finally, when his wife and friends urge him to accept, and Steinbrenner blathers on about loyalty, and the scout casts him a pitiful, searching look, Martin caves, and he agrees to return to New York.

Steinbrenner secretly brings out Billy and his wife and books them into a midtown hotel under assumed names. He informs Billy that he'll be unveiled as the new Yankee manager as the last introduction of the old-timers' game. Billy beseeches George to reconsider. He should be brought out earlier. He's a lifetime .250 hitter; he shouldn't be brought out on the heels of Mantle and DiMaggio.

Steinbrenner sweeps aside Billy's plea. The owner is wide and powerful, with an ego slightly larger than the island of Manhattan. He fancies himself an expert on Yankee pride, though he is, in truth, a wealthy shipowner from Cleveland.

Billy Martin, hiding in his hotel room with the air conditioner blasting, tunes in WMCA (570 AM), and hears Rizzuto call Bill Virdon's final game. The team performs solidly. Bonds doubles in the bottom of the first, scores on a sacrifice fly. An inning later, he drives a ball to deep center, and it's caught, but another run scores. Catfish pitches and gives up some runs, and with two outs in the ninth, the game is up for grabs when shortstop Fred Stanley makes a tumbling catch on the left-field grass and the Yankees win their third in a row.

Billy doesn't know what to make of these players. He wants to avoid snap judgments. He decides that the best thing, once he takes over the team, is just to soft-shoe it. He'll observe. He needs to identify the clubhouse lawyers, alibiers, and complainers so he can get rid of them in the off-season.

That night, as the Yankees quit the dugout and enter the clubhouse, they notice that the manager's little office is tightly packed with TV lights and microphones.

"Have you been fired, Bill?" the newsmen ask.

"I haven't been told anything," Virdon responds.

Watching from the lockers, Thurman Munson nods at the madness, and quietly asks Catfish his opinion.

"Well," Hunter whispers, "a new manager might make a difference in five or ten games a year, but I'd say the man doesn't know yet."

"If he knew, he would say so."

"One thing you can't doubt is the man's honesty."

"Yep."

"The thing that happened to us," Catfish confides to his catcher, "is that a lot of guys came back from being hurt before they were up to one hundred percent ready."

Thurman shakes his head in disgust. "They ought to tell the man if they're firing him."[2]

"Every time a team goes into a slump," Virdon is telling the newsmen, "you read that they'll fire the manager."

"The rumors are all over the city," the reporters persist. "The GM's been out of town on a secret mission the last few days. What's going on?"

"I have no idea," Bill keeps saying. "I had a routine talk with our general manager this afternoon, and he said nothing to me about any change." Time inches along, pregnant and sorrowful. It's like being murdered by a glacier, the way this thing is happening. Virdon notices the unusual number of photographers crowding into his small, hot office in order to snap his picture. "I've a feeling," Virdon unhappily observes, "you're not here because we just won three straight."

The reporters pack up and go.

The telephone in the manager's office rings. Everyone within hearing distance knows who it is even before Virdon picks it up. Of course, it's the GM. He asks the manager to come across the street to the Yankee offices when he is dressed.

Early the next morning, around the time Virdon returns to Shea to empty out his desk, Martin sends his wife out for a morning paper.[3] He needs last night's baseball results. His wife returns with the *New York Post.* It's like a sauna outside. It's already ninety degrees and not yet 7:30. The street itself is melting. Ladies are getting their heels stuck, they're walking out of their shoes. Billy pecks his wife on the cheek, then opens the sports section, sees where Boston won again, and curses. They've been on a tear, winning twenty-one of their last twenty-six games, leaving the Yankees ten games behind, with two months to play. This time, the Red Sox accomplished another last-minute turnaround, their twentieth this season. Detroit took the lead, seven to six, scoring four runs in the top of the ninth, and then Boston came to bat. Second baseman Denny Doyle beat out a hit to shortstop, continuing to second when the throw went wild. Yastrzemski singled. Zimmer waved Doyle home. The Tigers threw to the plate, but Doyle scored while Carl advanced to second on the play. The score was tied. The next batter, Lynn, was walked intentionally, and then Rice laid down a sacrifice bunt. The pitcher pounced on the ball. He whirled, thinking to nail Carl, but his eagerness spoiled his accuracy. He pegged it into foul territory. Carl turned the corner and kept going, winning the game from second base on a bunt.

In New York, the hours slowly pass. Temperatures climb.

Driving to the stadium, Thurman Munson hears the weatherman warn of a record heat wave. All over the city, but particularly in the tenement districts, fire hydrants are opened so that kids can frolic in the spray. New York's water pressure drops precipitously. Officials warn that fire-fighting efforts are being compromised.

Heedlessly, more hydrants are opened.

The radio also reports that the Yankees will hold a press conference before the old-timers' game and that Billy Martin is in town. This is how Munson discovers that Martin will be the team's new manager.

At Shea, the grounds crew hoses down the baked infield before the game and then turns the hose upon a cluster of shirtless fans in the left-field stands.

The clubhouse is steamy and crowded with Yankees, past and present.

And then, one at a time, the names are called and yesterday's heroes emerge, some crawling as if from a crypt, others jaunty in their stride, their firm historical bodies now flaccid. Lifting his cap, each is received with a standing ovation. They appear in their old uniforms, combinations of colors which call forth ancient loyalties and enmities. They gather like peacetime dignitaries on the foul line of a park in which none of them ever played: Pee Wee Reese, Whitey Ford, Billy Herman, Roy Campanella, Mantle, Ford, DiMaggio . . .

Then the new manager is announced and out of the dugout runs Billy Martin, a mustache on his face, wearing on his back his old number: 1 (freed up now since Bobby Murcer went west).

Some boo. After all, Virdon is candid, intelligent, and well liked. *Why replace him?* Last year, he steered a much weaker Yankee team to a surprisingly strong finish. He was voted 1974's AL Manager of the Year. *How can he suddenly be no good?*

For the most part, however, the new manager is greeted with applause. Fans see in this the healthy completion of a circuit. They agree with Mantle and Ford: this is where Billy belongs. It may do little toward improving the team's immediate pennant chances, but in this year of veteran homecomings — Tony C., Hammer, Dick Allen — it makes sense that the former brat of the infield now comes back as the inspirational hothead of the dugout.

Three other times Martin has taken over teams, but never with this much fanfare, emotion, sensation. Billy hasn't appeared on a Yankee roster since 1957. That was eighteen long years ago. He reaches deep in his heart where usually, reliably, the old man can be found taking beanballs to the head and body, but now there is nothing of that nature, there is no resentment anywhere, there is no blame, there is only an unfamiliar, subdued sort of empathy. Here is Billy, in the old man's shoes. Standing in 101-degree heat, he thinks of Stengel and is overcome. Later, Martin will admit to weeping, his tears mingling with his perspiration. One last time, the fatherless son wants to see the sonless father. He wants to thank the old man. He wants, more than anything, to forgive him.

In the two-inning old-timers' game, Billy mans second base. Two ground balls are hit in his direction. He fields them both flawlessly. His team of old Yankees wins, two to zero.

In the more meaningful contest that follows, Cleveland's Boog Powell drives a three-run home run in the sixth but Sparky Lyle comes in and shuts down the Indians. Bonds goes oh for four but Munson goes two for three. New York strings together five singles in the eighth and wins, five to three.

The next day, when things calm down, Billy finally has a chance to address his players. "When I'm managing, you'd better take your job seriously," he says, "or you won't be around long." The manager has noticed weak execution. His men are failing to hit the cutoff man or advance the runner. Too many of them aren't being aggressive on the field. "If you play for me, you play the game like you play life. You play it to be successful, you play it with dignity, you play it with pride, and you play it aggressively. Life is a very serious thing, and baseball has been my life. What else has my life been? That's why, when I lose a ball game, I can't eat after a game. Sometimes I can hardly sleep. If you're in love with the game, you can't turn it on and off like a light. It's something that runs so deep it takes you over. If I lose, I say to myself, *What if I had done this or that? What if so-and-so had done this?* You're second-guessing yourself, trying to reach perfection to where if a similar situation arises in the future, you handle it better the next time. As a manager I give one hundred percent of my effort, and I expect the same from my players. Any questions?"

Thurman Munson raises a hand.

"Yeah?"

"I call my own pitches," the catcher declares. "I've studied these hitters for a long time, and I know what I'm doing behind the plate. I know you like to call pitches sometimes. Frankly, I don't think you're as qualified as I am."

"Yeah?"

"Just gimme a few days to show you. You'll see I'm right."

"You got it. Anybody else?"

The team wins six of the first eight games that Billy manages.

In Milwaukee, on August 4, Rudy May is pitching. He's struggling a little. Thurman calls time and jogs out to talk to him. Out of the corner of his eye, Munson sees Billy trotting out to join the conference. It's the first time Billy has tried a visit to the mound. As he nears, Munson turns on him and snarls, half seriously, "What the hell are you doin' here?"

To Rudy May's amazement, Billy turns right around. He goes back to the dugout. He never says a word.

Rudy smiles gratefully at Thurman.

* * *

The Dodgers cannot endure this disappointing season. Already, their dreams of a repeat pennant appear foolish. Many of last year's standouts are injured. Mike Marshall, catcher Joe Ferguson, center fielder Jimmy Wynn, shortstop Bill Russell, and left fielder Bill Buckner are lost to the team for extended periods. Second baseman Davey Lopes acknowledges another, even bigger factor. "We have been destroyed psychologically by the way the Reds have been playing," the second baseman admits with cool candor. "I don't think we'll catch them."

The strain is especially evident in LA's clubhouse, where the players turn on Steve Garvey, who refuses to take part in their discouragement. Oblivious, he continues to be fabulous, to hit for distance and average, and to drive in runs. He disputes Lopes's contention that all is lost. Lopes, in turn, reveals that he and most of his teammates are sick of Garvey. The other Dodgers confirm this. None deny that Garvey is a gamer, dedicated to showing up, getting out there, and playing his absolute hardest no matter how he feels. They just don't like the guy's PR machine, the way he appears on magazine covers, with every hair in place, sitting ramrod straight before an apple pie sprouting American flags.

In so many unbearable ways, Garvey is too good to be true. He says what he feels and he means what he says. He is simple and straight and he possesses no apparent sense of humor. The Dodger players regard themselves as scrappy and tough, as athletes with attitude. They're distressed that, increasingly, Garvey turns out to be their spokesman.

To halt the Garvey-bashing, manager Walt Alston suggests a team meeting. Alston is old and slow. He views his main task as simply getting along with twenty-five men. He is incapable of dynamic problem solving. He was managing the Dodgers before even Frank Robinson was in the majors. Back then, as Alston tells anyone who'll listen, the uniforms were sewn out of heavy flannel, and the road shirts were scratchy, and on the front they read BROOK-LYN. Alston has never been particularly adept at relating to the concerns of his players. Since the 1960s, he's fallen more out of touch.

Alston has little to say to the youngsters who have come up through the farm system playing for the voluble Tommy Lasorda. Whereas Lasorda offers anyone a mighty embrace, Alston at most might shake one's hand to express gratitude.

Unsurprisingly, Alston's attempt at a team meeting clears up nothing. Garvey stands before the others in the locker room, he asks if anyone has a problem with him, and nobody answers.

The Dodger organization seeks to bury the story. They announce a big piece of news. They have finally succeeded in re-signing Marshall, who has been pitching for them this season without a contract. Marshall acknowledges the deal, but recommends that his peers should never pay attention to their uniforms. They must treat baseball as a summer job, a job in which they are paid to play a game and to wear the costumes of boys.[4]

This too flies in the face of Garvey, who loves to rhapsodize about the glory of his uniform and who insists that *Dodger blue* flows in his veins. "There is such a thing as a Dodger," Garvey often argues, "as opposed to, say, a Tiger or an Indian. A Dodger has interest not only in himself, but in the organization. He has a personality of his own, but once the game starts, he is strictly a team man. He's a player you can depend on, not flashy, but solid. And he's proud to be a Dodger."[5]

Garvey's teammate Andy Messersmith couldn't agree more. Messersmith, LA's best pitcher, loves his uniform so much that he wants a no-trade clause in his contract. The Dodgers balk at this demand. They are far more willing to reward Marshall's greed than Messersmith's loyalty. It will be their undoing.

All this breathy talk of uniforms — Carbo's adoration of Yawkey expressed as "playing for the uniform," the worry of Bonds that he doesn't look enough "like a Yankee" in his new pinstripes, Garvey's devoted rhapsodies — will soon seem quaint. Messersmith's desire to stay a Dodger will ironically send him away, and after 1975, in the wake of free agency, Mike Marshall's cynicism alone will stand affirmed. Eventually, even Steve Garvey will don a rival uniform and will close out his career batting against Los Angeles.

TWELVE

MAJOR-LEAGUE STANDINGS ON JULY 28, 1975

NATIONAL LEAGUE

East Division

	W	L	Pct	GB
Pittsburgh	62	38	.620	–
Philadelphia	57	44	.564	$5\frac{1}{2}$
New York	51	46	.526	$9\frac{1}{2}$
St. Louis	50	49	.505	$11\frac{1}{2}$
Chicago	46	56	.451	17
Montreal	40	56	.417	20

West Division

	W	L	Pct	GB
Cincinnati	66	36	.647	–
Los Angeles	54	49	.524	$12\frac{1}{2}$
San Francisco	51	50	.505	$14\frac{1}{2}$
San Diego	48	54	.471	18
Atlanta	43	58	.426	$22\frac{1}{2}$
Houston	36	68	.346	31

AMERICAN LEAGUE

East Division

	W	L	Pct	GB
Boston	60	40	.600	–
Baltimore	51	47	.520	8
New York	50	50	.500	10
Milwaukee	50	52	.490	11
Detroit	45	55	.450	15
Cleveland	44	54	.449	15

West Division

	W	L	Pct	GB
Oakland	64	37	.634	–
Kansas City	54	46	.540	$9\frac{1}{2}$
Chicago	48	51	.485	15
Texas	47	55	.461	$17\frac{1}{2}$
California	46	57	.447	19
Minnesota	43	58	.426	21

Everything's going well for Sparky Anderson. His Reds are playing gorgeously; even better, his son Lee is talking to him. By having that fight with his eldest, Sparky apparently cleared the air between them. They are now closer than ever. Lee calls him frequently, often for no reason at all. They both read the sports page closely, and in late July each notices the same thing: Bernie Carbo, of all people, is second in the American League in slugging percentage. After two hundred twenty at bats, he has forty-seven runs, forty-two RBIs, fourteen homers, and sixty walks.

Once again, it's tempting for Sparky to think about luring him back, to consider making a trade for Bernardo. His family would love that. But who could the Reds trade? Certainly Boston would accept George Foster in exchange for Carbo, but Sparky's not about to let go of Foster. It's true that in the field Carbo has the better arm, but at the plate, when Foster gets into a pitch, no one hits a ball harder than he does — not Willie Stargell, Willie McCovey, or Lee May.

And Sparky knows why Bernie's stats look so good: he's batting leadoff. This isn't something that casual observers like Sparky's kids would ever notice, but when Boston's manager places Bernie lower in the lineup, the player's average tails off and his ratio of walks to strikeouts changes for the worse. When he's down in the batting order, he swings at bad pitches. He tries to jerk every pitch out of the park. He feels he has to drive in runs. But put Bernie in the leadoff spot and he concentrates on getting on base.[1] The fact is, though, that Cincinnati has a lot of leadoff hitters. Sparky already has three. Boston doesn't have any, which is why they're putting Bernie there. And for now, yes, Boston's in first, but they won't be for long. Sparky's betting on the Orioles.

In his office at Riverfront, the manager talks to the press not about Boston's chances but about one of these three great leadoff hitters of his, the speedy Ken Griffey. Sparky predicts that Griffey won't hit a lot of home runs but will garner his share of doubles and triples and stolen bases. He'll also provide excellent defense in right field. Sitting on the lap of the manager at the time is Griffey's six-year-old son, his eldest. The boy bears the father's name; as Pete Rose has Pete Rose Jr., so Ken Griffey has this one, little Ken Griffey Jr. When together, the two frisky boys call themselves "The Juniors." They stake out the laundry room so that Eduardo Perez, son of Tony and the only one of the kids who is tall enough to reach the team's candy stash, is safe to steal them sweets. Reds' equipment manager Bernie Stowe dubs them the "Little Red Machine," and often asks aloud whether he's running a clubhouse or a child-care facility. Vickie Bench sighs when she hears of the children's mischief. "We hope to have some little Benches running around soon," she tells newsmen. "Not immediately, but soon."

Ken Griffey Jr. squirms out of Sparky's lap and helps himself to a soda from the manager's refrigerator. Junior is spoiled, but this is natural. His father grew up without a father, so the son gets anything he wants. They live in a large, new house in Cincinnati's western suburbs, with a spacious family room, a fireplace, a trophy display, and an exercise room with weight machines in the basement. Junior never feels awestruck to hang around Pete Rose,

Johnny Bench, or Joe Morgan. They are just his dad's coworkers. "Don't copy them," his dad often says. "Just be yourself."

Junior heeds the advice, for the time being, but quite soon a high-energy player will arrive in the majors and it will become hard for Griffey's eldest not to imitate that player's style, the way he lunges for stolen bases or snatches a fly ball out of the air with a backhanded windmill swipe, slapping his glove against his thigh. At the moment, that player is still a youngster too. Some mornings the boy's coach, Hank Thomasson, stands at the door of his house, turning the knob, letting himself inside. Thomasson does this all the time. He acts in the noble tradition of George Powles and Bill Peterson, white playground directors devoted to teaching a sense of community to ghetto children.[2] Peterson essentially raised Dave Winfield; Powles provided a reliable father figure for Frank Robinson and Curt Flood; but each sports director's true contribution, his legacy of influence, remains incalculable. There is a home, and there is a home plate; sometimes, they are the same.

Thomasson has a summer team that plays Connie Mack ball at Oakland's Bushrod Park. The team is named the National Association for the Advancement of Colored People, their jerseys boldly reading NAACP. Future American League outfielders Gary Pettis and Lloyd Moseby are on the team. Their catcher is Dave Stewart, who will be the ace of the A's one day. From behind the plate, Stewart can throw out guys on his knees. Rickey Henderson is the first baseman. Few on the team have money or fathers, but Thomasson does all he can to keep them motivated. Early every Saturday morning, he drives across town to awaken Henderson personally. Thomasson enters the house, nods hello to Bobbie, Rickey's mother, and pushes into Rickey's bedroom. He sets down the hot chocolate and glazed donuts on a bedstand. "It's time," Thomasson says softly.

Rickey is mostly legs, with a very short torso. He displays the greatest athletic ability Thomasson has ever witnessed. Henderson's an all-league, all-city, all-county, and all-state pick in four high school sports, but his passion is football. He dreams of being a running back for the Oakland Raiders and could easily realize that. Thomasson knows the scouts are watching. Once Rickey graduates he'll be offered football scholarships from all over. Professional baseball teams will seek to draft him as well, but Henderson's less enthusiastic about those prospects. He really only started to play baseball because Tyrone, his brother, pushed him into it (and worst of all, their first team was sponsored by a funeral parlor). Every boy with whom Rickey played back then was right-handed. Watching them swing the bat from the right side, the impressionable left-handed seven-year-old unquestioningly assumed that this was a rule of the game: everybody hits right-handed. He did the same.

Too late, Henderson hears that it's actually advantageous to bat left-handed, because you're a full step closer to first base, and most pitchers, being right-handed, throw curveballs that conveniently break toward you, rather than away. By the time Rickey learns this, though, he's comfortable where he's at, hitting righty and throwing lefty. This remains a combination, Thomasson knows, that baseball scouts abhor. In general, Thomasson doesn't think the scouts are as enthused about Henderson as they should be. They keep emphasizing what a helluva infielder Rickey would make, given his reflexes and quick feet, if only he gloved with his right hand. Being a lefty, Rickey is scratched from four of baseball's nine positions — catcher, second, short, and third — but, the scouts point out to Thomasson, he's too small to play first, and he's not a great outfielder. This kid, scouts say, will never make it. But Thomasson believes.

Late in July, Mr. and Mrs. Johnny Bench arrive in New York together, Vickie to check in with old friends, John to give a speech at a fight-cancer fund-raiser and to play three baseball games in Shea Stadium. Vickie attends the fund-raiser in a cream blouse and soft-rose pantsuit. Her hair is full and lustrous. The tabloids snap her dabbing her green eyes as her husband tells how, during his MVP season in 1972, while leading his team to the World Series, he secretly believed himself dying, because a spot had been found on his lung and a malignancy suspected; and when they opened him up after the season, finding a lung lesion but no cancer, they had to be careful not to cut his back muscles or he'd never be able to throw a baseball again. But now, thank merciful heaven, Johnny Bench is alive and strong and he's here and they applaud him, at the fund-raiser and everywhere else in town.

Sitting at Shea, Vickie observes it all with a certain distance, bemused yet dutifully tracking the dynamics, the flow of loyalty, of team pride, learning how the historical weave of grudges proves this set of guys is better than that set of guys, how and why us is better than them. It's all quite inane.

With envy in her eyes, Vickie watches an airplane ascend high overhead, bound for parts unknown.

It's like Dick Allen says: baseball does bad things to marriage. Probably, if Vickie knew that the current issue of the *Baseball Bulletin* featured an article on "The Danger Baseball Wives Must Face," she'd happily plunk down six bucks for a copy and lap up every bit of advice (except that she'd worry about being caught by paparazzi). Here is Vickie's experience: she knows her husband until the season begins, then he wriggles from her grasp and disappears beneath the waves, never to be heard from again. She and John do nothing now but fight. Something like a low-grade fever runs through the marriage, sapping her strength, leaving her dreary, impatient, hopeless, and angry.

Larry Flynt contacts Vickie's modeling agency, Wilhelmina, and offers $25,000 if Mrs. Bench will pose naked in *Hustler*.

Wearing a look of dismay, Vickie passes this news on to her husband.

"Why not do it?" John blithely replies.

Vickie trembles. Her head spins from the puzzling uncertainty of her circumstance. "You're joking."

"It's good money."

"Oh, lord." She drops her head in her hands. "You have got to be kidding!"[3] Johnny Bench, she suddenly grasps, has no intention of making any little Benches run around soon. It's like Curt Flood says: "If the ballplayer is married, it is a safe bet that his wife is discontented, jangled, and advisedly suspicious."

Opening the sports section, one usually expects a depiction of athletic grace and splendor. Instead, on the morning of July 30, the sports page of the *Tampa Tribune* shows an old, white man in a Yankees cap. He is dressed in vigorous color, a loud, checkered jacket, a tie illustrated with ballplayers.

Surprised by this sight, a suspicious, skinny ten-year-old named Dwight likely asks his father, Dan, about it. *What's this?*

His dad is the one to ask. He knows *everything* about baseball. He once was a semiprofessional ballplayer. Now he coaches a semi-pro team in their Florida neighborhood.[4] Their house is close to where the Detroit Tigers hold spring training, so the children are able to watch the greats in person, like Mickey Lolich, like Al Kaline. On Monday nights, Dan comes home from the phosphate factory and sits in his easy chair with a beer and a bag of chips in his lap, watching NBC's *Game of the Week* with shy Dwight beside him, and for hours they share the glories of the game, dissecting the clout of Dick Allen's swing or the obvious heart of Willie Stargell. It's a good time. Baseball was all Dan ever talked about with his father, and it's the same now with his son.

The photo in the *Tampa Tribune* is explained by its caption: *Casey Stengel celebrates another birthday.* An amusing thought — as if the Man in the Moon has birthdays, as if Casey's age can be determined by anything short of radiocarbon dating — as if he is mortal, and might one day disappear. The '56 Yankees called Stengel "the old man of baseball." Already, back then, decades ago. Just how old is he now? In human years, he's eighty-five; but in baseball years, he is eternal. He was pitching and catching by the time Babe Ruth was born. He got his first World Series hit when DiMaggio was two; his playing career ended five years before Mantle was born. "A Stengel," said one of Casey's cohorts, "is one creature what never dies."

Dwight reminds Dan of himself when he was a boy.[5] Dwight will use anything he can find as a ball so he can pretend he's in a home-run derby. Or he'll throw at a chalk-drawn circle on a brick wall as if he's in a pitching duel. Mostly Dwight occupies himself with daydreams. It's always baseball. He imagines he's Pete Rose or Rod Carew. He invents games in his mind. He lies in bed at night, throwing a tennis ball up in the air and catching it, over and over, until he falls asleep. He dreams he can throw like his grandfather Ucleese, a strong-legged, long-armed pitcher who wasn't promoted to the big leagues because he was black, and this was before Jackie Robinson.[6]

Dwight has made the all-star team in Little League. He plays third base. He's much smaller than the others but then they're all older. One of them, a twelve-year-old named Albert Everett, is five foot eight and 150 pounds. He not only throws hard but hits with power. Thanks to Everett, Dwight's all-star team goes undefeated. They win their Little League district, section, state, division, and region. When the team travels to Williamsport, Pennsylvania, for the final tournament, Dwight has to drop out, because all competitors in the championships must be eleven or twelve.[7] Dwight's place is taken by Casey Sheffield, another pint-size kid who's only slightly older. The final game is broadcast nationally on ABC–TV. While his team loses the Little League World Series by one run, Dwight watches along with Albert Everett's five-year-old brother, Carl, and Casey Sheffield's six-year-old brother, Gary, both of whom will play one day in the majors with Dwight. At that time, someone will ask Mickey Mantle who he would be, if he could be anyone, and his response'll come instantly: "Dwight Gooden."[8]

With his all-star jitters past, Randy Jones returns to San Diego and settles back into form. Over his next four starts, he surrenders only two runs in thirty-six innings. He gets fifteen ground-ball outs on July 22, eighteen on July 27, twenty-one on August 1, and twenty on August 6. "You're boring," his teammates tell him. "Really boring."[9] They tease him. His pitches are *so slow*. They speculate that he's throwing balloons up there, or feathers. They claim to have clocked his fastball at twenty-seven miles per hour, and debate how much they might accomplish in the long moments before his pitches find the catcher.

Once, after Randy beats the Braves in the first contest of a twi-night doubleheader, usherettes scatter $25,000 around the infield of Atlanta-Fulton County Stadium. Six attractive women appear, some in shorts, others in flared jeans, all wearing tight blouses. Over the public-address system, a man cries, "Go!" The women are allowed to keep every dollar they can cram into their clothes within a minute and a half. Their ninety seconds of mad scurrying is matched only by the desperation of the ailing Braves' front office, who pray for their salvation with promotional nights of this sort. Their team is performing so poorly that fans won't come unless there's a giveaway. The Braves hand out posters, helmets, bats, jackets, caps; they sponsor Teen Night, Family Night, Straight-A Student Night. Other struggling teams attempt similar things, with mixed results. Last year's Beer Night in Cleveland ended in a riot. ("The box score," one journalist dryly observed, "should have included arrests and injuries.") Houston had a rodeo that tore up their AstroTurf. Texas offered a free car that never materialized. Atlanta gave away Frisbees but the customers spent the game spinning them out onto the field, and then one of the contestants on Hot Pants Night stripped off her blouse and streaked.

A young Atlanta businessman watches it all in growing horror. He owns a local cable company. In the past, recalls the business-man, the Braves were a good enough ball club that they didn't need asinine gimmicks to encourage attendance.

The aggravated businessman turns to his people in accounting. He directs them to draw up a new fiscal plan. He proposes buying the last-place Braves. He'll turn them around. He wants to generate money for a championship by broadening the team's marketing. He will dispense with regional identities and arouse a national fan base. What he advocates will uproot the game and eradicate generations of tradition. New loyalties will be penciled in, loyalties unencumbered by any notion of neighborhood. Before they even become winners, his team will turn a profit, for they will be a product distributed through his own cable company. This is his vision. His name is Ted Turner, and before the year is out, he will own the Atlanta Braves.

THIRTEEN

MAJOR-LEAGUE STANDINGS ON AUGUST 18, 1975

NATIONAL LEAGUE

East Division

	W	L	Pct	GB
Pittsburgh	67	55	.549	–
Philadelphia	66	55	.545	$\frac{1}{2}$
St. Louis	65	57	.533	2
New York	63	58	.521	$3\frac{1}{2}$
Chicago	58	66	.468	10
Montreal	50	69	.420	$15\frac{1}{2}$

West Division

	W	L	Pct	GB
Cincinnati	82	39	.678	–
Los Angeles	65	57	.533	$17\frac{1}{2}$
San Francisco	61	62	.496	22
San Diego	55	66	.455	27
Atlanta	55	69	.444	$28\frac{1}{2}$
Houston	46	80	.365	$38\frac{1}{2}$

AMERICAN LEAGUE

East Division

	W	L	Pct	GB
Boston	74	49	.602	–
Baltimore	66	54	.550	$6\frac{1}{2}$
New York	62	59	.512	11
Milwaukee	56	66	.459	$17\frac{1}{2}$
Cleveland	53	65	.449	$18\frac{1}{2}$
Detroit	48	74	.393	$25\frac{1}{2}$

West Division

	W	L	Pct	GB
Oakland	74	48	.607	–
Kansas City	67	53	.558	6
Texas	60	63	.488	$14\frac{1}{2}$
Chicago	59	63	.484	15
Minnesota	56	67	.455	$18\frac{1}{2}$
California	55	69	.444	20

Luis Tiant has not seen his father in fifteen years. Once, ten years ago, he glimpsed his mother in Mexico, but she had to flee back home or risk being permanently exiled from her husband.

On August 21, 1975, Luis stands in Boston's Logan Airport with Maria, his wife of fourteen years, and their twelve-year-old, Luis, seven-year-old, Isabel, and one-year-old, Danny. Every television camera in New England is present. Luis can understand why they are there, but it still upsets him. This moment belongs to his family; this moment is private.

The international flight from Mexico City docks in the American Airlines gate. *What will my parents look like?* He wipes his brow with a handkerchief. *They will look older; don't be surprised.* He sees his father step off the plane. Luis puts his hands over his eyes. He weeps. *I wasn't going to do that.* He can't help it. His father is smiling. They embrace.

"Don't cry," his father whispers. "The cameras will see you."

"I don't care," says Luis. "That's the way I feel."

A writer approaches and, through a Spanish interpreter, asks Luis's mother whether her husband will be available to pitch for the Red Sox.

She considers. "It's been so long since he threw a ball," she answers skeptically. "He'd have to go into training."

"She doesn't understand baseball," her husband interrupts, and grins. "You tell the Red Sox I'm ready." He looks at his grandson Luis. "He's going to make a great ballplayer."

That night the Tiants have a lot to talk about, a lot to ask, a lot to tell, and a lot to remember. Luis and his father have a few drinks, a few cigars, and more than a few laughs. But Luis's mother is exhausted. She has to go to bed. She kisses her son good night. "I'm so happy," she tells him softly, eyes brimming. "I don't care if I die now."[1]

On Tuesday night, August 26, Senor Tiant gets his first opportunity to watch his son pitch. Before the game, a special ceremony is conducted. Luis's father is introduced. He receives a standing ovation. He goes to the mound, in a brown suit and a Red Sox cap, to throw out the first pitch. He removes his jacket and hands it to his son, who stands beside him, covered with goose bumps.

Tim Blackwell jogs out and squats behind home. Fisk is hurt again, of course, having this time split his finger on a foul tip. He'll be back soon. Until then, Blackwell and Bob Montgomery split the catching duties.

Blackwell flashes a signal to Luis's father, then the old left-handed New York Cuban goes into a full, graceful motion and fires a pitch — low and outside. He looks disapprovingly toward the plate, then calls for the ball again. Once more he goes into his windup and delivers — this time, bringing in some heat, right through the middle of the strike zone.

"Every one of his pitches had mustard on it," says Bill Lee admiringly.

The fans are on their feet again in a rousing salute as he dons his jacket.

"I'm ready to go four or five innings," he tells his son, "anytime."

Ted Williams (l) advising Carl Yastrzemski (r). In 1961 Carl inherited
Fenway's left field from Williams, who had played it since 1939.
(*National Baseball Hall of Fame Library, Cooperstown, N.Y.*)

Yastrzemski (l) advising
Jim Rice (r). Taking over
Fenway's left field in
1975, Rice stayed there
for fourteen years.
(*National Baseball
Hall of Fame Library,
Cooperstown, N.Y.*)

Longtime Boston Red Sox owner Tom Yawkey. In 1975 everybody knew that Yawkey had 200 million bucks; nobody yet knew that he had leukemia. (*National Baseball Hall of Fame Library, Cooperstown, N.Y.*)

Boston's Dwight "Dewey" Evans. The Red Sox believed they had one of the game's best outfielders in Evans; then, in 1975, Fred Lynn arrived. (*National Baseball Hall of Fame Library, Cooperstown, N.Y.*)

Cy Young Award–winning pitcher Jim "Catfish" Hunter became baseball's first free agent, and on December 31, 1974, he signed a five-year contract with the Yankees for the unheard-of sum of $3.75 million. (*National Baseball Hall of Fame Library, Cooperstown, N.Y.*)

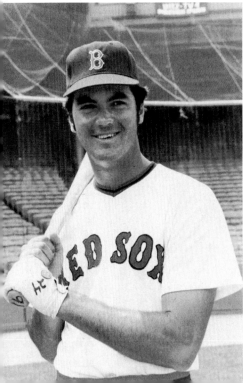

The 1946 champion USC Trojan baseball team, with coach Rod Dedeaux (first row, second from the left) and twelve-year-old batboy George "Sparky" Anderson (cross-legged in front, right). (*USC Sports Information*)

For most of the twentieth century, Casey Stengel embodied our national pastime. The sport was never the same after he passed away; it was as if all the uniforms that Casey ever wore came unraveled upon his death. (*Photo by Robert Kaufman*)

Billy Martin, the best manager in baseball — and he knew it. (*National Baseball Hall of Fame Library, Cooperstown, N.Y.*)

Third baseman Sal Bando was the heart of an Oakland A's dynasty that won five straight AL western division titles (1971–75) and three straight World Series (1972–74). (*National Baseball Hall of Fame Library, Cooperstown, N.Y.*)

Charisma, arrogance, muscle, and cunning: Oakland's right fielder Reggie Jackson.

Cincinnati's Johnny Bench was among the all-time best-hitting catchers, but after marrying model Vickie Chesser on the first day of spring training, 1975, he fell into a long, frustrating slump at the plate. (*National Baseball Hall of Fame Library, Cooperstown, N.Y.*)

Pittsburgh's Willie Stargell was one of several veterans shifted to first base in 1975 to make room for a younger outfielder; in this case, the big, wide, and swift Dave Parker. (*National Baseball Hall of Fame Library, Cooperstown, N.Y.*)

In 1975, under the tutelage of hitting guru Charlie Lau, young Kansas City third baseman George Brett hit over .300 for the first time. He went on to do it ten more times, retiring after twenty-one years with a lifetime average of .305. (*National Baseball Hall of Fame Library, Cooperstown, N.Y.*)

Center fielder Bobby Bonds was sent to the Yankees as the "new Willie Mays," but his year in New York came to be the most disappointing season of his life. (*National Baseball Hall of Fame Library, Cooperstown, N.Y.*)

Dodger pitcher Mike Marshall became the first reliever ever to win a Cy Young Award. The muttonchops on his jowls hearkened back to the dark ages of organized baseball, but his right arm looked to be a modern miracle. (*National Baseball Hall of Fame Library, Cooperstown, N.Y.*)

To compensate for the slumping Bench and Perez, second baseman Joe Morgan swung increasingly for power. He went on to win the first of his two consecutive Most Valuable Player Awards. (*National Baseball Hall of Fame Library, Cooperstown, N.Y.*)

The pride and joy of Cincinnati, Pete Rose played recklessly and dove headfirst into everything. (© *Bettmann/CORBIS*)

Don Gullett, who, despite missing two months of the season with a fractured left thumb, finished with a 15–4 mark. (*National Baseball Hall of Fame Library, Cooperstown, N.Y.*)

Twenty-four-year-old rookie reliever Rawly Eastwick, who, along with twenty-three-year-old lefty Will McEnaney, anchored Captain Hook's bull pen. (*National Baseball Hall of Fame Library, Cooperstown, N.Y.*)

Boston catcher Carlton Fisk awaits the throw at the plate; whenever he wasn't injured—which was rare—Fisk took so long to do everything that his teammates dubbed him the "Human Rain Delay."

Oakland's pitching ace Vida Blue won twenty-two games in 1975, marking his third twenty-victory season in five years.

In 1974 San Diego's sinker baller Randy Jones was 8–22 with a 4.46 ERA, the losingest pitcher in the majors. In 1975 he was 20–12, leading the league with a 2.24 ERA. (*National Baseball Hall of Fame Library, Cooperstown, N.Y.*)

Billy Martin (l) with Joe DiMaggio (r). Fired by the Texas Rangers in late July, Martin was introduced as the new manager of the New York Yankees before the old-timers' game, August 2, 1975. (*National Baseball Hall of Fame Library, Cooperstown, N.Y.*)

Pitcher Andy Messersmith performed his best with Los Angeles. He wanted to stay a Dodger forever. Instead, he inadvertently ushered in the era of free agency. (*National Baseball Hall of Fame Library, Cooperstown, N.Y.*)

Traded to the Expos, Dave McNally didn't feel good on the mound and retired in midseason, having never signed his Montreal contract. By the time the significance of this came clear, it was too late for baseball's owners. (*National Baseball Hall of Fame Library, Cooperstown, N.Y.*)

Sparky Anderson (l) and Pittsburgh's Danny Murtaugh (r) converse at Riverfront Stadium before the start of the National League play-offs. Both were highly successful managers despite their very different styles. (© *Bettmann/CORBIS*)

Boston's Luis Tiant pitching against the Oakland Athletics in the opening game of the American League play-offs. Employing a variety of arm angles, twists, and pirouettes, Tiant could throw six different pitches for strikes. (*AP/Wide World Photos*)

Cincinnati's George Foster (l), Dave
Concepcion (c), and Ken Griffey (r) in
Pittsburgh for the third game of the National
League play-offs. The three players stole a
total of six bases off the Pirates in game two.
(© *Bettmann/CORBIS*)

Boston's Bill "Spaceman" Lee with
his father, also named Bill Lee,
shortly before the start of game two
of the World Series. Old Bill enjoyed
coaching his son and continued to
do so even after Spaceman reached
the majors. (*AP/Wide World Photos*)

Fred Lynn making one of
his spectacular patented
running catches. This one,
off Johnny Bench in the
second game of the
World Series, closed out
the top of the sixth.
(© *Bettmann/CORBIS*)

Carl Yastrzemski fixes a stare on
his red stockings after his team
drops game two of the World
Series by a score of 3–2. The
Red Sox had not lost a meaningful game since the pennant race
became serious in August.
(© *Bettmann/CORBIS*)

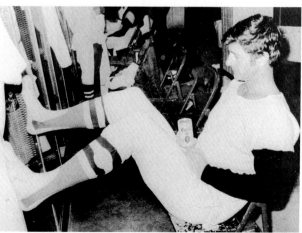

Interference? Carlton Fisk collides with Cincinnati's Ed Armbrister in the bottom of the tenth inning of game three of the World Series. Armbrister's successful sacrifice decided another one-run contest.

In the fifth inning of Boston's must-win game six, for seemingly the first time all year, Fred Lynn couldn't make a catch. Pursuing Ken Griffey's high drive, Lynn smashed into the wall, then slid to the ground. Two scored. Lynn's body went numb. He stayed in the game. (*AP/Wide World Photos*)

Carlton Fisk wills the ball fair, concluding what many call the greatest baseball game ever played: the sixth game of the 1975 World Series. (*AP/Wide World Photos*)

Johnny Bench congratulates Tony Perez after he smashes Spaceman's slop drop over the fence in the sixth inning of game seven, bringing Cincinnati within a run of Boston. (*AP/Wide World Photos*)

Sparky Anderson and Johnny Bench share a bottle of champagne
after game seven of the World Series. (© *Bettmann/CORBIS*)

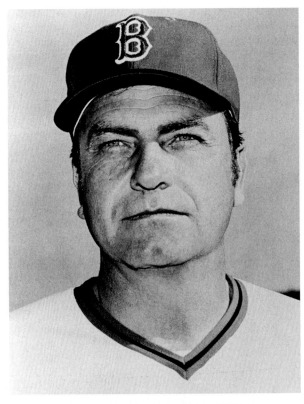

At the end of 1975, the *Sporting
News* named Boston's Darrell
Johnson the American League
Manager of the Year. An ordinary
strategist blessed with an extraordi-
nary team, DJ was out of a job by
the middle of the next season.
(*National Baseball Hall of Fame
Library, Cooperstown, N.Y.*)

They head back to the dugout.

Professionally, Luis is having one of his worst years. He won fifty-seven games for the Red Sox over the last three seasons, but now his back is killing him. He can hardly bend over. There is no way he can make the ball do the things he wants. His pitches sail in high, so that anyone can hit them. Tonight the weak-hitting Angels cue up to shell him. He loses, eight to two.

Up in the press box, local writers commiserate with the team publicist. It's an open secret: Luis Tiant's amazing comeback is finally over. He is washed up. Despite the support of the best hitting team in the American League, despite having Burleson, Lynn, and Evans behind him, Luis has won only two games since July 17. The press corps is aggrieved that Tiant's father didn't arrive in time to see his son when he was still dominant. "It's too bad," one of them says, with a sad shake of his head. "The old man arrived a year late. El Tiante used to be *so* good."

It's smoggy in Anaheim. Tiny annoying beetles buzz in the dry afternoon air of the stadium, drawn especially to Todd Larson, who's seated high up in the right-field grandstand. Todd attends the game this Sunday with his brother, Scott, and the McGwire family, who live in the cul-de-sac of a nearby town. Of the five McGwire brothers, Todd is closest in age, proximity, and interests to the big redhead called "Tree" — polite, with glasses, whose real name is Mark.

Todd spends the game either swiping at the beetles that hover around him or working to convince Tree to attend Damien High and play football for coach Dick Larson, his dad.

Tree is reluctant. He prefers baseball. He's a fastball pitcher, a good one. He's also a good hitter, very strong. He likes hitting home runs. Football's fun too, but he doesn't like the idea of practicing for four or five nights a week just to play one game a week. "It's a waste of time," Tree says.

Todd can sort of see his point.[2]

* * *

The story goes that Joe Stephenson, the scout who signed Bill Lee out of Rod Dedeaux's program at USC, was sitting at the kitchen table of the Brett household in El Segundo, June 1966, getting seventeen-year-old Ken Brett's signature on a Boston Red Sox contract, when Jack Brett said, "Okay, now here's the guy you should *really* sign," and pointed at his twelve-year-old, George. "Here's the hitter in the family," Jack assured the scout. "Keep an eye on him."[3]

After the victory against the Angels, George Brett brings his parents, Jack and Ethel, to meet his hitting instructor.

"So," Jack says stiffly, unclear on the protocol when addressing your son's guru, "you're Charlie Lau."

It's the first time George has heard his father say the name without an expletive.

Charlie Lau looks at them like a tired turtle.

The conversation that ensues is unremarkable in the extreme.

The night before, Jack and Ethel's other major-league son, Ken Brett, pitched for the Pirates, beating Montreal in extra innings. Ken's been struggling with a sore elbow. He's having an off year, though his team again seems capable of taking the NL East. With one son on a National League contender and another on an American League contender, Ethel Brett is surely in some kind of hell, imagining these boys of hers to be on a crash course. She hates to think about it, a championship series between Kansas City and Pittsburgh, her youngest battling her eldest while the whole world watches. This cruel fate appears likely, increasingly so, as the end of August finds both the Royals and Pirates battling for first in the different divisions of their different leagues.

Though his team almost always wins, Sparky continually fidgets with the batting order — testing, refining, expanding the depth of his bench. Foster might bat as low as eighth, or as high as fourth; sometimes he gets just a couple at bats and then is replaced in the field by Terry Crowley, Merv Rettenmund, or even Johnny Bench, or occasionally Foster moves over to right, or he doesn't start —

just pinch hits. Sparky's in the last month of the regular season, and still things are unsettled.

Tonight, against Randy Jones, Sparky starts Foster in center, batting third. Foster isn't used to being so near to the top of the batting order: it means that he begins the game on offense, which is an altogether different sort of mind-set. Awaiting his turn, Foster absently glances about. He sways to and fro with his thirty-five-ounce black bat, surveys those seated in regular intervals above. The stands are crammed with kids; he can sense their impish zeal even when grownups block them from his view. He can smell their peppermint breath.

There are children everywhere in Foster's world, asking him to write his name upon their belongings, yelling that he's wonderful. When, in looking up from the on-deck circle, Foster locates the face of a particular child, there is surely that sense of staring into something holy, like a radiant stained-glass window, like a pale moon chalked upon the late afternoon sky. Each beatific youngster must bring to mind biblical passages, strengthening Foster's resolve, igniting his concentration, so that he goes to the plate in rapture, with a prayer in his heart.

That evening Foster singles twice. Pete Rose just stares incredulously, goes oh for four, shakes his head. He used to doubt Foster's reliability, but he's begun to admire the guy. Still, Pete gets a little annoyed that the Riverfront fans, his hometown folks, who for years affectionately called his outfield post the "Rose Garden," now so readily call left field "Fosterville."

In every respect, Rose and Foster are complete opposites. They cut different figures at the plate. Pete stoops as if confronting Rocky Marciano, limply holding his pale, short bat, while Foster carries himself with dignity, raising high a dark, heavy bat. Rose loves television and junk food: the staples of his diet are Fritos, circus peanuts, cold hot dogs, cold hard-boiled eggs, cheesecake, pound cake, and Rice Krispies. He is a loud and vulgar carouser. Foster is what Casey Stengel calls "a milk shake drinker." He reads the Bible, performs calisthenics, and eats only healthy foods. He turns down caffeine, alcohol, and tobacco.

Foster doesn't get on base with the eye-catching frequency of Rose, but he's impossible for pitchers to take for granted. No right-handed Red has a higher batting average, and only Bench has more home runs on the team. Foster averages a hit a game — usually for extra bases — runs well, and often scores. When the Reds rally, as they seem to do several times each night, Foster is in the thick of it, drawing walks, pushing runners over, helping behind the scenes.

If Foster hits that well living a clean life, wonders Joe Morgan, *why doesn't he just lower his standards, settle for being above average, and mess around a little?*

If you live like Foster does, Bench says, *yeah,* of course *you'll hit home runs.* Stengel used to rib Bobby Richardson, the Baptist second baseman who sternly denounced the big league's propensity for unclean conversation, gambling, and promiscuity. "Look at him," Casey would say, indicating Richardson. "He don't drink, he don't smoke, and he still can't hit two-fifty!" But Foster's hitting a lot better than Richardson ever did.

Randy Jones steadily induces grounder after grounder, gives up one run, pitches the whole game, and beats the Reds. No other pitcher defeats them so regularly, but Sparky refuses to credit Jones; he feels his team is slacking off, which is an inherent danger of running away with the pennant. A week later, after becoming the first team in history to clinch the National League title this early in the season, the Reds go into a minitailspin and lose six of nine.

For the first month in many a season, the Athletics stumble, lose their motivation, and play below .500. The Royals alertly respond with an eight-game winning streak, the longest in team history. By the time they arrive in Oakland on September 8 for a three-game series, they are only five games back of the A's, the pennant race is heating up, and at long last Stanley "Hammer" Burrell corners Rickey and talks him into coming to a game at the Mausoleum and keeping him company in Finley's private box. Since Charlie now lives in Chicago, he has Stanley sit in his box and give him the play-by-play of the games over the phone.[4] "It gets lonely," Stanley admits, with a hangdog look.

Rickey sometimes feels intimidated by Stanley's vocabulary, and he doesn't usually like to watch sports as much as play them, but he agrees to come — after Stanley swears that Vida Blue is pitching. Rickey relates to Vida. They both prefer football to baseball. In high school, Blue threw thirty-five touchdown passes in one season, and he also struck out every batter he faced — twenty-one total — in a seven-inning game.

Stanley and Rickey get to the Mausoleum a couple hours early. Stanley dons a hat that identifies him as team vice president. Rickey looks at the field in the dying afternoon light. Vida Blue is nowhere to be seen, but Reggie Jackson is taking batting practice. Rickey also likes Reggie. *Reggie's a hot dog, just like me.* But whenever he talks to Reggie, he's always disappointed. Rickey doesn't care all that much about superstars, because he's pretty talented himself, and he usually doesn't want stuff like memorabilia, but on occasion he has asked Reggie for an autograph, and he always gets turned down. The last time this happened, he vowed, "You just wait, Mr. Jackson. One day you'll be asking for *my* autograph." Although this amused Reggie, he still wouldn't sign anything for Rickey.[5]

Stanley spends much of the game on the phone to Finley, describing the contest to the team's owner, but occasionally he has time to talk to Rickey, and he jumps into those moments with excited oratory. He tells Rickey how this Oakland team is easily the most underappreciated dynasty in baseball history, scarcely able each season to draw a million paying customers to their own ballpark, regularly playing before crowds of six thousand, rarely selling out at home.

Occasionally, as he dashes down to the dugout with a new instruction for Alvin Dark, Stanley will critique Finley's defensive moves to Rickey. On the whole, Stanley believes Finley has a good grasp of hitting and of baserunning tactics.

It's the pitchers who hate Finley most. Only Catfish Hunter ever succeeded in keeping Finley from affecting his pitching. Blue and Holtzman have been underpaid and too long manipulated, and neither one cares anymore. Finley has destroyed the game's joy for them. They pitch now because they are paid to, and are otherwise emotionless about their team's fantastic success.

Despite Stanley's promise, Vida Blue actually never takes the mound. It's a disappointment. Glenn Abbott starts instead. Paul Lindblad relieves him. Still, the game is tied, one to one in the eighth, when all of a sudden it takes a strange twist, it broadens horizontally, becomes a most suspenseful contest. The Royals put a runner on third with no outs. Everyone can see what's coming down; if the Royals seize the chance, if they push this run across, they will have an unbeatable momentum and they'll take the game, the series, the division, the league. It is just a run, and not even the ninth inning, but the people in the stands know with complete certainty that this is a pivot on which the season turns. If this man scores, Oakland's reign is over.

Charlie Finley commands Stanley to tell Alvin Dark to pull Lindblad and to bring out the fireman with the Bat Masterson mustache, Rollie Fingers. Rollie is not, by most accounts, a genius. Some charitably call him stupid. Finley doesn't care. Fingers is, in every respect, the best relief pitcher in the American League. It doesn't matter if he knows who he's facing. Put a baseball in his hand, point him at the plate, and watch him win.

"Get me three strikeouts," Finley orders Stanley, to order Dark, to order Fingers. "One ball on the ground and all is lost."

Stanley passes on the message.

Rollie nods his tin head, not hearing any instruction Dark gives him, and throws a perfect inning. He continues, throws five more shutout innings. The Royals never see another opportunity. In the fourteenth inning, the A's score on an error, a stolen base, and a broken-bat single. The Royals end up being swept in the series against Oakland and fall eight games out of first.

The AL West pennant race is over. Ethel Brett can breathe a sigh of relief. This year, at least, her sons won't face-off in the World Series.

Casey Stengel is admitted to Glendale Memorial. The hospital places him under observation and administers multiple tests. It's termed "a routine checkup."

That night, the vice president in charge of special marketing for a noted Dallas firm attends a cocktail party, saddening all who see him. His famous golden features are now ruddy and bloated, his sandy hair prematurely gray, his big heart broke. He is hobbled with arthritis. His children barely know him: he only occasionally visits their lives; they blame baseball for his dissolution, for taking their father away. His body is that of an old man although he is not yet fifty years of age.[6]

That night, once more, Mickey Mantle drinks too much. He can barely walk from years of injuries and alcohol. He passes out and dreams he's a Yankee again. He's wearing pinstripes as a checkered taxicab hurries him through the Bronx. They pull up to the stadium. The sky is some melodramatic color. He hears his name over the public-address system. He is needed at the plate. It turns overcast. A panic sets in. He is supposed to be batting, but he can't get inside. The clouds hang menacingly near, an unrelenting gloom. Blackbirds flap about in a frenzy. He is crawling through a hole. He can see Casey and Billy and Yogi, he can see his other teammates. He can't reach them. "Now batting," the announcer repeats peevishly, "number *seven*, Mickey Mantle." Casey throws him a disgusted look. Mickey tries to squeeze through the hole in Yankee Stadium. The birds are screaming pairs of scissors. Now he's completely stuck. . . .[7]

Mantle awakes, twisted in the damp bedsheets of his personal assistant. He is sweating like a pig. He reeks like a bottle. His wife, *well* . . . she probably misses him. He knows he should head home but he's too pooped to move. He drifts off again.

*   *   *

The character of the AL East pennant race has changed. Cleveland and Detroit are out of it. Milwaukee has crumbled. Under new manager Billy Martin, the badly wounded Yankees win fifteen games in August and sixteen games in September. But even that is not enough: the race becomes a 1974 rerun — Baltimore versus Boston. Orioles' manager Earl Weaver assures everyone that young Boston will characteristically collapse in the stretch and that his experienced team will overtake them. Once again, as with August and September of last year, the Orioles are suddenly superb. Most agree with Weaver that the Red Sox will choke.

Many things encourage such skepticism. Yastrzemski strains a ligament in his shoulder. Petrocelli suffers debilitating migraines and nausea. Both Carl and Rico endure terrible batting slumps in the second half of the season. Tiant's back is terrible, and he wins only one game between July 17 and September 11. Because of his split finger, Fisk spends nine days on the injured list. Bill Lee hurts his elbow and is sent to the bull pen. And Tony Conigliaro — Tony C., the most local of all the local boys to have worn the Red Sox uniform this season — calls a press conference to announce his final retirement from baseball.

On the night before he is due to start a crucial game against Jim Palmer and the Orioles, pitcher Rogelio Moret piles his Audi into a tractor-trailer that is stopped along the fog-bound highway, miraculously receiving only minor lacerations. (It's the second time this season that a Red Sox pitcher has nearly killed himself in a car, and it prompts player rep Bill Lee to ask the Red Sox front office whether, in the new player-owner agreement, there can be a provision for free driver's ed for players.)

A Baltimore disc jockey named Johnny Walker travels to Kenya and has a witch doctor cast an evil spell on the Red Sox.

Despite this, Boston continues to receive good hitting from Lynn, Rice, and Doyle, and strong pitching from Willoughby, Wise, and Dick Drago. The Red Sox hold fast against Orioles and witch doctors. Luis Tiant returns from a long period of rest. Suddenly, in the season's last few weeks, he is pitching as well as he has ever pitched. A suspicious *Boston Globe* headline asks: WHAT'S RIGHT WITH THE RED SOX?

They play Detroit on September 22. Their magic number is down to six (meaning that any combination of Boston wins and Baltimore losses totaling six will clinch them the American League East division championship). Pitcher Vernon Ruhle is on the mound for the Tigers. Ruhle has a reputation for running the ball in on hitters. In the second inning, he comes inside on Rice but Rice doesn't move. Ruhle's pitch hits him in the hand, breaking his fourth metacarpal. The Red Sox will in fact clinch the pennant, but once again, as in 1967, they will head to the postseason without their cleanup hitter.

As great as he is, with 977 RBIs and 319 home runs in eleven seasons, Dick Allen has never played in a World Series; neither, despite 2,430 hits in fourteen seasons, has sweet-swinging Billy Williams. But both have been members of classic choke teams: Allen, in 1964, when his Phillies, ahead by six with ten to play, lost to St. Louis; and Williams, in 1969, when his Cubs fumbled at the finish and lost first place to the Miracle Mets.

In 1972 the two reached personal bests, with Dick winning the American League's Most Valuable Player Award while Billy was named the *Sporting News'* Player of the Year. Both were in Chicago then, Billy with the fifth-place Cubs, and Dick with the second-place White Sox.

Now each is on a different team. Billy Williams is with Oakland, insuring that Joe Rudi and Reggie Jackson get pitches to hit, while Dick Allen performs much the same chore for Mike Schmidt and Greg Luzinski of the Phillies. Late in the 1975 season, neither is performing particularly well, but at long last both are on pennant contenders. Philadelphia is a few games behind Pittsburgh in the NL East while the A's are a few games ahead of the Royals in the AL West.

Sadly, this is how things remain. Predictably enough, the Pirates once again win the National League's eastern division pennant.

Of the two men, only Billy Williams receives a chance at post-season play.

Nineteen seventy-five is the most disappointing season in the life of Bonds, more disappointing even than 1970, when he set the major-league single-season strikeout record (189). This was to be *his* year. He was brought to town and dressed in pinstripes to mollify those New Yorkers agitating for a charismatic glittery superstar. He fails them and feels it keenly. He plays most of the year on one leg and does not become, as was predicted, baseball's first forty/forty man — forty home runs (more than any Yankee in a decade) and forty stolen bases (more than any Yankee in thirty years). He *does* become the first player ever to collect thirty/thirty over three separate seasons (with Bonds not yet thirty years old), but so what? That feels like a minor accomplishment. Now his doctors are hinting that surgery will be required on the knee, a terrifying prospect. Bobby would rather rest the leg and see if everything heals up. This is his intent when he buttonholes the manager before a game late in the season to inform Billy he can't play.

Billy takes the news without enthusiasm.[8] His expression is cold. *Goddammit, nobody tells me how to fill out a lineup card!* He wants to get rid of Bonds. In Billy's day, you played hurt every single day — you didn't run crying to Casey over some teeny bruise. . . . Not anymore, apparently. Martin makes a mental note to dump Bonds after the season is over. Bonds will make appetizing trade bait and Billy prefers not to harbor crybabies.

In Glendale Memorial Hospital, Casey Stengel tunes in Angels' radio, KMPC. The sixth-place Angels are ending their season in Oakland. It's Fan Appreciation Day. "Vida Blue now, completing his warm-up tosses," says the familiar voice of announcer Dick Enberg. "Blue looking for his twenty-second victory in this, his final tune-up before the American League play-offs get under way at Boston's Fenway Park. The future–Hall-of-Fame southpaw is matched against a journeyman right-hander, a new acquisition for the Angels, Gary Ross. After eight years in the majors, this will be Ross's sixteenth start, his only big-league appearance of the year."

Blue can't seem to get loose. His shoulder feels stiff. He reaches down for some heat and, in the process, surrenders a walk to Dave Chalk in the first. He slows up, concentrates on hitting the spots. Chalk is erased on a double play. He manages to go through the first three innings without giving up a hit, until the second time he faces Stanton, the Angels' cleanup hitter. Stanton bounces a ball forcefully at shortstop Campaneris. The high-strung, sure-handed Campy snags it, but then can't get it out of his glove. Stanton is aboard on the error. He takes off, steals second, and, with two outs in the fourth, California finally has a runner in scoring position.

Vida stays cool. He's working with a three-run cushion, thanks to Sal Bando's two-run single in the first and Reggie Jackson's solo shot in the third. His earned-run average is really in no danger. Whatever happens, he's only going five — the late-season A's policy.

An inning later, he still hasn't yielded a hit. Dark shakes his hand in thanks and dispatches him to the showers. Reggie gets agitated on Blue's behalf — *the guy's got a no-no going!* — until Bando assures Reggie that Alvin is doing the right thing.[9] Blue has to get his work in, that's all.

Blue shrugs. He cares little. Who's to say he'd get the no-hitter anyway? He doesn't even bother to see who's taking his spot on the mound. He saunters down the runway to the clubhouse and clicks on the TV, only to discover then that the Steelers' game can't be received inside the damned Mausoleum.[10]

Alvin Dark sends out right-handed reliever Glenn Abbott in the top of the sixth. "The fans," Enberg reports, with characteristic understatement, "lack appreciation." Everyone's hungry to see True Blue take his stab at immortality. Scorecards and programs are shredded and thrown; paper airplanes, cups, bottles, and crumbled napkins rain down; and Oakland Coliseum resounds with catcalls — just as, a year before, the Astrodome itself seemed to boo when the ill-fated Don Wilson was yanked for a pinch hitter after eight innings of exquisite no-hit ball.

This hostile reception flusters Oakland's new pitcher. Abbott hates going in. He's conscious of the no-hitter. He despairs of being the goat as the Angels' second baseman, Jerry Remy, steps in against him. Abbott hangs a curve. Remy punches a dribbler into the hole near short. It rolls slowly. Remy runs very fast. Bando cuts in front of Campy, grabs the ball, blindly releases it. His throw beats Remy to first by a split second.

"Well," says Enberg, "every no-hitter requires a defensive gem, and wouldn't you know it, Captain Sal has just provided it."

Abbott faces three, retires three, and Dark lifts him.

Rod Dedeaux enters Stengel's hospital room. They exchange casual nods. Shelved at the foot of the bed is Casey's medical chart. Dedeaux lifts it out, sits down. The tests indicate that Stengel has malignant sarcoma, a cancer of the lymph glands. The disease is centered in his abdomen.

"What's it tell ya?" asks Casey, though he already knows it all. He's wired to every sort of electronic gadget and run through with tubes. Against the bleached whiteness of sheets and starched uniforms and sterile bandages, Stengel looks more like an elephant than ever.

Dedeaux shrugs. "Says ten pennants in eleven years."

"But I ain't never won no all-star games, but nearly did that one Mr. Ted Williams broke his arm but wouldn't quit, oh that guy . . . *Wait!*" The KMPC commercial break is coming to an end. "Shhhh . . . Blue pitched a no-hitter for five."

"Yes."

"Dark pulled him."

Dedeaux agrees with Dark on this. "He had to."

"Yep, yep, yep," says Casey. "His guys gotta be ready for the play-offs, his pitchers. Everybody knows that, of course. Except the ballplayers. And the customers."

In the seventh, Dark sends in Lindblad, the veteran southpaw. Lindblad is slow. He hasn't been paying attention. He learns, from a glance at the scoreboard, that Oakland has three runs, and he figures that if California scores four, he'll get the loss. His intent is simple: pitch an inning, get the hell out. He doesn't realize there's a no-hitter on the line.[11]

Lindblad faces three, retires three, and Dark lifts him.

In the bottom of the inning, a young and distractingly pretty nurse passes through Stengel's quarters. She puts a straw into a cup of water and brings it near Casey obediently drinks.

The Athletics are up. The nurse fluffs pillows, straightens sheets. She is so lovely and smells so nice as she tucks a blanket about Stengel that Dedeaux nervously eyes the blood-pressure gauge on the wall.

Reggie bats in the seventh with Claudell Washington aboard. The left-handed Jackson faces a tall Mexican lefty, a rookie named Sid Monge. This is just the twenty-third inning of Sid's major-league career. He's given up eight runs in four appearances, and he's about to give up two more in one pitch. Reggie senses this, and waits patiently. When the pitch arrives, he wraps his famously grand swing around it and sends the baseball screaming across the hills toward Contra Costa County.

It's his second home run in four innings.

Dick Enberg stays calm. "And with that mammoth bash," the broadcaster observes, "in what is likely to be his final at bat of the regular season, Reggie ties the Boomer, George Scott, for the league lead with thirty-six round-trippers."

In the Oakland dugout, Dark is totaling up the year-end stats. He sees that Rollie Fingers needs one and two-thirds scoreless innings in order to lower his earned-run average below 3.00. That would be nice. Dark realizes he could use rookie Mike Norris for the first third of the eighth inning, and then bring in Rollie, thereby allowing him to face the minimum number of batters, but . . .

Ken Holtzman (the "Jew") crosses over, bets Rollie Fingers (the "Buzzard") five bucks that he'll ruin the no-hitter. That's how Rollie discovers he should start warming up to open the eighth.

Five dollars is a lot of money to a Finley employee, and both

Rollie's fastball and curveball are working. The Buzzard is feeling better than good right now — he could mow down the Hall of Fame, that's how good he feels — so he enthusiastically takes the Jew's bet, and after each successive out in the eighth inning, he smiles into the dugout.

Holtzman responds by clutching his throat in a choke sign.[12]

Over the next two innings, Fingers faces six, retires six, and earns five dollar bills.

Dave McNally grew up in Billings, Montana, and went back in July in order to run a Ford dealership with his brother. Because he walked away from the $85,000 he would've earned if he had remained in baseball, he was hailed by the newspapers as "a class act." He gave simple reasons for quitting: he couldn't do what he was being paid to do, couldn't pull his weight, couldn't do the job. He felt like he was "stealing money" from Montreal. "You know," observed the president of the Expos, John McHale, "if he weren't so honest, he could have signed the contract, even if he believed he'd be a lame duck for two years. That's what you have to admire about the man." For most of the 1975 season, the sudden retirement of Dave McNally was seen as an example of tremendous sacrifice and farsighted humility, the case of an athlete who set himself high standards and recognized his time to go.

As the season wore on, however, the story changed. The contract problems McNally had with McHale clearly nagged at him. With increasing openness, he admitted to a bitter disappointment with the Expos' front office. He recalled Montreal as "a bad situation from the very beginning." He never received what he'd been promised: a two-year, no-cut contract, a raise, a tax shelter, and moving expenses. He felt betrayed by McHale, so much so that when the Expos mailed him retirement papers, McNally stubbornly refused to sign. As a result, McNally, though carried on the disqualified list, remained under contract to Montreal.

McNally felt that nobody should be allowed to own the rights to where he could work. Frustrated, he got in touch with Marvin

Miller, the head of the players' union.[13] Together, McNally and Miller went over paragraph 10(a) in the Uniform Player's Contract: "If prior to March 1, the Player and the Club have not agreed upon the terms of such contract, then on or before 10 days after said March 1, the Club shall have the right by written notice to the Player to renew this contract for the period of one year." This was the renewal clause invoked by McHale, and consequently, unless and until McNally applied for voluntary retirement, he would be reserved by the Expos for the rest of his life. According to the owners, this clause said that a contract may be continually renewed, a year at a time.

Miller, however, had always disputed this. *One year*, he thought, *means one year only*. He contended that paragraph 10(a) was an option for a single year of service, after which the contract lapses. In order to validate this particular interpretation, however, Miller needed someone to play a year without a contract.

Several ballplayers nearly achieved this in 1974 — Bobby Tolan, Sparky Lyle, Ted Simmons. Each eventually came to an agreement with his club, inking a contract before any player grievance could be filed. But now, in addition to the retired McNally, Miller has another, an active player — Andy Messersmith of the Dodgers — who is ready to test the reserve clause.

Messersmith finishes the year with a 2.29 ERA, the lowest of his career. He leads the league in shutouts. He is third in strikeouts. His totals for complete games and innings pitched are the highest of any Dodger since Koufax in 1966. Although he's had three strong years in a row, he's proudest of this one. "This has been my best year from both a physical and performance standpoint," he declares. "The hardest part has been pitching with the unsigned contract hanging over my head."[14]

With the season over, Marvin Miller files grievances on behalf of McNally and Messersmith. Their hearings are slated for late November. The two pitchers approach the arbitrations with very different intentions. Essentially, Messersmith is bluffing. He has no desire to leave the Dodgers and hopes that the threat of an arbitrated grievance will at last scare them into granting him the no-trade clause he so desires. McNally, on the other hand, wants the reserve system taken down. He thinks it's unfair. A kid gets locked up by one team for life. An outstanding third-base prospect would never receive a chance to play if he was stuck behind a Brooks Robinson for his whole career. He could only hope to be traded, which might never happen; or worse, he could be traded and end up as McNally did, at the mercy of a liar like John McHale.

That night, Casey Stengel closes his eyes for the last time. He is pronounced dead on September 30 at 10:58 P.M.

His passing sounds the death knell for baseball's golden era, when a neighborhood was characterized by its team and a franchise defined by its traditions. After 1975 free agency will allow players to change clubs annually. Ancient grudge matches — what was meant, for example, when the Yankees beat the Dodgers or St. Louis swept Chicago — will lose all justification. The cheering ballpark, which in Stengel's day charged the home team with a nearly palpable energy, will no longer seem a factor in the play of a club. The fan is to be merely a spectator. Loyalties will become obsolete.

It's as if all the uniforms that Casey has ever worn come unraveled upon his death.

PART FIVE

THE POSTSEASON

OCTOBER 1

CASEY IS EMBALMED and his funeral calendared into major-league baseball's play-off schedule. He is to be put in the ground on the travel day between Fenway Park and the Oakland Coliseum. "Stengel might have enjoyed the humor in that," notes Bob Creamer of *Sports Illustrated*. "Funeral postponed because of game."

Gabe Paul, president of the Yankees, uses the time to perform calculations. Of the Yankee players managed by Casey, six became big-league managers, eleven became coaches, six became scouts, three became broadcasters, six became college baseball coaches, and two became baseball executives. Impressed, Paul concludes, "There's a great deal of Casey Stengel left in baseball."

OCTOBER 3

LAS VEGAS ODDSMAKER Jimmy the Greek gives Oakland six-to-five odds to win the play-offs. They'll win their fifth consecutive AL championship, he predicts, after losing one, probably to Tiant, who will start the first game for the Red Sox. He has become untouchable since returning from his back injury, throwing a near no-hitter September 11, and then shutting out the Orioles and Jim Palmer, winning the big games down the stretch before the eyes of his father.

Because the best-of-five series begins in Fenway Park, Alvin Dark would prefer to start a right-hander, a rock-solid veteran, his Tiant or Palmer. In truth, he wants to start Catfish Hunter, but of course they no longer own him. The Boston reporters ask team captain Sal Bando whether Finley's losing Catfish was the biggest blunder in the history of baseball. Sal thinks, and thinks some more. The silence is prolonged. By now, the newspapermen are laughing. "If it wasn't the biggest," Bando eventually replies, "I haven't heard of any bigger."

The two teams have played twelve games in the regular season and each has won six. But the A's possess the experience, the power, the speed, the deeper staff, and their bull pen is superior, with three of their relievers alone combining for 201 appearances, twenty-seven wins, and forty-three saves. Vida Blue won twenty-two games this season (his most since 1971). Billy North got on base a lot. Claudell Washington hit .308. Reggie homered thirty-six times. Roommates Bando and Gene Tenace slumped early in 1975, then changed bats in mid-August, Tenace going to a heavier bat with a thicker handle (à la Claudell Washington), Sal switching to a lighter bat with a thinner handle (à la Reggie Jackson), and both finished the season on hot streaks.

Dark has two starters with postseason experience, Blue and Holtzman. Holtzman is two and one in the play-offs and four and one in the World Series while Blue is one and two in the play-offs and oh and three in the World Series. Holtzman earns the first start, Blue the second; Dark reserves judgment on game three. When a reporter notifies Holtzman that he will start the play-offs, the famously icy pitcher denies having any reaction. "It doesn't matter to me when or where I pitch."[1] Like most of his teammates, Holtzman just wants the World Series bonus. Reporters are glad to discover that designated hitter Billy Williams, at least, hasn't been totally worn down by Finley. "I've waited fifteen fucking years for this," he shouts happily in the Coliseum clubhouse, after Oakland clinches its divisional pennant.[2] But he shouts happily alone.

Grateful reporters note that Tiant does not share Holtzman's indifference. Luis talks of pride in a life riddled with uncertainty. "No matter what," Luis reflects, "you no really known until you got an opportunity in October." They ask Tiant if he thinks he'll win. "Who knows?" he answers. "Strange things happen. A ball hits a pebble . . ."

The former manager of the Kansas City Royals, Jack McKeon, has been scouting the Red Sox for a month at the employ of Charlie Finley. He hands in his report, and Alvin Dark immediately flips to see what it says about the opposing starter. Dark quickly needs to track down a copycat pitcher to throw batting practice. "Luis Tiant," it reads. "He throws six pitches for strikes — fastball, curveball, slider, forkball, change of pace, and knuckleball — and nobody knows from which spot, overhand, sidearm, three-quarters."

That's all.

Dark nods. A bit terse, perhaps, but no denying the accuracy of its message. *There's no copycat available, because there's nobody anywhere who pitches like Tiant.* Dark managed Luis for a few years in Cleveland, a shady team that Tiant briefly made luminous. At the time, Dark was one of his pitcher's greatest detractors. He deplored Tiant's many mound motions, his fakes and twists and kicks. The southern Baptist couldn't entirely trust the kind, silly Cuban. Dark kept predicting an injury, "a strain somewhere," to which Tiant eventually retorted, "Motions no hurt my arm: getting no runs hurt my arm."

As for the Red Sox, they take batting practice against their own Holtzman copycats. Bill Lee throws a bit, just to show that he's getting his stuff back together and that his elbow is all better, and then Fred Lynn goes to the rubber, and he pitches a bit. Of all the players on Boston's roster, it is their rookie center fielder who best mimics Holtzman's ability to work the corners without ever using the middle part of the plate, Holtzman's talent for changing speeds imperceptibly on first a fastball and then a curve. Afterward, reporters ask Lynn if he's nervous about the upcoming games. Lynn smiles and shakes his head. The only time he was ever really nervous was his freshman year at USC, standing at the goal line, waiting for the opening kickoff with teammate Lynn Swann. And even then, once he touched the ball, he was all right.

Not many in the press believe that Boston actually has a chance against the three-time consecutive World Champion Oakland Athletics, but Petrocelli defends his team. The Red Sox had to beat back an almost miraculous Baltimore surge just to get here. "I think these kids have learned a lot in this race. It wasn't easy, but we were fine when it came to head-to-head confrontations. We proved that. All the time we had to hear people worrying that we would blow it. It hung over us, the pressure from our own fans and writers. After that, we should be prepared for anything."

"The only thing I'm worried about," Yastrzemski snaps, "is the wall and swinging the bat." Darrell Johnson is determined that Carl, despite his shoulder problems and his slump (he's hitting just .212 since the all-star break), will bat in the coveted number three position. DJ also names Carl as his starting left fielder. In his career of playing the wall, Carl has earned six Gold Gloves, but this season he has played left on only eight occasions. A day before the play-offs are to begin, Carl arrives early to workouts in order to take fungoes off the wall. He departs in the afternoon, goes to a dentist, has his root canal finished, and then returns to vote on postseason shares.

The team holds the balloting in the locker room. They're deciding who to reward with a share of their potential postseason proceeds. They award the grounds crew and clubhouse boys $500 apiece, give $1,000 to their batting practice pitchers and parking attendant. Some of the part-time players who saw limited action earn $500 or $1,000. The regulars automatically earn a full share, and they vote to give a full share to their trainer and traveling secretary, and vote full shares to Doyle and pitchers Willoughby and Jim Burton, three players who appeared midseason but contributed much.

Later, Rico runs into Tony Conigliaro, now a Providence sportscaster.[3] "Listen," Rico tells Tony C., "we voted on shares and . . ." Rico knits his brow in mock distress, comes straight to the point. "Well, you owe us twenty-five cents."

Joe Rudi's thumb throbs. Rudi, like Yastrzemski, was hampered by injuries after moving from left to first this year. Early in the season, with Tiant on the mound, Rudi somehow hurt the ligaments in his thumb. He missed six weeks because of it. Rudi reinjured it last week, swinging and missing at a cut fastball from Angels' pitcher Gary Ross. He has the thumb wrapped in adhesive and snapped into a leather gauntlet. He avoids batting practice.

This is Oakland's fifth straight year in the play-offs, Rudi thinks. *How much longer can it possibly continue?* There is a noticeable lack of any fan base in the Bay Area. A collective egotism functions in place of any team spirit. With Catfish having pulled a Houdini, his former teammates now scour their own contracts for an escape clause, for a loophole to exploit. On occasion, players telephone other teams and personally invite a trade. After beating Los Angeles in last year's World Series, for example, Reggie Jackson pitched himself to the Dodgers. Now, before the first AL play-off game at Fenway, Reggie stands in left field addressing the press corps. Musing over his value to another franchise, Reggie says, very deliberately, "If I go to New York, they'll name a candy bar after me."[4] It's far from the first time he has voiced the prediction, but it's the first time reporters have paid any attention or plumbed the depth of the quote. This genius for succinct observation is what sportswriters have come to expect from Reggie, and why they look forward to his annual involvement in baseball's October proceedings. He is a spotlight hog and a clutch player, but most important to the sportswriters, he provides his own copy.

Only a few of the reporters even recognize the false history behind Reggie's remark. The quote reveals his belief that the Baby Ruth candy bar was named for Babe Ruth, which it wasn't. "On the other hand," a wire reporter jokes to a lingering photographer, "Hanna-Barbera *did* name an animated bear after Yogi Berra, so maybe Reggie should've said that if he goes to New York, they'll name a cartoon character after him too. That'd be more correct, at least."

This is Reggie's last season playing for Oakland. Next he will go to Baltimore, and then to New York, where he will satisfy as the flashy superstar that Bobby Bonds was supposed to be. And he will, indeed, have a candy bar named after him.

During a game at Fenway earlier this season, Alvin Dark disagreed so heatedly with an umpire that he was ejected. On his way off the field, Dark dropped to his hands and knees and pulled up third base. He started to walk off the field with it, then turned instead and threw it into the stands.

Several of the looser types around the team — a few of the clubhouse boys, some of the jokers in the broadcasting crew — are now encouraging him to bring out the third-base bag during the player introductions, carrying it as if to return it.

Dark refuses, for the good of the team. He doesn't want to start the series with anything that might appear in the least disrespectful to the umpires.

OCTOBER 4

THE DAY IS BRIGHT AND WARM. At 1:00, Luis Tiant takes the mound. Oakland begins with Billy North: he flies out. Claudell Washington is next, and he strikes out; then Sal Bando strikes out, and the inning is over.

Juan Beniquez begins the Boston first. With Cooper at first, Beniquez is today's designated hitter. He's very nervous. Nothing in baseball equals the tension of a championship series. He stands deep in the box, feet close together, in a slightly closed-up stance. Holtzman delivers, and Beniquez takes a big stride, swings, flies out.

Suddenly, all of his tightness drains away.

Denny Doyle follows by grounding out. Holtzman is working fast. Two away, and Yastrzemski steps in.[5] His shoulder hurts. He can't hold the bat as high as he used to, so he's been working on a new stance, holding his hands low, then gradually raising them up as the pitcher gets ready to throw. It's proved to be a difficult adjustment. He's trying not to think about it too much. It's more constructive to be thinking about the pitcher just now, to go over his recent at bats against Holtzman. There was this spring, when the Red Sox played their two series against the Athletics — already a distant memory. There was May 13 in Oakland, when Holtzman came out of the bull pen with two out, the score tied, and the go-ahead run on third; he fanned Carl on three pitches, earning the victory. There was May 21 at Fenway, when Yastrzemski went to the plate with the bases loaded and hit a grand slam off Holtzman. This would be the most helpful thought at the moment, the one to cling to tightly. Carl allows a fastball through for a strike and bangs Holtzman's second pitch up the middle for the game's first hit.

Fisk steps in. He's taller than most catchers, and speedier. He sends a grounder bounding toward third. Bando backs up on it. The ball (as Tiant foresaw) hits a pebble. It skitters through, pursued by left fielder Claudell Washington. Carl, who is rarely a handsome sight to behold on the base paths, stumbles around second, lumbering toward third. He looks up. There's Zimmer, in the coaches' box. He's beaming. He's waving Carl in. It's beautiful. The Red Sox are supposed to be the turtles of the American League and the A's the hares, yet here is Zimmer, messing aggressively with the perception. His gamble changes the complexion of the game. Claudell Washington finds the ball, but his throw can't find the cut-off man: it goes over Campy and off Bando's mitt — two errors on the same ball. Carl scores. Pudge stops at second.

Lynn steps in. He grounds a ball to the left of rookie second baseman Phil Garner (who is nicknamed "Yosemite Sam" after the cartoon character because of his droopy red mustache and short stature). Garner moves after it. It takes a sudden hop and hits his bare hand, between the thumb and first finger. He kicks the ball into short right field, starts after it. He falls down. Zimmer sends Fisk. Lynn stays at first.

Three Oakland errors, two runs.

Billy North looks around. *Wow*, he thinks. *Heavy*. The tone is set. *The Red Sox are playing like the three-time world champions. We're playing like the Little Leaguers.*

* * *

Alvin Dark and his staff watch Tiant closely. They know how pitchers will type themselves. As soon as possible, they want to figure out what sort of game Luis is going to pitch. They're intent on uncovering Tiant's unconscious pattern, stripping away his embellishments, looking past his decorative head tosses and distracting twists and pirouettes, peeling him open to find his tendencies. After two innings, the Oakland coaches lean in together. Tiant has thrown fastballs — one-oh to North, oh-one to Washington, oh-one and oh-two to Bando, two-one and two-two to Reggie, oh-two to Tenace — and always for strikes. They decide that today's Tiant will throw hard, that he will pitch this game as a bringer of smoke and heat. They walk the bench and warn the players. They tell the A's to go up and attack Tiant as a fastball pitcher.

Suddenly, as if he has wiretapped the Oakland dugout, Tiant changes styles and begins throwing to spots with all kinds of stuff. Ahead by two runs, he sees no need to throw any two consecutive pitches at the same speed. Almost intentionally, he'll fall behind in the count, causing hitters to gear up for a fastball, and then he'll throw off-speed pitches for strikes. The batters never get settled, and they swing without timing.

Joe Rudi comes up to open the fifth. In his previous at bat, Rudi swung and missed at a sidearm slider, low and away, striking out. Now, as he spreads out in the batter's box, standing as always corner to corner, Rudi's thumb again begins to throb. He ignores it, takes two balls, fouls one off, then drills a single through the box for Oakland's first hit of the game. He holds at first as Billy Williams fouls out, holds there as Bert Campaneris flies out, and dies there as Yosemite Sam pops a foul that Fisk chases into the seats and gloves off a fan for the third out.

Dark is beside himself. Most pitchers have a spot during their windup when the white of the baseball first becomes visible, and once the hitter learns to focus on that spot, the ball appears to be coming half speed, which gives him enough time to adjust to the pitch and react with his bat. But today Luis is throwing from three, four, maybe five different spots. None of the Athletics know where the ball's coming from. In all the time he managed Tiant with the Indians, he never knew which way Tiant was going to throw the ball. And he still doesn't know. Dark tells himself that probably *Luis* doesn't even know.

In the top of the sixth, Tiant surrenders a leadoff double to Reggie Jackson.

"Tiant works quickly when nobody's on," A's broadcaster Monte Moore observes from the Oakland broadcasting booth. "Once somebody gets on base, it's like time slows down and you're tracking the game with a calendar rather than a watch."

Bill Lee rises in the bull pen. He starts to loosen up. As is his custom, he throws from well back of the mound until he's warm, then comes to the rubber.

Gene Tenace goes to the plate, having already homered off Tiant three times this year (twice in Fenway). Tenace draws a full count, then pops up weakly to right. Rudi slams the first pitch 380 feet to deep right center, where Evans, on the run, puts it away. Two down and Billy Williams is up. Jackson is now on third, shouting belligerently at the pitcher. Tiant ignores him, delivers a slow curve, high, ball one. Tiant glares down at the umpire and yells something. He throws a fastball, low and away. Ball two. Tiant goes into a grand corkscrew motion. Williams lines the pitch high toward the wall. Yastrzemski backs up. He counts, under his breath. Carl long ago paced off the number of steps from the warning track to the wall, even on a dead run, so he never has to take his eyes off Williams's drive. If he had to think about the wall behind him, the funny bounces, the exposed rivets, the two-by-fours, the tin, the holes in the scoreboard, it would play on his mind. He wouldn't be able to run up against it. Instead, counting, he goes back, back, back, and when he knows he can't run any further, he leaps and hauls in the ball, and the inning is over, and Tiant's shutout is saved.

In the bull pen, Bill Lee promptly zips on a jacket and sits down.

*   *   *

Ken Holtzman has given up only two singles, but Tiant's superb pitching, combined with Oakland's sloppy fielding, has Holtzman behind by two runs. In the bottom of the fifth, he throws one pitch. Beniquez pops out. He throws a second pitch. Doyle grounds out. He throws three pitches. Yastrzemski strikes out. Holtzman dominates until the bottom of the seventh, when Evans greets him by pulling a drive into left for a double. Cooper sacrifices him to third. The A's draw in their infield, but Burleson clobbers it through and past Bando; Evans scores. Dark removes Holtzman, brings in Jim Todd, then Paul Lindblad, then Dick Bosman. In sunshiny center field, North drops a fly ball. In blustery left field, Washington misplays a catch against the wall. Monte Moore watches in mortification from his broadcasting booth. "The Oakland A's won ninety-eight ball games this year," he gulps — and here his voice becomes a sheepish mutter of disgust — "none of them playing like *this.*"

By inning's end, the A's have set a new play-off record for errors, and the Red Sox lead, seven to nothing.

Bert Campaneris opens the eighth with a grounder to short that Burleson boots. Burleson is furious with himself. A double by pinch hitter Jim Holt moves Campy to third, and then Cooper's error on a North ground ball allows him to score. Runners on first and third, no outs. Tiant remains unruffled. He eliminates both Washington and Bando on swinging third strikes and then retires Jackson on an easy infield play.

As soon as Luis returns to the dugout, Burleson beelines for him. He blurts out an apology. Luis looks so calm that Burleson immediately feels better. "It's okay." Tiant smiles. "I know you were trying. We're going to win the game. That's all that matters to me. Don't let it bother you."

In the ninth, Tiant takes the mound amid a standing ovation. This is Fenway's most important game in eight years. The home team is winning. Delirious, the fans chant, "Loo-ee! Loo-ee!"

To the listeners back home, Monte Moore clarifies, "The sound you are hearing now is not booing."

Tiant walks the first batter, retires the second on a fly ball, induces the third to ground into a fielder's choice. Two outs, a man on first. Campy comes to bat while Tommy Harper appears on deck. A contact hitter with great speed, Harper is a Fenway favorite. Until this year, he played for the Red Sox, and his off-season trade to the Angels was one of Boston's least popular player exchanges. In mid-1975 the Angels sent him to Oakland. Now here he is, set to pinch-hit if Campy reaches.

Tiant's first pitch to Campaneris is called, strike one.

His second pitch is swung on and missed, strike two.

"Loo-ee! Loo-ee!"

Tiant looks over at the runner, then steps off the rubber. He glances idly at Oakland's on-deck circle. He spots Tommy, his best friend, preparing to bat next.

Tiant smiles.

Harper points at himself. *That's right*, he appears to say, *you've got to deal with me.*

On the mound, Luis giggles. He shakes a finger. *No, no*, he seems to be responding, *you won't get the chance.*

"Loo-ee! Loo-ee!"

Tiant goes into his stretch. It's an ornately twisted version. He motions with his arms, legs, shoulders, back, and head. At some point, he releases the pitch.

Campaneris swings, pops it up. Rico puts it away.

Tommy Harper takes his bats and goes inside.

Soon after, Alvin Dark faces a battery of writers in the main interview hall. He sees Tiant enter. Alvin smiles and ducks away from the microphones. He pats the pitcher on the head. "Luis," Dark gushes, giving him his due at long last, "you were just beautiful out there today."

Jerry Reuss throws better than anyone else on the staff of the Pittsburgh Pirates. He's an enormous blonde, six foot five, 215 pounds. Unlike most pitchers, who throw hard initially and learn control later, Reuss began as a finesse hurler. After the 1974 season, in which he won sixteen games, he put himself through a disciplined conditioning program. He showed up in the spring with a full beard, a good fastball, and a hard breaking ball. He had turned himself into a power pitcher, and raised his number of wins to eighteen in 1975.

The Pirates have made the postseason in five of the last six years. In 1970 and 1972 they lost in the play-offs to the Reds. In 1971 they advanced to the World Series and beat Baltimore. In 1974 Reuss started two games in the play-offs against the Dodgers, lost them both, and Los Angeles advanced.

This afternoon, the sky is free of clouds, a low sun visible between Riverfront's roof and uppermost seating arrangement. Bright daylight creeps across the field in uneven patches. The game opens with the mound and home plate in shadow, and a splash of unfiltered light between them.

Reuss's technique is to throw curves and sliders for strikes, and to make the hitters swing at fastballs out of the strike zone. With no score and one out in the top of the first, Reuss breaks off a magnificent curve. In the box, Joe Morgan has trouble picking up the ball. The count goes to oh and two. Reuss delivers four straight pitches on the corner. The umpire appreciates none of them. Morgan takes his base and Bench steps to the plate. Morgan steals second. Bench drives a pitch into left.

Pirate left fielder Richie Zisk sees the ball go from shadow to light, and then vanish.

Up in the Pirates' broadcasting booth, the voice of Nellie King falls. King is a tall man who once pitched for the Pirates. He's now been announcing games alongside the Gunner, Pittsburgh's fabled Bob Prince, for eight years. He's growing weary, as they all are, of dropping these play-off games to the NL West champions.[6] *Oh, for Roberto Clemente!* It's been sad to see the fans desert the team in recent years. And how doubly unfair this is, to start the crucial series in the visitor's park, with NBC forcing the game to begin amid 4:00 shadows. Bench is running to first. "Zisk can't make the play," King notes abstractedly. Then, "Yes! He does! A miraculous grab and what a play by Richie Zisk, that had double written all over it, and that's the toughest play, a line drive, Zisk was trying to pick it up, and how he found it, I don't know, and how he caught it, that's even a bigger question mark, but he sure did, a fine grab by Zisk in left field saving extra bases, and more important, the run."

Reuss induces Tony Perez to ground out on an oh-two pitch. The inning is over.

Giddy with momentum, Nellie King reminds his listeners that World Series tickets go on sale in Pittsburgh tomorrow afternoon. General admission seats are three dollars. Reserved seats are five dollars.

Despite a magnificent career, twenty-four-year-old Don Gullett (eighty and forty-one) has been cursed with postseason disasters (eleven appearances, two losses, zero victories). He determines that the postseason of 1975, a season in which he missed ten weeks with a broken thumb while still amassing a fifteen-and-four record, will be different. He retires the first five Pirates, before Big Dave Parker steps in.

Parker is more than a little conflicted to find himself in this situation. Parker was raised on Cincinnati's Poplar Street, a block from Crosley Field. Like the man on the mound, he grew up applauding the Reds. Parker worked at the ballpark as a teen, selling lemonade and hot dogs, in order to be near the game. He would wait in the players' parking lot, watching in awe as those first great black Reds, the outfielders, Frank Robinson and Vada Pinson, cruised up in white Thunderbirds with identical porthole windows and red interiors. Once Robinson gave Parker a fielder's glove from his trunk, thus cementing him as Parker's idol.

Now, the same season Frank Robinson first manages, Dave Parker finally plays every day. Cobra hits .308, drives in one hundred one runs, scores seventy-five runs, and bashes twenty-five home runs, but at season's end he's unhappy with the way he's swinging the bat. His timing is off. Gullett gets two easy strikes on him and then gives him a gift: he hits him in the ribs. With two outs, Pittsburgh has a base runner.

The sun has shifted once more. Pirate Richie Hebner enters a spotlight at home plate. Hebner is starting to get his stroke down, after a rough season of very little solid contact. Gullett works from the stretch. He delivers. Hebner swings. *Crack!* A base hit into the right-center gap. They wave Parker in. Griffey throws. It's close, but Cobra scores. Pittsburgh takes the lead, one to nothing. Weak-hitting shortstop Frankie Taveras follows with a two-strike single to left center that scores Hebner, two to nothing.

Reuss returns to the mound in the bottom of the second. He has the lead but no control. He doesn't get the calls. His positioning stutters. The strike zone seems to be shifting with the shadows. "What's wrong with these?" he calls down to the umpire. "I mean, too low, too high, outside, what?" A perplexed Reuss has two men on, no outs, and a two-two count at the plate when he hangs a curveball, and Concepcion lines it through the slatted lateral shadows into left.

Bob Prince assumes the microphone from Nellie King.

For the second time in two innings, Prince sees left fielder Zisk lose a line drive halfway through the infield and sort his way through sunshine. "Zisk going over," the Gunner says in his patented rasp. "Can he make the play?"

The broadcasting booth is receiving ever more complete accounts of today's game in Fenway, how the Athletics were defeated by the wind (which surprised Claudell Washington at the wall) and the earth (which surprised Sal Bando with strange bounces). Bob Prince can't help but suspect that now, in Riverfront, the Pirates are going to be defeated by other elements, by light, and by shadows. *It's such a crummy time of day to schedule a ball game. . . .*

"And he does! No way Zisk coulda seen the ball with that wicked sun, hit right at him, and it was by him, and he reached back somehow or 'ruther as he heard it come by or whatever, and he caught it. The Reds coulda been off and running with a ton of runs. Whatta catch!"

The shadows cut new angles. Now Reuss pitches with the sun in his eyes. Gullett steps in, swings weakly, grounds a ball past Hebner and the diving Taveras. A run scores; now it's two to one in favor of Pittsburgh. Rose grounds out, leaving the tying run on second.

Gullett retires the Pirates, one-two-three.

Morgan leads off in the bottom of the third. This is what he receives: ball, strike, strike, ball, ball, ball. It's Morgan's second walk of the game. He takes a big lead at first. Reuss sets, throws over. Morgan's back. Reuss sets, throws home. Morgan goes. The pitch is high. The catcher, Manny Sanguillen, loses the ball in the sun. He drops it. There is no throw; Morgan is safe at second. Again Reuss sets and throws home. Again, Morgan goes. The pitch is outside, ball two. Sanguillen throws, Morgan is safe. Two stolen bases on two balls to Bench. Proof yet again that Morgan makes things happen. He's at third with nobody out. Reuss is rattled. Ball three, ball four, and Bench is on first. There is activity in the Pirates' bull pen. Four walks, two in this inning. Perez up.

Time is called. The pitching coach comes out. Sanguillen and Stargell join him at the mound. They're slowing down the game so that a reliever has time to loosen up. Reuss, it is now clear, won't last. He's falling behind every batter. He's displaying no pattern to his pitches. The umpire breaks up their conference at the mound. The reliever isn't ready, so Reuss stays in for now. He delivers. Perez hits a one-oh fly ball to center for a base hit. A run scores. The game is tied. Nobody out, runners at first and second. Reuss gets two fly balls and two outs, but Bench is now on third.

Reuss rings up a two-two count on the next batter, Griffey, but his location remains awful, and the next pitch effectively ends the game. Griffey doubles it off the wall, and the Reds take the lead, four runs to two. Reuss gives way to Jack Brett's oldest son, Ken, who retires Geronimo to close the inning.

In the top of the fifth, the shadows shift once more. Now the right fielder stands drenched in sunshine. Taveras is on first. Gullett gets two quick outs, and then faces Al Oliver.

Prince remains on mike, indulging his way with nicknames and turns of phrase. "We need a bug on the rug," he tells radio listeners, meaning a skipping hit along the fast AstroTurf. "We got the Spider at first base," meaning Frankie Taveras. "If the Bucs get a bug on the rug, we got a run. The check. The pitch to Scoop," meaning Al Oliver. *Crack!* "And there's Scoop hitting a ball very deep into right center! Going w*aaay* back! W*aaay* back! And *iiit's* . . . caught! At the wall by Heronimo," meaning Geronimo. "You lucky rascal! Al Oliver hit that baby deep, took Heronimo right to the wall, a game of inches, the wind blowing to left, almost a two-run homer, instead inning over."

From then on, the momentum is against the Pirates. Their relief corps collapses. The Reds score again and again. It's six to two in the Cincinnati fifth, with one on and two outs, when Gullett steps to the plate for the fourth time. Larry Demery is pitching. On the oh-one pitch, Gullett swings a big rip, and connects. The ball sails deep to left field. Astounded, Gullett watches as he runs. He rounds first base. He's halfway to second when the ball clears the fence. It's his first home run in the major leagues. He raises a fist. He leaps into the air. The first-base coach sees this, worries that the ordinarily reserved Gullett has hurt himself, perhaps twisted his ankle. He is reassured once Gullett finishes circling the bases. Riverfront roars.

"D*aaaahhhh*n Gullett," rasps the Gunner bitterly. "It's the one Red you wouldn't think would go downtown on you." He sighs. "And they are enjoying this little fanny-kicking they're giving us."

The Pirates end up using four pitchers. Gullett allows Pittsburgh only one more run over the next four innings, completing the game for his first postseason victory. Cincinnati wins, eight to three.

Luis Tiant's frail father had been sitting behind the Boston dugout, moved greatly by his son's tremendous performance. Unnoticed but also in attendance at Fenway was the much-less-famous William Francis Lee, father of Bill Lee.

Just as Fred Lynn begot Fred Lynn, Carl Yastrzemski begot Carl Yastrzemski, and Luis Tiant begot Luis Tiant, so Bill Lee begot Bill Lee, showed his namesake how to fly kites and identify constellations and tie knots, but first and foremost he taught Young Bill to play ball. He had him out for his first throws. He coached him in Little League, and then Pony League. It wasn't until high school that Young Bill became a winning pitcher. After games, Old Bill would talk things over with Young Bill and tell him what he did and didn't do. Old Bill still does this to some degree. He was after Young Bill to settle down between pitches and to stop walking around the mound, stop pounding the ball in his glove. "That just gives the hitter confidence," he told Young Bill. "You should look the batter in the eye and throw the ball. Take command." Young Bill did, and now Old Bill is after him to knock more batters down and to run his screwball in on more of the left-handed hitters.

Old Bill's a dignified, gray-haired gentleman. He regards himself to be a lot like most people in the United States. He's worked for thirty-six years as a methods manager for a San Francisco telephone company. He steadily follows a course. He believes that this helps to hold the country together. Old Bill's a handsome and proud Republican, a Barry Goldwater supporter. He has flown out for the weekend to see his son pitch in the postseason. He has to be back in the office on Monday.

In Young Bill's small, conservative hometown, people are always approaching his father to ask, "How come . . . ? What happened . . . ?" They're puzzled by the way their quiet, sweet kid has turned out. They're curious what on earth could possibly have changed Young Bill into such an outspoken, controversial Spaceman.

Though proud of his well-read son, Old Bill gets their point. "Maybe if I were there more," he tells them, "maybe he'd listen to me more. But then, it would probably be just like any father-son relationship. He'd get sick of me and never listen to what I have to say."

OCTOBER 5

COLLECTIVELY, BANDO AND JACKSON go one for eight in the first game of the ALCS play-offs. It's embarrassing, emasculating. Bando is the club leader, and Reggie is its clutch power. The two men remind one another how they came back to win last year's pennant after dropping the first game to the Orioles. Aw hell, they've won four straight AL pennants and only once did they ever win the first game. . . .

In game two, the two are intent upon restoring their masculinity.

Reggie Cleveland, the sinker/slider pitcher, is making the start for Boston. Cleveland was red-hot in September: he won four, lost none, and pitched five scoreless innings of midgame relief in a crucial Baltimore series.

Bando comes to the plate in the first with two outs. Nobody's on. He hits Cleveland's two-strike pitch off the wall in left. Yastrzemski sweeps in gracefully. "I can play the wall in my sleep," he assures all. He casually snares the ball, gets it in fast. Bando is *just* safe at second.

*   *   *

Simultaneously, game two of the National League Championship Series gets under way. The sun is dim behind an overcast sky in Cincinnati, so the stadium is less troubled today by patches of contrasting sunlight.

Again, the two teams start left-handers: Cincinnati's Fred Norman against Pittsburgh's Jim Rooker. The Pirates disregard the published reports that these Reds are the most talented team since the 1955 Dodgers. They ignore rumors that Joe Morgan will soon win the NL MVP, the fourth time in six years that a Cincinnati player will capture the award. Instead, they remember that the Reds themselves came back to win the 1972 play-offs after dropping the first game to the Pirates. They remember too that the Mets came back to win the 1973 play-offs after dropping the first game to the Reds.

They also remember facing Fred Norman this season and chasing him in the first. He's a slap pitcher, that's all. Hitting him is completely different than hitting Gullett. You have to supply your own power, you have to wait, you have to take him to left field (if you're a left-handed batter) or right field (if you're right-handed), you have to wear him out.

True to shaky form, Norman surrenders consecutive two-out walks in the first. On second is Al Oliver. On first is Stargell. At the plate is Zisk, who has hit more home runs against Cincinnati this year than any other Pirate. Zisk goes deep on the first pitch, pummeling a high fly into left field. Foster follows it back. He catches it at the wall. Three outs.

At Fenway, Reggie Jackson comes to the plate with Bando at second and crushes a letter-high slider from Cleveland. Jackson stands there in the batter's box, intoxicated with self-admiration, watching the ball soar over the bull pen and into the right-field bleachers, a distance of at least four hundred and thirty feet.

Oakland two, Boston zero.

*   *   *

Rose opens the Cincinnati half of the first with a weak single off Jim Rooker. Morgan fouls out. Bench strikes out looking. Rooker throws over to first, Rose gets back just in time. Rooker throws a high fastball to Tony Perez for ball one. He throws a fastball on the corner for strike one. Perez hits the next pitch solidly into the second deck, and the Reds lead, two to nothing. Foster follows with a line drive to left. On the second pitch to Concepcion, Foster steals second. Concepcion singles up the middle, moving Foster to third. On the third pitch to Griffey, Concepcion steals second. Sanguillen is saved further embarrassment when Griffey grounds out to end the inning.

In the second, Norman easily retires the Pirates. Rooker easily retires the Reds.

In the third, Stennett gets aboard on an infield single. Sanguillen, swinging at a pitch around his eyes, hits into a double play. Al Oliver grounds out.

The Reds also go down in order.

In Boston it's the top of the third, and Sal Bando has his second chance. Again, two away, but fleet-footed Campaneris is on first. Bando hits a rising liner into left. It would be a home run in any other park, but in Fenway it's off the wall. Campy hustles to take third. Reflexively positioned, Carl gloves the ball on the carom and fires to third as he turns, in a single fluid motion, without even looking. Rico catches Carl's perfect throw — two inches off the bag, an inch off the ground — and Campy slides into it a millisecond later. Defying all odds, he's out. Yastrzemski silently trots back to position.

Still, Oakland two, Boston zero.

Stargell leads off the third with a double.

"Now let's start some tattooed thunder and lightning," crackles the Gunner over Pittsburgh's airwaves.

Stargell takes third on a wild pitch.

Jack Billingham warms up in the Cincinnati bull pen.

*   *   *

Reggie Jackson opens the fourth in Boston with a single. The next batter grounds smoothly to Petrocelli. Jackson, a former football star, comes into second as if he's Mean Joe Greene. He rolls Denny Doyle, but too late, because the double play succeeds.

Jackson slowly peels himself off the infield. He brushes at his uniform. "Sorry," he tells Doyle. "You okay?"

Doyle is tough as nails. There's a shooting pain down his right side, a dull ache in his ankle, but he's exceptionally proud. He looks testily at Jackson. "Who got up first?" Doyle challenges him.

Jackson nods and jogs back to the dugout. He's never really given that guy much regard, but now he's impressed by something in the second baseman's eyes, that light Reggie no longer sees in the eyes of his own teammates.

Doyle bats in the bottom of the inning, the Red Sox trailing three to nothing, thanks to some hitting by Rudi and Claudell. He still shows no effects from the flattening he took as he takes an outside pitch from Vida Blue. Ball one.

Sometimes Blue has trouble getting loose, but today he is cruising along with a shutout, showing good control, good velocity on his fastball. He's got a grimy spot on the left leg of his white uniform pants. It's a superstitious habit he has. Before every start, Blue bends over for a handful of dirt on the mound, then rubs it on his leg. Many managers have asked umpires to investigate the spot, assuming that it disguises a gel with which he doctors his pitches. The umpires all say the same thing: it's just ordinary dirt.

Blue throws a breaking pitch that backs Doyle out of the batter's box, then slices across the plate for a called strike. The count goes to one and one. He throws Doyle another curve. This one gets popped up behind Yosemite Sam at second.

It falls for a base hit, and everything unravels from there.

At Riverfront, Norman walks Zisk on four straight pitches.

Parker strikes out. Hebner smacks a ball up the middle. Zisk is an obvious out at second, but his slide takes out Concepcion, whose relay throw to first goes into the dugout. Stargell scores, making it two to one in favor of Cincinnati. Taveras grounds out with the tying run at second.

Foster, with three hits, a stolen base, and two runs in the series, leads off the Cincinnati fourth with a bloop single to shallow center. Concepcion follows with a bloop of his own to shallow right. Griffey dribbles a single through the left side, scoring Foster, making it three to one, Cincinnati.

"Three straight hits that just make you *sick* to look at 'em," Bob Prince mutters.

On the one-one pitch to Geronimo, Griffey and Concepcion advance on a double steal. Geronimo strikes out, Norman flies out, Griffey scores, Rose flies out. After four innings, the Reds lead, four to one.

With one out in the fifth, Rennie Stennett hits a weak single. Sanguillen pops up a two-and-oh pitch to center. Al Oliver walks. With two men on, the tying run comes to the plate. Stargell watches a ball, a strike, another ball. He swings and misses, he fouls off a curve. Norman strikes him out on the next pitch, inning over.

With Doyle at first and no outs in the fourth, Carl Yastrzemski comes to the plate. The announcement of his name over the public-address system shakes loose a thunderous ovation. Carl receives it stonily, dawdling outside the batter's box. The sun is low, as it was after a harvest in his youth. *I wonder what potatoes are fetching this year.* When he was little, just a kid playing stickball on the farm with stones or hitting peewee potatoes fungo-style, the break-even point was $1.75 a hundred weight. His family made a killing with their potatoes during the Korean War, then the market crashed. . . . Through it all, there was the guiding deliciousness of the *czarnina* of his grandmother. *Makes my mouth water.* It is strange how sometimes Carl can flash on her cooking, a quick taste, a memory so vivid and divine, the picture of her tiny fingers stained darkly with juice as she pushes the stone from the purple flesh of the plums that make her famous dumplings. . . .[7]

Carl steps into the box and hits the first pitch over the wall. It's his first opposite-field home run of the season. The score is three to two, with Oakland in the lead.

Vida Blue kicks around behind the mound, clearing his mind.

Fisk steps in and doubles. Lynn steps in and singles. Rico steps in.

Blue lifts the rosin bag, slams it down in agitation.

Finley sends out Alvin Dark. Blue does not want to leave, but Finley/Dark yanks him anyway. Needing a double-play ball to kill this big inning, Oakland goes to sinker baller Jim Todd. Rico obligingly hits into a double play, but meanwhile Fisk trots down the line and ties the ball game.

Oakland three, Boston three.

Pittsburgh's twiggy and bespectacled sidearmer, Kent Tekulve, relieves Jim Rooker in the Cincinnati fifth. Tekulve has one victory and two losses on the year. Against Cincinnati, he has a 6.21 ERA. Now, with a runner on second, he strikes out Bench. With runners on first and third, he strikes out Foster on a breaking ball, and then gets Concepcion to ground out. Tekulve is out of the inning: two hits, two left, no runs.

In the sixth, a Pirate again singles with no outs, but Norman again gets what he needs, a double play, followed by a groundout, and then Pittsburgh takes the field.

In Boston, after Cecil Cooper starts the bottom of the fifth with a double off Jim Todd, Rollie Fingers pops from the A's dugout and strides out to begin warming in their bull pen. Fingers pitched in seventy-five games this year and had ten victories, six defeats, and twenty-four saves. The Buzzard figures largely in the late-season nightmares of New England. A baseball scavenger, he beat the Red Sox three times this year (two times in two days in late August), and earned a save another time. In seventeen and two-thirds' innings against them, Fingers gave up two runs while striking out twenty Red Sox.

With Burleson up and Cooper at second, Finley/Dark pulls Todd and inserts Fingers.

"I've had the pleasure of broadcasting every one of Oakland's games this season," says Monte Moore, "and, for the life of me, I can't remember Fingers ever coming out as early as the fifth inning."

Fingers retires the side, the game rolls into the sixth inning, the momentum belongs to the A's. Sal Bando bats again. He has already doubled and singled off Cleveland today. This time he rips another one deep to left. Again, a home run in any other park. Again, Carl plays it masterfully off the wall to hold Bando to a single. Reggie steps in, and Doyle, anticipating a double play, flips off his sunglasses and hands them to the umpire.

Darrell Johnson has other plans. He pulls Cleveland. He brings in Rogelio Moret, who throws a lot like Vida Blue. Jackson flies out, Tenace fouls out, Joe Rudi doubles, Bando holds at third. Claudell Washington steps in. Tie score, two on, two out, one ball, one strike, and Washington bounces it up the middle. Burleson is a blur: he moves, he grabs, he pivots, he throws, that's three.

And now a very determined Carl Yastrzemski comes to bat, it's the bottom of the sixth, and momentum has switched sides. With one out, Carl doubles off the wall, Fisk scores him with a base hit to left, and Boston takes the lead, four to three.

In Cincinnati, Tekulve still throws for Pittsburgh in the bottom of the sixth. Griffey rips a three-two change-up into right for a base hit. There are no outs.

Tekulve throws over to first, Griffey's back safely. He delivers, ball one. He delivers again, Griffey goes. The pitch is high, ball two. Sanguillen throws, not in time, and Griffey is at second with Cincinnati's eighth stolen base in the series. Geronimo walks. A pinch hitter bats for Fred Norman, the bunting specialist Ed Armbrister. Tekulve delivers a called strike to Armbrister. Sanguillen sees Griffey stray off second base. As the catcher rises and throws across to the bag, Griffey fakes, as if to dive back, then suddenly breaks for third. The infield is caught sleeping. Griffey has it stolen easily.

"I can't believe this," says Bob Prince. "Holy Toledo."

With one strike, still no outs, and Griffey now at third, Sparky no longer needs the sacrifice, so he calls back Armbrister and announces a new batter, Terry Crowley. Pittsburgh's manager, Danny Murtaugh, a patient man with a hawk nose, hazel eyes, and a face craggy as a landslide, responds predictably. He pulls his pitcher in favor of a left-hander, Ken Brett, to face the left-handed Crowley. Long minutes pass. The players warm up and position themselves. Sparky then immediately replaces Crowley at the plate with the right-handed Merv Rettenmund, thus reseizing the advantage.

After all the changes and the many delays, Ken Brett finally goes into his stretch, sets at the belt, looks at Griffey on third, delivers home, and is called for a balk. Another run scores, making it five to one in favor of Cincinnati, and Geronimo is on second.

Prince sighs. "They're making us look like Little Leaguers."

Rettenmund flies deep to right. Geronimo tags and goes to third. Rose flies to shallow right. Geronimo tags and goes home. Parker throws and Geronimo is out, ending the inning on a double play.

Sparky brings in reliever Rawly Eastwick to start the sixth. The Pirates go down in order.

Murtaugh brings in reliever Bruce Kison, who won two big ball games down the stretch against Philadelphia. Kison walks Joe Morgan, who takes second for Cincinnati's seventh steal of the day.

"This is an embarrassing afternoon of baseball," the ever-partisan Prince observes.

Rogelio Moret has only a one-run cushion when he opens the seventh by walking pinch hitter Tommy Harper. Harper, one of the speediest base runners in history, is not the kind of guy you want on first with no outs. He stole more bases (seventy-three) in one year (1969) than any American Leaguer since Ty Cobb. As a result of playing three years for Boston, Harper knows the Fenway infield intimately. He grabbed more bases in 1973 and 1974 (eighty-two total) than the entire Red Sox roster stole in 1975 (sixty-six total).

Darrell Johnson pulls Moret. Dick Drago comes on.

Dark pulls his batter. Billy Williams pinch-hits.

Harper takes a healthy lead off first. Drago looks in at Fisk, throws over to first three times. Harper is always back in time. Drago turns to the plate. Low, ball one. Foul, strike one. Drago looks over, throws over. Harper dives. *Safe.* Williams waits patiently at the plate. Drago studies Harper some more, then delivers a slider, high and inside, to Williams. *That's my pitch!* gloats Williams, but his timing is off and he merely fouls back for strike two. Williams steps out and takes a short stroll, muttering to himself. He fouls off another, then takes one outside for ball two. Drago throws to first. Harper dives back. *Safe.* Throws again, Harper back in. *Safe.* Drago delivers a high fastball, Williams swings and misses — he's out.

One away, and Billy North the batter.

Drago checks on Harper. Throws to first, Harper dives back. *Safe.*

And now Dark decides Drago has had enough of these quick tosses to Cooper.

Oakland puts on the hit-and-run. Harper takes off with the pitch. The infield shifts around to cover second, thereby leaving open unguarded holes through which North can slap a hit. All this movement reduces the chance of an inning-ending double play while allowing a simple grounder to advance a runner two bases, or to score him. The batter, however, can't be fussy; he must hit whatever is thrown. Drago's pitch is far from ideal. North gets under it. He lines out to Lynn. Harper, all the way around second, is doubled up easily, and the inning is over.

Rico steps in against Fingers in the bottom of the eighth. He has fanned and bounced into a double play today. His count goes to three balls, two strikes. He hits the pay-off pitch high into left field.

Rudi runs back as far as he can. At the scoreboard, he looks up. He sees the ball clear the top of the wall and ricochet off the light tower. Home run. Boston five, Oakland three. Rudi keeps staring up, watching crows fly, and clouds like dirty cotton. He takes some time before returning to his position. The smell of hot dogs wafts down from the stands. The sun slowly settles in the west. The day bears a grumpy quality.

In Cincinnati, Bench flies out. Perez grounds through to left field. Morgan scores. Foster grounds into an inning-ending double play, but Cincinnati leads by a score of six to one, which is exactly how it stays. Eastwick picks up the save, Norman the victory. Big Red Machine indeed.

Charlie Finley sits, grimacing, in a box near the third-base dugout. His lemon-yellow jacket is very loud. He is not. Boston leads, six to three, in the top of the ninth. Inconceivably, the underdog Red Sox are about to go two games up on his world champions.

Behind Finley, in Section 29, the hometown fans stand. They begin to sing. "Good-bye, Charlie," they sing. The rest of Fenway Park joins in. "Good-bye, Charlie. Good-bye, Charlie. We hate to see you go."

At the conclusion of the merry taunt, Finley stands. He surveys the crowd in his Ray Charles sunglasses, and then he waves, and he smiles.

The crowd replies warmly. Finley seems a good sport. He can take a joke.

It is never in the nature of Danny Murtaugh to worry. Three times, over three decades, he has quit as manager of the Pittsburgh Pirates, and four times he has been brought back. His moves are familiar. He does not surprise the opposition. His trademark is patience. Over a much stronger foe in 1960, and again in 1971, Murtaugh guided his guys to a world championship. Like Darrell Johnson, Red Schoendist, or Walter Alston, Murtaugh largely leaves his ballplayers alone to play. His style is muted, in conscious opposition to the overstrategizing, the anxious interference, the risky plays of a Sparky Anderson, a Gene Mauch, or a Billy Martin. Murtaugh also happens to have been the first manager to field an all-black team.

Sunday night, after two straight losses, the Pirates fly home. Calmly, Murtaugh reminds his players of how they rallied to win the World Series in 1971, after dropping the first two games to Earl Weaver's tough Orioles. Besides, if left-handed pitching is indeed an advantage in a short series, then the Pirates, despite being on the brink of elimination, still have the edge. Their three best starters are southpaws while Cincinnati has just two. In game three, Sparky must, however reluctantly, start a right-hander, the veteran Gary Nolan. Murtaugh can respond confidently with a twenty-one-year-old who was pitching triple A in June, a dark-eyed sliver of a man named John Candelaria.

OCTOBER 6

RICK WISE HAS WORKED in twenty-four cities, appearing as a pitcher from Montreal to Houston to San Diego, from Milwaukee to Baltimore to Boston, but his parents, who live in Portland, Oregon, have never yet seen him win a major-league game. They fly south to Oakland to watch their son start game three of the American League Championship Series.

It's Alvin Dark's decision (but it isn't really: it's Charlie Finley's, no matter). The word is given that Ken Holtzman will start game three on two days' rest. Holtzman, as usual, has no response. "Okay," he says; he can pitch without much of a break, whereas Vida Blue takes longer to recover. But Holtzman knows that the two times this season he started on two days' rest, he lost.

Reporters locate Tom Yawkey in Oakland's Mausoleum. He observes his team working out in advance of the third game. He waves off their questions. "I'll let my players do the talking," he tells them. "I'm just here to watch."

*   *   *

Thousands of admirers, friends, neighbors, and local youths file through a mortuary on the outskirts of Los Angeles to view the corpse of Casey Stengel — gargoyle face, bowlegs and all.

The funeral's weather is soggy and miserable. And yet, as soon as the mourners enter the Church of the Recessional in Forest Lawn Memorial Park, there is audible snickering, there are scarcely smothered guffaws. Choice linguistic exploits of Stengelese are recounted in whispers, mumbles celebrate the joyous sprawl of his comedic antics, the sparrow that flew out in 1919 when Stengel doffed his cap to the crowd, or the one-knee conclusory slide of his inside-the-park home run in the 1923 World Series, which Casey always felt compelled to demonstrate, no matter how formal the surroundings.

The audience honors the great man with the irreverent laughter he so loved, nudging one another knowingly, until Bowie Kuhn steps up to the podium. Kuhn frowns. The giggles subside. "Casey Stengel helped us not to take ourselves too seriously," the rump-faced man reads aloud. "And when you think of all the things he could have been, and been outstanding at, to have him one hundred percent in baseball was a wonderful thing for us. He made more fans for baseball than any other man who ever lived." Kuhn reads on, honoring Stengel as an American folk hero whose legacy will survive "as long as little boys play the game of baseball and as long as this cynical age has some room in its heart for laughter."

Rod Dedeaux speaks next. "Well," Dedeaux starts, "God is certainly getting an earful tonight."

The audience roars appreciatively. It's a quote from last week's *LA Times*, in which columnist Jim Murray characterized Stengel as a rubber-faced figure from a Grimms' fairy tale, and imagined the cacophony his arrival set off at the pearly gates: "There's an applicant out here of indeterminate national origin, speaking a language we do not know, nonstop, wearing a wrinkled uniform with the logos of ten teams on it, bright blue eyes which he winks incessantly, cereal-bowl haircut, and a straw suitcase, carrying a bottle and a bat and he says he knows Heinie Groh personally and he has a lineup card in his hand. . . ."

Dedeaux looks out and realizes how many of Stengel's so-called enemies — Howard Cosell, Phil Rizzuto, Jerry Coleman, and Joe DiMaggio — sit before him now with tears in their eyes. He chokes up, regains control, and goes on.

"The Ol' Perfessor is an apt name," Dedeaux says. "Casey saw himself as a teacher. That's what he loved doing most. That was the secret of his greatness. He wanted to develop men of character and ambition and he did.

"To know Casey," he says simply, "was to know you could never forget him."

Dr. Kenneth Carlson, a Methodist minister, concludes the service with a prayer. Twenty-seven pallbearers, among them Billy Martin, Tommy Lasorda, and Maury Wills, escort the casket outside.

Mickey Mantle is tracked down at a Dallas golf course and pressed for his thoughts on Stengel's passing.

Mickey thinks of the old man grabbing him by the scruff of the neck, shaking him hard, and saying, "Don't let me see you do that again, you little bastard!" He recalls failing to run out a ground ball, and Casey's jeer: "All it means is a player running ninety feet and if he can't hustle for ninety feet at the salaries they're paid these days something's got to be wrong." Mickey knows he threw bats after striking out, and kicked watercoolers, and this drove the old man crazy. Rebellion taints all his reminiscences of Casey Stengel. Despite the years of helpful tips and teachings, Mickey can't recall a bit of the old man's wisdoms, for he stubbornly refused to listen.

Mantle reshoulders his golf bag, gives a distant look. "He was like a father to me," he tells the press. He grins shyly and returns to his game.

OCTOBER 7

JOHN CANDELARIA is the son of Puerto Rican parents, a tall, stick figure whom Pittsburgh calls their "Candy Man." They hand him the ball Tuesday night, this rookie left-handed pitcher, and here is what happens: Pete Rose, Joe Morgan, Johnny Bench, and Tony Perez strike out. George Foster flies out. Davey Concepcion hits a hanging curve for a home run. Ken Griffey, Cesar Geronimo, and Gary Nolan strike out. Rose and Morgan fly out. Bench strikes out. Perez and Foster fly out. Concepcion strikes out. Griffey grounds out. Geronimo and Nolan strike out. Rose flies out.

And this is what happens when Nolan pitches Tuesday night: Rennie Stennett flies out. Richie Hebner boards with a line drive. Al Oliver pops up. Willie Stargell strikes out. Dave Parker flies out. Richie Zisk strikes out. Manny Sanguillen and Frankie Taveras fly out. John Candelaria strikes out. Stennett, Hebner, Oliver, and Stargell fly out. Parker fouls out. In the fifth, Zisk and Sanguillen board on successive line drives. Pinch hitter Ed Kirkpatrick fouls out, Candelaria strikes out, and the inning ends.

After five, Cincinnati leads, one to nothing.

*   *   *

By game time in Oakland, the sun no longer shines on the dugouts, but it remains tough in the outfield until the third inning, when it moves past the bleachers, blanketing the whole field in a chill shadow. The sun is out of the Mausoleum, and paints the distant Oakland hills with Popsicle light as Cecil Cooper leads off the fifth inning against Holtzman. Both starting pitchers are looking sharp, but the defense behind Holtzman has been sloppy, so already he's behind on an unearned run, one to nothing. (This season, Wise and Holtzman each lost no-hitters in the ninth; Wise because of a home run, Holtzman because of his fielders.)

Cooper has been up once today; in the second, with two outs, he swung on the first pitch and flew out to center. He stands in, watching the pitcher tug the peak of his green-and-gold cap. Holtzman delivers. Cooper fouls it off for a strike. The organist in the Mausoleum plays a whole note. Holtzman delivers a second pitch. Cooper swings through it for his second strike. The organist ascends a full step and plays another whole note, louder. Cooper swings through another pitch; he's out, and the organist breaks into a few happy measures of song. One away.

Holtzman starts off the next batter, Burleson, with a smoking fastball right down the middle. Strike one. He wastes a pitch, a low breaking ball, then tries to sneak one inside. *Mistake.* Burleson gets around on it and sends the ball skipping over the third-base bag, down the chalk into left for a double.

Beniquez enters the batter's box. Holtzman looks at Burleson at second, doesn't throw. He deals with the batter. The count to Beniquez goes full. Holtzman stays cool. He stares in. Beniquez flies out to right center. Two away.

Burleson holds at second.

Doyle bats. Holtzman starts him off with a sinker and Doyle takes it for ball one. Holtzman follows with an outside pitch. Doyle reaches out, shoots it down the line in right, a mirror image of Burleson's hit. (It's Doyle's sixth hit off Holtzman in the past four days.)

Burleson rounds third and scores.

Boston two, Oakland zero, still two away, another man on. Yastrzemski hurriedly moves Doyle to third with a base hit to right field.

Charlie Finley is not in the Mausoleum tonight. He had business in New York City, so he's there, watching on the television through a special hookup. Of course, he is on the telephone with Stanley the entire time. Now he figures, *Holtzman is finally showing the effects of pitching on two days' rest.* Fisk is due up, so Finley dispatches Dark to the mound. Holtzman is removed. Relief pitcher Jim Todd throws one pitch. Pudge bloops a little Texas leaguer, it falls for a hit, Doyle scores, Carl moves to third. Boston three, Oakland zero. Having given up three consecutive two-out singles and with Fred Lynn due up, Todd is replaced by a left-handed reliever, Paul Lindblad. Lynn swings and misses, strike one. Lynn swings and misses, strike two. Pudge goes. The throw down to second is not in time. Lindblad sets, looks. Carl is off third, bouncing on his tiptoes. Lynn is at the plate, focused. Lindblad winds and unloads and his two-strike pitch dies before the plate and scoots past the catcher, *wild pitch!* Then Carl's hunched and he's running, snarling, and Lynn is waving him home and backing away, and Zimmer is exhorting him in the background, gesturing like a mad prophet. Lindblad races in, and the three converge on home at once — the ball, the runner, and the pitcher. The ball hits the sliding Carl, and it glances away. The slide upends Lindblad, who shrieks and falls on Carl. The umpire calls Carl safe. Boston four, Oakland zero. Fisk takes a big turn at third.

Bando runs in, shamefaced, to recover the ball.

Following two long and sloppy games in Cincinnati, the third game in the National League play-offs is, of all things, a richly taut pitching duel. The Pirates are down by one in the bottom of the sixth and there's one away, when Richie Hebner drills a two-strike pitch off the end of his bat. It strikes the pitcher's glove, rolls toward second, and Hebner is safe at first. Al Oliver steps in. Earlier in the season, Scoop homered off a Gary Nolan fastball, down and away. Now, from the stretch, Nolan sets at the belt. He looks around. Bench hangs a sign. Nolan delivers a fastball, down and away. Oliver swings big. It's a fly ball deep to left center. Foster goes back, at the warning track, but it's gone. Two to one, Pittsburgh, on their first home run of the series.

Now, at last, a national audience grasps the important role played by Pittsburgh's pitching. All season it's been outstanding, and all season it has gone unnoticed. In the bottom of the eighth, Ken Griffey takes a curve for strike one. He takes a fastball at the letters for strike two. He chases a bad pitch, an outside breaking ball, for strike three. Candelaria — who was pitching minor-league ball just a few months ago — has his thirteenth strikeout victim, tying Tom Seaver for the National League Championship Series record.

Solemnly, Candelaria continues to work. He has a slight over-bite. His dark ringlets of hair provide a shaggy halo of sorts. Geronimo swings and misses, strike one, swings and misses, strike two, looks and leaves, strike three. Two outs, eighth inning, two to one in favor of Pittsburgh, and Candaleria has just tied Joe Coleman's major-league championship series record of fourteen strikeouts.

But abruptly, the magic is extinguished. Merv Rettenmund pinch-hits for Cincinnati's pitcher. Rettenmund has batted once previously in these play-offs, and he did nothing. Tonight, he walks on four straight balls. Rose comes up, he guesses a first-pitch breaking ball, is right, and sends it over the wall in left. Now it's three-two, Cincinnati, with home runs accounting for all the scoring in the game.

In Oakland, Boston is leading, five to one, in the top of the eighth, with one on and one out, when the Red Sox finally start to unravel. Doyle boots an easy grounder, putting runners at the corners with Bando at the plate.

The Mausoleum erupts, a madhouse of sound. "CHARGE!" the

people scream, as the electronic scoreboard instructs. "CHARGE!" They blow fierce blasts on long plastic trumpets. They send full rolls of toilet paper unspooling across the outfield, and the tissue rapidly spreads around to litter the drafty park, eddying and buffeting on the infield, sailing around the upper decks, about the press box.

Doyle trots to the mound, apologizes quickly to Rick Wise.

The infield positions itself back for the double play. Obligingly, Bando sends a ground ball to short. But the routine play handcuffs Burleson — he can't find the ball. Everybody's safe, a run scores, and now Reggie Jackson is at the plate, representing the tying run, with Joe Rudi on deck. Wise should be in the dugout, but instead he's working with two on and one out.

The crowd is screaming at the top of its lungs. The fans cannot contain themselves. Several, appearing lost, dash out onto the field. Time is called. Now they throw everything they have at Yastrzemski, the old guy — they pelt left field with bottles, and cardboard, and fruit, and wrappers. He stands in the deluge of debris, hands on his hips, glaring.

Carl's mother, Hattie, watches angrily. She has grown weak over the course of this season, becoming an invalid, and now, at Tom Yawkey's courteous insistence, she and her husband, Carl Sr., sit high in the regal booth reserved for the visiting owner while Yawkey holds a seat down among the natives. (Of course Yawkey too is gravely ill, but he hides this, because gentlemen don't complain.) Yawkey sits with Dick O'Connell, along the first base side, amid a contingent of pennant-waving Sox supporters. Rick Wise's mother and father sit with them. Someone's banner proclaims GO BOSOX STUFF IT UP THEIR A'S.

The field is cleared, the game resumes. Reggie lines a base hit down the power alley in left center. The air howls. Carl angles at the ball full tilt, like a man after a bunny, seeking to intercept it from the side. He dives, his nose in the grass, skidding on his belly through pillowy rolls of toilet paper, glove outstretched, and the ball bounces once, and then settles in his glove. He elbows himself up. He throws. He holds Reggie to a single, but another run is in.

Boston five, Oakland three.

Finally, after seven and a third gallant innings, Wise is done. Drago relieves him, fires one pitch, gets the double play, inning is over.

John Candelaria has left the game to a warm ovation, and the Reds are now three outs from the pennant as Willie Stargell leads off for Pittsburgh in the bottom of the ninth. Stargell has already struck out twice and popped to third. His count goes to one strike, one ball. Cincinnati's defense moves around to the right. The shortstop Concepcion plays on the bag at second. Morgan stations himself near first. Fighting the shift, the left-handed Stargell taps an easy single through the infield hole into left.

Now Murtaugh calls time and inserts young, fast Willie Randolph at first to run for Stargell. The next batter is Dave Parker. He strikes out on three pitches. Sparky brings in Rawly Eastwick to face Richie Zisk. As Eastwick warms up, Cincinnati's infield huddles. The crowd claps rhythmically to the organist's rowdy polkas. Foster, Geronimo, and Griffey meet for a discussion in the outfield. Randolph uses the opportunity to run up and down the right-field line.

Eastwick climbs up on the mound. He faced the Pirates two days before and got ahead of every batter, throwing nothing but fire for three scoreless innings. Rawly checks Randolph at first. He delivers, and Zisk hits the first pitch for a single. The tying run is at second. The winning run is aboard.

Manny Sanguillen pops out, two away.

For the first time, Sparky Anderson allows himself to think: *We're gonna win.* He feels this as a constriction in his chest, like a sob.

But Murtaugh refuses to make it easy. He sends up a pinch hitter. Crazy with the suspense, Pirate fans begin hurling trash. The umpires call time. Someone throws out a Frisbee. Eastwick's arm cools while the field is cleared. He walks the next two batters. A run scores. The game, knotted at three apiece, goes into extra innings.

Sparky is unaffected. His breast remains seized with a sense of impending victory. In extra-inning games this year, his guys won eleven of fifteen while their guys won only four of eleven. *We'll win.*

Drago is still pitching for Boston in the bottom of the ninth. If he can induce three outs and preserve the two-run lead, his team will go to the World Series, but it's no easy task. Oakland has a knack for clutch rallies.

Drago faces Billy Williams. He throws a ball, a strike, a strike, a ball, and then Williams hits a pitch off Drago's shin. It bounces crazily at Cooper. Drago hustles over to cover first. Cooper throws. Drago squeezes it. One away. Drago bleeds through his stocking from where the ball hit, but he doesn't feel a thing.

Drago next faces Gene Tenace, who pops out to Burleson. Two away. Drago faces Billy North. He throws four straight balls and walks him, and then faces Jim Holt, who has tremendous power —

Darrell Johnson goes to the mound to calm his pitcher.

Drago listens, sighs, relaxes. He looks in at Pudge for the sign, nods, winds, delivers, and throws three straight balls. Drago has misplaced the strike zone. He is one pitch away from putting the tying run aboard.

The fans begin to pepper center field with firecrackers and Roman candles. The grass erupts with light and sound. Fred Lynn hops around skittishly.

Perhaps the crack of gunpowder snaps Drago into focus. He throws a fastball: strike one. He throws another fastball: strike two. The count to Holt is now full. The Red Sox crouch excitedly on the top step of the dugout. Drago throws another fastball: fouled back. The count remains full.

Behind the Oakland dugout, people hang a Red Sox ballplayer in effigy.

Ned Martin is at the microphone, broadcasting to forty-seven radio stations in New England on behalf of the Red Sox. A middle-aged man, Martin has a penetrating gaze and a bulbous nose that hints at rhinophyma. "We may never get out of here alive if they win tonight," he mutters to the broadcaster beside him, Jim Woods.

More smoke curls up from explosives in the outfield.

"Maybe not," agrees Woods, who makes a show of sounding determined, "but I'm gonna try."

Drago throws a final fastball: a ground ball to second. The pitcher mechanically pursues the play to first. Doyle charges, comes up with the ball. He throws. Cooper has it. *We're going to the World Series!* Drago jumps and punches the air. Cooper pounds the ball in his glove. He looks momentarily disconcerted. The realization dawns, and abruptly he's leaping into Drago's arms.

The whole team spills onto the field. Some wear windbreakers. They embrace in a group hug before the dugout, bouncing and shouting happily, a blur of red hats.

Rick Wise's parents have at last seen him win.

Ken Griffey Jr. is at home listening to the radio. Junior is exploring superstition. He discovers that by crossing his own fingers at the right time, he somehow influences distant events, and helps his dad succeed. (As a consequence, Ken Griffey has had a fabulous series.) Saturday at the park, Junior crossed his fingers in the bottom of the third, and his dad hit a two-run double, giving the Reds the lead, sending Reuss to the showers. By crossing his fingers opportunely during the second game, Junior helped his dad steal three bases.

His dad leads off the tenth inning. The score is tied. Pittsburgh has a new pitcher, a left-hander, Ramon Hernandez. Junior waits. It is important that he not cross his fingers until just the right moment.

On the radio, Reds' play-by-play man Marty Brennaman advises fans against meeting the team at the airport. "In the event of a postgame celebration tonight," says Brennaman, a slender young man with a sweeping head of hair, "don't go to the airport, do not meet them there, they won't be seen at all, they'll be taken directly to Fountain Square, where a welcome-home ceremony is planned. There'll be a man on the Square shortly after this game. If the Reds win this game, fans are invited to head downtown and join the fun. The Reds will probably be getting downtown about two or two-thirty in the morning, tomorrow morning."

Hernandez throws two curves. Both break nastily. Griffey swings at each and misses. The count is oh and two.

"Here we go," says a small listener in Ohio. *The moment is now.* Junior crosses his fingers.

A man with worn features and rheumy eyes watches from a seat above the outfield on the rim of the terrace level. He hasn't been this near to Ken Griffey in many, many years. He intends to get closer.[8]

His name is Buddy Griffey. He is Ken's dad. He abandoned Ken and Ken's five siblings when they were young. Buddy's wife Ruth had to raise the children alone. Ruth took odd jobs; she collected welfare. Her children learned to do without and to work on their own to make ends meet. Ken worked in a grocery store, a steel factory. He read meters for the local electric company. Dogs chased him; he carried six cans of Mace spray to protect himself. All this time, Buddy was nowhere to be found. Now he wants to make up for it. He has traveled to downtown Pittsburgh to buy a three-dollar general-admission ticket from a store called CG Murphy's. He wants to reassert his role in his son's life.

The count holds at oh and two as Hernandez rubs up a new baseball. He climbs back atop the mound. He goes for the rosin bag.

Buddy Griffey went to high school with Stan Musial. Both were athletes, but Buddy was the standout. Really! Once he gets to speak with his dear son Ken, Buddy will tell him all about it. He will unburden himself of all the wisdom gleaned from a life spent eluding responsibility. He's coming home now. It'll be better than it ever was. He'll make up for all the lost time. With apparent casualness, Buddy will let on how very much Musial envied him, and they will laugh and laugh about this, as Ken's dad recalls his days as a star in tiny Donora, Pennsylvania.

Hernandez shakes off Sanguillen's sign. He shakes it off again. He winds up and delivers.

Buddy has his fingers crossed (it's the one thing he shares with Junior, besides his last name).

At the plate, Ken surprises everyone — his father, his son, his opponents, his manager. With two strikes, he squares around. He bunts. Sanguillen is caught unaware. He comes up with the ball, but his throw is low.

Ken safely crosses the first-base bag.

Next, Hernandez balks Griffey to second. Geronimo sacrifices him to third — one out. Sparky sends up pinch bunter Ed Armbrister. But Armbrister doesn't bunt — he swings away, and against a drawn-up infield, he swats a lazy fly to center. Two outs, but Griffey scores. Rose singles. Morgan doubles. Bench flies out, and the game goes to the bottom of the tenth with Cincinnati in front, five runs to three.

Sparky brings in Pedro Borbon to pitch.

Richie Hebner was out of the lineup three times this year. He's been trying to redeem his season with a big play-off series. So far, so good. He already has two hits in the game. He's one of the few Pirates, along with Zisk (the other white-skinned Pirate regular), who remembered to bring his bat to the play-offs, and it's been the one time the white Richies have dominated the bat-breaking lineup of sluggers known in Pittsburgh as "The Lumber Company." Parker has remained uncomfortable at the plate, going hitless. Taveras, who displayed a lot of patience in the clutch down the stretch, has done nothing. Sanguillen, with a .328 batting average and a .451 slugging percentage on the year, has hit just .167 in this series. Stargell and Oliver have failed to hit their weight.

Borbon rocks, kicks, and delivers three screaming fastballs at Hebner. Three straight strikes, one out. Al Oliver steps up. Scoop grounds the first pitch toward Morgan at second. *Two away*. Now Stargell would come to the plate, except that Randolph ran for him in the ninth, so it's the second-string rookie Randolph who bats, with the Pirates down by two runs, bases empty, tenth inning, and the

Reds an out away from the National League pennant. Randolph receives the same first pitch as Scoop, also grounds it to Morgan — the play is made. The Reds mob Borbon: they have swept the Pirates. In four days, they will play Boston for the world championship. The immediate consensus in the press box is that the Red Sox don't stand a chance.

Without expression, Willie Randolph jogs through the pandemonium to the Pirate dugout. No one knows, but that was his sixty-third and final at bat wearing the gold and black of Pittsburgh. The Pirates have the great Rennie Stennett to work the keystone; they won't keep Randolph. Shortly, he will be folded into a postseason trade with the Yankees, who'll exchange their troublesome Doc (Medich) for Pittsburgh's troublesome Dock (Ellis) and Ken Brett. Thurman Munson'll be ecstatic, remembering Randolph from spring training in Puerto Rico, the guy moving to his left and right with ease, showing tremendous range on the field. Randolph, a sullen figure jokingly called "Mr. Personality," will be a throw-in, as Armbrister was thrown in by Houston, as Carbo was thrown in by St. Louis — a throw-in who will rise to extraordinary prominence elsewhere.

This is the last postseason game for Danny Murtaugh, who'll die next year, as well as the final Pirates' broadcast for Bob Prince and Nellie King, who'll be fired inexplicably in a few days, breaking their hearts. Prince has spent twenty-eight of his fifty-eight years broadcasting Pirate games in the tristate area over KDKA and the Westinghouse network. Stargell and a few other ballplayers will lead a parade of protest through the streets of Pittsburgh, demanding that the Westinghouse network rehire the Gunner. Over ten thousand Prince supporters will turn out. Stargell will address the crowd. "A job in baseball is unlike most other jobs," he'll explain. He'll look out at the sea of faces, and for the first time see himself as a leader, as kin to his Seminole ancestor, War Chief Osceola. "In baseball, you're asked to give your heart, not just your time. The game doesn't pay its nonplaying employees well, especially when they're asked to work upwards of one hundred hours a week. They

just right, and his dad was gonna be delighted, and they got this little hill out there in center field and the beer tastes good and the people are just great, especially in the summer, and then Casey concluded his soliloquy with, "Oh, didn't I tell you? We traded you to Cincinnati."

A hardy group of New England sports fans departs home for one of two destinations: either the airport, to welcome home the American League champions, or Fenway's ticket office, to await the sale of World Series tickets. They bring picnic chairs, wool blankets, sleeping bags, magazines, crossword puzzles, and playing cards. Their chests bear buttons with likenesses of Rice and Lynn, who they proclaim to be the "Gold Dust Twins." At the airport, nearly two thousand of these people, mostly students, wait for fifteen hours through the night, they tape homemade bedsheet banners all over the concourse, they allow the state troopers to clear a path from the gate to the stairs, they cheer madly when the Sox plane descends, they greet the players by name, they pat backs, they shake hands. Gloomy old men wearing white buttons with red block letters that proclaim YAZ SIR, THAT'S MY BABY are heard to mutter that this is nothing compared to the welcome the team received in 1967. At Fenway, thousands more are standing for days on the sidewalk of Jersey Street, waiting for the box office to open and a handful of six-dollar standing-room tickets to be made available. Most of the good seats are already in the hands of corporate sponsors, media, major-league employees, and elected representatives. Gloomy old men wearing oversize buttons that proclaim THE *ONE* AND *ONLY* SPLENDID SPLINTER are heard muttering that this doesn't compare to the ecstatic anticipation of awaiting World Series tickets in 1946.

OCTOBER 8

TOM YAWKEY is chauffeured from the airport to the Ritz Carlton amid the growing rosy light of dawn. He crawls into bed, falls fast asleep while reading scouting reports. He always goes through them. These reports on the Reds are particularly concise, very easy to read. Still, he's too tired. He's growing sicker by the week. This is the most exhausting time in his life.

Later, Yawkey shows up at Fenway. He continues to smoke cigarettes against doctor's orders. He chats with Darrell Johnson in the manager's office. A reporter sticks his head in. "Can I throw something at you?"

The owner's blue eyes pass warmly over the reporter. He assents.

"Would you say," the reporter then asks, "that Carl Yastrzemski is the best all-around player you have ever had?"

"Well . . ." Yawkey's gray eyebrows arch toward the ceiling. The names scroll through his mind. *Jimmie Foxx. Bobby Doerr. Joe Cronin.* "I know that Ted Williams was *such* a great hitter . . . Joe

DiMaggio told me he was the greatest hitter he ever saw . . . And Ted could field better than a lot of people think . . . But the best all-around player?" Yawkey douses his cigarette, rubs his short-clipped hair. "Yes, Carl does more than the rest ever did, I'm sure of that. Certainly."

OCTOBER 9

AT THE PRE-SERIES WORKOUT, Boston's pitching arms are rounded up — Richard A. Drago, William F. Lee, Rogelio Moret, Richard H. Pole, Diego P. Segui, Luis C. Tiant, James A. Willoughby, Richard C. Wise — and herded inside to watch replays of the Big Red Machine. The recordings are on videocassettes, the latest technology, which requires an immense apparatus of electronic equipment.

"Cincinnati will come to the plate," a Red Sox coach predicts. "They'll see what you have. They'll like to watch. They usually score late in the game, after they've seen everything a pitcher has got. They're patient learners. So be sure to hold back something special for later at bats."

The pitchers nod. They huddle close. On a flickering screen, Johnny Bench homers at the hour of darkness. Joe Morgan scurries about the bases pell-mell. Tony Perez carries the club on his shoulders. Pete Rose takes out the pivot man. A Boston scout draws away their attention, clearing his throat. His voice echoes off the brick walls as he reads aloud from the batting reports. He warns the pitchers not to give too much to Rose, to throw nibblers to Morgan, to display confident control against Bench, to work the corners on Perez. . . .

Bill Lee raises his hand. "So, we pitch around Rose, pitch around Morgan, pitch around Bench, and pitch around Perez. Correct me if I'm wrong: it sounds like the best strategy is to start the game with the bases loaded, five runs in, and their pitcher at the plate."[10]

The room explodes with laughter. Darrell Johnson, observing from the back of the room, stalks off. *Clubhouse lawyers, funnymen, agitators . . .* He'd be happy if just once the Spaceman showed some respect.

The manager emerges into the dugout. He walks out to the field. Most of his guys are taking BP or shagging flies. The air is tangy with sea salt. Overhead, the clouds are clumped like clotted cream. Zimmer stands in the outfield, beneath billboards that advertise television and whiskey. He looks abstracted. There's something on his mind.

"What are you thinking?" DJ asks.

"Well," replies Zim, "I gotta hunch."

"Yeah?" The manager knows his third-base coach is a gambler, maybe not as big a gambler as Tiant, who has bookies threatening him with death when he takes the mound, but still Zim likes to play the odds on the dogs and the horses, and really it's not so different once you upgrade it to humans.[11]

"It's a risk," Zim quietly admits. "You ain't gonna like it."

"Go on."

"I saw a lot of these Big Red guys when I was in the other league." Zim used to manage the San Diego Padres. "They're pretty much a free-swinging team."

"Great, great. We got the pitchers inside, we're telling them Cincinnati is patient at the plate. Now you say they're free swingers."

"I gotta hunch," Zimmer whispers with significant inflection. "I think a lefty who keeps the ball down and throws a lot of off-speed stuff might give them trouble, especially in our ballpark, with this grass we got here."

DJ looks at Zim as if he's mad. "Wha . . . ? Oh no! I am *not* starting Bill Lee. Is this what you're asking? Zim, Zim, Zim . . ." For a moment, Zimmer expects to be ordered to take a cold shower. "You're not using your head, here. That's your soft spot speaking."

The left side of Zim's skull does in fact bear a tender area from when he was a player and got beaned a lot.

"Okay, okay."

The manager squints doubtfully. "You don't like what Lee adds to the bull pen?"

Zim says nothing. He understands Johnson's reluctance; there ain't nobody in baseball he dislikes more than Bill Lee. Lee has this ego; he thinks he's Casey Stengel, but Zim knew Casey — hell, Don Zimmer made the first error in the history of the New York Mets while playing third base for Stengel — and although Lee mimics Casey's glib, cruel sarcasm exactly right, he ain't as approachable, he lacks Casey's whimsical sense of sportsmanship, that joy in teamwork that Casey used to sell the game and that Sparky Anderson still uses. *Bill Lee just likes to lay them fancy words on folks.* If Lee wants to get down on himself, which he does often enough, that's fine, but he usually does it just as an excuse to get down on someone else. Lee will joke that he gets along well with Darrell Johnson because they have similar drinking problems, crap like that, a backhanded slap, and then he'll lay into DJ for leaving his starters in too long, and 'cause he ain't establishing any sort of order in the bull pen but instead just going with whoever has the hot hand at the moment — *as if DJ had a lot of options this year! What with his relievers out there always getting hit in the face or crashing their automobiles.*

"You would agree with me," says Johnson, "that Lee didn't pitch especially well in the last month of the season?"

Zim looks at the empty bleachers. He smiles wanly. "Yeah, his elbow, I know. It's just . . ." He hesitates. "Think about it. The Spaceman starting game two. That's my recommendation."

"Ah, shit."

"I'm just asking: think about it."[12]

DJ grunts. He knows that Don Zimmer is right, but he hates admitting it; his skin crawls at the idea of giving Lee the chance because the Spaceman is *such* a royal pain in the ass and he's got that mouth just made for a media circus. But he's also got that Marvelous Mel Parnell finger, that strange middle finger that enables him to throw the crazy sinker, which is how he's become the most consistent left-handed winner in Fenway Park since the days of Parnell, who bewildered the bats of Stengel's Yankees back in the forties.[13] The ability to throw a ball that breaks away from right-handed hitters and then jam them inside with a fastball — this is what Lee offers, and this is what Darrell Johnson keeps picturing, when at last he addresses the notepads and microphones to reveal that he's made a decision on the starters, that he's going with Tiant in game one and Lee in game two.

The newsmen's response, as expected, is that DJ is already desperate, possibly drunk.[14] Bill Lee has not made an appearance since the next-to-last game of the regular season. He has not started a game in three weeks. He has not won since August 24.

Johnson admonishes the newsmen for their lack of faith. "Bill Lee," he solemnly intones, "is a *tremendous* competitor." He looks hard at the scribblers. "Anybody who saw what he did to Catfish Hunter in Yankee Stadium back at the end of July knows *that.*"

Watching the manager work to defend his most obnoxious player, Zimmer shakes his head. "I hope to hell this works," he mutters to himself.

Bernie Carbo is seated with Sparky on a groundskeeper's bench in right.

"I've, uh . . . I've got something on my mind I'd like to say." Carbo draws a deep breath and steadies himself. "There was this once, you said to me, *Bernardo, you think I'm always picking on you. Someday you're gonna play for someone else and you're gonna see that I care about you, I care what happens to you now and later in your life.*" Bernie scratches his head, ruffling his thick black hair. Suddenly, he laughs. "I was immature, you know? I really didn't get what you meant."

Sparky eyes Carbo curiously. He's surprised to hear sentiments of this nature from the intemperate man whom Bill Lee so aptly describes as "pure oxygen looking for a flame."[15]

"Guess —" Bernie coughs. "I guess I've grown up. I, um . . . I just want to thank you for everything you've done for me."

"Now," Anderson replies, "let me tell *you* something." He strokes his chin, and sucks his teeth meditatively. He considers how best to put it. "You played for me when *I* was still immature." Sparky remembers keeping Carbo's longhair friends out of Riverfront because of their dilated pupils and embroidered jeans.[16] "I also have to admit to you I think I've grown up. I appreciate what you've told me, Bernie, but I want you to know we all have faults. As soon as we realize that, we become what is commonly known in our society as a man."

His words sound a melody over the staccato crack of baseballs on bats.

Sparky sighs. The two men stand. They eye each other closely.

Carbo feels the hairs begin to stir on the back of his neck, and becomes aware of the impending ceremony around him: the grooming of the grass, the scrubbing of the wooden scoreboard, the fitting of new bulbs into the light stanchions, the advance preparation of hot dogs and popcorn, the vendors active in the streets beyond, the pennants, the banner headlines, the 76 television crews, the 738 print reporters, the hundreds of column inches. . . . He senses himself as part of something grand, something more immense than even Tom Yawkey. *I love my uniform,* he suddenly thinks, with the allegiance of a child.[17] "Well," Carbo says at last, "I should go."

"Yeah."

It seems for a second they might hug. Instead, they shake hands.

"Good luck, Sparky."

"Good luck to you, Bernardo."[18]

Sparky looks up as he strolls in from right field. The press await him at first base. He approaches and they, living up to their name, press in all around. They know he's starting Gullett in game one and Billingham in game two, but now they also know Johnson's starting Tiant in game one and Lee in game two, and they want Sparky's reaction.

Sparky says little about Lee. Privately, he admits it's a smart move. He spies Zimmer's influence at work. Bill Lee is a lot like Randy Jones, and nobody looked better defeating the Reds this year than Randy Jones. And deep down Sparky remains a bit unsure about Billingham, and for that reason he would just as soon steer clear of the subject of the game two starters. Billingham led the staff in victories until around six weeks ago, when inexplicably his mound rhythm soured, his pitches sailed in high, he gave up an average of six or seven runs a game, he lost five of six decisions. Lately Billingham has been working with the pitching coach; he's been throwing a lot and he certainly appears to be a pitcher who can get the requisite ground balls in Fenway Park, but who really knows? *Everything's a goddamn crapshoot in this game.*

Sparky keeps this to himself. Instead, he takes up the topic of game one, the matchup of innocence versus experience, his flame-throwing southpaw against their junk-balling righty. He doesn't want to make a mockery or a farce out of the World Series, Sparky insists, but he has seen this Tiant pitch out of a stretch with a man on, and Anderson's bothered. It isn't the way Tiant flutters, bringing his hands down to his waist; it's when Tiant stops his hands at the waist, then drops them another notch before throwing to first. "That's a balk as far as I'm concerned," Sparky tells the newsmen. It's ingenious. The papers print everything Sparky says, and before the Series even begins, he gets into the mind of the umpires. With calm cunning, he plants the seed of a doubt. The Reds are the fastest team in the league, stealing 168 bases in 205 attempts, but if Tiant maintains anything like the mastery he's displayed in his previous four outings, then the extra base provided by a balk would be a godsend.

Moving on from Tiant's illegal moves, Sparky makes sure that everyone knows about the great Don Gullett. "He came up to me before one of the play-off games and asked my permission to shave," Sparky informs the press. "I mean, he's been in the major leagues for six years now and still asks me something like that . . . incredible! This is some farm boy, some polite farm boy. He'll *yessir* and *nosir* you to death if you ain't on your guard. He came to us at the age of nineteen and hasn't changed a bit. Great boy, a gentleman, poised, some pitcher. He'll pitch a great game, I say." Sparky looks without expression at the Green Monster that shortens left field so ridiculously. "That wall won't bother him."

OCTOBER 10

Hourly, more patriotic bunting is heaped upon Fenway Park, and more debates break out about Tiant's hesitations and Lee's seriousness.

Dr. Warren Bennis of the University of Cincinnati telegraphs the presidents of the University of Massachusetts, Boston University, Northeastern, Boston College, MIT, and Harvard. "We'll bet you a case of Cincinnati's famous hot German sausage," he writes, describing what are popularly known as "metts," "against any suitable Boston delicacy on Cincinnati taking the Series."

The young governor of Massachusetts, Michael Dukakis, bets Ohio governor James Rhodes twenty pounds of codfish against a bushel of Ohio corn that the Red Sox will win. Rhodes refuses. "I don't want to take the guy's fish," he explains.

Luis Tiant gathers the usual crowd of friends at his home in Milton for a home-cooked dinner of white rice, black beans, and ham croquettes. Luis enjoys being the host. He feels absolutely wonderful. The guests drink and laugh. They stay late. His family goes to sleep. At 2:00 A.M., the party finally disperses. Luis pads around to all of the bedrooms, checking on everybody, tucking blankets under chins, turning off lights. Here are his children, his parents. Here is his wife. He slips into bed beside her. Lying there, snuggling in her warmth, Luis thinks. There was the time he was eighteen and his father was telling him there was no money in baseball, and warning him against this love of the game, for it would embitter his heart, and Luis remembers trying out for the hometown Sugar Kings anyway, being rejected, and feeling crushed, and accepting $150 a month to pitch in far-off Mexico City. And in Mexico, all the time that thirty-two-year-old attorney-turned-guerrilla Castro was taking over Tiant's homeland on the front page of weeklies such as *El Figaro* and *Deporte Ilustrado*, the picture of sensational pitcher Luis Tiant filled the back pages. This was the time and place in which Luis became mesmerized by the jewel of Maria, and they married, but their honeymoon to Cuba was called off when Castro began refusing his citizens the right to leave the island, and Luis grew afraid of being trapped in his birthplace and had to accept that his parents might never meet his wife. In the winters he pitched for the Puerto Rican or Venezuelan leagues; in the summers he pitched in the United States for "the great leagues" (as they were called back home), but there were always seasons of June–August pitching inconsistencies, and there was always this palpable sadness to the holidays, because he couldn't see his parents, he couldn't send them anything, and talking on the phone was hard: he could never really say the things that were on his mind. And all the while that Luis played baseball in the United States or Venezuela — his parents stuck out of reach — the light of his life, gentle and beautiful Maria, remained in an apartment in Mexico City, where she raised their son, Luis, and daughter, Isabel, all by herself.

Finally, like a flower, the 1968 season blossomed, and his mother at last saw her only child by going to a neighbor's house in Havana to watch him pitch in the all-star game. She cried the whole time Luis was on the mound because she wanted to reach out. She wanted to touch him, and she couldn't. He ended that year with the lowest ERA in the American League since fire-thrower Walter Johnson's 1.49 in 1919, and then Alvin Dark, his manager with the Indians, forbade him from pitching over the winter, and in 1969 Luis returned with adhesions, a sore shoulder, a stiff elbow, a pulled muscle in his side, and he lost twenty games, so Dark traded him to Minnesota. Then Luis hurt his back, and he misplaced his fastball, and he couldn't regain his control and couldn't win games and couldn't help but think of his father dying and never having the chance to see him again, because his father was almost seventy and was still going to work every day, pumping gas at a garage. He lived only ninety miles away from the United States, a distance Luis could nearly cross on foot, but Luis couldn't even send his father a dime for a cup of coffee on Christmas, couldn't do anything to make life any easier for his parents. Around then Luis pulled a muscle in his rib cage and bombed out of spring training, and everyone figured that he just didn't have it anymore, that he had nothing left. It was March 1972. The Twins completely dropped him. He even flunked a tryout in the minors with Atlanta and was released by two teams in four months.

And then another blossom opened, for Darrell Johnson glimpsed Tiant's potential, and Johnson was the manager of the Louisville Colonels, which was Boston's entry in the triple-A league, and Johnson convinced Dick O'Connell that Luis was making a complete recovery, so O'Connell quickly brought him to Boston. Tiant lost a lot of games at first, and an assemblage of crew cuts and beer bellies in the Fenway bleachers kept yelling unkind things whenever he warmed up, and Luis felt rejected and crushed, until he ended that year with the lowest ERA in Boston since submarine-thrower Carl Mays's 1.74 in 1917. Now the fans in tumultuous Fenway applaud his every pitch, his every step, jump to their feet even when Luis merely reaches down to pick up the rosin bag, but he always thinks of the crew cuts and beer bellies in the bleachers, and this keeps the applause from going to his head.

And so, he is in his own home. He has his Maria and the children with him; he has his parents; he has so many good friends; and he has his career. There were many years when he had none of these, when everything seemed wrong. Now everything is right. There is no more he can ask for. He and his family will awaken in the morning and go to the park. After pitching professionally for sixteen years, after hundreds of games in the American League and hundreds more in the Venezuelan leagues, Luis will start the World Series. In all his life, he's never been this happy. All his prayers have been answered at once. He thanks God, he closes his eyes, and he sleeps like a baby.[19]

OCTOBER 11

CINCINNATI	BOSTON
Rose, *third base*	Evans, *right field*
Morgan, *second base*	Doyle, *second base*
Bench, *catcher*	Yastrzemski, *left field*
Perez, *first base*	Fisk, *catcher*
Foster, *left field*	Lynn, *center field*
Concepcion, *shortstop*	Petrocelli, *third base*
Griffey, *right field*	Burleson, *shortstop*
Geronimo, *center field*	Cooper, *first base*
Gullett, *pitcher*	Tiant, *pitcher*
(Carroll, *pitcher*)	
(McEnaney, *pitcher*)	

Somewhere along in the second inning of game one, the rain ceases.[20] Foster is on one knee in the on-deck circle, with his hand on his hip, watching Tiant, when suddenly he grasps the abundance of green in right field, the lack of foul territory, the crosswind that blows from right to left, the unspeakable nearness of the fortress wall in left — all these strange things — and realizes that this park requires a different style of ball game, and for the first time he wonders if his guys are prepared.

Nobody has scored yet, but everything already seems hard for the Reds and easy for the Red Sox. Cincinnati keeps hitting line drives that get caught while Boston keeps hitting Gullett, which isn't even supposed to happen; he's probably the best left-hander in baseball, but on this damp, raw day, he keeps falling behind, keeps trying to hit the outside corner and keeps missing, and Red Sox keep getting on base, and then he keeps pitching his way out of danger. Granted, Boston can't seem to score, but two of their guys get thrown out at home while none of the Reds even get aboard.

Tiant is nothing like what they were led to believe. Before the game, the Reds were shown tapes of the pitcher blowing the ball past Oakland, and they were told to expect 80-percent fastballs, but today Tiant throws sliders, curves, change-ups, and knuckleballs, and he seems to go into convulsions as he pitches. With all of Tiant's motions, Foster really has to concentrate just to find the ball. He returns to the dugout, chagrined after lining out to Cooper in the second, and, seeking sympathy, he finally says something aloud; he complains about Tiant's wiggles and jiggles to his teammates on the bench.

Pudgy, white Pete Rose eyes the muscular, dark Foster and makes a dismissive gesture. Rose feels differently. "I don't watch that stuff," Pete sniffs. "His head could roll off and I wouldn't notice."

"All he has is a lot of legs and arms," Ken Griffey tells Foster encouragingly. "He can't overpower you."

"But he uses that off-speed stuff so well. It —" *makes me look bad,* Foster almost says. He catches himself, swallows, and says instead, "It gets me off balance."

Griffey nods. Due on deck, he taps a batting helmet onto his head and steps out.

Rose looks again at Foster and, at last, takes a grudging swipe at compassion. "Yeah, yeah, yeah," he grumbles at Foster. "I know. Shit, we ain't got nobody in the National League like this, somebody who can throw spinning high curveballs that take two minutes to come down."

Foster cherishes Rose's intent.

For three innings, Tiant breezes through the entire Cincinnati lineup without a trace of difficulty. Then, with one out in the fourth, Joe Morgan bats for the second time. Tiant turns his back on him and comes around with a big, slow, overhand curve for a called strike. The next pitch is a high fastball. Morgan lines it to center. Lynn retrieves it on a bounce.

Morgan, the fastest Red of all with sixty-eight steals in seventy-eight tries, has reached first. People are thinking what Sparky has told them to think: Tiant pitches illegally with a man on. Now Sparky's got a base runner who'll prove it to the world.

Both dugouts come to attention as Tiant wiggles his hands. He sets. He nods at Johnny Bench in the batter's box. He flexes his legs, steps off the rubber. He looks at Morgan. He returns to the rubber. He winds up. He throws a low, sidearm pitch to Bench, who fouls it down third.

Tiant looks again at Morgan, throws to first base. He gets the ball back, throws over to first, gets the ball back, throws over to first. On the third pick-off attempt, he catches Morgan leaning toward second. Cecil Cooper tags his elbow but umpire Nick Colosi fails to see it and calls Morgan safe. Tiant gets the ball back, flexes his legs, stops, flexes his legs again.

He throws over. Morgan dives.

"Balk!" cries Colosi.

Morgan puts his head down and jogs into scoring position.

Tiant marches up to the umpire, livid. Luis has never been called for a balk in eleven years of major-league pitching! "How that balk?" he screams, and he's embarrassed to hear that even his rudimentary English is failing him. "How that balk?"

"Is balk!" Colosi shouts back. "Is balk!"

Tiant harrumphs, then trudges back up the mound. He needs two more outs. Bench is at the plate, Perez is on deck, and Morgan is at second.

Luis throws a high, overhand strike and it's fouled directly back.

Essentially, any pitch Bench hits into fair territory will advance Morgan. Luis takes a breath, he throws a strike at a three-quarter angle and it's fouled high into the left-field seats.

Second baseman Denny Doyle comes over to the mound, with his buttery-soft, alabaster skin and flaming red hair, to calm the pitted and pockmarked pitcher. Denny intones a few unremarkable assurances. His eyes are resolute, his mouth firmly set, his complexion creamy. Luis nods and touches Doyle's face thankfully, almost effetely. He then throws three pitches low and outside. Bench doesn't swing. The count is full.

Bench is not bothered by Tiant's bump-and-grind motion. He just pretends he's hitting Juan Marichal; it's the same sort of challenge, the head feints, the body fakes, the multitude of variations, every pitch different. Marichal played mostly for San Francisco. He won more games in the 1960s than any other pitcher, but Bench always had pretty good luck against him.

Bench fouls off the next two pitches.

Tiant moves the ball around, he puts it within an inch or two of where he wants it every time, and Bench keeps fouling it off, again and again, and all the while Tiant has to keep a close eye on Morgan because the guy can steal third as well as anybody.

On the thirteenth pitch, Morgan takes off, but Bench fouls out to Fisk. Morgan returns to second. Tiant gets two quick strikes on Tony Perez. The crowd chants, "Loo-ee! Loo-ee!" Perez strikes out looking at a fastball. Morgan is left standing at second, frozen in annoyance. He waits there as Concepcion brings him his fielder's glove.

In the sixth inning, with one away and no score, Morgan doubles. The situation repeats. Again, as in the fourth, Luis has to get Bench and Perez with Morgan at second.

Bench drives a ball to the right of Burleson. Morgan is sure to score, except that Rico happens to anticipate it, he's going to his left on the pitch, and he makes a quick play to get Bench at first, so Morgan stays where he is.

Tiant then strikes out Perez, this time with breaking pitches, so again Morgan is stranded in scoring position.

Young men and women in wool hats and winter clothing watch the game for free while perched precariously on the Windsor Canadian billboard above Fenway's center field. They watch from fifty feet above Lansdowne Street, five hundred feet from home plate. They can see the ballplayers blowing on their hands to stay warm, but cannot see that Pete Rose is the only player not wearing long sleeves. They can see Gullett's motion, how he pitches with a minimum of excess, moving as if in fast motion, throwing the ball like he's throwing a punch in a John Ford Western, reaching low from his shoestrings. They cannot see Gullett's fastball, how it rides in or sails away, nor can they see Gullett's face, with his chaw, his brows knitted, his look helpless. They can see the Reds stinging the ball and the Red Sox walking. They can see that Boston is leaving just as many on base as Cincinnati. They can see the score, spelled out in lights above the grandstand. It remains tied at zero.

In the top of the seventh, Foster again faces Tiant, and must be once more unsure what he's gotten into. The truth is, he's spoiled. He's become accustomed to pitchers who focus on the catcher's mitt as they release the ball. This Tiant, he winds up and then pulls the ball out of thin air, releasing every pitch from behind his glove and hand, each time from a new angle, at a different speed. If Foster looks into the stands for the simple comfort of a child's face, he finds instead thirty-five thousand frenzied mouths smelling of beer and yelling "Loo-ee! Loo-ee!" without end. *This was supposed to be the initiation of a sacred event.* It feels like he's dialed into a primitive folk ritual that will conclude with his dismemberment.

He singles.

Concepcion follows with a shallow blooper to left. It's a certain single to everyone but left fielder Carl Yastrzemski. He behaves as if, since 1961, he's been stationed beneath Fenway's Green Monster to catch exactly this type of hit, which in a way, he has been. Carl alone thinks he can catch it. He digs deep but he's off balance. He trips, hits the ground with a knee, and goes down grabbing blindly at the ball. And yet his glove is exactly where it needs to be, and the ball plops right in. Carl snaps his mitt shut and elbows himself up to a kneeling position. His hat is off and the fans glimpse the face. It is striking how old Carl looks (no one would ever guess it by his fielding). The front of his uniform is soiled, but the baseball he raises, which he has dedicatedly kept from touching the unclean ground, is pure white.

In the visitor's dugout, Sparky spits. *You have to expect that from Yastrzemski.* If not for Carl, Sparky would have runners at second and third with no outs. Sparky signals for Foster to steal, and he tries, but Pudge cuts him down at second. Griffey then doubles, which just figures. *If not for Yaz, if not for Fisk, I'd have two runs from that double!* Geronimo receives an intentional pass, bringing up Gullett. With two outs, Sparky has the pitcher swing away, and Gullett connects for a nasty, twisting flare toward right, except that Denny Doyle is playing the way Oakland's Dick Green used to, without great speed but alert, anticipating everything, and now, running, he stabs Gullett's drive for the third out.

Gullett retrieves his mitt and goes to the mound. Bottom of the seventh, score still tied at nothing apiece, and Tiant the leadoff batter.

Luis has not even bothered to take batting practice today. In his two previous plate appearances of the game, he has struck out and, to much merriment, earned a walk. Now, Luis expects to view more jumping fastballs. But for some reason, Gullett tries a change-up, which comes in high and hangs there, so Tiant swats at it, and it rolls all the way out to left without brushing against anybody's glove. It's Tiant's first hit since 1972.

Dewey Evans, up next, bunts down the right side.

Gullett grabs the ball.

"Go to second," Bench instructs him.

Sparky Anderson will later use this instant to illustrate the philosophy he got from Branch Rickey, that luck is a residue of design. "When you make a mistake," he'll explain after the game, "you pay for it with a loss." He'll be sitting in the manager's office, with a plate of cold cuts and potato salad on the desk before him. "Don Gullett slips, and everything changes."

The pitcher has lost his footing. His throw is off balance.

Tiant is making for second as fast as he can. Ahead of him, Concepcion moves into position and prepares for the throw.

Tiant suddenly tastes fear. Of all things, he's afraid to slide. He isn't sure he remembers how; it's been so long. He approaches the base and quickly crumbles, folding himself into second.

The throw from Gullett hops into center.

Men on first and second, no outs.

Doyle is next. On the first pitch, he squares around, fouls off one of Gullett's outstanding fastballs.

Boston's options have everyone perplexed. *That's Luis Tiant on second base, not Lou Brock.* Tiant barely found second. *Now Darrell Johnson expects him to take third on a sacrifice bunt?*

Shortstop Dave Concepcion anticipates another bunt attempt. He shifts over near second base.

Doyle watches a hole open up between second and third. His manager removes the bunt sign. Doyle sees his pitch, down and away. He reaches out. He punches it through the hole into left. Everyone advances safely.

Now Yastrzemski is up. The bases are loaded, still no outs. Of all things, Tiant is at third base, with Pete Rose making inquiries into his well-being.

The crowd is fantastically loud.

At third, Zimmer cups his hands around the pitcher's batting helmet. "ANYTHING HIT IN THE AIR," Zimmer shouts at the hole in Tiant's earflap, "YOU TAG UP! COME BACK! I DON'T WANT YOU CAUGHT HALFWAY."

Gullett unleashes a marvelous heater, down and in, but Yastrzemski has it timed and sends it on a line to Griffey in right. Like the rest of Cincinnati's outfielders, Griffey is positioned too deeply. He can't make the play. He catches the ball on a bounce.

Tiant staggers around bewildered in the base path, tripping in the dirt, spinning in the chalk dust. First, he cuts back toward third, then he digs for home.

The screaming crowd now stirs a layer of laughter into their beastly roar. It's gone from high drama to hysterical slapstick. Griffey throws home. First baseman Tony Perez, seeing Tiant cross the plate, jumps and cuts off Griffey's throw. It's very much the proper thing to do except that, unknown to Perez, Luis has missed home. Concepcion races across the infield, hollering that Perez must throw to Bench. The shortstop is unable to make himself heard above the Fenway tumult.

Fisk is on deck. He observes Tiant's failure to touch the plate. Everyone is yelling. The noise is like a hurricane. "Tag the plate!" someone shouts. Pudge motions. He tries to grab Tiant's shirt.

"Hurry up, Luis!" Darrell Johnson screams.

Realizing his mistake, the pitcher backs casually around Bench. He jumps on the plate for the game's first run.

It's the most dramatic baserunning since Stengel won the first game of the 1923 World Series by hitting a two-out, inside-the-park home run on a three-two count in the ninth. It was Casey's biggest hit ever, for he ran it with his shoe slipping off, and he ended it with that one-knee slide and a comical wave of his hand at the 55,307 in attendance.

The bases loaded, Sparky pulls Gullett, brings in Clay Carroll. Fisk walks, making the score two to nothing in favor of Boston. Sparky pulls Carroll, brings in McEnaney. Lynn strikes out, but Rico singles, four to nothing. Burleson singles, five to nothing. Cooper flies out deep to Griffey, six to nothing. And then Tiant once more comes to bat. He strikes out. The inning ends.

The park is on its feet for the last two innings. "Loo-ee! Loo-ee!" Tiant is fired to the hilt. His chest broadens, filled by the ovation. He tugs his cap and continues to make the pitches he needs to make. Cincinnati goes down in order in the eighth and in the ninth. Just like that, with 113 pitches, Tiant has dismantled the Big Red Machine. In the process, he has thrown the first complete World Series game since 1971. It's his fifth key victory in a row. He has now pitched thirty-six straight innings in Fenway Park without allowing an earned run.

And still, Sparky remains unimpressed. He admires only heat, a good snappy fastball, and doesn't respect Tiant's junk-ball shenanigans. He thinks of John Candelaria blowing away his men with ferocious stuff in the third game of the play-offs — now *that* was pitching. "This was the weakest five-hitter I've ever seen," says the manager outside the clubhouse. "I don't know how many shots we hit right at people, shots that were caught or turned into outs."

"We kept hitting the ball," Pete Rose sighs, "and they kept catching it and catching it."

"I'll give Tiant credit though," Sparky allows. "He put nine zeroes up there on the scoreboard and I don't know how much better you can do," he says, before adding cryptically, prophetically, "The only thing they won is one game."

After Tiant, Boston has Bill Lee and Rick Wise, pitchers whose powerfully simple names rekindle the promise of Carl Mays, Joe Bush, Sam Jones, Babe Ruth, the monosyllabic Anglos who won Fenway Park its last World Series pennant in 1918. Lee will start the next game — tomorrow, Sunday afternoon — while Wise is to pitch the third game in Cincinnati on Tuesday evening. Cincinnati may think that it has the better starting pitching, because six of their pitchers won ten or more while only five Boston pitchers accomplished this feat, but each of these two Red Sox has more victories (Wise nineteen, Lee seventeen) than anyone on the Reds' staff.

That night Luis quietly entertains family and friends in Milton. His father plays with the children and then takes a seat in the corner of the downstairs game room. Alone with his thoughts, he sits, a sallow cast to his features, looking at once haunted and proud. He pinches a lit cigarette between his long, slender fingers. People come and go. His son happens by, having finished a game of pool.

The old man reaches out and plucks at Luis, like Fisk tried to do earlier, in the bottom of the seventh. Now it brings down his son and the cue stick he's holding. Luis sits on his father's lap. They exchange a look of devotion, of gratitude. His father pats Luis on the arm.

No one said life was fair. No one ever made any promises whatsoever. Life for Tiant's father has been nothing but struggle, and sorrow, and strife. Now his only child, his one son, has emerged victorious. He loses control and begins to sob.

Luis is also sobbing.

This day has meant everything to them.[21]

OCTOBER 12

BILL LEE AGAINST JACK BILLINGHAM in game two provides a curious matchup of sinker-ball pitchers, one right-handed, one left-handed, both lousy lately. Both have given up historic home runs to Henry Aaron. The Hammer's shot off Billingham was number 714. It came on Aaron's first swing on the 1974 season, and it tied Ruth's all-time home run record. Asked how he handled it, Billingham shrugs. "You do what everyone else does in the ballpark. You just turn your head and watch the ball sail over the wall." His casual indifference infuriates the quote seekers; Billingham seems so lackadaisical that he's nearly dead. Surely he's worried about his reputation, about being regarded as the one who gave up the Hammer's record-tying homer? "Nah," says Jack. "Hank won't be remembered for his seven hundred fourteenth homer and neither will I. He'll be remembered for the last homer he hits."

Bill Lee agrees. Aaron hit his final homer of 1975 off Lee, at Fenway, against a stiff breeze, on the afternoon of September 14. At the time, the Hammer was presumed to be retiring from the game. Lee was comforted to think that he would go down in history for something, even if it's just for surrendering the last blast of the home run king's career, number 745. But after the game, Aaron announced his firm intention to return in 1976 to play for Milwaukee. "I'm mad," Lee admitted. "I threw him his last home run pitch, and thought I'd be remembered forever. Now I'll just have to concentrate and throw him another."

CINCINNATI

Rose, *third base*
Morgan, *second base*
Bench, *catcher*
Perez, *first base*
Foster, *left field*
Concepcion, *shortstop*
Griffey, *right field*
Geronimo, *center field*
Billingham, *pitcher*
(Borbon, *pitcher*)
(McEnaney, *pitcher*)
(Rettenmund, *pinch hitter*)
(Eastwick, *pitcher*)

BOSTON

Evans, *right field*
Doyle, *second base*
Yastrzemski, *left field*
Fisk, *catcher*
Lynn, *center field*
Petrocelli, *third base*
Burleson, *shortstop*
Cooper, *first base*
Lee, *pitcher*
(Drago, *pitcher*)
(Carbo, *pinch hitter*)

Before the second game, a sportswriter runs across Lee in a corridor beneath the park. He asks the pitcher if he thinks it'll rain.

"Yep," snaps Lee. "Otherwise, we'll have a dry planet."

Naturally it rains today. After all, Bill Lee is pitching. Although Lee calls himself "a mediocre ballplayer with a positive outlook," the truth is he's a hurler literally chased by dark clouds. The Red Sox players call Fisk the "Human Rain Delay" because he takes so unbelievably long to do anything — to recover from injuries, to shower, to dress, to get into position, to call for a pitch — but the nickname works for Lee too.[22] Hand him the ball and watch the weather roll in. One game he threw this season lasted six hours when inclement weather continuously interrupted. His last victory came in a downpour, August 24, against the White Sox, with Lee slipping all over the mound, going down while grabbing at ground balls, throwing from a seated position, finishing flat on his back, and, for his twenty-third consecutive inning, not giving up an earned run.

As secretary of state, former Harvard professor, and — ominously — Yankee fan Henry Kissinger throws out the first ball in game two, Lee is playing pitch-catch in the bull pen. A fan in the bleachers leans across the railing. "Hey, Spaceman!" he hollers. "Feelin' good? How do you figure your chances of winning?"

"My chances of winning?" Lee takes a toss from the bull pen catcher. He shrugs. "Fifty-fifty." Lee picks up his jacket, jogs in. He climbs the mound, begins to kick holes in it. He warms up, throwing softly to Fisk. It's pouring rain. There's a gale blowing in off the top of the wall. If this wasn't the World Series, the game would be called and played on some other day, bright with sunshine, with birds singing. But too much advance planning is involved. Championship games aren't lightly rescheduled.

With hungry-wolf eyes, the Reds watch Lee from their dugout. They cannot believe what they are seeing. He is throwing so much *junk!* Most of the players are laughing. They behave as if they might soon shove one another aside in their eagerness to feast at the plate.[23]

Pete Rose leads off and Lee strikes him out.

Morgan grounds to Doyle.

Bench flies out to Lynn.

Just like that, the Red Sox are up. Cooper bangs Billingham's first pitch over Foster's head in left. Given the wind, Foster isn't sure how to play the ball. He stumbles. The footing is treacherous. *Will the ball hit the top of the scoreboard? Or the board itself? Or roll in the corner? Or stop? Or bounce around?* He decides to play the ball on the rebound. He permits it to kiss the wall and he relays it in. Cooper is safe at second. Doyle follows with an infield hit. Sparky telephones the bull pen and, in response, several Cincinnati pitchers rouse themselves and begin to play catch.

In the coaches' box at third base, Zimmer is awfully pleased with the developments at hand. Lee appears to have his old command back. (Zim has never rooted so hard for Lee to pitch well.) And now, with no outs, they have runners at the corners and Yastrzemski at the plate. Zim is careful to speak with Cecil Cooper at third. The coach cannot forget Boston's mishaps on the base paths the day before, such as Dewey in the first inning trying for home, against Zim's specific directions, and getting nailed.

"If the ball is topped in front of the plate," Zim patiently instructs Coop, "then you may stay, if you think you can't get home. But if it's hit on the ground — go!"

Cooper nods as if he understands.

Yastrzemski hits a chopper over the mound. Billingham leaps, spears it, looks at Cooper, throws to Concepcion to force Doyle. Joe Morgan sees Cooper break for the plate and then freeze. "Home," he tells the shortstop. Concepcion fires to Bench and they've got Cooper in a rundown.

Zimmer is irate. *Why even waste your breath talking to these kids?* He recalls Bill Lee's joke, that the only way to turn the Red Sox into a running team would be to draft beautiful women into being their base coaches. Only then would the ballplayers pay attention.

Cooper is tagged out. Yastrzemski takes second on the play, and Pudge singles him home.

Lee makes the run stand up. As with Tiant in game one, the pitcher retires the first ten Reds in order. He's locked in a flow, coasting, getting people out. His mind spins about randomly. He runs into trouble in the fourth when, with one out, Morgan comes to bat. Morgan twitches his left elbow in the batter's box in order to keep his swing loose; Lee thinks he resembles a chicken with one good wing. When Morgan walks, the storm rumbles overhead with apt theatricality. Again, the game verges on a rain delay.

Lee's brain awakens to the dismal situation. That's the first warning sign, the flood of consciousness, the return of absolute awareness. Dedeaux used to admonish him about this. He'd stress that, when Lee was on the mound, he would have to cut off his head and let his body do the work. "Stop thinking," Dedeaux would insist, "or you'll hurt the ball club."

His old teacher proves once more to be correct, as a worried Lee starts to make his pitches too fine. Bench singles to center. Morgan takes third. Tony Perez hits a slow bouncer, and before it even gets to Burleson, Morgan has crossed the plate.

With difficulty, Bill Lee locates a window in his head, flips up the latch, opens the window, and lets all his concerns out. He submerges himself in the task at hand. He makes his way down the lineup without surrendering another run. He's back in business.

The score remains tied, one-one, in the sixth inning, when the top of the order comes to bat in the figure of Pete Rose.

Lee has been having terrific luck this year with his new pitch, the surprise "eephus" that he calls a "slop drop" or "sludge curve," the high, arching, off-speed pitch that descends from the upper atmosphere in no particular rush. No one has managed good contact with it.

Rose squats in the batter's box, as he was taught by his father, in order to reduce the strike zone; Lee thinks he resembles a simian taking a shit.

Fisk calls for the eephus. Rose casually singles it to center field for his first base hit of the Series.

Morgan follows by slapping a one-one curveball to right. It's on the ground, in the hole, and behind the runner. It's ideal for advancing Rose to third. First baseman Cecil Cooper zealously throws himself at it. He gets it, grabs it, and forces Rose at second.

Bench is up to bat, Morgan on first.

One out, one on, one run apiece. The Spaceman works to keep his mind out of it.

Pudge calls for another eephus.

Morgan gets a good jump on the slow curve. He breaks for second. He gets four steps into muck before realizing he has no traction.

Fisk throws. Doyle tags. Morgan, who has stolen two more bases this year than the entire Red Sox team, has been caught stealing for the first time since August 30.

Despite the glum weather, the capacity crowd breaks into a merry jig. *Pudge nailed Little Joe!* The black umbrellas dance. The

yellow ponchos dip and sway. The ovation is tumultuous, the loud-
est heard yet. The roar lingers even as Bench lines a shot past Lee
and into center field. Lynn charges. He fights his way forward,
squishing through mud with every step. His cleats throw up huge
divots. Bench's line drive sinks fast before him, and Lynn struggles
toward it, staggering, stumbling. He resembles a man stabbed in
the back. At last he pitches forward, arms out wildly before him.
He arcs downward, the ball arcs downward, and they come
together in a moment of exhausted effort. Lynn hits the ground as
if throwing himself on a blaze, as a man determined to smother a
rally with his own body. He lies sprawled on the ground, number
nineteen, face in the grass. The particular success of his endeavor
remains unclear. Lynn exhales and then, hands flat against the
grass, pushes himself up. He stoops to retrieve his hat, nonchalantly reveals the baseball gripped in his glove, and jogs in.

Jack Billingham's been matching Lee in strikeouts and ground-
outs. In the bottom of the sixth, he surrenders a one-out single to
Yastrzemski.

Fisk, up next, runs the count full. Yastrzemski takes off on the
next pitch, forcing Concepcion to break toward second just as
Pudge hits a perfect double-play ball, a grounder to short that Concepcion is now out of position to field. The ball spits through the
infield, and the runners advance.

Next, Lynn flies to Griffey in short right. Carl holds at second,
Pudge at first.

Now Petrocelli is up. The crowd trembles with excitement. They
begin to chant. "Ree-co! Ree-co!" Thick puffs of what look to be
smoke sweep through, as if from a nearby battlefield.

Rico singles up the middle, scoring Yastrzemski. Two to one.

Evans walks. The bases are full.

Sparky removes Billingham, inserts Pedro Borbon.

Borbon comes out to throw in the park for the first time since,
some years ago, on a dare, he hurled a baseball from Fenway's
home plate to the bleacher seats in center field without a single

warm-up toss. (The team physician, appalled, never forgave him.) Borbon is well rested. He feels just as bullish as ever. He gets Burleson to fly out and end the inning.

After Griffey strikes out to close the top of the seventh, Bowie Kuhn quits his first-base box to stand at the edge of the Red Sox dugout. It's wretchedly wet now. The commissioner can barely see second base through the rain. He wipes his glasses.

The icy wind blows rain into the press box. It's just too cold and wet. Most of the journalists grab their scorecards, their flasks, their attaché cases, and head into the protected corridors, where they can watch the action on the overhead monitors.

Several park patrons file out and onto the stools of neighborhood bars, Copperfield's, or the Eliot Lounge. They'll see the game's finish on television.

Pieces of unloosed fog drift past the stands, splintering the light of the ballpark into its aggregate hues, wreaking havoc with the perception of distances.

Kuhn brings in the teams and orders the grounds crew to roll out the tarpaulin.

Leading by a score of two to one, the Red Sox retreat to their locker room, pursued by Mr. and Mrs. Kissinger, who in turn are pursued by a phalanx of Secret Service. Lee, glancing at the secretary of state, sees the thick, wavy hair and mistakes him initially for Fred Lynn's father. Then, when he realizes who it is, Lee feels he should demand to know, in reference to recent grain deals made with the Soviet Union, where all of his wheat is going. He restrains himself. The Red Sox are a little awed by this presence in their midst. Kissinger sits on a table, with his famously strained smile and heavy horn-rimmed glasses, signing autographs. He looks like a papa bear in a necktie and a three-piece suit. At one point, he informs one of his agents that he has to go to the bathroom. Several of the Secret Service inspect the facilities.

"They have to check out the john before he uses it," Lee explains to Drago in a knowing whisper. "Make sure no revolutionaries come up through the plumbing."[24]

For a time, after the rest of his club has gone inside, Sparky stays in the dugout, pacing. He looks up at the kids clinging to a Windsor whiskey billboard. Sparky admires their persistence, despite the damp and freezing wind — their dedication. *They're doing more than we are.* He spits. *We have two more innings, six more chances at Lee.* All Sparky can think of is Cleveland in 1954 — Al Rosen, Bobby Avila, Larry Doby — when they couldn't generate anything against the Giants and they lost in four straight.

Presently, he retires to the clubhouse. "Settle down," he tells his players. "Keep calm." It's not much in the way of a pep talk, but then again, he's a baseball manager, not a football coach. He rarely has the chance to address the team at halftime; he hasn't perfected the craft. What he wants now is to get their minds off the scoreboard. He doesn't want them to guess what he's thinking — *Cleveland, 1954* — he doesn't want them to think they're losing. Jack Billingham has pitched too well for them to believe they're losing. They're a run behind — so what? They came from behind forty-seven times this season! They can do this. This shouldn't be hard.

The weather is bad everywhere. It's a miserable, murky Sunday afternoon. All across the nation, people are indoors, flipping around the channels. Fifty million people have tuned in to this game. NBC is nervous about losing the audience if the rain delay continues. They're digging around for entertaining visuals. They can't go into the Red Sox locker room because Kissinger is there, performing some mysterious function of state alongside what seems like three hundred Secret Service agents. Instead, they take a camera down to the Reds' clubhouse. Johnny Bench is interviewed. He is asked what he'll look to do in his next at bat. Bench explains that he's been trying to pull the ball all afternoon, but Bill Lee keeps pitching him outside and away from his strength, and getting him out. "I think I'll take him to the opposite field," Bench admits candidly.[25]

Fifty million Americans absorb this information. None think to warn the Sox that Bench will be fighting the shift and swinging like a number-two hitter.

By the time Bill Lee learns of Bench's new strategy, it'll be too late.

Play resumes after twenty-seven minutes. The score remains two to one. In the top of the ninth, Bench comes to bat. Lee delivers a fastball two inches outside, one inch above the knee. Sure enough, Bench stretches out and slices it off the end of his bat for a double to right. Later Lee will be asked if he had a particular strategy in mind. "Sure," the pitcher will answer. "I was trying not to walk the first man up."

Darrell Johnson strolls to the mound. Gratefully, Lee gives him back the baseball. One pitch into the inning, and he's gone. That's Johnson's job, to come out and get him in situations like that. Unfortunately for DJ, Lee will never ask to be taken out; he's not like Tiant, who'll tell the manager to keep an eye on him if he's feeling vulnerable. Lee will take the ball when it's offered and throw as long as he's asked. But here again, Lee faults the manager for unusual patience in the starter. "When," Lee will later ask rhetorically, "in the memory of organized baseball, has a left-hander who's already thrown eight innings come out to face a Hall of Fame right-handed batter after a rain delay like that?"

With a one-run lead in the ninth, none out, and three right-handed Reds due up, the manager's choice is obvious: Drago. All year, the right-handed Drago has been their bull-pen ace. He had fifteen saves in 1975; the rest of the staff had sixteen. During the scary nights of August and September, when the Orioles seemed nightly to creep closer, when Boston's lead was being threatened in the final innings, it was Drago who walked in from the bull pen and reliably shut down the opposition. He did it earlier this week, against Oakland.

Tonight, he almost does it again. Perez grounds out to Burleson,

Foster pops up to Yastrzemski. Drago fires a fastball past Concepcion. *Strike one.* The park rises to its feet, applauding. Drago misses outside, one and one. The applause renews. Even Kissinger is now sporting a Red Sox cap. Two more strikes and Boston will be two games up on the Big Red Machine.

Knowing that Concepcion likes the ball high, Fisk sets up low and outside. But Drago misses the target, his fastball sailing up and in around the batter's throat.

Concepcion, who made the last out yesterday in game one, doesn't want to be the last out again. He chops madly at the ball, drives it into the dirt in front of Drago. Fisk relaxes. He figures it's playable, it'll get stuck in the mud like every other ground ball this afternoon. Instead, it hits something and skips wildly over Drago's head. Bench runs in to tie the score, two to two. Doyle gloves the ball, but there's no play. Concepcion is on first.

The crowd promptly sits down. Kissinger removes his cap.

Knowing that Concepcion will attempt to steal second, Fisk sets up high and outside. Drago delivers home. Concepcion breaks. Burleson breaks. Fisk's foot slips in the mud. (*Luck is a residue of design,* Sparky thinks again.) The catcher's throw is low. The ball hits in front of the bag. Burleson grabs it and pushes his glove at Concepcion.

"Safe!" cries umpire Dick Stello.

"No!" cries Burleson.

"You missed!" Stello retorts. "You didn't tag him!"

"There's no way I missed! That's not true! I tagged him on the back!"

It's the first stolen base Boston has given up in weeks.

Drago gets the ball. He turns back to deal with the little left-hander Griffey. Drago throws him two good fastballs. Griffey can't catch up. He fouls them both back. The count goes to one and two.

Knowing that Griffey can hit the fastball, Fisk calls for a breaking ball. Drago shakes him off.

Griffey's six-year-old is seated on the third-base side with Birdie, his mother, and Craig, his little brother.

"C'mon, Dad!" says Junior. He crosses his fingers. He leans forward, watching intensely, then tries to cross his brother's fingers for him, but Craig starts to cry because it hurts and Birdie tells him to stop doing whatever he's doing and to just watch his daddy bat.

"But —" Junior starts.

"Enough," his mother replies firmly.

Junior wants to see somebody hit the Green Monster. All this excited talk about how close Fenway's left-field wall is, and nobody from Cincinnati has even gotten it out there, his dad most of all. His dad hasn't even hit a ball out of the infield all day.

Until now. His father correctly guesses fastball. He gets it where he likes it, high and away, and he punches it through the alley in left center.

Concepcion comes around to score the go-ahead run, three to two.

Griffey stands on second base, his heart pounding, looking up in the stands. That was the biggest hit of his life. He beams at his eldest boy, gives him a big wink.

"When I grow up," Junior tells Craig breathlessly, "I'm gonna play for the Cincinnati Reds."

In Copperfield's and the Eliot Lounge, the mood curdles. Everything had been so festive until Concepcion got that lucky hit and then the second-base umpire blew the call on Burleson's tag. Now it's a morgue, and the spirits that had fired their hopes are making their heads hurt.

Drago walks Geronimo to get to the relief pitcher, Rawly Eastwick, who grounds into a force play for the third out.

In Riverfront Stadium, there is applause. The Cincinnati Bengals, the football team that shares Riverfront with the Reds, have just finished playing before a sellout crowd of 51,220. The field is empty, but the fans don't leave. Instead, throughout the Cincinnati stands, locals play transistor radios as the second game of the World Series goes into the bottom of the ninth, with their guys leading by a run.

Eastwick has good movement on the ball. Quickly, Burleson fouls to Griffey in short right, Carbo (batting for Drago) lines weakly to Foster, and Cooper pops to Concepcion.

It is over.

Journalists descend upon Boston's locker room. They point out to Carl Yastrzemski that the Red Sox have not lost a game like this since the pennant race became serious in August.

Carl answers as best he can. Yes, he is disappointed at the loss. . . . No, he can't gauge what this means. . . . He pulls his double-knit jersey up over his head and heaves it toward the laundry pile. Journalists read frustration into this action; it is the tired throw of an aging star wondering how many more postseasons he'll see. He unties his cleats. Someone opens a Coors for him. He lights a filtered cigarette. He pulls his knee braces down around his calves, lowers himself into a wooden folding chair.

At harvest time, his favorite task was always loading the trucks. He savored the challenge. It required a certain concentration to do it right, concentration and determination, the same things that make him such a fine ballplayer. The truck would chug down the rows, belching smoke while bags of potatoes were handed up, bags weighing upward of seventy-five or eighty pounds, which then quickly had to be stacked eight high in the back of the truck.[26] Hard work.

"I don't mind hard work," Carl says aloud, apropos of nothing. The journalists dutifully jot it down. Yastrzemski slouches so as to rest his feet up against the metal frame of his locker, fixes a stare on his red stockings, and sips grimly from his can of beer.

The press has established an interview room underneath the left-field stands. Several hundred of them are seated when Bill Lee enters. Usually, the managers come, and a few representatives from the winning team. They've never had a loser come in before. Lee is urged to get up before the microphones. He looks around and smiles. "This is just like *A Clockwork Orange.*"

"What do you mean?" a newsman asks.

"I feel like I've been shot with some strange drug and you're watching how I react."

There's a moment of quiet as the scribblers transcribe this. "How did you feel out there?" someone then yells.

"I had good vibrations . . . a definite sense that things were going to be good . . . a spiraling type of feeling."

"Do you blame Drago for losing your game?" asks another.

"Fuck, no," scoffs Lee. "Drago did one hell of a job. We were one out away from victory. There was just that one ground ball. When that ball gets put on the ground, it either hits a hole or a glove. The law of averages. You don't mess with the law of averages."

"Spaceman, do you throw many fastballs?"

"The one Bench hammered into right," he says with a blank look. "That was my best fastball."

"What other pitches do you throw?"

"I have the usual assortment: curves, sliders, screwballs, and three kinds of fastballs — slow, semiquick, and slower. After that, I start going to my junk."

"What was your worst pitch today? The pitch you threw Bench in the ninth?"

"No. My worst pitch was with three and two on Morgan when I walked him."

Another newsman wonders about Lee's pro-Garrity remarks earlier in the season. "Have you been involved in the busing problem here?"

"Involved?" Lee blinks. "How, as a tail gunner on a bus?" He lolls his head around, trying to loosen up his neck, then continues. "No, but I do go to South Boston every Monday night as an Army reserve recruiter and I talk to the people there. They know where I stand. Maybe busing isn't the answer but try it at least. People got to live together. The blacks, the Puerto Ricans, everybody. We live together on a ball club with no fists raised . . . except once in a while."

"Mr. Lee, the Series now continues on to Cincinnati, where the Reds have triumphed sixty-four times this year, the best home record in the history of the National League. Is your team worried?"

"Not at all. We'll come back. What the Reds don't realize is that we're a great AstroTurf team. Just ask the Kansas City Royals. We've got the ground-ball hitters, a shortstop who throws hard, and a second baseman with range. We're just as good as they are."

"What is your overall impression of the Series so far?"

"Hmmm . . ." Lee gives it some thought. "Tied."

"What do you think of Riverfront Stadium?"

"It's another one of those concrete donuts made by a pharmaceutical company."

"Are you always this downhearted after you lose a World Series game?" one reporter asks.

"Ah now, why be downhearted?" Lee retorts. "I did my best, and I lost. I'll still be alive tomorrow, barring a traffic accident. And now, if you'll excuse me, I have to get some ice and vodka for my arm. It, uh . . . it opens the pores."[27]

OCTOBER 13

IN THE MIDFORTIES, before he became Sparky, George Anderson begged to be the batboy for the University of Southern California. A poor student, Anderson knew there was no way he could ever get into college. He was smart, but not in that way. He knew the reputation of USC's sports programs, and he loved their baseball team particularly, and he wanted to glean whatever he could from just watching and listening. He communicated this to the baseball coach, whose name was Rod Dedeaux, and Dedeaux welcomed him in, and Anderson stayed to learn from him for five years. Nearly twenty-five years later, there remain just two people in the world who don't call George Anderson "Sparky." One is Carol, his wife; the other is Dedeaux, Anderson's oldest friend in baseball. When the World Series comes to Cincinnati for games three to five, Sparky discovers an unsettling fact. Dedeaux is traveling with the Red Sox party, staying with the Red Sox entourage, even sitting with the Red Sox rooters. Sparky says he understands, with Bill Lee and Fred Lynn both Red Sox and Dedeaux disciples.

Still, Sparky is hurt. His managerial style is heavily indebted to Dedeaux.

The men from the Cincinnati news outlets ask Pete Rose if he's glad to be home, and how he liked his trip to Boston.

"The lobster was good," he quips, "but the weather was worthless."

Rose generally feels that the papers are making too much of the change in cities while grossly underestimating the significance of the change in parks. It's true that Boston is the land of colleges, the seaport of Irish-Catholic Democrats, and now the Series comes to the country of pork, soap, and beer, the sleepy river town of German Protestant Republicans. But both cities are enthusiastic and loyal baseball towns, and that's all that really matters, so in that sense they aren't so dissimilar. The fields are truly the difference because Cincinnati has AstroTurf, and the lines at Riverfront are equal distances, and there are few surprises.

Rose started with the Reds in Crosley Field, which was Cincinnati's version of Fenway, a quaint, creaky, character-laden neighborhood joint with inadequate seating capacity, crummy parking options, an asymmetrical tract dictating an asymmetrical playing field, patron views blocked occasionally by poles. The flaws of Crosley Field were addressed in the design of Riverfront, a clean piece of architecture with twice the number of seats, an added parking structure, improved ingress and egress. Everyone was happy. Pitchers liked the fence distances, fielders liked the truer bounce of artificial turf, base stealers liked the swift track. No Reds' face lit up more brightly to see their new home than that of Pete Rose, who confirmed his destiny with a glance at the broad alleys of the outfield. With more of his hits likely to squirt safely through the infield on the speedy carpet, and all that room off center to deposit bloopers and bleeders, Rose spoke with increasing cockiness of being able to surpass Ty Cobb's all-time hits total of 4,191, a sacred record assumed by generations of baseball fans to be as unassailable as DiMaggio's fifty-six-game hitting streak. And a decade from this moment, after Rose amasses more of everything else — more at bats, more games, more National League doubles, more automobiles, more breasty mistresses, more paternity suits, more gambling debts — he will in fact succeed in the inconceivable: he will amass more hits than Ty Cobb. In 1985 Riverfront will resound with a tumultuous ovation as their native son stands on first base after hit number 4,192. Steve Garvey will extend his G.I. Joe–hand and thank Rose for the memories. For the first time, Pete Rose will not know what to do on a ball field. His team's batboy, Pete Rose Jr., will jog out to extend congratulations. Young Pete will later recall this as their first-ever hug. Looking in the sky, Pete Rose will see his own square-jawed father sitting up in heaven, in front of Ty Cobb. Another first: Pete Rose will cry in front of his son.

Right now, though, it's 1975, and everywhere Pete turns, people want to shake his hand, they want him to sign his name alongside "2,547," his current hits total. *Two thousand five hundred forty-seven, that's nothing!* He is surrounded, but he is also stranded, a cocky visionary, alone in his impossible confidence. Only he can see that someday he will hold the record. Nobody believes more in Pete Rose than Pete Rose — and even then, truth be told, he believes only because his father never did.

OCTOBER 14

ARRIVING NOW IN THE BIRTHPLACE of one of the major league's oldest franchises, the World Series renews as a face-off of right-handed comebacks, Gary Nolan pitted against Rick Wise.

Jim Rice travels with the Red Sox. He's been suiting up for each game and sitting in the dugout. Despite his size and strength, he can contribute nothing.

Tony Conigliaro bumps into him in the hotel dining room. They exchange hellos. Tony comes close and motions at Rice's bandaged wrist. "I know how you feel," he says quietly. "Just be proud of what you accomplished in the regular season."[28]

"Okay," Rice responds. "Thanks." He really isn't sure why Tony sounds so solicitous. Boston's got a lot of good, young players. They have the nucleus for a great team. It's not as if there won't be more postseason appearances. There'll be other times for Jim Rice to shine.

Rice returns to his meal. He shares a table with a Boston sports-writer. A man holding five baseballs walks over. "Which one of you is Jim Rice?" the man asks.

Rice immediately points at the sportswriter.

"I'm sorry that I don't know your face, Mister Rice," the man tells the sportswriter. "Football's really more my bag. College foot-ball. The Buckeyes, they're my guys. Anyway, would you be super enough to sign these baseballs for my children and their friends? They're very big fans."

"Of course," the sportswriter murmurs. He writes "Jim Rice" upon the balls. The man thanks him profusely, bows, and goes.

The sportswriter gives the ballplayer a hard look. "Just make sure you have tomorrow's column in by ten-thirty tonight," he instructs Rice. "And it better be super."[29]

BOSTON	CINCINNATI
Cooper, *first base*	Rose, *third base*
Doyle, *second base*	Griffey, *right field*
Yastrzemski, *left field*	(Rettenmund, *pinch hitter*)
Fisk, *catcher*	Morgan, *second base*
Lynn, *center field*	Perez, *first base*
Petrocelli, *third base*	Bench, *catcher*
Evans, *right field*	Foster, *left field*
Burleson, *shortstop*	Concepcion, *shortstop*
Wise, *pitcher*	Geronimo, *center field*
(Burton, *pitcher*)	Nolan, *pitcher*
(Cleveland, *pitcher*)	(Darcy, *pitcher*)
(Carbo, *pinch hitter*)	(Carroll, *pitcher*)
(Willoughby, *pitcher*)	(McEnaney, *pitcher*)
(Moret, *pitcher*)	(Eastwick, *pitcher*)
	(Armbrister, *pinch hitter*)

That night, at 8:45 P.M., the president of the United States, Gerald R. Ford, steps before a Republican dinner gathering in Hartford, Connecticut. "For those of you who are interested," he begins, "the

Red Sox are ahead, one to nothing." After the crowd's applause subsides, the president elaborates. "I'm told that Carlton Fisk hit a home run."

The home run is the most satisfying yet in young Pudge's life, not only because it's the very first home run hit in this tightly contested World Series and puts his team ahead, but because the person nearest to him at the time he hits the long, second-inning shot to left is Johnny Bench. Pudge wants badly to outdo Cincinnati's legendary clutch slugger, and now, of the two catchers, it is he, Fisk, who has homered first.

The next time Pudge returns to the batter's box, with one out in the fourth inning, Bench acknowledges receiving the message loud and clear: he has Gary Nolan pitch around Fisk to get to Lynn. With Pudge on first, Lynn singles to right. Griffey throws toward third, but Fisk is already safe. Lynn takes a wide turn at first. On a grass field, he'd be able to take second on that play; the ball wouldn't get so quickly to Griffey. Mulling this over, Lynn's concentration lapses. Cincinnati's sharp-eyed shortstop notices: Concepcion intercepts Griffey's throw to Rose with a snap of his mitt and relays the ball instead to Perez. Lynn quickly cuts back toward the first-base bag but slips on the wet artificial turf. He is out.

These are the precise fundamentals that allow Cincinnati to neutralize their leaky pitching, the instant ability of their infielders to detect a baserunning mistake and, thinking as one, take advantage of it. This happened in game two, when Morgan saw Cooper hesitate on the base path, when Bench caught Evans straying off second base; it happened in game one, when Lynn tagged up on a pop-up to short center and headed home, when Evans futilely tried to score from second on a single. Each action resulted in an out, each depended upon perfect execution and telepathy between Concepcion, Morgan, and Bench, and each deflated an incipient Boston rally.

If Concepcion hadn't picked off Lynn, there'd be runners at first and third, and the infield would be out of position to field the

Petrocelli grounder that immediately follows. Instead, with two away and Pudge on third, Joe Morgan can play Rico deep, and when he bounces up through the box, Morgan scampers back, snags it behind second, spins, throws, and nips Rico at first.

An elderly woman watching channel thirty-eight in Marble-head, Massachusetts, questions whether the pillow she traditionally hugs for good luck is still working.[30] The Sox have not scored and the inning is over. She looks at it another way, though, and sees her influence at work. For it's not as if the Reds have much to crow about. Rick Wise knows that they like the ball inside, so he keeps the ball away. He's got his good fastball going and, just like Tiant and Lee in the earlier games, he zips through the lineup. He gets through eleven Reds without giving up a hit. In the fourth inning, a gambling cup is passed about the press box. Setting aside their press handouts and stat sheets, the writers stuff in dollars, taking bets on which Red will break up Wise's no-hitter. No one imagines that Cincinnati can go much longer without a hit, though of course the Reds are well aware that Wise no-hit them in 1971, and quite nearly no-hit them a second time.

With two outs in the bottom of the fourth, Wise faces a slumping Tony Perez. Cincinnati's all-time RBI leader hasn't managed to get a hit in the Series. He's batting today in the number-four spot, with Bench in the number five, so as to get some better pitches to hit. He lined out to Lynn in his first at bat; this time he draws a walk.

Sparky observes Cooper playing back, knows that Wise has a poor move to first, figures the game is still young, his guys are behind, and Wise is working on a no-hitter, so he decides to send Perez. He relays the steal sign to the third-base coach, who relays it to Tony, who is so astonished that he checks three times to make sure he received it correctly. He has stolen twenty-nine bases in twelve years; his one stolen base this year was on the back side of a double steal. Dutifully, he gets a big lead. When Wise throws a slow breaking ball, Perez takes off. Fisk's throw is late.

They'll later ask about his baserunning times. "I don't know how fast I am," Tony will say. "But if anybody tries to time me going down to first base, I'll kill him."

Wise scowls fiercely through his steamed-up glasses. He is a vain man, tart and humorless, and Perez's surprise steal displeases him immensely. Perez, of all people, daring to run on him! Wise depends upon his mean reputation to challenge the hitter with hard strikes and a savvy pitch selection. *Does nobody fear me?* First he was traded to St. Louis in exchange for Steve Carlton and everybody felt Philadelphia got the better deal. Then he was traded to Boston for Reggie Smith and the consensus was that St. Louis received a bargain. This year, he won nineteen games, the most on Boston's goddamn staff, then he easily beat Oakland in the playoffs. He should be, by any objective standard, one of the most feared and admired pitchers in organized baseball. Instead, he earns the game three assignment. Instead, Tony Perez steals on him as if Wise was some slow-armed Sammy Nobody. . . .

Flustered with unusual doubts, Wise hangs a slider to Bench, who drives it screeching into the night for Cincinnati's first hit. The ball crashes against the facade in far-off left center with a blasting sound that reasserts Bench's superiority, in every way, over Fisk. On one hit, the Reds now lead, two to one.

A high school girl in Roxbury looks askance at her blue nail polish. She put it on last Saturday when the Red Sox won their first game. She figured it was a good-luck sign, and these two teams being so close, all possible magic must be mustered on the side of Boston.[31]

And her magic was working for a bit there. How else to explain the early departure of Gary Nolan? Before the game, his mind was sharp, his emotions profound. And then, suddenly, his neck was stiff. (*This was, of course, the doing of my blue nail polish.*)

By the top of the fifth, she notices that her polish is chipping, the Red Sox are losing, and Wise's concentration is disintegrating. He lets another breaking ball get up, and Concepcion dispatches it over the wall in left center. Geronimo follows with a blast into the right-field stands. The bespectacled Wise fans the opposing pitcher next, but he gives up a triple to Pete Rose, and he's yanked.

The girl debates repainting her nails as Darrell Johnson brings in Jim Burton, a poor choice. Griffey walks. Morgan hits a sacrifice fly to score Rose. Now Reggie Cleveland replaces Burton and, with Griffey at second, strikes out Perez to end the inning. Cincinnati is on top, five to one.

In the sixth, she has the cotton balls out and the acetone at hand, with a bottle of a new color nearby, when Pat Darcy (pitching in relief of Nolan) walks Carl Yastrzemski on four pitches. She stops what she is doing, and Darcy walks Fisk. She puts away her nail-polish remover. Darcy uncorks a wild pitch and each runner advances. Lynn flies to Foster in left center. Yastrzemski tags up. The score is five to two.

Reggie Cleveland gets three quick outs in the bottom of the inning. He's due to bat in the top of the seventh with the bases empty and two outs.

"Carbo!" Darrell Johnson calls. He sends Bernie out to pinch-hit for Cleveland and instructs Willoughby to get loose.

Bernie finds himself in the batter's box, facing big Clay Carroll, his old bunk mate. *Hiya, Hawk!* Carbo nearly hails the hillbilly in greeting. Before the Series, he asked Hawk for an autograph. He wouldn't be comfortable asking that of just anyone, but Hawk is a good friend; he signed a picture with wishes for the best of luck.

The first pitch is a fastball and Carbo nails it over the left-field wall, for which a girl in Roxbury whom he's never met feels responsible. She's grateful she kept her nails blue.

As he rounds the bases, Bernie spies another old buddy, Pete Rose. Bernie made a lot of friends on the Cincinnati team, which is natural, since he's so outgoing and sincere. His affection for Rose probably ran the deepest. Pete greatly resembles Carbo's dad — the big, strong arms, the husky body, the work ethic, the arrogance (which time and again proves not to be arrogance so much as a factual assessment). Bernie was always terrified of his dad. Now, as he nears the bag of dirt that is third base, Bernie can't resist a little taunting.

"Don't you wish you were that strong?" he shouts at Rose, who tells Carbo, politely, to go fuck himself.[32]

Carroll later seizes back the autographed photo and rips it into a thousand pieces.

Boston enters the ninth trailing by two.

Will McEnaney has relieved Carroll, who relieved Darcy, who relieved Nolan. Petrocelli lines a single to center. Rawly Eastwick relieves McEnaney, and now Evans is up. Zimmer, in the third-base coaches' box, maintains a running mutter over the chalk with Rose. The third baseman is exultant, supremely confident of victory, but Zim warns him to be prepared. Zim knows how often Dewey Evans is underestimated. (Evans even underestimates himself.) In truth, bringing in Eastwick greatly facilitates the situation: Dewey can get a better rip at a fastball than at McEnaney's breaking stuff. Boston's right fielder has been promising to let his bat go out after the ball more.

"Watch," Zim murmurs, "Dewey'll hit it out."

Eastwick felt good warming up in the bull pen, but now he doesn't have anything. He isn't concentrating. He isn't throwing right. He isn't doing anything right. His fastball is terrible. It isn't moving, it isn't fast. It is just dead. It's high and inside when he introduces it to Dewey Evans, who pounds it deep to left.

George Foster follows it to the wall. He looks up, incredulous, as it clears the fence. Despondent, Foster leans against the wall for solace. Their four-run lead is gone; the score is tied. Foster touches the wall tenderly, an intimate gesture, almost lonely. He quietly thinks of the wall, this outfield wall he knows so well; how could it betray him? He doesn't know what to make of it. Slowly he turns, starts back to his position. His hands dangle uselessly at the ends of his arms.

An elderly woman in Marblehead clutches her good-luck pillow and apologizes abundantly for ever doubting its awesome power.

Rose gulps, stares wide-eyed at Zimmer.

"Told you so!" Zim sings out. He smiles, and spreads his hands.

Well, Eastwick blandly tells himself, *some people are just going to hit the ball. You can't get everyone out.* But Rawly has been weakened, Morgan can see that. As Dewey circles the bases, as the

Boston dugout pours out in riotous celebration, Joe strolls to the mound.

"Listen now," Morgan says quietly. He places a steady hand against the small of Rawly's back. "The same thing happened against Pittsburgh, and we won. Okay?"

Rawly blinks. He takes off his cap and kicks the rubber. "Okay." His voice is hoarse with shock and holds a note halfway between disbelief and pleading. He raises his head. *Bear down. Keep pitching.*

Burleson loops a single to center, but Willoughby sacrifices, Cooper flies out, and Rawly's out of the inning. He swallows hard and runs in. He feels okay. That's the thing about Joe. He picks them up all the time.

In the tenth, the magic looks to be favoring the Sox. With no outs and Doyle aboard, Yastrzemski comes to bat. Darrell Johnson ponders a risky strategy — having Carl perform a sacrifice bunt. It'll be like Tony Perez stealing second, the last thing anybody expects. A big power threat dribbling weakly before the plate. Rose will sure as hell be surprised! It'll be like Bench bunting, and never in Pete's life has he seen Bench bunt; you just don't do it. The eyes of the Boston manager gleam darkly with the satisfaction of an imminent ambush. *They'll be throwing the ball all over the place. Even lardass Denny Doyle should make second, maybe third on that.* But DJ folds his arms and, for now, signals nobody, not Zim in the third-base box, not Carl at home. He'll allow Carl to get to a one-strike count before ordering him to lay down the surprise attack.

Eastwick foils DJ's scheme by immediately presenting Yastrzemski with a dead fastball, high and outside, which Carl can't resist. He powers it to dead center, Geronimo leaps at the fence and catches it.

Fisk hits into a double play.

The tie continues into the bottom of the inning. Geronimo leads off by grounding a single to center just out of Doyle's diving reach. Fisk's mind locks in on Geronimo. This guy looks like a runner, but he only stole thirteen bases all year. How dangerous could he be?

Fisk imagines getting the double play, or, better yet, nailing Geronimo if/when he dares to steal. Pudge is eager to show up Bench.

Up to bat comes a pinch hitter, Armbrister. Pudge remains oblivious. Ed Armbrister has what, seven pinch hits in his entire career? Pudge can't recall. When Armbrister squares around to bunt and bounces one high before the plate, Pudge pounces. "Fair ball," cries home-plate umpire Larry Barnett. "The ball is in play." Pudge, still thinking of the lead runner, of nailing Geronimo, runs into Armbrister, who has stutter stepped while exiting the box. It's a clumsy moment. Having come off the bench, Armbrister is not as heated as Fisk; he backs up uncertainly. Pudge barehands the ball. He's standing next to Armbrister, but he does not tag him. Instead, he aims one down to Burleson at second — *Geronimo!* — and, of all things, rifles it into center field. Automatically Pudge spins, starts down the first-base line to back up the — but there's Armbrister again! The guy's still running to first, Christ! Fisk clips the back of his calf. Armbrister nearly trips, but stumbles safely to first.

Of the thirty-two million viewers, Rod Dedeaux, from his seat just above the visitor's dugout, most likely knows what will immediately transpire. It is, after all, something he drills into each of his boys, several merciless hours in the sun every day spent backing up second, and one of his all-time best baseball children is in position right now. Fred Lynn gets the ball. Of course. Alertly, as always, he's sprinting up the middle when Fisk overthrows Burleson. Lynn scoops it and, being left-handed, fires it to third without pivoting. Dedeaux thinks Geronimo is out, but he is ruled safe. Rico keeps the tag on him, though, and Geronimo overslides. Rico feels a brief, calm exhilaration. He looks up, but there's no umpires around to call the runner out. They're all turned and watching Pudge.

The two collisions with Armbrister have the catcher rattled: he's a take-charge fellow, an agent of anticipation; he doesn't care for these sorts of surprising intimate contacts. Now he's livid. A guy on second and third and still no outs! Fisk's petulant posture rings so convincingly that every viewer suddenly feels the same thing —

Armbrister got in Fisk's way. He interfered. The Red Sox manager sprints out but seems unable to recall the names of the players involved. "I'm telling you the man interfered with that man on the play!" he screams at the home-plate umpire. Fisk gets into it, a belligerent bulge of chewing tobacco in his cheek, but has to stop arguing with the umpire in order to spit. The manager marches up the line to holler at the first-base umpire awhile, then comes back home, desperate to make these men in black see Fisk's, and his, and now every viewer's, version. "I'll tell you one thing," Johnson snarls in disgust. "It's a lousy operation. And you know that!" The home-plate umpire shakes his head, begins to disagree, but the manager cuts him off. "A lousy operation!" Johnson shouts one last time, retreating to the dugout.

If the same play had happened to me, Sparky admits to himself, *I would have gone apeshit.* He coughs a smile into his fist. *Guys in the bars love plays like that; they'll be shooting the shit about that call until next spring.*

Bench feels Fisk showed poor judgment. *He should have tagged Armbrister after the collision, then worried about the other guy.* But that's Pudge, he doesn't take the easy out, no sir; that's just not his way; he's goddamn Carlton Fisk; his name is loaded with obscene-sounding consonants; he won't surrender even a sacrifice bunt, he has to try to turn it into something spectacular, an inordinately difficult double play, even with the game on the line.

Boston brings in its fifth pitcher, Rogelio Moret, who walks Pete Rose intentionally to load the bases. Merv Rettenmund, a World Series veteran, then bats in place of the less-experienced Ken Griffey. Boston's infield shortens up and the outfield plays shallow. With a high kick of his right leg and a wide swoop of his left arm, Moret strikes out Rettenmund. Joe Morgan is next. Moret gets two strikes on him. Joe is waiting for something to punch, a ball he can hit in the air. He gets it. With a swing every bit as fluid and stylish as sweet DiMaggio's, Morgan sends the ball over the head of Fred Lynn to score Geronimo.

The Reds are up, two games to one, in the Series.

Pudge spins, hurls his catcher's mask in a rage. It hits the back-stop and lodges in the screen behind home plate.

President Ford has meanwhile departed the Republican dinner in Connecticut. His glistening limousine races down the midnight streets of Hartford. Police neglect to guard an intersection. A puffy-eyed teenager in a yellow automobile fails to stop. He broadsides the president. Ford is unhurt. The news is flashed up on the message board of Riverfront. Sparky notes an irony. "Isn't it strange," he says, winking at one of the batboys, "a baseline collision is gonna get remembered longer than a collision that took place on the same evening involving the president of the United States?"

Armbrister's controversial bunt also will be remembered longer than the ninth-inning comeback home run by Evans, the record-tying barrage of six total home runs, the first consecutive home runs by number-seven (Concepcion) and -eight (Geronimo) hitters, the first night pinch-hit home run (Carbo). In the visitor's club-house, despite the tense and unprecedented exchange of clutch World Series slugging, the bunt is all anyone will discuss.[33]

The players sit slumped in front of their lockers, chewing and spitting brown juice on the green carpet. Most are in only baseball trousers and black-sleeved undershirts, but Pudge still wears his gear, his chest protector and shin guards. Tonight the Human Rain Delay moves even slower than usual, as if he cannot accept that the game is finished. "This is fucking brutal," Fisk blurts finally. Then he stands, scoops up three magazines from his locker, and flings them across the room. His words tumble out in a rage. "He bunted the ball, it shot right up in the air, he stood there, I had to go up for a rebound over him to get the ball, he stood right there, I probably tagged him, pushed him out of the way to throw, he's out of the box, three feet in front of the plate, it should have been a double play. And he said, *no interference.*"

The pitcher Willoughby stands nearby in muddy cleats. "You had the ball," he remembers. He's the sidearm, sinker-throwing, short-relieving right-hander who was on the mound at the time, and he saw the whole thing from a distance of sixty feet. "The man went charging into you. It very obviously *was* interference."

More players are standing now, pacing and muttering. There is an encroaching steamy mist and the sound of water pattering against tile.

Yastrzemski nods and spits.

"I don't know," says Rico. He's distraught, sitting on the edge of an equipment box. "It looked that way." And then Petrocelli, the reliable peacekeeper, throws his sweatshirt on the floor. "Why should I say I don't know? Of course I know. It was interference, pure and simple. Millions of people saw it."

These close games tend to bring the Red Sox close together. Two tough losses in a row, both at the last minute — the club blames the rookie umpires. There was the balk call on Tiant in game one, the blown call on Concepcion's ninth-inning steal attempt in game two, and now, worst of all, this. "Barnett's call," says Willoughby, "that was a travesty to the game of baseball."

"I'm an infielder," Pudge asserts. He's viciously angry now. "I'm fielding the ball in front of the plate. He can't run into me. Do I got to wait till the ball hits the ground to field it? It's just like a pop-up between the plate and first. I'm an infielder fielding the ball and he stands right in my way and I probably tagged him pushing him out of the way. I don't even recall that."

Bill Lee, kicking agitatedly about in shower clogs, is convinced he saw Pudge tag Armbrister.

"No interference call," Willoughby points out, "no out call, we lose the game."

Lee nods. He looks meaningfully at Drago and Carbo, his mutinous buddies, his simpaticos. "We should put baseball back in the hands of the people."

Willoughby snorts. He scores the Series on three fingers: "Reds one. Red Sox one. Umpires one."

Recalling the bonus awarded to the Series victors, Carbo leaps to his feet. He's never been one to hide his feelings. "Motherfuckers!" He's worried about his share of the spoils. "The umpires are taking ten thousand dollars out of each of our pockets!" he screams. "How about if *they* don't get paid when *they* don't perform the way *they* should?"

Pudge keeps talking. "— he ran flush into me, really like smashing into a linebacker. It might as well be the Cincinnati Bengals out there playing the Patriots. It's a fuckin' shame to lose a game on a play like that. All it takes is a little bit of guts to call that play. The most important series of the year and you have to lose it like that. That's a double play right there, and they score the winning run. He's got to get out of my way. If he stays in the box, there's no argument. But he's in fair territory, in front of the plate. Barnett said there can't be interference on the play. Why can't there be? You might as well throw a body block at the catcher, then run to first."

Drago is also stirred up. This is what he does. He throws hard and talks loud. When he's not relieving, his job is to be the obnoxious one. He's the main holler guy on the bench, more than Bernie or the Spaceman. With gleaming eyes narrowed and mustache sneering nastily, he insults opponents. He spreads masculinity-impugning innuendoes. He rattles nerves and ruins concentration. He plays mind games.[34] Just now he is standing with fists balled up, heaping extravagant curses upon the umpires, asking why they don't let the players choose who gets to work the Series.

Lee continues moving throughout the locker room, screaming. He begins to believe that a more strenuous argument from their manager might have made a difference. "Darrell didn't give it his all," he insists hotly. "If it had been me, I would have climbed up Barnett's back and bitten his ear off. I would have van Goghed him."

Luis Tiant pads in from the shower, towel clutched about his waist, cigar stuffed in his mouth. He lacks patience with these crybaby complaints. Coming from his background, going through the heartsick separation of family, his perspective is big. He sees what's important. This isn't.

He loves this team, these guys; they're all strong individuals, all very distinct. Now they're going to have to come together as a unit, amid the tension and publicity, and help each other over these hurtles. Tiant's particular specialty is physical comedy: he's the clubhouse cutup, the clown who'll throw a bucket of ice water on you when you're in the shower or on the john, or he'll put a match to the paper you're reading, he'll tease and cajole and make a hilarious show of himself to get everybody laughing — this is how he works, because humor, he believes, is crucial, whereas bitching and moaning isn't at all constructive.

"Look," Tiant says, "you feel so violent about umpire, you should go over and lynch him. I am man, I will lead you. Come on! Come on!"[35]

The vision of this gnarled man, hairy and stinky and nearly naked, with a beaten body so full of suspicious bones that it cracks and snaps with any motion, smoking a long Cuban cigar as he leads them in the first post-Series lynching of a baseball umpire — this subdues most of them. They aren't laughing, but neither are so many upset anymore.

Yastrzemski, however, stays angry. Usually Tiant's most reliable partner in pranks and pratfalls and locker-room shenanigans, Carl really wanted to win this game. It reminds him of how they got jobbed out of game one of the 1967 World Series because a scheduling conflict cut short their batting practice, or how they lost the 1972 pennant from a calendar screwup. When you win on the field but lose anyway, it'll hang you. And this game, goddammit, they deserved this one. Carl recaps the game's heroics in his head: *Wise's three no-hit innings early and Willoughby's three shutout innings late, one and two-thirds' perfect innings of relief from Reggie Cleveland, the home runs by Fisk, Carbo, and Evans . . . pearls before umpire swine who can't even read the rule book.* "So *this* is the World Series?" Carl scoffs.

Tiant shrugs, draws on his cigar, and begins to whistle.

"Next year," Carl continues, "the Series is going to be between San Diego and the Angels. Yeah, it'll be their turn. The umpires aren't chosen on merit; maybe the teams shouldn't be either." He recites a short history lesson, reminding everybody that this was the same Larry Barnett who, in Baltimore in September, called Carl safe at home even though earlier in the play the second-base umpire already had called him out.

Yastrzemski is personally affronted. Besides blowing the Armbrister call, Barnett punched him out on an ankle-high three-two pitch in the eighth. Carl hates nothing more than being called looking. It shouldn't happen, as long as the umpires respect his knowledge of the strike zone. Earlier in the season, when a home-plate umpire failed to display this respect, calling him out on a shitty pitch from Ed Figueroa, Carl knelt and buried home in dirt, piling it high atop the plate with both hands. He got thrown out of the game, but that was worth it. After all, no umpire ever dared to punch out Ted Williams on strikes.

"The best teams in baseball are in this Series," Carl says, "but the best umpires aren't. They take turns, no matter how competent they are. Why don't the teams take turns? Next year, how about San Diego and the Angels playing, no matter where they finish?"

"There's going to be a great outpouring of sympathy for us," predicts Lee. "The country is going to go crazy. The people of Fairbanks, Alaska, are going to start sending letters to Bowie Kuhn, start calling his house. There's going to be such an outcry that we're going to have to play the game over tomorrow. You wait and see."

The switchboards at the *Boston Globe* are in fact jammed with callers seeking a way to get in touch with the commissioner of baseball. In Prospect, Ohio, where Larry Barnett lives with his wife and daughter, the police are alerted by the FBI. Plausible threats have been made against Barnett's family. One telegram arrives from an anonymous gambler who promises to avenge the money he lost from Barnett's failure to call interference. The Boston police guarantee Barnett round-the-clock protection should the Series return to Fenway. "It is probably an understatement to say there are people in Boston who don't like him as an umpire," admits police department spokesman George Landry, "but to threaten violence against him personally is another thing."

OCTOBER 15

THE OVERCAST MORNING finds Tony Perez and his wife, Pituka, in downtown Cincinnati, happily strolling and shopping together, and taking full advantage of the newfangled pedestrian conveniences.[36] Tony wears a flexible raincoat, tan slacks, a white shirt, and loafers. He hoists an umbrella over Pituka, who is dressed in a colorful pantsuit. Tony is not usually one to accompany his wife on her shopping ventures, but he is superstitious. Things haven't been going right for him, so he's changing his way of doing things. Yesterday he stayed home and rested. That didn't help. Today he goes out.

Tony hasn't had a base hit since October 5. In the first two games of the play-offs, he went five for eight. Then, against John Candelaria, his bat went cold, he lost his swing, his timing. Against the Red Sox, he has struck out five times, lined out three times, grounded out once. Batting cleanup, he is oh for ten in the first three games of the World Series.

He and Pituka wander about downtown. People gasp in adoration. They rush up to the Mayor of Riverfront; they clap him on the back. "We're with you," they enthuse. "You're gonna be fine, Tony. Don't you worry!"

Thirteen miles up Interstate 75, at the Ramada Inn in Sharonville, Ohio, Luis Tiant sits serenely in a similar swirl of activity. Radio crews clomp up the stairwells. Broadcasters lay heavy, black cables around the room, down the corridor, out the lobby. Generators purr in the street, truck engines rev and rattle. Elevators and toilets are backed up, several telephones are ringing. Somebody called room service. The maid would like to clean the room. Sharonville, usually such a sleepy suburb, has never seen anything like this. People surround Tiant — ballplayers vehemently reading newspapers aloud, the network crew, cameramen, team representatives, journalists. The room is filled with nervous bodies, polyester pants, hollering mouths, waving arms, checkered jackets, shifting emotions.

Amidst it all, Luis meditatively sips a cup of black coffee. His buddy, Felix, sits beside him at the small courtesy table. Felix is geared up by the hubbub and unnerved by Tiant's refined composure. Felix makes nervous sounds, wipes his wing-tip shoes anxiously on the hotel's immaculate carpet. Luis appears not to have a care in the world.[37]

Tonight, on three days' rest, Felix's dear friend, this old, chunky right-hander with the Fu Manchu mustache, will try to beat the team of the decade an unprecedented second consecutive time.

If he succeeds, the Series will be even, two games to two, and Boston will be guaranteed a sixth game at Fenway, a chance to be cheered by their own overwrought fans and aided by the eccentricities of their home park.

If Luis fails, the Red Sox will be down, three games to one, and recovery almost impossible, given that they have still another game to endure in inhospitable Riverfront. They will be regarded as a team that displayed at first far more spunk than was predicted, but understandably couldn't overcome the shock of losing two straight games from unsteady umpiring.

Luis is honestly a little worried, but only about the gray skies.

There's a 40-percent chance of showers, with temperatures predicted to be in the low sixties. He doesn't like the rain. He prefers to pitch on hot days. But he'll try pitching in the rain and he'll see what happens. If he loses, he loses.

"What's the matter with you?" Felix asks him. "Don't you have any nerves in there?"

Luis laughs. A gambler, a clown, a superstar, he is also a religious man. He tends to address situations like these with proverbs. *"Ud tiene dos bolsillos en la vida,"* he answers Felix. *"Uno para ganar y el otro para perder. Ud debe llevarlos con dignidad."*

> *You are given two pockets in life.*
> *One is the winning pocket and the other the losing pocket.*
> *You must carry them both with dignity.*

BOSTON	CINCINNATI
Beniquez, *left field*	Rose, *third base*
(Miller, *left field*)	Griffey, *right field*
Doyle, *second base*	Morgan, *second base*
Yastrzemski, *first base*	Perez, *first base*
Fisk, *catcher*	Bench, *catcher*
Lynn, *center field*	Foster, *left field*
Petrocelli, *third base*	Concepcion, *shortstop*
Evans, *right field*	Geronimo, *center field*
Burleson, *shortstop*	Norman, *pitcher*
Tiant, *pitcher*	(Borbon, *pitcher*)
	(Crowley, *pinch hitter*)
	(Carroll, *pitcher*)
	(Chaney, *pinch hitter*)
	(Eastwick, *pitcher*)
	(Armbrister, *pinch hitter*)

That night, to the watchful eyes of Fred Norman, the losing pocket seems the source of most of Tiant's pitches. It's the bottom of the first. The Boston starter is having trouble keeping the ball down. Cincinnati's mound is high and Tiant can't step down in the manner he prefers. This upsets his control. He can't get his breaking ball over.

Norman talks fast, has opinions. He's short, he's left-handed: he's got a lot to make up for. Tonight he's fired up, he's ecstatic to be starting game four, he'll admit that readily. In truth, he would've preferred an earlier assignment. He wanted game two. (After all, he won game two in the play-offs.) He didn't get it, his feelings were hurt; that's all in the past now. Maybe Billingham *was* better suited for Fenway, because Norman can get the fly-ball outs; he's great at Riverfront — the hitters chase the screwball, they swing off balance, they pop the ball up.

Tiant draws a full count on Rose, their leadoff batter. As with the beginning of game one, the two rotund, veteran gamblers, Rose and Tiant, square off. A ceaseless series of foul balls ensues. In game one, Rose eventually grounded out to Doyle; this time, after ten pitches, he grounds it safely past Doyle.

Norman's smile widens, bringing a hard, flat sheen to his eyes.

Griffey bounces a ball through to deep left center, scoring Rose. Rounding second, Griffey observes that Lynn is still chasing down the ball. He tries for third.

Norman shakes his head. He disagrees with Griffey's gamble. In this situation, there's no difference between him being on second or him being on third.

That is big, big mistake, Tiant thinks. *You no run on Freddie.*[38]

Lynn fields the ball at the fence. He slings a swift parabola from deep center and hits Burleson. The Rooster swiftly completes the relay. Griffey is out at third.

Norman knows how perfect execution, big throws, timely plays of this sort, they make all the difference. This *could* have been a very large Reds outburst. This *could* have meant an early exit for Tiant, as Morgan follows with a walk, and Bench scores him with a long double to deep right center.

Tiant escapes. He's down by two runs, but he stays in the game.

Two runs, Norman calculates, *should be plenty*. He scrambles out to the mound with renewed fervor. He matches Tiant junk ball for junk ball. For three innings, he keeps giving up hits, but the Red Sox keep leaving men on. He feels unbeatable, ready to mow down the whole American League tonight. This feeling lasts exactly thirty-seven minutes, and expires in the top of the fourth, when both Fisk and Lynn single, and Evans triples to tie the score.

Norman expects Sparky to barrel out of the dugout and snatch away the baseball. The pitcher can see Borbon warming up in the bull pen, signaling that he's ready. *Why not bring him in?* Borbon works the same way a mousetrap does. There's a blur of movement, and then you're out.

Sparky doesn't appear. Grateful for the vote of confidence, Norman turns to face the next batter, Burleson.

Rick Burleson may be batting eighth in Boston's lineup, but he's the only player on either World Series team with a hit in every postseason game. All year, he's been the unheralded one, the battler, the small guy with the snarl under the mustache. On the field, nothing escaped him. He'd run over to the mound whenever the situation looked grim and command the pitcher to have the ball hit to him. "I'll take care of it. I'll turn two on these sons of bitches."[39] When Yastrzemski made the all-star team this summer, he was embarrassed; the honor, he said, should go to someone like Burleson. The Red Sox have no backup for Burleson: according to Bill Lee, he's their least-expendable player and it's true — they have depth at every position except short-stop. This season, Burleson played in all but thirty-six of the team's total innings. And now, he is hitting .467 for the Series.

Norman's first pitch looks like a pregnant watermelon. Burleson smashes it into left center.

Norman curses softly.

George Foster fields Burleson's hit contemplatively, with an almost earnest consideration for the welfare of the baseball. Burleson, taking advantage of Foster's conscientiousness, hustles into second on what should have been a routine single.

Sparky saunters out. "Well, did you see that?" the manager asks easily, as if he and Norman were just watching a game together over a couple Burgies. "The good players, you see, they got an instinct for the extra base."

"Yeah," sighs Norman dejectedly. His face is pallid, coated faintly with sweat. He's in no mood to admire the opposition. He's overcome, but that doesn't say the half of it. He hands Sparky the ball.

"Ah, you did your best." Sparky pats his pitcher on the arm. "Don't worry, we got these guys. We just have to throw some water on the fire first."

In comes Borbon. As usual, he appears skeptical, or about to spit. Behind his back, he twists his wrist around the ball. With a sharp snap, he untwists, flings it forward, and fires a mistake to Tiant, who sends the ball back through the box for a single. Beniquez follows with a check-swing dribbler. Perez fumbles it for his third error of the Series. Burleson scores. Yastrzemski hammers a drive to right center that Geronimo approaches fearfully. It falls in. Tiant scores.

A double that should have been a single, a single by a pitcher who never bats, an error that should've been an out, a lazily fielded fly: Boston leads, five to two.

But luck doesn't long remain with Boston, for Tiant still struggles. With two outs, Foster grounds up the middle. Doyle fields it hurriedly and throws off balance. The ball bounces past Yastrzemski at first. Foster takes second. Concepcion follows with a blooper to left center that falls between Burleson, Lynn, and Juan Beniquez. Cringing, they nearly collide, and then Geronimo sends one twisting to the left-field corner, which Beniquez misplays into a triple.

The lead is down to a run, with luck apparently running out, when Tiant walks Rose to begin the fifth.

Griffey hits a drive to right field. Evans tries to fool Rose. He turns his back on Griffey's hit, behaving as if it's a home run. Dewey learned this ruse from Yastrzemski, who specializes in a series of decoys he calls "dekes." This worked earlier in the season to double up a runner in Chicago, but it doesn't fool Rose. Evans catches the ball on the warning track, but Rose has moved only a few feet off the bag.

Morgan walks.

Now even Fisk believes that Tiant is lost. *He just isn't pitching his typical game. He doesn't have his control.*

Perez hits a grounder up the middle just to the left of second base. Doyle makes an exceptional play to get to it. His throw just beats Perez to first.

With runners at second and third and two outs, Bench comes to bat. Darrell Johnson wants Bench intentionally walked. The guy hammers home runs like Mickey Mantle, and first base is open. DJ doesn't want to tell Tiant how to pitch, though. The manager respects Luis too much, and Luis respects Bench too little, so bravely, perhaps ill-advisedly, he pitches to the slugger, challenging him, and Bench flies out.

Boston still leads, five to four, but they can't seem to score any more runs. Tiant, pitching without his stuff, visibly tired after surrendering four runs in his first four innings, increasingly confronts the prospect of having to hold Cincinnati scoreless at home for the last five innings, a truly fantastic scenario. Men constantly get on base, and Tiant has to keep working from a stretch. He's stuck in a leaky boat, bailing frantically; he keeps crashing his car and extricating himself; he's a boxer on the ropes who won't go down.

While Tiant works to throttle the Big Red Machine, Sparky brings Rawly Eastwick in to pitch. Eastwick has been credited with both of the Reds' Series victories thus far. Tonight, he faces nine Boston batters and briskly retires them in order. If his team gets him two runs, he'll set a World Series record with three consecutive victories. Eastwick is young and tall and fast, and each time Tiant retakes the mound afterward, he looks, by contrast, even older, even shorter, even slower.

In the ninth inning, Geronimo leads off with a single to right. Sparky sends up Armbrister to pinch-bunt for Eastwick.

It's the first time Pudge has been near Armbrister since the previous night's events. He thinks about saying something to him, something snide and crude. Then he thinks, *Why go into that kind of garbage?* He knows Armbrister is going to lay it down. He just wants him out of the way.

Fisk gets his wish.

Armbrister pushes his bunt further up the field than he did the night before. He leaves the batter's box quietly and efficiently. His sacrifice is completed without incident. One out, Geronimo on second. Pete Rose is up. Tiant walks him.

Darrell Johnson visits the mound.

Luis notices that there is nobody warming up in the bull pen. He's touched. There is no undulating, adulating crowd to inspire him, no chants of "Loo-ee! Loo-ee!" He has already thrown 156 pitches tonight, enough work for two and a half pitchers, yet clearly his manager still trusts him to finish.

"How do you feel?" asks DJ.

"Him," Luis gestures at Geronimo on second, "he hit a punk curve. I throw only now fastballs."

Fisk is there. "He's getting faster," Pudge chimes in. "These are the best fastballs all night."

Tiant looks at the catcher with a curious, sad smile.

"Deal with one at a time," DJ instructs them, rather obviously. "Griffey is next. Morgan, after that."

"I give my best." Tiant shrugs wearily. "If they beat me, hell with it."

"Okay then."

"I do job. It is why you pay me."

DJ pats him kindly. "You're my man, Luis."

Other than the unprecedented amount of soda with which he's been lavished while rooting for his father's team, Ken Griffey Jr. hasn't enjoyed much about tonight's game. Sitting above the Reds' dugout with Craig and his mother, Junior has seen his father thrown out at third in the first, bounce to the pitcher in the third, fly to right in the fifth, and ground to second in the seventh. Now, in the ninth, his father comes up for the last time. He's due for a big hit. The situation is identical to game two, with the winning run aboard.

The Reds always play their smartest at the game's end. As Little Joe says, they never lose their cool. They're the great comeback team. They won twenty-three regular-season games in their final time at bat; they did it two more times in their play-off against the Pirates; and they did it in games two and three of the Series.

Tonight, the dirt around home plate appears unsettled. His father floats in the dusty air, suffused with a golden light. Every detail about him is clear, and his face seems immortal and beautiful.

"Come on, big fella," Junior hisses. He asks his mother's permission to cross Craig's fingers for good luck.

Birdie shoots him a cold look and refuses.

Junior doesn't like this pitcher. He's fat, ugly, and old. He sweats and spits too much. The top of his uniform is drenched with perspiration. He scowls down at Junior's father, his face distended from the fist-sized wad of chewing tobacco in his mouth. He rotates toward second base, kicks a leg toward left field, pushes his arm toward right field, then delivers a pitch toward home. He throws four pitches: three balls, one strike.

His fifth pitch appears ideal. With obvious delight, Junior's father jumps on it and sends it soaring out toward the center-field fence.

The home crowd gasps.

Rawly Eastwick has been sitting in the dugout, breathing the festive air, resting his limbs, tasting the wonder. He's been preparing postgame remarks for the reporters, trying to think what it means to win so many World Series games in your debut season. Now he stands and watches intently. Griffey's shot is tremendous, traveling more than four hundred feet into deep center. Rawly doubts it'll leave the park, but it will definitely score two to win the game, giving Eastwick his third consecutive Series victory.

Unless . . .

Fred Lynn is running full tilt at the wall, his left eye trained on the ball. From his days as a star defensive back in football, Lynn retains an excellent ability to sprint forward while looking backward.

Alone in the stadium, Tiant does not watch. Instead, he looks at the crowd. There is nothing Luis can do now. It is out of his hands. If he is to lose, he will lose. He must not fear it. Anticipation and pressure — this, to him, is fear. Fear is useless. If he loses, he loses. This is fate. So he does not watch. He gauges the crowd's response. He relies upon Freddie.

Junior sees the man in center run, sees his hands go up in stages, sees him arrive at the warning track. Desperately, the center fielder stretches. The ball descends over his left shoulder. He hooks it on the very tip of his webbing. He slaps his free hand down on top of the glove.[40]

A sudden expulsion of breath issues from the stadium, the dying groan of an elephant nailed by a freight train.

Tiant knows: Freddie did his job.

Rawly Eastwick is as astonished as anyone. The game came down to a matter of inches. If the rookie Lynn misses, if the rookie Eastwick wins. That was it.

Lynn's momentum carries him forward two strides. He crunches against the fence briefly and whirls around. He throws to Burleson. No one advances.

Cleveland, 1954, Sparky thinks again: *Vic Wertz, Willie Mays, that whole fiasco.* Other than Lynn being left-handed, it's the same play.

Still, that's only the second out, and the situation remains promising. A man on first, a man on second, and Joe Morgan up.

Tiant spits five spurts of chewing tobacco and delivers a fastball. Ball one.

Geronimo, on second base, sees a chance to help their cause. Tiant isn't paying him any attention. He could take third. He tries to let Morgan know his intentions without making too big a deal out of it, but he doesn't get his message across. On the next pitch, he takes off.

It never occurred to Morgan that Geronimo would be going. It's poor strategy. If Geronimo steals third, it opens up a base, and the Red Sox simply walk Joe in order to pitch to Perez, which is eminently preferable, since Tony is hitless against Boston. Morgan is surprised; more than that, he is bothered. Out of the corner of his eye, he glimpses Geronimo flitting across the infield and his concentration lapses. Tiant's pitch certainly appears good; it's a fastball at the knees. Morgan swipes at it distractedly. He connects. The ball travels very high but comes down quite close. Yastrzemski gloves it.

In Rochester, Minnesota, neighbors hear a woman screaming and call the police. Officers speed over. Guns drawn, they hammer at the woman's door in alarm. She answers, surprised. She appears uninjured. Officers tell her about the neighbors' concern. The woman laughs. "That was me cheering," she explains. "I'm a Red Sox fan. They just evened the Series."[41]

Tiant trudges tiredly into the locker room, tosses a red helmet on the top shelf, settles on a stool, and lights up a cigar. The reporters ask him how he does it. What's his secret? Luis slumps forward, his mustache almost touching his kneecaps. "I no have secrets." His words drift upward through a haze of smoke. "I believe my religion. I believe in God."

A stereo set plays gentle music. The clubhouse is quiet and happy.

Bill Lee happens past. "My impression of the Series," he says, "is that it's tied again."

In Cincinnati's clubhouse, there is numb admiration. The Reds no longer question Tiant's tenacity or guile, as they did after Saturday's shutout.

"We tried the same play in the ninth that won for us Tuesday night," Rose notes ironically. "It didn't work this time because Armbrister bunted so well."

One of baseball's crappiest communicators, Darrell Johnson, mounts the interview stage beneath Riverfront Stadium's grandstand. He announces a change of plans, of course; he's always doing that, or else muttering vague, bland answers that no one can fathom.

Reggie Cleveland will start game five instead of Bill Lee.

"Lee is not ready," Johnson says dully.

The scribblers can't grasp the strategy of countering Cincinnati's starter, the great Don Gullett, with Reggie Cleveland, a guy with a weight problem who did a lot of good work in September, but got hit hard in the play-offs.

"Reggie is the best available," DJ snaps. He seems, gradually, to realize that this praise is faint, at best. He falls silent for a few seconds. He holds up a hand. "These guys are a great fastball-hitting team, but Reggie has a great slider, and he can beat those guys if we can get a few runs off Mr. Gullett, who looked fair against us in Boston."

Johnson announces that Bill Lee will pitch the sixth game on Saturday, and if there is a seventh game on Sunday, it goes to Luis Tiant. The manager abruptly leaves the room, taking no further questions.

Journalists ask Tiant whether he could even stagger to the mound with what amounts to two and a half days' rest, following a game in which he threw 163 pitches. "You better believe I'll be ready," Luis says, his eyes glittering like droplets of ink. "If I have to throw three thousand pitches, I'll do it somehow."

"This team will win," Zimmer assures the press. His voice is hearty and hale; his round, jowlish cheeks are flushed with gladness; his moist palms twitch. "I have never been more confident in my life."

OCTOBER 16

At THE CALIFORNIA HOME of Alvin Dark, the telephone rings. It's Charles Finley.

"I'm not going to rehire you for 1976," Finley informs Dark.
"Do you have any questions?"

"None at all," says Dark.

It's the second time Dark has been fired by Finley, who has fired
more managers than any owner in baseball history.

Over the years, 127 ballplayers left Cuba to play in the United
States, most ending up with the Washington Senators. This exodus
ceased once Castro assumed power. Now only four Cuban major
leaguers remain. Last night, at Riverfront, half of them faced off —
Tony Perez against Luis Tiant. Tony had four at bats. He struck
out. He flied out. He grounded out twice to the infield. He is now oh
for fourteen. He learns, in this manner, that shopping downtown
with Pituka before a game doesn't necessarily improve his batting
average. He's desperate. He's running out of routines to alter. The
next day he stays home until nearly game time. He sleeps a lot.

Pituka delivers a pep talk as he departs. She tells him, "This is going to be your day!"

BOSTON	CINCINNATI
Beniquez, *left field*	Rose, *third base*
Doyle, *second base*	Griffey, *right field*
Yastrzemski, *first base*	Morgan, *second base*
Fisk, *catcher*	Bench, *catcher*
Lynn, *center field*	Perez, *first base*
Petrocelli, *third base*	Foster, *left field*
Evans, *right field*	Concepcion, *shortstop*
Burleson, *shortstop*	Geronimo, *center field*
Cleveland, *pitcher*	Gullett, *pitcher*
(Willoughby, *pitcher*)	(Eastwick, *pitcher*)
(Griffin, *pinch hitter*)	
(Pole, *pitcher*)	
(Segui, *pitcher*)	

That night, after Tony fans in the second inning, Sparky reminds him about Dal Maxvill.[42] In the 1968 World Series, Maxvill, a weak-hitting infielder with the Cardinals, set a record by batting twenty-two times without a hit. "I have complete confidence in you," Sparky says with a straight face. "You'll get that record yet."

"I no want the record," Tony replies. "I trade it for a hit, I swear."

Boston takes the lead in the first inning. Doyle, the slowest creature on the face of the earth, earns a triple by grounding into the right-field corner, where, like a scared turtle, the ball plunks itself down, retracts its limbs, sits, and waits. Yastrzemski follows with a fly ball to Griffey that scores Doyle.

After that, Gullett bears down. His fastball is moving nicely. He's got velocity and control and good location. His arm is loaded with springs and plutonium, and he jettisons balls in a fog of move-ment, as a cat pounces, or a hummingbird flaps. Gullett's game face, as always, is one of terrific apprehension, but he's feeling fan-tastic. He blows down one Boston player after another.

The Reds, meanwhile, have difficulty getting anything going

against Cleveland. In the first, with one out and Rose on third, Bench flies to left. Pete being Pete, well, he's going home on anything. He tags up. Juan Beniquez throws it on a line. Of course, Rose loses his helmet. He slides tail-first, unusual for him, but he's meaning to kick the ball out of Fisk's hand. He doesn't succeed. Pudge's tag is quick and careful. Pete's hair catches the wind. It stands on end such that it appears, for a moment, as if Fisk is electrocuting Rose by applying glove with ball to inner calf.

The score remains Boston one, Cincinnati zero. Cleveland breezes along. He has two outs in the fourth when Tony Perez comes to bat for the second time. They've been pitching Perez outside, so now they decide to mix it up. On the first pitch, Pudge calls for an inside fastball. Cleveland misses. Perez does not.

"Reggie didn't get it in," Perez later explains, "so I hit it out."

His slump is over. The score is tied.

It remains one to one in the fifth, when Cleveland makes another mistake. With two outs and two strikes on Gullett, Reggie hangs a slider. Gullett singles to center, Rose follows with a double, Beniquez overthrows Burleson, and the Reds take the lead, two to one.

Cleveland continues to throw well and lose. He makes seventy-three pitches, only nineteen of which are balls. He gets ahead on every batter. Five separate times he has two strikes on a batter before surrendering a hit. The sixth inning opens with a full count to Morgan. Reggie makes a perfect pitch, but the umpire disagrees and Morgan is aboard.

Seven times Cleveland throws over to Yastrzemski at first. Seven times Morgan gets back safely. Reggie throws home, gets strike one on Bench. Four throws over to first, and four times Morgan is safe. Reggie throws home. Foul ball, Morgan going. Strike two. Five throws over, Morgan safe each time. Reggie throws home. Foul ball. He throws home again. A perfect double-play ball to second but Doyle doesn't see it. The second baseman loses the ball in the white of Bench's uniform. It scoots past him into the outfield. Evans picks it up, throws it over Petrocelli's head. Still no outs. Cincinnati ahead by a run, men on second and third, and Perez up next.

Darrell Johnson comes to the mound. He instructs Cleveland to strike out Perez (one for sixteen) and then walk the next batter, George Foster (five for sixteen). Cleveland gets a ball and a strike. Tony pops the next one up high. It drifts foul. Pudge runs out from under his mask, pursues the foul to beside the Cincinnati dugout. The ball begins to descend over Bowie Kuhn, where the commissioner sits between NL President Chub Feeney and U.S. Secretary of Commerce Rogers Morton. Fisk dives over the photographers' box. He lands, fully extended, atop a group of cameramen. He misses the ball by a few inches, extracts himself, fetches his mask, nonchalantly comes back behind the plate.

Tony is impressed by the catcher's hustle. "Nice try," he says.

Pudge grunts. *Two strikes now.* He sets up low and away. Cleveland delivers high and inside. "I'm sure," Tony will apologize later, as if vaguely ashamed of himself, "Reggie didn't want to put it there." It's really only the pitcher's third mistake of the night, but by far his costliest. Tony drives it off the facing between decks in left center for his fourth RBI. The crowd, numbering 56,693, is the largest ever to attend a baseball game in Cincinnati. They rise to give Tony a standing ovation as Cleveland departs, with the score five to one in favor of Cincinnati.

Reggie was the first Canadian to start a World Series game. He was also the first one to throw sixteen times to first base on one batter. He now becomes the first to be knocked out of a Series game.

Gullett, in the meantime, is pitching like a young Koufax. This isn't the same Gullett that Boston saw in game one; this is the boy with the fantastic bullet ball, the pitcher with the best active record in the game, the delight of the Cincinnati staff, the overpowering southpaw who can, according to Rose, "throw a baseball through a car wash without it getting wet." After surrendering Doyle's triple in the first, Gullett throws almost exclusively fastballs and retires the next sixteen batters. With one out in the eighth, Evans gets Boston's second hit, but he's stranded when Burleson flies out and Doug Griffin, batting for the pitcher, lines out.

Reliever Dick Pole opens the eighth for Boston. Pole is an intense redhead, twenty-four years old, a right-hander. This is his first postseason appearance. He's not nervous, not a bit. He anticipated that he might be — he thought he'd be scared to death — but he comes out and he feels fine. The mound, however — *the mound feels wrong*. It's different from the one he was using in the bull pen. He can't find his rhythm.

Bench leads off. Pole gets a strike on him, but is low with four pitches. He's so uncomfortable that his feet are leaping off the mound with every pitch. After Bench takes his base on balls, Pole throws four straight dirt balls to walk Perez. Darrell Johnson waves in Diego Segui and that's it for Pole: one strike, two batters, nine pitches. "If you were looking for the opposite of someone's World Series dream, this was it," Pole insists in the clubhouse after the game. "It was as embarrassing as you could imagine. This whole season I've been up and down and up and down, and when I got going good, I got smacked in the head. And now this." Pole is shaken, remorseful. "I don't know. I just hope I get a chance to redeem myself." He doesn't. He never appears in another postseason game for the rest of his major-league career.

In the ninth inning, Gullett's pitch count reaches triple digits. Finally, he begins to tire. He gives up three straight hits, making the score six to two, Cincinnati.

Sparky grows antsy. He needs to quash this incipient comeback; he has to stop this. After all, his is clearly not the only team skilled at last-minute rallies. *Look at game three, that Evans homer squaring it up just when things were seeming so rosy.*

He checks with Billingham, who is charting the pitches.[43] They agree: Gullett's leaving too much out over the plate. Sparky thinks he's maybe trying too hard, because the kid has this tendency to put on the kill when he's going for that last out, and it turns him a tad sloppy.

The manager remembers this morning: the bedraggled man — the broad chest, the unkempt mustache, the haze of insects — threatening him in the street if the Reds blow it this time.

With two outs in the ninth, two men on, and Petrocelli at the plate, Sparky decides what to do. He sends Gullett to the showers and brings in his other raw source of heat, Rawly Eastwick.

That's managing — knowing your moment, knowing your options, knowing the odds.

Eastwick blows three consecutive strikes past Rico, earning a save to go with his two wins in the Series.

Cincinnati now has a three-game-to-two advantage.

Darrell Johnson discourages any complicated postgame analyses. "Don Gullett beat us," the Boston manager admits. "Nothing else did." Bench says he's never seen the pitcher throw a better game. Gullett tells reporters, "I want to thank my Maker for giving me the ability to go out there and pitch."

The Series returns to Fenway with Boston mired in a must-win situation.

OCTOBER 17

I T RAINS .27 INCHES in Boston. The sixth game (Lee v. Billingham) is scheduled for 1:00 P.M. tomorrow afternoon. On the flight home, reporters ask Lee about the poor forecast. The lanky pitcher taps at the storm clouds outside the cabin window. "That's my kind of weather," he replies.

"Don't the Reds have the advantage, since they've already batted eight innings against you?"

"I expect they're going to hit me a little better," Lee admits. "So . . ." He pauses and thinks. His face suddenly brightens with a plan. "We'll have to score more runs."

"Might the pressure prove too great for you?"

"I don't know," Lee says at once. "I've only had five days' rest, you know, and that's not much rest. I had twenty-six days to rest before my last start."

"Won't you be nervous, starting a game on the edge of elimination?"

Lee nods. "I'll be nervous, yeah. But I'm nervous every day of my life." He accepts a drink from the flight attendant. "This is my way of working it out. Some guys beat their wives. I talk a lot."

The jet begins its descent. It lands to the sound of applause. Logan Airport is jammed with thousands waving banners and chanting,"Loo-ee! Loo-ee!" A scrawny white man with a tumbleweed Afro holds a sign that proclaims BILL LEE IS *NOT* CRAZY.

A vast crew of NBC engineers returns to Boston, along with a contingent of sportswriters, the commissioner's entourage, the Cincinnati front-office staff. They discover prices have skyrocketed as the hotels, bars, restaurants, and garages profit from the situation.

Jimmy the Greek, still respected despite picking the wrong team to win the ALCS, lists the Reds as eleven-to-ten favorites to win the sixth game and clinch the World Series.

"We're swinging the bats real good now," Pete Rose agrees, "and the majority of the players, I'd say all of 'em, feel we're going to wind it up by Saturday. That sounds cocky, and I don't mean it to be. What I'm saying is we're thinking we're gonna beat 'em Saturday in the right way, if you know what I mean."

Joe Morgan tries to untangle his friend's talk. "Right now we're in the driver's seat," Morgan explains. "We have the champagne going for us now. If we get rained out Saturday, it'll just be a stay of execution. If we don't get 'em Saturday, we'll get 'em the next day."

Bench is so certain of a swift finish that he brings only one change of clothes to Boston.

Of the Reds, only George Foster is worried. He believes they play better when they're behind. Now they're ahead. Foster looks at the Red Sox, who have to sweep both games in order to win the Series, and wishes the situations were reversed, because Cincinnati knuckles down only when consequences are serious. They're still going to have to enter that enemy shoebox and take a game. Boston is not about to surrender easily.

* * *

A small prop plane flies over Fenway, hauling a banner that says THESE ARE THE TIMES THAT TRY MEN'S SOULS.

OCTOBER 18

IT RAINS 1.97 INCHES in Boston. The sixth game is rescheduled for tomorrow afternoon at 1:00 P.M.

Four or five Red Sox players come to Fenway to receive their mail. Fisk, alone, comes to work out. He runs in the rain. He takes batting practice off the machine under the bleachers.

Lee remains nonchalant about the weather. "I think an extra day will be good for my elbow," he tells reporters. "I like it."

Interviewed on a radio program, Lee is prompted to speak frankly about Darrell Johnson. He does more than that. He launches an ill-timed vituperative rant. *The pitchers*, Lee explains, *don't respect the manager.* He relays the complaints of Drago and Moret, that nobody in the bull pen knows what his job is supposed to be because there's no official short man. Lee expresses the belief that his team made the World Series despite the interference of its fumbling manager. "Darrell Johnson," says Lee, his voice dripping with acid, "has been falling out of trees all year and landing on his feet."

After the season, Moret will be traded to Atlanta. Drago will be sent to California as "the player to be named later" in the Denny Doyle trade.

Darrell Johnson, despite being selected as the *Sporting News'* 1975 Manager of the Year, will be fired eighty-six games into the 1976 season and replaced by Don Zimmer.

Zim will feud with the Spaceman for three years, until finally Lee is shipped from the team he loves to Montreal, the only baseball town with a less hospitable pitching climate than Boston.

OCTOBER 19

IT RAINS .31 INCHES in Boston. The sixth game is rescheduled for tomorrow night at 8:30 P.M. The managers announce new starters. Boston will start Tiant instead of Lee, and Cincinnati will start Nolan instead of Billingham.[44]

Lee is furious with Darrell Johnson. The manager defends his decision. "If a man put a gun to my head and said I'm going to pull the trigger if you lose this game," DJ vows, "I'd want Luis Tiant to pitch that game."

Billingham's spirit is shattered. Sparky assures him he'll be needed in relief. "If Nolan doesn't get going right off, and there's a left-hander at the plate, I'm sending in Fred Norman, but if there's a right-hander at the plate, then you come in."

Bill Lee's father is in town to watch Young Bill pitch a World Series game. Old Bill has to be back at work by Tuesday. He has to fly out of Boston on Monday.

He won't be able to watch his son pitch.

Young Bill takes his father to Fenway on Sunday afternoon,

once the rain subdues. It's misting a little. The wind whips in from the northeast. The field is a quagmire. The grounds crew empties the tarp for the fourth time.

He hands Old Bill a catcher's mitt. They play catch on the sidelines. Old Bill wears a brown leather jacket and Bally shoes. After several minutes, he squats. His son goes through a repertoire of pitches, gradually throwing harder and harder. "We should have played today," Young Bill calls out. "This is my weather." He fires off a few sinkers. "We could have played, and no one could have hit a home run."

There lingers the distinct likelihood that this quarter-hour of tossing to Old Bill could be the last pitching the Spaceman does this season.

In the meantime, the Reds have accepted an invitation to work out at the playing field of Tufts University. They don their uniforms and charter a bus. The driver gets lost in Somerville. He pulls into a service station. Sparky Anderson jumps out to ask the attendant for directions. The attendant's jaw drops. "You're the Cincinnati Reds!" he exclaims. Hearing of their predicament, he points the team in the direction of Tufts.

The driver immediately gets lost again.

That night, Tiant attends a hockey game, Bruins v. Maple Leafs. Boston Garden chants his name and shakes with applause. The owner of the Leafs slips him a new supply of Cuban cigars.

Luis reveals that he's been bothered by a cough and a chest cold, as have several other players, but he doesn't think it will affect him too much.

OCTOBER 20

IT RAINS .25 INCHES in Boston. The game is rescheduled for tomorrow night at 8:30 P.M. "If it rains a few more days," notes one sportswriter, "Jim Rice's hand will be healed enough to play."

The delays begin to wear on even Rose. His first winter speaking engagement is scheduled for Wednesday in Louisville. In a snappish mood, he expresses concern about the loss of income.

On the other hand, Fred Lynn declares that his team feels less pressure now. The rains have relaxed them. Cincinnati's indomitable momentum has dissipated. Rick Burleson sits at home with his feet up. The days are languid and without purpose. The sky is gray, the drizzle eternal. There is no sun to bring the hours into focus. All nervousness vanishes. Asked what the delay means to him personally, Lynn looks ahead to the Buffalo Bills on Monday Night Football and candidly responds, "It means I get to watch the Juice on television."

OCTOBER 21

WHEN CARL YASTRZEMSKI'S MOTHER, Hattie, asks her physicians how long she has, they say: *It depends*.[45] They talk about the immeasurabilities of the malignant appetite, the abnormalities of cellular division, the role of her immune system and healthy tissue. They tell her about the rate of metastasis. Essentially, they don't answer her question. It puts her in mind of these men who surround her, these athletes with their strong Polish bones, these family ballplayers, these roundabout Carls, her husband, her son. Is there never an easy answer with these men? It seems at times that they'll tell her everything but what she wants to know.

The game remains scheduled for tonight at 8:30 P.M. The sky clears. Fenway's head groundskeeper assures everyone the field will be ready. He has brought in helicopters to deposit five tons of an absorbent compound called "Turface," which will soak up the moisture. He speaks of a strong wind out of the west-southwest that will dry the ground.

Hattie travels into Boston to attend. She can hear the scalpers working Kenmore Square. They're selling reserved grandstand seats for sixty dollars apiece. Bleachers cost thirty-five dollars and standing room tickets are twenty-five dollars. Street vendors peddle handmade Tiant T-shirts. Tom Yawkey dispatches several employees to help Hattie into Fenway, as there is not yet any access for the handicapped.

Sparky Anderson denies that his team fears Tiant. "Lord," he tells reporters, "we've faced pitchers in the National League, like Andy Messersmith, every bit as tough as Tiant, and beaten them." No one in Boston believes Sparky. A banner in the bleachers proclaims LOO-EE FOR PRESIDENT. Hattie is caught up in the excitement. She applauds everything Tiant does, from taking batting practice to walking to the bull pen. She sits in a wheelchair next to her husband, Carl Sr., in the section directly behind the Red Sox wives. Her son's blond wife, Carol, sits in the row directly ahead of them.

Hattie would like to know something, but she doesn't think she can ask Carol, and she knows better than to ask her husband unless she wants to endure an explanation that extends all the way from Casey Stengel to Fred Lynn. Hattie can understand why Darrell Johnson is starting her son, Carl, but she doesn't see why DJ is starting Cecil Cooper, who's in a batting slump, instead of Bernie Carbo, who's hitting well. The manager could put Carl at first base, instead of out there protecting the shin of the wall. *Ah, well. More of the mysteries and manners of the majors.*

Hattie spent the summer in a hospital bed, questioning doctors. The surgery left her weak. She listened to a transistor radio. She drew comfort from her son's team. Gradually, as they gained the pennant, her strength returned. She insisted upon attending the play-offs in person. This is her ninth game over the last few weeks, and though — given her continued frailty — the task has been extremely difficult, it has also provided a healthy distraction.

CINCINNATI

Rose, *third base*
Griffey, *right field*
Morgan, *second base*
Bench, *catcher*
Perez, *first base*
Foster, *left field*
Concepcion, *shortstop*
Geronimo, *center field*
Nolan, *pitcher*
(Chaney, *pinch hitter*)
(Norman, *pitcher*)
(Armbrister, *pinch hitter*)
(Carroll, *pitcher*)
(Crowley, *pinch hitter*)
(Borbon, *pitcher*)
(Eastwick, *pitcher*)
(McEnaney, *pitcher*)
(Driessen, *pinch hitter*)
(Darcy, *pitcher*)

BOSTON

Cooper, *first base*
(Drago, *pitcher*)
(Miller, *pinch hitter*)
(Wise, *pitcher*)
Doyle, *second base*
Yastrzemski, *left field/first base*
Fisk, *catcher*
Lynn, *center field*
Petrocelli, *third base*
Evans, *right field*
Burleson, *shortstop*
Tiant, *pitcher*
(Moret, *pitcher*)
(Carbo, *pinch hitter/left field*)

The game opens at night.

Ray Nolan cheers his moonfaced son, Gary, that he may avoid a stiff neck in this outing.

The elder Luis Tiant watches without expression from the stands. He is dressed as always in a brown leather jacket, brown trousers, and a brown fedora.

Rose is the first batter. He hits a short fly ball to left. Carl races over. He makes a sliding catch for the game's first out. In the bottom of the inning, with two away and still no score, Carl comes to bat. This is Hattie's superstition: during her son's at bats, no matter the degree of difficulty, she stands. Carol has her own superstition. She goes away for the fourth inning. She did this once and her husband hit a home run.

Now, in the first, Carl lines a single to right off Nolan. Fisk grounds a single to left. Lynn homers into the bleachers over the pitching mound of the Boston bull pen. The Red Sox lead, three to nothing.

Darrell Johnson thoroughly trusts and depends upon Tiant's ability to confound Cincinnati. Across the diamond, in the other dugout, Sparky wastes no such faith on his starter. He yanks Nolan after nine batters, sticks in Norman. With two outs, Norman walks the bases full. Sparky brings in Billingham, who strikes out Petrocelli.

Billingham begins the next inning by putting two men on. Tiant sacrifices them over. Billingham gets Cooper and Doyle to ground out, and escapes harm.

With the pitcher due to bat in the top of the fifth, Sparky pulls Billingham (one and one-third innings). He sends up designated bunter Ed Armbrister.

Luis walks him.

Rose singles, and then Griffey hammers a ball toward the 379-foot mark in left center. Lynn runs a long way, extends his glove, and at the last minute leaps. Fenway is roaring. But the ball soars over his glove, and Lynn soars into the wall.

The roar abates.

Lynn slides sickly to the ground. He lies there, motionless. The only thing he feels is regret over missing the darn fly. Otherwise, he is completely numb. The moment is fraught with peril. The crowd stands as one, mortified. A hush falls across New England. *Lynn is hurt!* Yastrzemski rushes to his side while Evans retrieves the ball. Griffey slides safely into Rico's shoes with a two-run triple. He is the first player to score off Tiant in Fenway in forty innings.

Boston's trainer runs to the outfield. After a few minutes, the sensation returns to Lynn's appendages. Groggily, he gets to his feet. "You were lucky," the trainer tells him. "There's some tin on the wall right where you hit yourself. That cushioned the impact." The trainer wants Lynn removed for tests at a hospital. Lynn shakes him off. He'll be sore tomorrow. He'll have months to recover. There's no way he's leaving. He used to play football, after all; getting flattened is nothing new. He insists upon remaining in the game.

Bench singles off the wall. Griffey trots in, and the score is tied, three to three. Perez strikes out to end the frame, and the Reds take the field with Clay Carroll as their fourth pitcher in five innings. He gets three outs, then is yanked for a pinch hitter and replaced on the mound by Borbon. The tie holds. Cincinnati three, Boston three.

Griffey and Morgan open the seventh by swatting consecutive singles off Tiant. Boston's manager goes to the mound. Bench and Perez are due up. *At last,* thinks Sparky. He knows DJ's timidity about pulling starters, but Sparky fully anticipates that, by now, any reasonable manager would bring in a new arm. DJ doesn't. He chats with Luis for a bit. He makes sure that his pitcher is all right. He leaves. Both Bench and Perez fly out, but then Foster follows with a double off the center-field wall that scores two. This seems such an avoidable outcome to Sparky that he cannot fathom what Boston's manager might be thinking. And still, he stays with Tiant to open the eighth. Geronimo wraps the first pitch around the right-field foul pole and into the stands to make it six to three, Cincinnati.

"He made a bad pitch to Foster and then another to Geronimo," laconic Darrell Johnson will summarize later. "You can never tell how fast a man can lose it. Sometimes it just happens."

Tiant departs. "Loo-ee, Loo-ee," the crowd grimly chants for the last time, as Rogelio Moret, tall and black with dark brown eyes, takes over pitching duties. He is two things you never want a pitcher to be: fragile and accident-prone. He has a great arm but erratic control, both off and on the mound.

The moon rises, a pumpkin on the right-field horizon, but a vast sullen heaviness settles over the stands, an air of dejection. Surely the gods give no clearer signs than these that their miracles are all used up: Rico strikes out weakly with the bases loaded, Coop goes oh for five, scoring opportunities are squandered, Burleson appears inattentive and commits an error, Lynn is bruised from chasing a triple into the fence, Tiant is chased by a home run, and now there's a scrawny Puerto Rican pothead pitching on behalf of Boston.[46]

In the press box, Dick Schaap, the editor of *Sport,* begins collecting the ballots for the World Series MVP. These will determine which Red wins the prize — *Eastwick? Morgan? Griffey? Rose?*

The bottom of the eighth arrives, with the Reds still ahead by three runs, and Borbon pitching. On notepads, or manual typewriters, hundreds upon hundreds of sportswriters begin to compose game accounts, the fall of Tiant, the wounding of Lynn, the discouraging sight of the fading Sox, the painful acceptance that Yawkey again is the loser. . . .

They glance up to see Lynn single off Borbon's leg and Petrocelli walk. Sparky pulls Borbon. Rawly Eastwick comes in. His stuff is awesome. He strikes out Evans.

Unsurprised, the writers return to drafting an obituary. Boston is down to its last five outs of 1975.

Still, two on.

Rick Burleson steps in against Eastwick.

Darrell Johnson watches impassively. His mind is racing. *I've gotta get Sparky to yank fuckin' Eastwick!* Eastwick already has two wins and a save in the Series. He's throwing faster tonight than ever before.

An idea comes to Johnson. He sees a chance. The relief pitcher is due up after Burleson. If Johnson were to send in someone like Bernie Carbo, send a left-handed pinch hitter to the plate, that would force Sparky's hand. One thing about Sparky, he's by the book. He'll be unable to resist changing pitchers. *Sparky'll bring in his lefty, and I'll raise the wager. I'll pull Bernardo, put up Juan Beniquez.*

He calls Bernie out of the clubhouse, where he has been swinging a weighted bat and doing exercises.

"Carbo, get out there. Beniquez, get warm."

"Right," Yastrzemski quietly encourages the manager. *This is correct.* "Right, right, right."

Bernie steps out to the on-deck circle. He gets what's going on. He isn't going to hit. He's a decoy. He watches Eastwick deal with Burleson. He doesn't bother to warm up.

Eastwick's first pitch to Burleson is low for a ball.

Gazing off, with the bat on his shoulder, Carbo muses how a home run now would make him the first guy in Series history to hit two consecutive pinch homers in a night game. And a home run now would tie the game up, change everything. But truth be told, he'd just as soon not be batting. Or even pretending that he is about to bat. He's never faced Eastwick before. He doesn't know what to expect. But he's certain he needn't prepare himself in any way. He too knows Sparky will never manage against the book: left-hander against left-hander, right-hander against right-hander. Bernie's just waiting for Sparky to come out of the dugout and pull Eastwick, then Bernie can walk back and sit down and Beniquez can hit.

Bernie Carbo was an only child, and often, as a pawn in a moment of psychological intrigue such as this, he flashes on his parents fighting. He saw that a lot when he was little, before they divorced, and afterward his father turned into a bitter man who spoke jealously of Bernie's baseball talents, and never once complimented his son.[47]

Burleson is retired on a line drive to left.

Sparky is four outs away from his first world championship.

"Now batting for pitcher Rogelio Moret," Fenway announcer Sherm Feller booms. "Number one, Bernie Carbo."

Subdued applause. The crowd seems mostly satisfied that their team didn't roll over, but no one sees the need to drag this out unnecessarily. The Big Red Machine will win, of course. They're the better team.

Eastwick steps off the mound. He too is waiting for Sparky. He knows he's not going to be allowed to face Carbo. It goes against the book, and if Sparky is anything, he's by the book.

The wait lengthens.

Sparky is informed that McEnaney is loose in the bull pen. The manager can bring him in to face Carbo. *I should. McEnaney retires lefties.* But Sparky suspects the opposing manager. *McEnaney comes in, Johnson counters with Beniquez, short wall in left — don't let Beniquez bat.* He can see Beniquez catching a piece of a pitch and lofting it over the Green Monster. *Wouldn't take much effort.*

Sparky will not let this happen. He won't give Beniquez the chance to be Hal Smith, who batted in an identical situation fifteen

Octobers earlier, bottom of the eighth, man on second and third, his team four outs away from losing the World Series, and goddamn-Cracker-Jack-surprise Smith hit a home run. That game concluded with Bill Mazeroski's little Texas-leaguer line drive over the fence in left off Ralph Terry — that was the home run everyone remembered, but it took lowly Hal Smith to set the stage for Mazeroski's heroics. Most bitter Yankee defeat ever. Hell, it got Casey Stengel fired.

"Come on," the umpire yells at Carbo in the on-deck circle. "Come on. It's time for you to hit."

Carbo steps gingerly into the batter's box and pushes some dirt around. Both he and Eastwick continue to peek into the Reds' dugout.

Still no Sparky.

Sparky is thinking about how, in eleven years as manager of the Yankees, Stengel took his team to nine pennants, but he dropped one to Pittsburgh and it cost him his job. *You get Hal Smith out, and a home run from Maz in the bottom of the ninth means squat. . . . If I bring in McEnaney, and they go to Beniquez, and if he hits one over that damn wall, it'll mean the end of me.* Sparky spits tobacco at the floor of the dugout and snorts. *I just will not be able to live with myself.*

He likes these odds, Carbo and Eastwick as opposed to Beniquez and McEnaney.

Eastwick hasn't even considered how he might pitch Carbo. He knows that the book says to pitch him away. He looks to Bench for instruction. He throws a slider.

Bernie watches it for a strike, then lets two inside pitches go by as balls. He feels a mad mixture of things — pride, glee . . . mostly terror. *Shit, shit. Be selective. Don't lunge.* He swings at a pitch, and he misses. The count goes to two balls and two strikes. *Shit, man, don't strike out!* He is still stunned that Sparky is going to let him hit. He forgets for the moment that the decision also belongs partly to his own manager. *Don't pull your head out, don't get all fouled up, don't let things get to you.*

Bernie was sure Sparky would bring in a left-hander. *Is this a test?* Is Sparky testing him to see if he can handle the situation? *Fuck him, here we go. Every pitch is a new game.* He tries to remember what he read of Williams's philosophy on zone hitting.[48] *Until you have two strikes, you don't touch any pitches unless they are in the outlined zone.*

Unfortunately, Bernie has two strikes.

At that point, the philosophy abandons you to your instincts.

Fortunately, Bernie picked up a lot about pinch-hitting from Matty Alou when he was with the Cardinals. Alou's theory was *come in swinging.* You need the hit. You're only going to get one pitcher's mistake while you're up there, and you have to take advantage of it. You can't think you're going to get more than one mistake, because you're not.

The next pitch is a strike. Bernie fouls it off.

Bernie's whole career has just been a struggle to stay in the lineup. When he's in the lineup, he struggles to stay there. When he's out of the lineup, he struggles to get in. That's it, his whole career.

Don't strike out, Bernie tells himself.

Right then, Sparky figures out what to do. *McEnaney.* He'll put in McEnaney now. With a two-two count, Darrell Johnson wouldn't dare go to Beniquez.

But, having thought this, Sparky doesn't move.

Cincinnati is one strike away from the ninth.

Bernie knows Bench. He guesses fastball. He thinks Bench wouldn't dare call for a two-and-two slider.

Bench does.

It starts inside. It jams Bernie. At the last minute, he sees it dipping into the strike zone. He frantically waves his bat toward the ball. *My God. I just took the single worst swing in the history of baseball. That was more embarrassing than the swing I took in Philadelphia that time, when I hit the home run and fell flat on my back.[49] It was more embarrassing than when I lost hold of the bat and it went into the third row of the box seats beyond the visitor's dugout in Wrigley Field.*

"Ball," the umpire begins to say, before realizing that Carbo has chopped and tipped the ball back over Bench's head. The umpire changes his call. "Foul ball!"

Immediately, Bench argues.

Wow. Bernie was certain that he missed the ball. He almost turns to thank the ump. *I must have just hit it out of his mitt.*

Seeing Bernie's awful swing, the Boston dugout fully and finally grasps that they are dead. "This guy isn't going to be able to do anything," Fisk glumly tells Yastrzemski.

Carl agrees. "No," he says. "He isn't."

Carbo steps out of the box to get it together again, steps back in. Once more, he's thinking fastball.

Pitch him away, Eastwick reminds himself. *The book says, pitch him away.* He goes into his stretch. As the ball leaves his hand, he senses an incorrect balance. He tenses his fingers. The ball squirts from his grasp. *Oh, no.*[50]

Fastball, waist high and inside. Bernie takes the swing of his career. He connects. The ball sails over second base toward center field. Bernie rounds first base.

Geronimo turns, starts toward the bleachers. He runs a few yards, then stops and watches. He sees a thousand arms reach skyward. The ball drops among them.

Carbo can't conceive of what he has just accomplished. He is so full of feeling his mind locks up. He moves like a windup toy, performing a home run trot with a head full of only clock springs.[51] He doesn't speak to anyone in the infield, even to acknowledge his father, who's positioned at third.

Strangers all over New England are hugging.

From the mound, Eastwick winces toward the section of seats where his last pitch landed.

Fuck. Sparky is speechless. *Fuck, this is hard.* He nearly keels over in the dugout. *This game of baseball, this is no goddamn game, this is masochism. One minute Eastwick has two wins and two saves and is a shoo-in for the World Series MVP, then he throws a mistake and now he's the goat. What makes this so hard? Is it true, we can't win the big one? Baltimore in the 1970 World Series, they tore us up. Oakland in 1972, we should've won that. . . .*

"Hey," a Reds' bench coach shouts, so sharply it startles Sparky out of his downward spiral to despair. "You know what we forgot?" Overhead, the park is bellowing its approval. Anderson and the bench coach sit next to each other. "We forgot about Bernie's swing, that inside-out swing he has."

Born a left hander in a suburban Detroit neighborhood, Carbo was taught not to pull the baseball because there were never enough fielders to cover the whole outfield, and so right field was an automatic out.

This lets it out. Abruptly, Anderson can't find enough expletives, no level of cursing satisfies him. *I didn't take Bernie seriously. I was too worried about goddamn Hal Smith, I was so sure he was Juan fuckin' Beniquez. Why, why, why? I should have brought in McEnaney.*

"Boy, he sure slugged the crap out of that fucker. Right down Carbo's Alley."

I should be happy for him. That's my pet project Bernie Carbo right there, the June hitter, the wrong-field hitter, tying the score. If I were a bigger man, I might take some of the credit and share in Bernie's success.[52]

Don Zimmer knows baseball as an activity performed over a languorous expanse of time, but a shift has taken place, focusing, firing, grasping the game's loose folds, pulling them taut, eliminating the innate sprawl of the sport. It now feels certain that Boston will win. Drago swaggers in, records three quick outs. Doyle leads off the bottom of the ninth with a walk. He makes it around to third on a single by Yastrzemski.

Two on, no outs, tie score. Sparky pulls Eastwick. He brings in McEnaney, who walks Fisk intentionally and pitches to Lynn.

Zim talks to Doyle at third. He reminds the base runner: "Bases loaded, nobody out. Anything that looks like a line drive, you can't go nowhere. We can't have you getting doubled up here. Anything in the air, I'll watch it while you just tag up."

Lynn hits a twisting fly ball to shallow left. Zim starts down the line. "Tag up!" he yells to Doyle. Foster catches the ball on the left-field line. Zimmer signals for Doyle to hold at third. Foster is only 180 feet from home, and he has a landing strip to guide his throw straight to Bench.

Doyle breaks for the plate. Zim assumes he's faking it, but Denny just keeps going. He may be the slowest guy on the team, but he remembers that the scouting reports advised them always to run on Foster.

"No!" screams the third-base coach. "No! No! No!"

Foster's throw is perfect. It's close, but Doyle is out. Two away.

"Hey, Popeye!" Rose hollers at Zim. Rose has a nickname for everyone. He calls Perez "Doggie." He calls Foster "Yahtzee." He calls Bench "Hands." "Popeye! How many times do you have to tell a guy not to go? Hunh, Popeye?"

Later, Denny will explain that he heard Zimmer yelling "Go! Go! Go!" This excuse will frustrate Zim, for it's identical to the one Dewey Evans gave in the first inning of game one. Zim specifically told Doyle, "You can't go nowhere."

As Rico ends the ninth inning with a groundout to Rose, Zimmer decides that if they lose this game, he'll dress fast and flee the clubhouse before the media gets there.

The last thing he wants to do is to criticize Doyle for losing a World Series.

The next thing Carbo knows, he's out in left field in place of Yastrzemski, who's been moved to first base. It's six to six in the top of the tenth, Concepcion on second. Foster has grounded out, Geronimo has struck out. Two away.

Sparky is burning through his pinch hitters. He's tried Chaney, Crowley, and Armbrister. Now he sends up Dan Driessen, who hits a ball down the line in left.

A ball hit high down Fenway's left-field line has a tendency to drift back toward fair territory. Bernie sprints over; the ball blows back. He reverses, sticks out his gloved hand. The baseball obligingly falls into his mitt. Inning over.

Bernie almost thanks the ball. He's scared shitless over how close he came to blowing that catch. He tries shrugging it off. He comes running in. He takes a seat next to Yastrzemski in the dugout. "Carl," Bernie softly confides, "I almost missed that ball."

The Red Sox are batting in the bottom of the tenth. Evans hits a smash that Darcy knocks down; he's thrown out. Burleson pops out. Two away, and Bernie is up again.

"I don't believe it," Bench says. The catcher is still trying to understand how Bernie, after those pathetic swings, managed to get around on a classic Eastwick heater and send it to deepest center, and send them into this infernal, eternal tie. Bench doesn't especially *love* the game of baseball: he's not like Rose, this is just something Bench is good at, a job at which he excels, his chosen manner of income. Tonight Bernie Carbo, of all people, the man Cincinnati signed before Bench in the 1965 draft, took money right out of the catcher's pocket. "I just don't believe it."

"John," Bernie replies with a smile, "me neither."

Hastily, Darcy strikes Carbo out, and the inning is over.

Pete Rose is in heaven when he comes to bat in the eleventh. He can't restrain himself. He turns to the catcher. "Some kind of game, ain't it?" he calls happily.

"Yeah," Pudge grumbles back, "some kind of game."[53]

An off-speed pitch from Drago falls in for a strike.

Rose now directs his attention to the pitcher. "Throw harder!" he screams at Drago. "You can't beat me with that slow crap."

Drago beans him. "Way to hang with the slow crap," he yells, as Rose sprints to first.[54]

"Look at that," Zim marvels to DJ. "He even runs it out when he's hit by a pitch."

Griffey comes up and drag bunts Drago's two-one pitch up the first-base path. Fisk pounces, disdaining the sacrifice. He fires the ball to Burleson. It's the play he tried to pull on Armbrister after the third game went into extra innings. This time it works. Rose is forced at second.

One out, and Griffey at first.

Now Morgan comes up and drives Drago's two-two pitch toward the seats in right. The ball shoots off his bat so swiftly, with such force, that Griffey doesn't even look up; he simply takes off.

Out in right, Dewey Evans is playing Morgan "deep and full," as the scouting reports recommend, because he's a line-drive hitter. Dewey feels that gauging this sort of hit, a level smash right at him, is one of baseball's most difficult tasks. He has only a second to decide where the ball will be. He senses it going over his head as soon as it's hit. He takes off. He doubts he can reach it. He races back anyway and cuts hard to his left. Just as the ball flies into the bull pen for a home run, Dewey, who is nowhere near, awkwardly leaps and, staggering in midair, snags it. He lands with his free arm pinwheeling for balance. He looks like a dancer in a show. Dewey's glove hand is so madly extended that Sparky expects it to be holding a top hat.

Sparky — who has seen what, forty or fifty thousand fly balls caught in his lifetime, who has seen Brooks Robinson stab Johnny Bench rockets, who has studied the brilliance of Clemente in right — immediately knows that this is the single greatest catch he has ever witnessed.[55]

Morgan halts, almost to first. Usually, when Joe hits it down the line like that, it hooks. This one doesn't. That's a homer in any other ballpark! Nowhere else is the right-field line, in effect, 380 feet. He glares hotly at Dewey. *I was about to win us the World Series!* He cannot believe this.

"I just stuck my glove up," is how Evans remembers the experience, "and the next thing I knew, I was throwing the ball in."

Dewey's second display of profound clarity on the play is his immediate whirl. With his mind on the runner, he heaves the ball toward the infield.

Griffey has frozen in disbelief, midway between second and third.

Dewey's throw is way off-line. It veers wide, to the grandstand side. Yastrzemski bounds happily over to retrieve it. Carl is flushed with the exuberance of being part of a famous play in the making. Griffey isn't even back around second yet. At the right of the coaches' box, he gets his glove on the ball. Praying that someone is there to receive his relay, Carl looks up. He finds Rick Burleson covering first base, having hustled over from shortstop, the only teammate with the presence of mind to act. The impossible double play goes nine-three-six.

Drago has thrown three scoreless innings. The game heads into the bottom of the eleventh, still six to six.

Rick Miller bats for Drago in the bottom of the eleventh.

Darcy is entering his second inning of work. He is Cincinnati's eighth pitcher of the evening. Sparky has only Gullett and Clay Kirby left in the bull pen, and he doesn't trust Kirby anymore, and he has to keep Gullett for tomorrow, if necessary.

Darcy retires Miller on a fly to left, Doyle and Yastrzemski on consecutive rollers to short, and the inning is over.

Game six now stretches to three hours and forty-five minutes in length.

In Boston's theater district, the plays and musicals have emptied. Theater patrons arrive at the parking lot to get their automobiles but find themselves enthralled by what they observe on the minitelevision in the attendant's shack. They press in for a view, unwilling to grab their keys and start their vehicles for fear that they'll miss a second of this live drama. When Rick Wise enters the game in the top of the twelfth, many of those milling about the parking lot begin to boo. "No!" one cries. Wise has given up thirty-seven home runs this season, most of them in Fenway. More recently, he has expressed bitterness over not getting another start in the Series. Jealously, he insulted the Spaceman. Wise may not be a very good sport, but he's a right-hander, he's well rested, and he's what Darrell Johnson needs right now.

Bench fouls to Fisk.

Perez grounds a single to center.

Foster loops a single to left.

In his field box seat at Fenway, an eighty-seven-year-old man named Duffy Lewis fidgets impatiently. He's one of the last surviving members of the world champion Red Sox. He threw out the first ball this evening. He used to play left field alongside Tris Speaker and Harry Hooper, the best outfield to play in Fenway until Lynn, Rice, and Evans. Ball games went more quickly in Duffy's day. There weren't so many pitching changes. He played in game two of the 1916 World Series when Babe Ruth and Sherry Smith dueled for the most innings of any Series competition, a game Boston finally pulled out in the bottom of the fourteenth. Duffy doesn't remember that game lasting nearly as long as this one.

With one out and two on, Wise gets Concepcion to fly out and strikes out Geronimo. The game Boston must win now goes into the bottom of the twelfth.

Pudge scurries to the dugout. He unhooks and removes his equipment. He's Boston's first batter. As Pudge grabs a bat and heads back out, sixty-one-year-old David Conant watches on television, in Pudge's hometown of Charlestown, New Hampshire. Conant has known Fisk since birth. His wife used to change Pudge's diapers.

Fisk is on deck, swinging, and twitching, and talking excitedly to Lynn. "I'm gonna try to drive something off the wall," he tells Freddie. "You just knock me in, that's all you gotta do. I'm gonna double and you knock me in."

Fred Lynn nods. "Okay, Pudge," he says.[56] It's almost identical to a conversation held twenty-four years earlier in the Polo Grounds, also between an infielder, Bobby Thompson, and a rookie center fielder, Willie Mays, who was batting after him.

Darcy warms up with weak tosses to Bench. Each throw blows a little more sadness in the catcher's direction. *This isn't major-league stuff,* Bench realizes. *We're gonna lose.* Bench looks toward the dugout. He gives Sparky a small shake of the head, as if to warn, *This guy's got nothing.*

At a house on Central Avenue in New Haven, Connecticut, a Yale professor named Bart Giamatti watches TV with his wife, Tony. Giamatti is noted for his fond affection of Machiavelli's power poems and for an insuperable love of the Red Sox.[57]

The television displays Darcy finishing his warm-up, then cuts to Pete Rose chatting with Boston's third-base coach, Don Zimmer. Giamatti looks without fondness or affection at Rose, perhaps baseball's greatest practicing Machiavellian, the man who said, "Somebody's gotta win, somebody's gotta lose, and I believe in letting the other guy lose." Charlie Hustle is, to Giamatti, self-obsessed, rough-edged, money-mad, and one-dimensional.

Giamatti sighs heavily. He has no idea what in the hell Rose and Zimmer could be talking about just now.

"Hey, Popeye," Pete Rose is calling excitedly over to Zim. (Rose and Zim are both Cincinnati-born. They attended the same high school. They have lots to talk about.) "Win or lose, Popeye, we're in the fuckin' greatest game ever played!"

"Yeah, yeah. Boy, you sound like a little kid in the candy store, you . . ."

With no confidence whatsoever, Johnny Bench drops into a squat behind home plate. He's trying to fathom how to get Pat Darcy's pitches all the way to his mitt without them first getting jumped on. The challenges are three: to retire first Fisk, then Lynn, and then Petrocelli.

Pudge steps in for the sixth time tonight. He's twice been intentionally walked. It would figure that if he's going to accomplish anything dramatic, he would wait until the game enters its fifth hour; after all, he's the Human Rain Delay. Why rush when you can take twelve innings? Pudge digs a foothold in the batter's box. He rows his arms back and forth several times. He grasps the bat overhead with both hands. He stretches. He swings his hips to both sides. He pulls his jersey. He touches the bat all over. He slowly blows out a breath. He cocks the bat.

Darcy's first pitch is a ball, low and away.

Fisk steps out. He repeats his whole routine, the rowing, the grasping, the stretching. He returns to the box.

Bench feels the fingers of the umpire resting upon his back. He calls for a fastball, down and in. They need a strike. He just wants Darcy to get it over.

Through the metal grating above an air duct in the clubhouse, the Spaceman is being secretly observed by a rat.

The landfill beneath Boston is riven by a vast array of subterranean tunnels, home to more than eleven million rodents. The heavy rains, flooding the network of dens and warrens, have sent the rats to the surface to seek new quarters.

Young Bill Lee sits in the training room with his left arm stuck in the diathermy machine.[58] He stayed in the dugout until Carbo hit the home run, and as soon as he saw that, Bill knew that they'd win tonight, and that he would need to ready himself for tomorrow's start. He's immensely pleased. He loves to pitch, plus he's got something he learned from his father (it was reinforced by Dedeaux): *Be the first one out there, whether you're playing for chalk, marbles, or the World Series, and shoot for perfection in performance.*

While his arm warms up, Bill reads a magazine article about black holes. The rat coldly watches. It stands on its hind legs, touches the grate with its whiskers. It sniffs the air, twitches. Bill turns the page of the magazine. The rat blinks a few times, taking the measure of things.

Another rat from the same family surfaces amid mud and darkness inside the Fenway scoreboard. An NBC cameraman named Lou Gerard is stationed there. His camera frames a shot of Darcy on the far left with Fisk on the far right and Bench squatted between them. Gerard hears something squeaking in the damp shadows at the base of the Green Monster. He jumps for a flashlight. The beam reveals the biggest rodent he's ever seen.

"Lou," Harry Coyle is saying into Gerard's headset. Coyle is the granite-nosed director. He used to be a bomber pilot. He's taciturn when sober, sentimental when drunk. He has directed all but four of the televised World Series. "Lou, you there?" Coyle was the first to adopt the center-field shot, the first to look at a ballpark as a camera might, inspecting it for blind spots. He has framed and lit every baseball memory since 1947. "Lou, you gotta follow the ball wherever Fisk hits it, got that?"

"Harry," Gerard croaks. He's shaking. He hears the gnashing of teeth. "There's a rat right here next to me, it's the size of a cat, and it's moving closer."

"Shit," Coyle barks. "What are you gonna do?"

"Maybe," says Gerard, "I oughtta just stay on Fisk and, uh . . . let's see what happens."

"Good then."[59]

At that moment, half of the television sets being used in California and New York are tuned to NBC.

To Coyle, the trickiest thing about Fenway is its shadows. As a piece of architecture, it's a filmic nightmare. Irregularities abound. The odd angles and abrupt corners translate on camera as patterns of uneven brightness that make Coyle's head ache: the ball rolls past third base through half-shadows of greens and grays, the white is sometimes lost in brown. He's always cognizant of the large light tower that prevents the first-base camera from recording any play made by the shortstop. The tower is recessed such that it catches the rimmed lip of the roof and sends onto the field of play — into deep, left-most left field — a triangular slab of shadow. It's an old shadow, and very black — black as the broken thumb of Smoky Joe Wood, who prematurely lost his pitching career when he took a spill on wet infield grass, black as the leg of Carl Mays after Ty Cobb bowled him over and spiked him while beating out a bunt, black as the career-terminating injuries to Hughson and Ferriss and Lonborg, black as the eye of Tony C. and the wrist of Jim Rice, and yes, naturally, as black as the ink on Babe Ruth's Yankee contract. It's a shadow comprising all the things that kept the Red Sox from being world champions since the days of Duffy Lewis, a dank haunt in which all their failures and tragic figures fly.

This is the shadow into which Carlton Fisk golfs the second pitch of Pat Darcy, his low offering. Harry Coyle picks the perspective of the home-plate camera. Sixty-six million NBC viewers see the baseball disappear for a split second. They squint into the dark, waiting to see what Fenway's fabled shadows will give them.

Uncharacteristically, Fisk cannot run. He can only proceed toward first base while bouncing, once, twice, three times, and gesticulating. Frantically, he waves his arms, like a man guiding a plummeting airplane around his house. He commands the shadows to part.

At 12:34 A.M., the ball reappears and crashes off the mesh attached to the left-field foul pole for a home run. The ball ricochets onto the field. George Foster waves his glove at it, discouraged, catches the rebounding ball, and keeps it in his garage for the rest of his life.[60]

The parking lots in the theater district burst with a deafening ecstasy. *Rick Wise is the winning pitcher!* The liquor stores, thank God, are open until 1:00 A.M. People dash in for champagne and they spill over the boulevards, popping corks like crazy.

David Conant skips down the lamp-lit avenues of Charlestown. The chill autumn air is rife with the scent of wood smoke and leaf mold. Conant unlocks the Episcopal Church, scurries inside, and begins to ring the bells.[61] The minister angrily awakens. He chastises Conant. "That's a hell of an idea," the minister snaps. The police shake their heads. All these Red Sox fans are crazy.[62]

In New Haven, Bart Giamatti's three kids are supposed to be asleep. Knowing the game is in extra innings, they're too excited to stay in bed. They prowl the hallway, eavesdropping, while their parents watch NBC in the master bedroom. After Fisk hits the home run, the kids pour excitedly into the room. Bart and Tony are happily yelling. The kids pretend to have no inkling of what is happening. The family ends up bouncing on the bed together with arms raised, singing and shouting and laughing.

The Fenway organist, John Kiley, breaks into Handel's "Hallelujah Chorus." The crowd sings along as Kiley follows with "Give Me Some Men Who Are Stouthearted Men" and "The Beer Barrel Polka" and "Seventy-Six Trombones." The fans run deliriously onto the field while Pudge is still rounding the bases. "I straight-armed somebody and kicked 'em out of the way," he recalls, "and I touched every little white thing I saw." Joe Morgan calmly stands there, making sure that Pudge succeeds in getting to each base, still hoping they can win this game, as if they're in Ohio and there's still another half inning to go.

When Gerard stops by the production truck a short time later, the entire 140-person crew is giddy. They can't stop congratulating him. "Nobody's ever had anything like this!" they scream. "You're going to see what happens after this!"

As he promised Coyle he would, Gerard kept his lens on Fisk. He fixed on the swing and then followed the batter when Pudge, like everybody else, couldn't tell if his drive would fall fair, if it was a home run, if this must-win game, once lost, and then tied, now belonged to Boston.

The rain gave them a rat, which gave them the fright that gave them the shot that gave them the future look of sports coverage.

Recorded on tape were a few seconds of intense, contradictory emotions tearing through Pudge's face: disgust, sadness, anger, hope, ecstasy. Over and over again in replay, the mouth opened. The neck rippled. The brow raised. The eyes widened. The jaw dropped. It's the single greatest reaction shot Coyle has ever seen. It tops Berra leaping into the lap of Larsen after his perfect game. Until now, everyone has assumed that the point of sports coverage is to follow the ball. This notion of following a single individual in order to capture his feelings is revolutionary.

Fisk's mad, spontaneous, desperate dance beneath the nearly

full hunter's moon becomes a television moment everyone remembers, a sequence that is credited with reawakening interest in the national pastime, and even is said to heal the rift of the sixties by allowing fathers and sons to talk once more. It has other results, less welcome. Henceforth, memories of sporting events will become increasingly more visual and less visceral. Viewers will always, first and foremost, remember how the participants felt before they recollect their own particular response. The rampant close-ups will emphasize personalities and superstars. The individual will be cut adrift, his contributions visually isolated, just as, symbolically, free agency will cut the players from the teams, and Ted Turner's tactics will isolate teams from traditions.

Later, and forever, Fisk's waltz — heavy, hopeful, resurrected — will be thought of as a last dance, a slow, beautiful trot as old-time baseball turns out the lights.

Sparky gathers up his stuff. He leaves the locker room. He overhears Joe Morgan talking like Pete Rose and inspiring his teammates, saying that things are now in their favor, they got the best eight guys out there and Don Gullett, one of the finest pitchers in baseball, right there in the middle tomorrow, they're exactly where they want to be, it's gonna be fine. Bench is telling a reporter how Fisk's hit wouldn't even have been a homer in their park, because it's fifteen feet further down the left-field line, and the drive was hooking.

Yeah. Sparky walks up the runway to right field where his bus awaits, muttering. . . . *Game fucking seven! Baseball championships shouldn't be decided by a single game. Baseball is about fuckin' clumps of games, batting averages, fielding tendencies, fuck, evolving consistencies, balancing averages, fuckin' playing on the side of statistics. The Super Bowl is a single game; the World Series is a best-of-seven series. There's a reason for that! Anything can happen in a single baseball game. The weather changes, size and speed of clouds, dew point, brightness of day, wind direction, all these things matter, the condition of the whole field now plays a significant role, advantage is lost. . . .* His guys comprise the best team in the western hemisphere right now, and he can't manage to win the World Series with them? It's inconceivable. By the numbers, Cincinnati has Boston outmanned at every position but one, they have a better infield, a better left and right fielder, they make fewer errors, more double plays, they draw more walks, steal more bases, score more runs, win more games. They have more good starters, a better bull pen, a lower team ERA. Yet the Red Sox have fought back from a one-two deficit, then from a two-three deficit. . . . *And here, now. Who in the world is possibly gonna be able to sleep tonight? Maybe someone in bum-fuck nowheresville will sleep, yes. Who'd predict they'd hit a home run before we would? Who knew Dewey Evans was gonna grab that hit by Morgan, that had to be the best catch I've ever seen in my life, period, absolutely. And all this time I thought Beniquez was gonna be Hal Smith and all along it was Bernie fuckin' Carbo, The Village Idiot, my son. Well, wayta go, son. At least you didn't fall on your ass after you hit this one out. You've come a long way. Goddamn. . . .*

Somebody places an arm around Sparky's shoulders. "Skip, that's the greatest game I ever played."

Sparky looks up, blinks. Big strong hands, dark auburn hair, sparkling brown eyes. *Peter Edward Rose.* Sparky could weep. "Peter," he replies, "how can you say that? You know something, I'm not going to sleep one minute tonight. And you're telling me it's the greatest game you ever played?"

"Here again, Skip, Fenway Park beat us. Call it home-court advantage or whatever, but we fouled out at least four times, and there just ain't enough of foul territory in this little park for that to happen." Rose finds it impossible to remain angry over the outcome of a baseball game. "What the hell, it was the best advertisement for baseball you could ever have. Woo, momma! I mean, Christ! You couldn't have any more exciting things happen than that. This was *the* greatest game in World Series history and I'm just proud to have played in it. If this ain't the number-one pastime, I don't know what is. My son and me'll be talking about this one for a long time to come."

"Right."

"Listen, Skip," says Rose, "I tell you what. Relax. We're going to win it tomorrow."[63]

Back at the Statler-Hilton Hotel, Sparky calls California. It's earlier there, his wife is still awake. She braces him for some bad news. "I hate to tell you, but everyone here was pulling for Bernie Carbo."[64]

OCTOBER 22

DEWEY EVANS awakens to find a terrific fuss being made about how he turned Morgan's home run into a double play. "It was okay, I guess," he mumbles. Dewey is a lot like Rico; he doesn't enjoy the spotlight, and he'd just as soon it moved on. "I got a greater thrill out of Bernie Carbo's home run in the eighth. That put us back in the game and it couldn't happen to a better guy. Bernie Carbo carried this club for two months early in the season. He deserves the credit for last night."

CINCINNATI	BOSTON
Rose, *third base*	Carbo, *left field*
Morgan, *second base*	(Miller, *left field*)
Bench, *catcher*	(Beniquez, *pinch hitter*)
Perez, *first base*	Doyle, *second base*
Foster, *left field*	(Montgomery, *pinch hitter*)
Concepcion, *shortstop*	Yastrzemski, *first base*
Griffey, *right field*	Fisk, *catcher*

(continued)

CINCINNATI	BOSTON
Geronimo, *center field*	Lynn, *center field*
Gullett, *pitcher*	Petrocelli, *third base*
(Rettenmund, *pinch hitter*)	Evans, *right field*
Billingham, *pitcher*	Burleson, *shortstop*
(Armbrister, *pinch hitter*)	Lee, *pitcher*
(Carroll, *pitcher*)	(Moret, *pitcher*)
(Driessen, *pinch hitter*)	(Willoughby, *pitcher*)
(McEnaney, *pitcher*)	(Cooper, *pinch hitter*)
	(Burton, *pitcher*)
	(Cleveland, *pitcher*)

Reporters surround Sparky. They ask him if he knows which Gullett will show up for tonight's game: the tentative one from game one or the hero from game five? Sparky is bemused that this is what it comes down to, two left-handers pitching for the championship of baseball in the alleged graveyard of southpaws. But he reveals no doubts whatsoever about his admiration for Gullett. "I tell you what," Sparky insists, "I don't know about that fellow for the Red Sox, but sometime after this game, my boy's going to the Hall of Fame." As Sparky commonly predicts a Hall-of-Fame destination for his players, this is singularly unremarkable; Stengel did the same with many of his youngsters.

Bill Lee is not impressed. "I don't care where Gullett's going." Lee shrugs. "After this game, *I'm* going to the Eliot Lounge."[65]

Lee takes a moment to fan the fires of rivalry between his guys and Cincinnati's guys. "Make no mistake," Lee announces to the press. He wants to remind everyone that this World Series has thematic significance. "It's a morality play," he instructs, "good versus evil, liberal versus conservative, right versus wrong, population planners versus population exploders."

He is asked about his philosophy of pitching.

"My philosophy?" Lee coughs. He scratches his chin. "My philosophy: love of good." He gesticulates expansively. "That will come clear by the end of the game."

Lee receives a shamrock pin from Dapper O'Neil before the game. It's a good-luck charm, Lee figures. Lee is flattered by the gesture, touched that the antibusing advocate, with whom he had so loudly clashed earlier in the season, would send this gift. Lee pitches the game with the shamrock pinned to his uniform and, as usual, the game begins promisingly for Boston. Lee retires Rose, Morgan, and Bench in order, and then Carbo leads off the bottom of the first with a double. It's a drive that hits the wall in left center, Boston's first touch of the Green Monster in the Series. With one of last night's heroes in scoring position, and three outs left in the first inning of the seventh game of the World Series, everything for Boston in 1975 is perfect for the very last time.

Doyle bats second, flies out to Griffey in right, and here the re-criminations begin, because Bernie neither tags up nor advances. His momentary immobility launches the first of an ageless series of what-ifs and could've-beens, initiating the gloomy, recursive loop of blame that plagues Boston's championship aspirations. Almost thirty years later, wistful figures haunting the barbershops of Boston will mumble, with mouths turned down and heads shaking, "If only B*eh*nie C*ah*bo had taken th*eh*d . . ." For if he had, he would've scored on the next play, when Yastrzemski grounded out to second base. Instead, when Fisk strikes out to end the inning, Bernie is stranded.

Carbo behaves alertly in left the next inning. He cuts George Foster down when he tries to stretch a line drive off the wall into a double. Many viewers forgive him his first-inning mistake; none forget.

A string of other defensive gems from Boston keeps the game scoreless. In the second, Petrocelli shuffles to his left to throw out Perez on a close play. Concepcion follows with a slow roller; Burleson charges, tosses off balance to first. Yastrzemski, pulled off the bag, grabs the errant throw and just manages to tag out quick Concepcion. In the third, the Red Sox turn two to erase Geronimo and Griffey, then play a sharp grounder off Lee's leg for the last out.

Gullett comes to the mound in the bottom of the third, lacking concentration. He's fast but wild. "When he's on the road, away from his old Kentucky home," admits Sparky, "he does have a tendency to press and overthrow."

With one out, Gullett walks Carbo. Doyle singles Bernie to third and Yastrzemski singles him home. Doyle makes third on the play. Carl sneaks into second.

Now Fisk is up. He barely slept after last night's game. It was the most emotional experience of his life. He got home at 4:00 A.M., got to sleep at 7:00, got up at 10:00.

Sparky would rather not gamble on Fisk's exhaustion. He instructs Bench to have Gullett walk the right-handed Pudge intentionally.

The bases are loaded for Lynn. When the left-hander gets called out on strikes, Sparky looks like a genius. Two outs, one run in; hey, Cincinnati can recover.

But Gullett's control remains, at best, elusive. He goes three and oh on the next batter, Petrocelli, then fights back to three and two.

Dave Concepcion calls time to complain about a light in a television booth at the top of the backstop screen. After play resumes, Gullett is rattled. He throws five straight balls, walking in two.

Boston leads, three to nothing, with the bases still loaded, but Gullett strikes out Burleson to rekindle Boston's self-flagellating recriminations. Three left on base, another valuable opportunity squandered, if only, what-if, etc. The recriminations continue to pile up until, by the top of the fifth inning, the stands have fallen silent. They were waving their Spaceman T-shirts in the bleachers, but no more. Bill Lee can't figure it out. The audience seems scared to applaud. They're waiting for the other shoe to drop. *Perhaps it's out of consideration for Tom Yawkey*, the Spaceman speculates. Perhaps they don't want the old man getting too confident for fear that, should his team yet again fail at the last minute, his heart won't be able to withstand the shock. No, but it's more selfish than that. *It's paranoia.* Lee feels it creeping through the stands, and he knows it owes no small inspiration to Cincinnati's boundless optimism, to what Bench calls their "inner conceit."

The fifth opens with Concepcion and Griffey getting aboard on consecutive singles. There's no outs. *And here it comes.* . . . Lee feels Fenway girding itself for imminent disappointment. It's infuriating. He's throwing a sinker/slider shutout here and stubbornly they hold their faith in abeyance. They act as if their boys aren't ahead by three in the fifth inning of the seventh game of the World Series. It's surreal. The team edges closer to its first championship in sixty-seven years while the defeatist fans watch mutely, wondering just how the Red Sox will fuck it up this time.

Back in April, when Los Angeles was three games up on the Reds, Pete Rose said, "The Dodgers are in first place, chasin' us." This evening, despite watching the Red Sox chase Gullett in four innings and take a commanding three-and-oh lead, all the fans can see are blown scoring opportunities. Even after Lee strikes out Cesar Geronimo, and gets pinch hitter Merv Rettenmund to rap into a double play that closes out the top of the fifth, Fenway seems to be moaning with murmurs of how Carbo should've advanced, and Burleson shouldn't have fanned, and pointing out how Lee got to third with one out in the fourth and then couldn't score.

When Lee and Dewey Evans both fly out to deep center field in the bottom of the fifth, stranding three more Boston base runners, the fans know they're leading but they can't shake this suspicion that the Red Sox are still chasing the Reds. They're too afraid that Cincinnati is merely toying with them, as a cat will allow a mouse to lounge before killing it. They have heard what Joe Morgan says, that you're allotted twenty-seven outs in this game, and that his team will generally pull the game out after using up twenty-six of them. They believe Little Joe.

Morgan comes to bat in the sixth, with Rose on first after a leadoff single. Morgan flies to Evans in shallow right.

Rose holds.

Bench comes to bat.

With the Reds consistently hitting Bill Lee to the right side of the diamond, Boston's coaches move Doyle off second base and into the hole.

Lee throws a perfect sinker. It tails off, low and away.

Bench connects, and hits a two-hopper to Burleson, who turns to toss it to second but has to wait while Doyle waddles over from his deep position. At last, Doyle receives the ball from Burleson, he steps on the bag for the force, he pivots to turn two — and then he catches a swift impression of Pete Rose barreling at him, big as a thoroughbred, with smoke billowing from his nostrils, and his dark eyes full of hate. The prevailing cynicism at last comes to fruition. Doyle flinches as he relays to first. He misses the outstretched glove of Carl Yastrzemski by about forty feet. "The throw got away from me," Doyle explains later. "It got away like the whole damn thing."

The ball soars into the Boston dugout and lands squarely in Don Zimmer's lap. Zim immediately fires it across to Fisk but the damage is done, Bench is on second, and Bill Lee is furious. *That was a perfect double-play ball.* He should be out of the inning! Instead, the Reds stay alive and now Tony Perez gets a swing.

Lee has thrown his slop-drop eephus three times in this game, twice for a called strike, once for a pop-up. He threw it past Perez in the first, though he was warned by his coaches before the game that if he tried the eephus, Perez would cream it.

Now, a flicker of complicity passes between Lee and Fisk.

Up until that moment, the most famous eephus pitch in Fenway Park was thrown on July 9, 1946, when Rip Sewell faced Ted Williams at the end of the all-star game, and Williams drove it out of the park for his record fifth RBI of the day.

Lee winds up and throws. The ball drifts toward home. Lee has always managed his use of the pitch very strictly. This time he's made a grievous miscalculation. For the rest of his life, he will be questioned about this particular pitch. Adamantly, he will refuse to second-guess himself. "If you live by the slow curve," Lee will always insist, "you die by the slow curve."[66]

Twenty-five years later, Perez will remain convinced that the slop drop got him to the Hall of Fame. Standing alongside Pudge and Sparky on the podium in Cooperstown, he will begin his induction speech by turning first to Fisk, to thank him for calling this pitch.

It's exactly what Perez has been hoping to see again. He times it beautifully. "He counted the seams of the ball as it floated up to the plate," Lee will remember, "checked to see if Lee MacPhail's signature was on it, signed his own name to it, and then jumped all over it."[67]

Perez leans back and knocks it over the fence. It lands on Lansdowne Street, near where Williams deposited Sewell's eephus. Cincinnati two, Boston three.

Lee gets Foster to fly to Evans, but Boston goes quietly in their half, adding nothing.

The seventh inning opens with the Red Sox still ahead by a single run.

Concepcion is promptly erased on a ground ball to Burleson, and Griffey replaces him in the batter's box.

Lee looks in. Pudge signals for a sinker. Lee nods.

The rumble and sputter of police motorcycles filters into the park from outside.

Lee leans back, brings his hands over his head, turns to first, raises a leg. He falls forward. The ball rotates as it leaves his hand. The seam burns his thumb. A blister immediately rises. *All it takes is one pitch.*

After the game, Lee explains how a blister is a second-degree burn, caused by friction or heat or pressure intensity, how a blister on the thumb adversely affects control, how a thumb is the most important digit on the hand of any sinker-ball pitcher, how a thumb is all that keeps us from being quadrupeds, and without thumbs we'd be apes swinging in the trees.[68]

Lee walks Griffey on four straight pitches and then stares down at his left thumb morosely. Darrell Johnson comes out. Learning of the blister, DJ immediately calls for relief.

A group of Spanish-speaking men talk excitedly in the bleachers as the long-striding Rogelio Moret hurries to the mound. "Moret!" they shout. "Moret! Moret!"

It doesn't take long for Griffey to steal, even with left-handed Moret on the mound. Fisk makes another poor throw. It's their ninth straight steal off Pudge.

Armbrister walks and up comes Rose, who hits a hard drive to center field. Lynn charges, but there is no hope of getting Griffey at the plate, and the game is tied, three to three.

Moret then walks Morgan, and Darrell Johnson emerges once more. Johnny Bench is up. Moret is dismissed in favor of Jim Willoughby.

It is, in retrospect, the addition of Jim Willoughby along with Denny Doyle that made pennant winners out of the Red Sox (just as adding Foster and Eastwick rendered Cincinnati impregnable). Indeed, Dick O'Connell will be selected as the *Sporting News'* 1975 Executive of the Year, his most oft-mentioned contribution the midseason acquisition of Doyle and Willoughby.

Coming into the seventh with the score tied and the bases loaded, Willoughby has continued success. He gets Bench to foul out to Fisk.

Bottom of the seventh. Clay Carroll is pitching in relief of Jack Billingham. Fisk strikes out, Lynn and Rico ground out.

Top of the eighth. Cincinnati returns again to battling Willoughby. Perez pops up, Foster and Concepcion ground out.

Bottom of the eighth. A man in the bleachers, his beige cap pulled tight and a lumberjack shirt hanging over his pants, stands on his seat. "Let's go!" he bellows. Those around him respond with quizzical expressions. Some paid scalpers as much as sixty dollars for tonight's bleacher seat.

Darrell Johnson is desperate for a base runner. He lucks out as Evans works Carroll for a leadoff walk. Burleson is up next. DJ instructs him to bunt. He misses twice. On the third pitch, the Rooster swings and bounces into a double play.

Willoughby is supposed to hit next, but DJ calls him back to the dugout. It's true that, against Willoughby, Cincinnati's right-handers haven't managed to get anything out of the infield, but they have a couple tough left-handers due up in the ninth. DJ tells Cecil Cooper (one for eighteen) to get up there and pinch-hit for Willoughby. Although there's no one on base and there's two outs, DJ wants to win this thing. He needs a hit. "Standing still at three-three," the manager will justify the decision later, "is no way to win a ball game. The key to the game is to put runs on the board."

Cooper pops up to third.

The deciding game rolls into its final inning with the score still tied.

Darrell Johnson, who has succeeded all year despite baffling strategies, takes one last gamble. He brings rookie left-hander Jim Burton in from the bull pen. Burton has one victory and two losses for the entire year. He's made only one postseason appearance, pitching one-third of an inning in game three, walking Griffey and retiring Morgan on a fly, before being replaced by Reggie Cleveland.

Burton enters the game, spreading ripples of concern throughout New England. Fenway remains quiet, mulling it over. Everyone hears the wooden chattering of Maria Tiant's *matraca*, that huge noisemaker she's been twirling constantly since the play-offs with Oakland. The *matraca* is so much heavier than a baseball, Luis jokes, that his wife now possesses the strongest arm in the family.

Ken Griffey opens the ninth by earning a base on balls against Burton. The apparent smallness of it disappoints Griffey's eldest, who is watching at home in Cincinnati. Junior wanted to see his dad pound another one to deep center like he did in game two's ninth (which won the game), or in game four's ninth (which Lynn barely caught), or in game six's fifth (which Lynn chased into the wall). Those were significant hits; they rang with consequence. *A walk can't be that important*, gripes Junior.

Carlton Fisk sees it differently. He and his guys basically have the big guns neutralized, but their inability to keep the speedy little guys — Griffey, Geronimo, Concepcion — off the base paths is a perceptible disadvantage.

Next, Geronimo casually bunts, pushing Griffey over to second with the rudimentary sacrifice that the Rooster couldn't accomplish last inning.

Next, Driessen bounces to the right, advancing Griffey to third. How important was the walk? The Reds have two outs, but the winning run now stands ninety feet from home and Rose is up.

Darrell Johnson emerges. He and Fisk converge on the mound to shout in Burton's face. This is supposed to help. They think they're being supportive. They proffer advice on how to pitch to Pete Rose. They suggest that he make Rose chase high fastballs.

"Okay," says Burton. The meeting breaks up.

Burton walks Rose on four pitches.

Joe Morgan merrily digs in. Two outs, ninth inning, tie score, men on first and third: he was hoping to come to the plate. He's been on deck with his elbow twitching excitedly, just praying that Rose will allow him the opportunity to win the game.

Burton makes a good pitch for strike one.

Morgan fouls the next pitch for strike two.

Burton follows with his best pitch, a slider, low and away. He throws it perfectly. There are only a few people in the world with wrists quick enough to handle it. Unfortunately, one of them is at bat. Morgan fights it off. He flicks his bat. He doesn't connect very well. The ball wobbles toward short center, dying all the way.

Burton looks back. He sees that Lynn can't get to it in time. He experiences a bottomless disappointment, he's heartsick and empty. Griffey jogs in to score the tie-breaking run.

Bill Lee paces the dugout, watching history repeat itself. He can appreciate the exquisite symmetry of this moment, because Cincinnati also won game two, his other start, with a two-out, seeing-eye single in the ninth off a reliever.

Reggie Cleveland replaces Burton. Cleveland walks Bench to reload the bases, and then gets Perez to fly out.

Sparky's end move is to bring in his own rookie left-handed reliever, Will McEnaney, to start the bottom of the ninth. The Red Sox have three outs left in 1975. A desperate Darrell Johnson sends Beniquez up to pinch-hit, but Juan flies out. He sends Montgomery up to pinch-hit, but Monty grounds out.

The last batter is Carl Yastrzemski.

Hattie stands, and Fenway follows her example, clapping as one.

McEnaney, on the mound, nearly gnaws his glove. It's astonishing! He can't believe it. He's twenty-two, the youngest activated player on either roster, and here he is, wrapping up the World Series. It's in fact his second mind-blowing experience of the month, the first being the birth of his first child a few weeks before. It kept McEnaney sleep-deprived for much of the Series as a consequence. McEnaney was grateful for the rained-out weekend before game six, which allowed him finally to catch up on all his lost slumber. Now he's a father, and well rested at that, and all he has to do to preserve Cincinnati's first World Series victory since 1940 is to retire the greatest clutch performer in the history of the Red Sox.

This is something that every father's son dreams of doing one day. *Just don't walk him*, McEnaney thinks.

Carl is thinking: *Home run.*[69] He wants to tie the game. He studies the situation. McEnaney is a left-handed sidearmer with a sinker ball. *Wait until the last possible second before swinging. Don't open up too quickly.* Carl waits. McEnaney makes a mistake. He gets the pitch up. But Carl drops too soon. He gets under the ball. Instead of driving it, he gets underneath it. It travels to deep center. The crowd roars. Now they're thinking: *Home run.* But McEnaney watches Geronimo, sees that the center fielder has stopped backing up and is settling in for a catch. McEnaney snatches off his own cap, shouts, pulls his cap back on. He dances straight at Bench, leaps into his arms. The catcher swings him around. All the Reds are hugging one another. No one is covering the bases. "If Geronimo had dropped the ball," Rose says afterward, "Yastrzemski would've gone all the way."

If I hadn't dropped down quite as much, thinks Carl, *I would have hit it out.*

Geronimo makes the catch.

"I was on a Rocky Mountain High," McEnaney later recalls. "I was way out somewhere."

In a rooftop box, a bareheaded old man watches the dissolution of another dream. "Well," Tom Yawkey says mildly, turning to the fellows gathered around, "I guess it wasn't meant to be." His gray jacket is drawn tight around his neck. There's a trace of moisture in his eyes. "We could have won in four straight, but ah . . . I'm proud of my players. They fought right to the end. That's a helluva ball club that beat us."

He'll be dead before the next season ends.

As soon as Cesar catches Carl's fly ball, the ballpark goes mad. Chaos erupts. Thousands upon thousands of young, male so-called baseball fans explode onto the playing field, fluttering about in delicious liberty. Some want souvenirs. Some want revenge. They generally possess strong feelings about losing the World Series, but their energy can't find its outlet. If there were shop windows and merchandise, they'd be looting. Instead, they grab dirt from the infield, they tear turf from the outfield. They run around the dia- mond, shouting, with their shirttails streaming behind them. They hurl expletives and rolls of toilet paper into the late-night air. They begin to pull up the bases, a true example of base stealing.

Vickie Bench watches from above Cincinnati's dugout, where she is seated beside the wives of the other Reds players. Vickie folds her arms over her tight-fitting blouse such that no one can read the name of her husband spelled out in sequins across the front.[70] A red-bearded student dashes past, hoisting a chunk of ballpark sod over his head. "This is a piece of Carl Yastrzemski territory!" he yells to no one in particular. "This is a kilo of Fenway green." The police are badly outnumbered. Again and again, they try unsuccessfully to shape the mob and sweep it toward an exit. Members of the Tactical Patrol Force escort the pitchers in from the bull pen. Luis Tiant appears unmoved.

A nasty fight breaks out at the base of the Green Monster. Groundskeepers in brown windbreakers try to keep people from smashing apart the scoreboard. Policemen don riot helmets and rush to help. Through the swarm of color and movement, Vickie catches a glimpse of the final score and sees again CIN 4, BOS 3, which confirms it, we won, yes, they lost. *So this is how it feels to be victorious.*

"Isn't this wonderful?" gushes Robin Plummer, the wife of Bench's backup catcher.[71] She keeps a pink-and-white toy bunny in her purse for good luck.

"I think it's terrible," snaps Rose's wife, Karolyn, who's alternately shooting home movies and blowing sharp blasts on her silver whistle.[72] Karolyn keeps a red painted rock in her handbag for good luck.

So, all of their good-luck charms worked. Tonight Vickie's husband and his friends are world champions. *Let jubilation reign.* Possibly, if Vickie were in Cincinnati just now, where exuberant tens of thousands have been pouring into Fountain Square since Rose tied the score in the seventh — lighting firecrackers, and singing happily, and blaring horns, and snarling traffic — possibly Vickie would feel more of something.

A young man emerges from the Red Sox dugout, with bushy eyebrows and wide, Glen Campbell sideburns. He wears tan slacks, a Sox cap, baseball shoes. His shirt is blue, with no. 9 and, inexplicably, the word COACH on the back. All around him, officers are chasing people, tripping and handcuffing them. Obliviously, the man starts to loosen up on the warning track. He runs wind sprints. Not a soul molests him. He sets off on a jog, around the rim of the field, and as he nears Vickie, she recognizes him as the twenty-three-year-old, brown-eyed wonder boy, Fred Lynn. He jogs back to the Boston dugout, stretches out his side a little, then vanishes.

And now, dutiful to the end, Vickie flees, returns to Manhattan. "Johnny Bench is a great athlete," she tells the world, "a mediocre everything else, and a true tragedy as a person."

Karolyn Rose's marriage endures a bit longer.[73] Karolyn accepted, when she married Pete, that she was his third love. "First there's baseball, second there's his car, and third there's me." That was okay with her because all she wanted to be was a good wife and mother. But then their daughter, Fawn, was born. Apparently

Karolyn didn't know how much Pete disliked Fawn; rather, Karolyn felt herself being relegated to fourth place. And then their son, Petey, was born, so then Karolyn dropped to fifth. "Fifth place," she explains soon after divorcing her husband, "was too low in the standings."

OCTOBER 23

AT 12:35 P.M., thirty-five thousand people, enough Bostonians to fill Fenway to capacity, converge on City Hall Plaza to salute their latest impossible dream. Dukakis is there, a figure of scorn since recently breaking a campaign pledge and raising taxes. The dark-haired governor tries to welcome everyone with a few remarks. The crowd shouts him down. They're in no mood for politicians. They crave the candor of Young Bill Lee, who tells the story of game seven as "Well, I went out there and threw the shit out of the ball, but we made a couple of mistakes and we lost," they want his irascibility, finding out after the game that the shamrock he got from Dapper O'Neil was not a good-luck charm but a symbol of ROAR (Return our Alienable Rights, an antibusing group): "Well, I wore Dapper's goddamn shamrock! And we lost with it. So that must prove that their ideology is all wrong, hunh?!"[74] Or they'd even prefer the unflappable Darrell Johnson, who disregards the loss because it took a weak shot to decide the other team's superiority. "The man hit a blooper into center off the end of the bat."

The manager shrugs. "There's not much you can do about something like that."

The masses have congregated to cheer for men, not squirrels — for public losers, not backroom compromisers. "Sit down, you turkey!" They make gobbling noises toward Governor Dukakis. "Take a backseat, you bum!"

Red Sox broadcaster Ned Martin introduces the manager. Johnson thanks the crowd for their support.

Martin introduces Yastrzemski. Carl is here to represent the invaluable veteran contributions — Rico, who played errorless ball in the seven World Series games and batted .308; Tiant, who started every Red Sox victory; and Carl, who played half the Series in the infield, half in the outfield, and batted .310.

"Let's not look back," Carl tells them, "because for the next four or five years, this team is going to be a contender." *With all these great young kids, every game is going to mean something for some time. Jeez, from now until I retire we're going to be in a pennant race.* "We're going to win that Series yet."

Martin introduces Burleson, who smiles, and waves, and thanks the city on behalf of the future, the team's gritty youths — Fisk, Lynn, Rice, Evans, Cooper, Moret.

Lastly, the broadcaster introduces Bill Lee, "the space cowboy from southern California," who comes to the microphone to talk about how Charlie Brown and Linus view winners and losers. Lee speaks for himself, and maybe also his heroic cohort in clutch slapstick, Bernie Carbo. After the mob scenes of the last two nights, he still half expects to get torn in two. Inevitably, he segues into the topic of ecology. "Boston has a harsh environment," Lee points out. "There is a harsh spring and winter. And when baseball comes, it's the herald of summer." He looks around. A cloud passes overhead. There's much more he could say . . . *Last night, a dead man won the $1 million Massachusetts lottery, the Soviet Union parachuted the first spacecraft onto the surface of Venus, and England lost Arnold Toynbee, the great historian. Meanwhile, fistfights between white and black students continue unabated in the corridors of*

Boston's Hyde Park High . . . but now is not the time. It's a question of appropriateness. Casey Stengel had to learn the answer. Now Bill Lee has learned it too. "I want to thank everyone for coming. Make sure you pick up everything."

Followed by their fans, the team files into City Hall, where a twelve-foot-by eight-foot cake model of Fenway awaits. The cake contains three thousand eggs, four hunded pounds of flour, and three hundred pounds of butter. It dwarfs the one at Johnny and Vickie's fairy-tale wedding, the cake with which Cincinnati began its season.

OCTOBER 31

ARLY IN THE DAY, two Bay Area high schools, Oakland High and Oakland Tech, meet on the football field. It's Oakland High's homecoming game. They're the best team in the league while Oakland Tech is oh and five on the season.

Everyone expects a blowout.

Oakland High kicks off. A skinny back catches it at the two yard line. He fakes, shuffles, fakes, and then zooms off. He runs straight into Oakland High's secondary and straight out the other side. He carries it all the way, a ninety-eight-yard touchdown on the opening kickoff.

His name is so long it spills off the back of his jersey and around the side. It looks as if he is called "Henderso."

Oakland Tech goes on to beat Oakland High twenty-four to twenty in the upset of the season. Rickey Henderson is named Doten Pontiac Athlete of the Week. He will end up rushing for 1,100 yards that season, scoring at least one touchdown in every game. Scholarship offers will pour in from UCLA, UNLV, Arizona State, all over the Pac Ten, more than twenty in all. It will be a dream come true until the Oakland Athletics select him next in the major league's June draft.

"I want you to play baseball," his mother, Bobbie, will tell him. She's a nurse. She sees too many hurt kids come in, sporting concussions and broken clavicles, all bashed up and ruined. She believes that Rickey is too small for football. She's worried about his health.

"Momma," he will tell her, "you know how much I love football."

"Yes."

They'll argue for hours.

"Momma," Rickey will say finally, "I'll leave it up to you." He feels sure that she'll defer to his dream.

"Fine," Bobbie will snap. "You're playing baseball. Subject closed."[75]

Rickey will start to cry.

CONCLUSION

THERE ARE CERTAIN BASEBALL seasons in which the sport and the business of our national pastime dramatically intersect to reinvigorate the game. In 1920, for example, the faith of fans was tested by the Black Sox scandal. Into the breach stepped baseball's first commissioner, Kenesaw Mountain Landis, as well as the unimaginable Babe Ruth. Baseball was saved. After VE- and VJ-Day, baseball's return to prewar glory was in doubt; by 1946 fans were distracted, athletes were underpaid, owners were nervous. A bold move by the Dodger front office put a black man on their triple-A team in Montreal, and again, thanks to Branch Rickey and Jackie Robinson, baseball was saved.

Nineteen seventy-five is another such year.

The season had begun propitiously, with attention lavished on Cleveland's sold-out Opening Day game, all eyes fastened on Frank Robinson as the first black manager strolled to home plate to exchange lineup cards. Frank was batting in the DH slot. In his first time up, in the first inning of his first game of the season, he hit a two-and-two fastball over the left-field fence for a home run. The

crowd of fifty-eight thousand roared loud and long. Jackie Robinson's widow, Rachel, danced in the stands alongside Commissioner
Kuhn, who humbly hogged all the credit for Frank's breakthrough
advancement. The papers ran pictures taken in the late fifties of the
two Robinsons together, young crew-cutted Frank chatting with
prematurely gray Jackie.

This self-congratulation on the part of Major League Baseball
eventually runs its course, and by season's end Frank Robinson is
nobody special, just one more mediocre manager of a so-so team.
The next Jackie Robinson is not, it became apparent, an Indian.
No. He is a Yankee. His name is Catfish Hunter.

Like Jackie, the symbolic importance of Catfish on the field
nearly overshadows his greatness as a player. Hunter is a pioneer of
free agency, a harbinger of things to come, baseball's first million-
dollar superstar. The garish spotlight of New York that once shone
on Robinson — the player scrutiny, press sarcasm, and public suspicion — now focuses on Catfish. The success of the first free agent
in 1975 is as doubtful and as crucial as that of the first black major
leaguer in 1947; it's easy to imagine a public hostile to free agency
if Catfish is anything other than superb. But he is. Like Jackie, Catfish excels masterfully, retiring batters, mowing down all reluctance, reticence, and resistance. His outlandish raise is earned as
few ever will be and eases the transition into baseball's next era.

Though Hunter does have a Jackie Robinson–like season, it is
Jim Palmer who receives this year's American League Cy Young
Award. The two started four games against each other in 1975.
Each won two, lost two. Their season totals prove virtually identical,
but Palmer, possessing a slightly lower ERA, nabs the award.

Every other year, the effectiveness of the right-handed Palmer
had been bolstered by the presence on the Baltimore staff of the
left-handed Dave McNally. In their nine years together, McNally
and Palmer had pitched in five league-championship series and
four World Series. Between 1969 and 1973, the two starters were
responsible for 194 regular-season Oriole victories.

This year, as Palmer accepts his second Cy Young Award,

McNally can only read about it in the papers. He is far away, it seems, but not so far that he can't be found by the president of the Montreal Expos, John McHale, who shows up in Montana one day late in 1975, offering McNally a $25,000 bonus if he will sign a contract, then and there, with the Expos.[1] McNally can keep the bonus, even if he never pitches again. But if he signs, his name will be removed from the grievance that has been filed by the players' union.

McNally reflects on this. Twenty-five thousand dollars is a lot of money. Even if he wins the suit, he doesn't stand to make a dime, since he is out of baseball now. But if he takes McHale's payoff, Messersmith will be isolated, left to file the suit alone. Rumor has it that the Dodgers are very close to satisfying Messersmith, and if they succeed, and both Messersmith and McNally sign contracts, their case will collapse, and nothing will ever change. Owners will continue to ignore the wishes of their employees; players will still be held hostage to the whims of management.[2]

McNally turns down McHale's offer.[3] O'Malley breaks off negotiations with Messersmith. The hearing commences November 21 at Manhattan's Barbizon Plaza. The neutral arbitrator, Peter Seitz, cuts a grandfatherly figure, dressed as always in a three-piece suit, with long, flowing gray hair. Witnesses testify for days. "I gave a sermon on the history and importance of the reserve system and the grave consequences of its elimination," Bowie Kuhn remembers. "I had the feeling no one was listening." Chub Feeney predicts that if the two pitchers win their case, "We might not have a World Series." Walter Alston says, "If Messersmith is declared a free agent, then baseball is dead."

Marvin Miller responds that the only issue presently under debate is whether a baseball athlete can play out his option in one year, or whether the option can be perpetually renewed without the athlete's consent.

Seitz does not enjoy this case. He is a kind man in a tough position. He agrees with Miller but sympathizes with the baseball establishment. He can anticipate no pleasant outcome. He strongly encourages the owners to bypass this arbitration and instead take up the issue directly with the players' union. "I begged them to negotiate," Seitz recalls. They wouldn't. "The owners were too stubborn and stupid. They were like the French barons in the twelfth century. They had accumulated so much power they wouldn't share it with anybody."[4]

On December 23, Seitz issues his decision. Messersmith and McNally are free to negotiate and sign with other teams, as is any major leaguer who plays a season without signing his contract. The automatic renewal clause in every ballplayer's contract lasts a single year, no more. Free agency is here.

The golden era of baseball, when the owners controlled the labor pool, is over. Now, more plainly than ever, the game is a business. The owners are no longer brothers but open foes, each tendering a rival bid for the experienced talent that will annually come available. The players are no longer teammates but mercenaries who will seek the pay of movie stars. While Dave McNally keeps selling Fords in Billings, his life entirely unchanged by the Seitz decision, Andy Messersmith is eagerly courted by George Steinbrenner. Ultimately, the pitcher signs for a million dollars with the new chief of the Braves, Ted Turner, who models himself after marketers such as Steinbrenner and Finley, and who will prove to be representative of the new type of owner, the diversified investor, the wealthy hobbyist.

Fortunately for all concerned, the country is just then recalling a profound affection for its national pastime. It happens suddenly, like the lifting of a curse, and just in time for America's bicentennial. The fans surge back, as they had in the twenties for Ruth and in the forties for Robinson; it occurs now because of the evident fulfillment of Hunter's promise, and the improbable near-upset of the '75 Series, and the sight of Fisk waving the ball fair.

Why does that Series resonate so? The Sox were underdogs, full of old-time personality, playing for a veteran owner in a quirky, prewar ballpark. For seven close games in October, they fiercely battled their antithesis, the heavily favored Big Red Machine. After free agency, every team with money will model itself on the Reds — a roster of future Hall of Famers, playing their game under high expectations in a concrete behemoth, a high-stakes scene of mob intimacy. Cincinnati represented the future; Boston, the past. They collided in 1975.

Despite the gloomy predictions of Kuhn, Feeney, and Alston, baseball will not die. But will the uniform continue to matter? Perhaps, after 1975, the uniform will mean more than ever. Before the Messersmith-McNally decision, the player donned his uniform as an inmate might don a set of prison clothes. Even with his name printed on the back, what he wore identified him by his owner and spoke of his helpless condition. He had signed a contract as a boy and so was bound to wear this uniform until he got traded, or died.

In the future, no player will long wear a uniform against his will. He will be permitted to change sides regularly, if he chooses. He will belong because he wants to belong. Some will simply chase dollars, but others will join certain teams to satisfy deeper yearnings. Like his father, Barry Bonds will achieve his greatest accomplishments as a Giant, dressed in black and orange. Ken Griffey Jr. will pull on the red stirrup stockings of Cincinnati, think of his dad, and smile. Dwight Gooden will perform most of his career in New York, where his father and grandfather dreamed of playing.

But what of Rickey Henderson, the fatherless one? He will find a father figure in Billy Martin, just as Billy found his in Stengel while playing in Oakland. Martin will be managing the A's during Henderson's first full season. Together, they will nearly take the team to the World Series in 1981. The next year, Billy will give Rickey the green light to run whenever he wants. Granted this freedom, Rickey will steal more bases in one season than any player in history. Martin will lose his job, of course, but he and Henderson will be reunited later in the eighties, both of them wearing Yankee pinstripes. Presently, Henderson will return to the A's in a midseason trade, but before Martin dies, on Christmas Day, 1989, Billy will watch Rickey and Mark "Tree" McGwire lead Oakland to its first world championship since the dynastic days of Reggie, Rollie, Rudi, and Catfish. Finley will be long gone. This time the championship will be earned by free and happy players.

The champagne will taste especially sweet that year.

NOTES

PART ONE: THE PRESEASON

ONE

1. Cataneo, *Tony C.*, pp. 108–111.
2. *Ibid.*
3. *Ibid.*
4. Hunter, *Catfish*, pp. 2–3.
5. Primary sources for Catfish negotiations include Ibid., pp. 126–150; Libby, *Catfish*, pp. 1–41, 146–163; Stambler, *Catfish*, pp. 8–18; Paul Hemphill, "The Yankees Fish for a Pennant," *Sport*, 1975, pp. 54, 63–71; Stout, *Red Sox Century*, p. 354.
6. Yastrzemski, *Baseball*, p. 76.
7. Hunter, *Catfish*, p. 9.

TWO

1. "Ebbing Flood," *Sports Illustrated*, August 1975, pp. 6–7.

THREE

1. Primary sources for the last year of Stengel's life include MacLean, *Casey Stengel*, pp. 180–184; Robert W. Creamer, *Casey Stengel*, pp. 330–332; Nicholson, *Casey Stengel*, pp. 174–177; Allen, *You*

Could Look It Up; Ted Thackrey Jr., "Casey Stengel, Baseball Great, Dies of Cancer," *Los Angeles Times,* September 30, 1975; "Casey Stengel Dies of Cancer at Eighty-Five," *Los Angeles Times,* October 1, 1975; "Morning Briefing," *Los Angeles Times,* October 3, 1975; "Morning Briefing," *Los Angeles Times,* October 4, 1975; "Baseball Ignored Casey in His Final Days," *San Francisco Examiner,* October 2, 1975; Wells Twombly, "There Was Only One Casey and He'll Never Die," *San Francisco Examiner,* October 1, 1975.

All accounts agree that Stengel was then living mainly in his memories.

"Casey," writes Nicholson (p. 175), "had lost a lot of his zest for life and just let [his house] go to hell. He couldn't cook, so he was eating out of cans. He didn't know how to wash or iron, so he slept in the same unkempt bed for months. Fan mail and utility bills piled up unanswered. He had been showing signs of senility for several years, but in this, the last year of his life, he was very erratic. He stayed in his room, listening to the radio and arguing with disembodied voices: 'You're full of shit and I'll tell you why.' He stuffed wads of bills — a thousand dollars here, five thousand there — into cubbyholes around the house including suit pockets, bureau drawers, closets, suitcases, even the fireplace."

2. Henderson, *Off Base,* pp. 26–27.

FOUR

1. Primary sources for the relationship between Johnny Bench and Vickie Chesser include Hertzel, *The Big Red Machine,* pp. 131–134; Jeanne Parr, *The Superwives* (New York: Coward, McCann & Geoghegan, 1975), pp. 277–283; Johnny Bench with William Brashler, *Catch You Later: The Autobiography of Johnny Bench* (New York: Harper & Row, 1979), p. 170; Kay Gilman, "Cincy No Place for a Broadway Johnny," *New York Daily News,* August 18, 1974; Rosemary Davis, "Johnny and Vickie Swing to Same Pitch," *Cincinnati Enquirer,* January 30, 1975; "Bench, Beauty: Bumpkins?" *Canton Repository,* February 2, 1975; "A Whirlwind Romance — Bench Will Wed Model," *Sporting News,* February 8, 1975; "Mrs. Bench's Game Plan: Johnny's in 'Clean Up,'" *Sunday Press,* February 16, 1975; Dick Young, "Vickie's Vegas Gamble Hits Honeymoon Jackpot," *New York Daily News,* February 24, 1975; Rosemary Davis, "Bench Fans Await Star's Wedding," *Cincinnati News,* February 27, 1975; Leonard Lewin, "There's Another Side to Johnny Bench," *New York Post,* July 23, 1975.

2. Young, "Vickie's Vegas Gamble."

3. Anderson, *The Main Spark,* p. 164.

4. "Vickie: Marriage 'Broke My Heart,'" *The State*, February 2, 1977.

5. Milton Richman, "Sparky 'Like Father' to Bernie Carbo," *Cincinnati Enquirer*, October 16, 1975.

6. Jeff Lenihan, "Baseball Helps Carbo Deal with Personal Tragedies," *Times Union*, November 6, 1989.

7. Pepe, *Talkin' Baseball*, p. 173.

8. Bill Madden, "To Hell and Back," *New York Daily News*, June 3, 1993.

9. Pepe, *Talkin' Baseball*, p. 209.

10. Cataneo, *Tony C.*, pp. 217–218.

FIVE

1. John Garrity, *The George Brett Story* (New York: Coward, McCann & Geoghegan, 1981), p. 122. Also Ross Newhan, "Royal Treatment: Brett Proved Father Correct with Illustrious Twenty-One-Year Career and Election to Hall of Fame," *Los Angeles Times*, July 25, 1999.

2. Primary sources for the relationship between Bobby and Barry Bonds include Muskat, *Barry Bonds*; Rambeck, *Barry Bonds*; Sullivan, *Sports Great Barry Bonds*; Savage, *Barry Bonds*; Michael Goodman, *Barry Bonds*; Harvey, *Barry Bonds*.

3. George Sullivan, *Bobby Bonds: Rising Superstar* (New York: G. P. Putnam's Sons, 1976), pp. 16–17.

4. Dick Schaap, "Bobby Bonds Brings His Act to Broadway," *Sport*, July 1975, p. 29.

5. Ibid., p. 28.

6. Ibid., pp. 29, 34.

7. Sullivan, *Bobby Bonds*, pp. 13–14.

8. Drucker, *The George Foster Story*, pp. 66–68.

PART TWO: THE SEASON'S FIRST HALF

SIX

1. Ibid., pp. 69–70.

2. Wells Twombly, "Bobby Murcer Jumps over to Candlestick," *Sport*, n.d., pp. 38–50.

3. Murray Chass, "Padres' Jones Fires Blanks," *New York Times*, May 31, 1975.

4. Anderson, *The Main Spark*, pp. 150–153.

5. Ibid., pp. 165–166.

SEVEN

1. Tiant, *El Tiante*, pp. 182–187.
2. Marty Bell, "You Can Go Home Again," *Sport*, n.d., p. 55.
3. Cataneo, *Tony C.*, p. 222.
4. Peter Gammons, "Lefty Lee Blue-Chipper on Bosox Mound Staff," *Sporting News*, June 14, 1975.
5. Diane K. Shah, "Sky the Limit for Bosox Bill Lee," *Dow Jones-Ottoway News Service*, August 23, 1974.
6. Fred Lynn, telephone conversation with author, July 20, 2001.
7. Lee, *The Wrong Stuff*, p. 133.
8. Dave Anderson, "The Other Free Agent," *New York Times*, February 29, 1976.
9. Ibid.
10. "McNally Quits: No More Oomph," *New York Post*, June 10, 1975.
11. Dan Coughlin, "Pride Was Worth More Than Money," *Plain Dealer*, May 5, 1980.
12. "McNally Improves," *Sporting News*, July 19, 1975.
13. *New York Times*, June 28, 1975.
14. Lee, *The Wrong Stuff*, p. 130.
15. Ibid., p. 131.
16. Munson, *Thurman Munson*, p. 112.

EIGHT

1. Anderson, *The Main Spark*, p. 168.
2. Pete Axthelm with Vern E. Smith, "The Amazing Randy," *Newsweek*, June 21, 1976, p. 57.

NINE

1. James S. Kunen, "Billy Martin Will Never Finish Last," *Sport*, August 1975, pp. 26–27.
2. Newhan, "Royal Treatment."
3. Garrity, *The George Brett Story*, pp. 122–125.

PART THREE: THE ALL-STAR BREAK

TEN

1. *Atlanta Constitution*, July 16, 1975.
2. Sheryl Flatow, "Steve Garvey of Los Angeles," *Sport*, n.d., pp. 81–82.
3. Yastrzemski, *Baseball*, p. 244.

4. Phil Collier, "Altar Boy Jones Works Padre Hill Miracle," *Sporting News*, September 6, 1975.

5. Kuhn, *Hardball*, p. 150.

PART FOUR: THE SEASON'S SECOND HALF

ELEVEN

1. Lyle, *The Bronx Zoo*, pp. 23, 26–27.

2. Murray Chass, "Lethargic Attitude Blamed by Some for Yank Decline," *New York Times*, August 3, 1975.

3. Martin, *Number One*, pp. 19–20.

4. Sullivan, *Bobby Bonds*, p. 118.

5. Flatow, "Steve Garvey of Los Angeles," pp. 86–87.

TWELVE

1. Tim Horgan, "It Happens Every Spring," *Boston Herald American*, May 19, 1975.

2. Don Freeman, "Winfield's the Name, Hitting's the Game," *Sport*, n.d., p. 70.

3. "Vickie: Marriage 'Broke My Heart,'" *The State*.

4. Gooden, *Heat*, pp. 10–12.

5. Tom Callahan, "Dr. K Is King of the Hill," *Time*, April 7, 1986, p. 56.

6. Ibid.

7. Richard Woodley, *Rookie* (Garden City, N.Y.: Doubleday, 1985), pp. 18–21.

8. Callahan, "Dr. K Is King of the Hill," p. 54.

9. Phil Collier, "Padres' Jones Forging Brilliant Hill Log," *Sporting News*, August 23, 1975.

THIRTEEN

1. Tiant, *El Tiante*, pp. 194–196.

2. Rains, *Mark McGwire*, pp. 11–20.

3. Newhan, "Royal Treatment"; also Garrity, *The George Brett Story*, pp. 123–125.

4. Henderson, *Off Base*, pp. 29–32.

5. Ibid., p. 9.

6. Falkner, *The Last Hero*, pp. 200–203.

7. Mantle, *The Mick*, p. 235.

8. Martin, *Number One*, pp. 21–22.

9. Glenn Schwartz, "Four-Hurler 'No-No' Caps Fine Season for Awesome A's," *San Francisco Examiner*, September 29, 1975.

10. Ibid.

11. "Four A's Pitchers No-Hit Angels and Set Record," *Los Angeles Times*, September 29, 1975.

12. Schwartz, "Four-Hurler 'No-No' Caps Fine Season for Awesome A's."

13. Rich Marazzi, "Dave McNally Had an Impact on Baseball On and Off the Field," *Sports Collectors Digest*, June 6, 1997.

14. Ross Newhan, "Messersmith Signs Off on No. 19," *Los Angeles Times*, September 28, 1975.

PART FIVE: THE POSTSEASON

1. Glenn Schwartz, "Holtzman A's Starter in Opener," *San Francisco Examiner*, September 26, 1975.

2. Glenn Schwartz, "Oakland's Sweetest Divisional Title," *San Francisco Examiner*, September 25, 1975.

3. Cataneo, *Tony C.*, p. 224.

4. Pepe, *Talkin' Baseball*, pp. 198–199.

5. The thoughts and strategies of Boston's players and coaches come from published newspaper accounts of the time — primarily the *Boston Globe* and *Sports Illustrated* — as well as from Lenihan, "Baseball Helps Carbo"; Zimmer, *Zim*, pp. 107–115; Lee, *The Wrong Stuff*, pp. 132–141; Yastrzemski, *Baseball*, pp. 245–251.

6. Primary sources for thoughts and strategies of Pittsburgh's players, coaches, and announcers include Smizik, *The Pittsburgh Pirates*; Stargell, *Willie Stargell*, pp. 166–172; Hall, *Dock Ellis in the Country of Baseball*; Adelman, *Out of Left Field*; and newspaper accounts of the time (primarily the *Sporting News* and *Sports Illustrated*).

7. Yastrzemski, *Yaz*, pp. 33, 37.

8. Bud Collins, "Ken Griffey — Once a Meter Reader, Now a Red Sox Beater," *Boston Globe*, October 13, 1975.

9. Stargell, *Willie Stargell*, pp. 2–3, 171–172.

10. Lee, *The Wrong Stuff*, p. 135.

11. Stout, *Red Sox Century*, p. 356.

12. Zimmer, *Zim*, p. 111.

13. Larry Claflin, "Odd-Ball Lee Puts Bosox Rivals Behind Eight Ball," *Sporting News*, July 14, 1973.

14. Stout, *Red Sox Century*, p. 371.

15. Lee, *The Wrong Stuff*, p. 133.

16. Lenihan, "Baseball Helps Carbo."

17. Pepe, *Talkin' Baseball*, pp. 192–194.

18. Richman, "Sparky 'Like Father' to Bernie Carbo."

19. Tiant, *El Tiante*, pp. 216–217.

20. Primary sources for the World Series thoughts, comments, and strategies of Cincinnati's players and coaches include Pepe, *Talkin' Baseball*, pp. 172–210; Anderson, *Sparky!*; Anderson, *The Main Spark*; Hertzel, *The Big Red Machine*; Walker, *Cincinnati and the Big Red Machine*; as well as published newspaper accounts at the time, primarily from the *Cincinnati Enquirer, Boston Globe, Boston Herald, New York Times, San Francisco Examiner, Sporting News,* and *Sports Illustrated.*

21. Tiant, *El Tiante*, p. 219.

22. Lynn, telephone conversation.

23. Lee, *The Wrong Stuff*, p. 136.

24. Ibid., p. 137.

25. Ibid.

26. Yastrzemski, *Yaz*, pp. 37–38.

27. Ray Fitzgerald, "He Takes a Bit of Lee-way," *Boston Globe*, October 13, 1975.

28. Cataneo, *Tony C.*, p. 225.

29. "World Series Notebook," *Boston Globe*, October 18, 1975.

30. *Boston Globe*, October 20, 1975.

31. Ibid.

32. Dave Nightingale, "He Just Won't Let a Hero's Halo Fit," *Chicago Daily News*, October 22, 1975.

33. Cliff Keane, "Fisk: It Was Like Smashing into a Linebacker," *Boston Globe*, October 15, 1975; Peter Gammons, "Reds Win in Tenth, 6–5, as Red Sox Scream 'Foul,'" *Boston Globe*, October 15, 1975; Ray Fitzgerald, "After Tumult, the Shouting," *Boston Globe*, October 15, 1975.

34. Mark Ribowsky, "Baseball's Bench Jockeys Wage Verbal War with Inspired- and Telling- Venom," *TV Guide*, May 3, 1980.

35. Wells Twombly, "Tiant: You Cannot Pitch if You Have the Fear," *San Francisco Examiner*, October 16, 1975.

36. Lowell Reidenbaugh, "Series Sparks," *Sporting News*, November 1, 1975.

37. Tiant, *El Tiante*, p. 221.

38. Twombly, "Tiant: You Cannot Pitch if You Have the Fear."

39. Lee, *The Wrong Stuff*, p. 129.

40. Wells Twombly, "Fielding Hero Lynn Suddenly Got 'Tight,'" *San Francisco Examiner*, October 16, 1975.

41. *Boston Globe*, October 20, 1975.

42. Peter Gammons, "Perez's Bat Is Smokin', So's Gullett . . . Sox Fall, 6–2," *Boston Globe*, October 17, 1975.

43. "Gullett 'Lost a Little Bit' but Not Soon Enough," *San Francisco Examiner*, October 17, 1975.

44. "Rain Stops Series Again; Sixth Game Tuesday Night," *San Francisco Examiner*, October 20, 1975.

45. Yastrzemski, *Baseball*, pp. 81, 243.

46. "Ex-Pitcher Moret Fights Battle of His Life," *Star Sports*, January 27, 1987.

47. Madden, "To Hell and Back."

48. Ed Gillooly, "Carbo Heeds Williams' Tip," *Boston Herald American*, May 19, 1975.

49. Earl Lawson, "Now Only Reds Grinning at Ex-Clown Carbo," *Sporting News*, September 12, 1970.

50. "Eastwick Forgot 'Book,'" *Sporting News*, November 8, 1975.

51. Nightingale, "He Just Won't Let a Hero's Halo Fit."

52. Hertzel, *The Big Red Machine*, pp. 10–12.

53. "Fisk Homer Climaxes Thriller," *San Francisco Examiner*, October 22, 1975.

54. Ribowsky, "Baseball's Bench Jockeys."

55. "Evans' Sensational Catch Balks Reds," *San Francisco Examiner*, October 22, 1975.

56. Fred Lynn, conversation with author, Carlsbad, Calif., July 9, 2001.

57. Reston, *Collision at Home Plate*, p. 101.

58. Lee, *The Wrong Stuff*, p. 140.

59. Alan Schwartz, "A Shot Seen 'Round the World,'" *New York Times*, October 15, 2000; also "Coyle Left Lasting Mark on Sports TV," *New York Post*, February 21, 1996.

60. Pepe, *Talkin' Baseball*, p. 208.

61. *Boston Globe*, October 23, 1975.

62. "After Fisk's Swing, Church Bells Ring," *San Francisco Examiner*, October 22, 1975.

63. Pepe, *Talkin' Baseball*, p. 209.

64. Ibid.

65. Lee, *The Wrong Stuff*, p. 140.

66. Dave Nightingale, "What Blistered Lee Wasn't Just His Thumb," *Chicago Daily News*, October 21, 1975.

67. Lee, *The Wrong Stuff*, p. 141.

68. Hecht, "Lee Tosses Some Gripes," *New York Post*, October 23, 1975.

69. Yastrzemski, *Baseball*, pp. 250–251.

70. "Vickie: Marriage 'Broke My Heart,'" *The State*; also Barbara Walder, "Johnny Bench on Marriage . . . and Divorce," *Philadelphia Inquirer*, October 20, 1976.

71. *Boston Globe*, October 23, 1975.

72. Ibid.

73. Reston, *Collision at Home Plate*, pp. 116–120.

74. Nightingale, "What Blistered Lee Wasn't Just His Thumb."

75. Henderson, *Off Base*, p. 44.

CONCLUSION

1. Miller, *A Whole Different Ball Game*, p. 245.

2. Tracy Ringolsby, "'Last Victory' Still a Gem for McNally," *Sporting News*, August 1, 1981.

3. Anderson, "The Other Free Agent."

4. Miller, *A Whole Different Ball Game*, p. 251.

SELECTED BIBLIOGRAPHY

BOOKS

Aaron, Hank, with Lonnie Wheeler. *I Had a Hammer: The Hank Aaron Story.* New York: Harper Collins, 1991.

Adelman, Bob, and Susan Hall. *Out of Left Field: Willie Stargell and the Pittsburgh Pirates.* New York: Two Continents Publishing Group, 1976.

Allen, Dick, with Tim Whitaker. *Crash: The Life and Times of Dick Allen.* New York: Ticknor & Fields, 1989.

Allen, Maury. *Memories of the Mick.* Dallas: Taylor, 1997.

———. *You Could Look It Up: The Life of Casey Stengel.* New York: Times Books, 1979.

Anderson, Sparky, with Dan Ewald. *Sparky!* New York: Prentice Hall, 1990.

Anderson, Sparky, with Si Burick. *The Main Spark: Sparky Anderson and the Cincinnati Reds.* Garden City, N.Y.: Doubleday, 1978.

Cataneo, David. *Tony C.: The Triumph and Tragedy of Tony Conigliaro.* Nashville, Tenn.: Rutledge Hill, 1997.

Christopher, Matt. *At the Plate with Ken Griffey Jr.* Boston: Little, Brown, 1997.

Clark, Ellery Harding. *Red Sox Forever.* Hicksville, N.Y.: Exposition, 1977.

Creamer, Robert W. *Casey Stengel: His Life and Times*. New York: Simon & Schuster, 1984.

Drucker, Malka, with George Foster. *The George Foster Story*. New York: Holiday House, 1979.

Falkner, David. *The Last Hero: The Life of Mickey Mantle*. New York: Simon & Schuster, 1995.

Flood, Curt, with Richard Carter. *The Way It Is*. New York: Trident, 1970.

Gooden, Dwight, with Bob Klapisch. *Heat: My Life on and off the Diamond*. New York: William Morrow, 1999.

Goodman, Michael. *Barry Bonds*. Mankato, Minn.: Creative Education, 1997.

Gutman, Bill. *Ken Griffey Jr.: A Biography*. New York: Pocket Books, 1998.

———. *Ken Griffey Sr. and Ken Griffey Jr.: Father and Son Teammates*. Brookfield, Conn.: Millbrook, 1993.

Hall, Donald C., with Dock Ellis. *Dock Ellis in the Country of Baseball*. New York: Simon & Schuster, 1989.

Harvey, Miles. *Barry Bonds: Baseball's Complete Player*. Chicago: Children's Press, 1994.

Henderson, Rickey, with John Shea. *Off Base: Confessions of a Thief*. New York: Harper Collins, 1992.

Hertzel, Bob. *The Big Red Machine*. New York: Prentice Hall, 1976.

Hunter, James, with Armen Keteyian. *Catfish: My Life in Baseball*. New York: McGraw Hill, 1988.

Jackson, Reggie, with Bill Libby. *Reggie*. Chicago: Playboy Press, 1975.

Koppett, Leonard. *The Man in the Dugout*. New York: Crown, 1993.

Kuhn, Bowie. *Hardball: The Education of a Baseball Commissioner*. New York: Times Books, 1987.

Lawson, Earl. *Cincinnati Seasons: 34 Years with the Reds*. South Bend, Ind.: Diamond Communications, 1987.

Lee, Bill, with Dick Lally. *The Wrong Stuff*. New York: Viking, 1984.

Libby, Bill. *Catfish: The Three-Million-Dollar Pitcher*. New York: Coward, McCann & Geoghegan, 1976.

———. *Thurman Munson: Pressure Player*. New York: G. P. Putnam's Sons, 1978.

Lyle, Sparky, with Peter Golenbock. *The Bronx Zoo*. New York: Crown, 1979.

MacLean, Norman. *Casey Stengel: A Biography*. New York: Drake, 1976.

Macnow, Glen. *Ken Griffey Jr.: Star Outfielder*. Springfield, N.J.: Enslow, 1997.

Mantle, Mickey, with Herb Gluck. *The Mick.* Garden City, N.Y.: Doubleday, 1985.

Martin, Billy, with Peter Golenbock. *Number One.* New York: Delacorte, 1980.

Miller, Marvin. *A Whole Different Ball Game: The Sport and Business of Baseball.* New York: Birch Lane, 1991.

Munson, Thurman, with Martin Appel. *Thurman Munson: An Autobiography.* New York: Coward, McCann & Geoghegan, 1978.

Muskat, Carrie. *Barry Bonds.* Philadelphia, Pa.: Chelsea House, 1997.

Nicholson, Lois P. *Casey Stengel.* New York: Chelsea House, 1995.

———. *Ken Griffey Jr.* Philadelphia, Pa · Chelsea House, 1997.

Owens, Tom. *Ken Griffey Jr.: A Super Center Fielder.* New York: PowerKids, 1997.

Pepe, Phil. *Talkin' Baseball: An Oral History of Baseball in the '70s.* New York: Ballantine Books, 1998.

Rains, Rob. *Mark McGwire: Home Run Hero.* New York: St. Martin's Paperback, 1999.

Rambeck, Richard. *Barry Bonds.* Plymouth, Minn.: Child's World, 1995.M

Reston, James, Jr. *Collision at Home Plate: The Lives of Pete Rose and Bart Giamatti.* New York: Harper Collins, 1991.

Robinson, Frank, with Dave Anderson. *Frank: The First Year.* New York: Holt, Rhinehart, & Winston, 1976.

Rolfe, John. *Ken Griffey Jr.* New York: Bantam Books, 1995.

Rose, Pete, with Roger Kahn. *Pete Rose: My Story.* New York: MacMillan, 1989.

Savage, Jeff. *Barry Bonds: Mr. Excitement.* Minneapolis, Minn.: Lerner, 1997.

Schneider, Russell J. *Frank Robinson: The Making of a Manager.* New York: Coward, McCann & Geoghegan, 1976.

Smizik, Bob. *The Pittsburgh Pirates: An Illustrated History.* New York: Walker, 1990.

Sokolove, Michael Y. *Hustle: The Myth, Life, and Lies of Pete Rose.* New York: Simon & Schuster, 1990.

Stambler, Irwin. *Catfish: The Three-Million-Dollar Arm.* New York: G. P. Putnam's Sons, 1976.

Stargell, Willie, with Tom Bird. *Willie Stargell: An Autobiography.* New York: Harper & Row, 1984.

Stout, Glenn, and Richard A. Johnson. *Red Sox Century.* New York: Houghton Mifflin, 2000.

Sullivan, Michael John. *Sports Great Barry Bonds.* Springfield, N.J.:
Enslow, 1995.

Tiant, Luis, and Joe Fitzgerald. *El Tiante: The Luis Tiant Story.* Garden
City, N.Y.: Doubleday, 1976.

Twyman, Gib. *Born to Hit: The George Brett Story.* New York: Random
House, 1982.

Walker, Robert Harris. *Cincinnati and the Big Red Machine.* Blooming-
ton, Ind.: Indiana University Press, 1988.

Yastrzemski, Carl, with Al Hirshberg. *Yaz.* New York: Tempo Books,
1968.

Yastrzemski, Carl, with Gerald Eskenazi. *Baseball, the Wall, and Me.*
Garden City, N.Y.: Doubleday, 1990.

Zimmer, Don, with Bill Madden. *Zim: A Baseball Life.* Kingston, N.Y.:
Total/Sports Illustrated, 2001.

PERIODICALS
For years 1974–76

Baseball Digest	*New York Post*
Boston Globe	*New York Times*
Boston Herald	*San Francisco Chronicle*
Cincinnati Enquirer	*Sporting News*
Los Angeles Times	*Sports Illustrated*
Milwaukee Courier	*Tampa Tribune*
New York Daily News	

ACKNOWLEDGMENTS

I AM GRATEFUL to my agent, Richard Abate, for thinking up this book and then believing that I was capable of writing it. If it is readable at all, the credit must go to my editor, Geoff Shandler. I cannot stress enough how fortunate I was to receive the insights and suggestions of two men as perceptive as Geoff and Richard.

The difficult task of copyediting this mess fell to the kind and patient Karen Landry. Quite simply, there is no one on this planet who could have done as good a job.

Editorial assistant Elizabeth Nagle also helped enormously, steadying me with her smart, sturdy manner.

Thanks to Fred Lynn, Dick O'Connell, Bill Lee, Rawly Eastwick, and others who took the time to talk to me.

Librarians everywhere encouraged me, as certainly they encourage every writer simply by treating books as good and (occasionally) important things. Special thanks must be extended to Deborah Ormon and her hardworking staff at the North Quincy branch of the Thomas Crane Public

Library, as well as to Timothy J. Wiles and his eager coworkers at the A. Bartlett Giamatti Research Center of the National Baseball Hall of Fame and Museum, including Eric Enders, Claudette Burke, Rachael Kepner, W. C. Burdick, Nadine Karel, Patricia Vignola, Brand Vawter, Brian Moynahan, Matt Schoss, Carl Cambria, Dan D'Addona, and Eric Poulin.

My barber, Bob Ciulla, and the various patrons of Squantum Cutters offered reminiscences and opinions. I always left Bob's shop laughing, wildly enthusiastic to return to this book.

I learned much about the game from my brothers, Marty and Jim. They managed my Little League team one year. We did pretty well; more important, we had much fun.

Most of all, I must thank Hannah Ross, my beautiful wife. I simply could not have written this without her support. Thank you, sweetheart.

INDEX

Aaron, Henry "Hank," "Hammer," 28, 68, 115, 116, 118, 135, 239–240; batting average, 71

Abbott, Glenn, 156, 161–162

Allen, Dick, 87, 107, 135, 144, 145; as MVP, 159; quoted, vii, 107; traded, 20, 21–22, 75–76

Allietta, Bob, 80

all-star games, 115–120

Alomar, Sandy, 51

Alou, Matty, 305

Alston, Walter "Smoky," 10, 100, 104, 120, 342, 344; relationship with players, 105, 137–138, 197

American League (AL): in all-star games, 116, 119, 120, (1975 lineup) 117; best players, 15; championship, 170, 199; East and West, 18, 45, 85, 94, 156, 158–159, (standings) 46, 68, 71, 78, 97, 109, 116, 128, 140, 149; innovations, 8, 19; Manager of the Year (1974), 135; MVPs, 21, 110, 116, 159, 214. See also entries for teams belonging to

Anderson, Albert, 45

Anderson, George "Sparky," 33–35, 43, 60, 66, 76–77, 99–100, 102, 197, 326; and Carbo, 37–38, 44–45,

140–141, 221–222; and Foster, 53, 55, 61, 74–75, 140, 152–154; as player, 23; in play-offs, 195, 198, 207–208, 211; relations with son, 63–64, 140, 213; and relief pitching, 104–107; and World Series, 223–224, 231, 234–248 passim, 253–254, 259, 265–266, 274–277, 284, 287–288, 294–295, 298–313 passim, 318–324 passim, 330

Anderson, Lee, 45, 63–64, 140, 141, 213

Anderson, Mrs. George (Carol), 34, 45, 253, 320

Anderson, Shirlee, 107

Arlington Stadium, 111, 122

Armbrister, Ed, 53, 102, 212; in play-offs, 194, 195, 211; in World Series, 264–267, 270, 277–278, 281, 300, 308, 310, 328, (in lineup) 257, 273, 299, 322

Astrodome, 88, 161

AstroTurf, 18, 75, 82, 147, 186, 251, 254

Atlanta Braves, 75, 99, 106; position in NL, 67, 96, 108, 127, 139, 148; Turner buys, 147, 343

Avila, Bobby, 246

Baltimore Orioles, 11, 45, 71, 89, 91, 94, 121, 170; best players, 46, 341; finances, 18; in play-offs, 188, 247; position in AL, 68, 97, 109, 128, 140, 149; uniforms, 62; winning streaks, 44, 158, 172; in World Series, 182, 198, 214, 307, 341

Bando, Sal, 29, 161, 162, 170, 171; in play-offs, 176–178, 180, 184, 188–190, 194, 204–206

Barnett, Larry, 264, 267–270

Barton, Marvin, 37

Baseball Bulletin, 144

Batista, Fulgencio, 72

batting averages, 64, 71, 74, 154, 211, 214, 275; Billy Martin's view, 109–110

Bench, Johnny, 30–37, 40, 42, 60, 76, 77, 142, 143–144, 152, 218–219, 310; in all-star game (1975), 117, 118; in Hall of Fame, 247; in play-offs, 182, 185, 190, 193, 197, 202, 205, 211; standing of, 63, 64, 65, 98, 154, (MVP) 33, 143, 214; in World Series, 231–232, 234, 236, 241–247 passim, 251, 258–260, 263–265, 274, 277, 285–290 passim, 300–301, 304–314 passim, 318, 323–333 passim, (in lineup) 229, 240, 257, 273, 284, 299, 321

Bench, Mrs. Johnny (Vickie Chesser), 30–37, 40, 42–43, 141, 143–144, 332–333

Beniquez, Juan, 46, 81, 82, 85; in play-offs, 176, 180, 203; in World Series, 276, 285, 302–305, 330, (in lineup) 273, 284, 321

Bennis, Dr. Warren, 225

Berra, Yogi, 33, 97–98, 101, 115, 174, 317

Bevacqua, Kurt, 94

Billingham, Jack, 105, 106, 107; in play-offs, 190; in World Series, 223, 239–246 passim, 274, 287, 289, 294, 300, 328, (in lineup) 240, 322

Bishop, Max, 9

Black Sox scandal (1920), 340

Blackwell, Tim, 85, 150

Blanks, Larvell "Sugar Bear," 99

Blue, Vida, 78, 123, 155–156, 160–161, 171, 194, 199; in all-star game, 116–118; in play-offs, 191, 193

Bonds, Barry, 50–52, 90

Bonds, Bobby, 50–52, 53, 81, 89, 93, 129, 132, 135, 174; in all-star game (1975), 117, 118; batting average, RBIs, 71, 90; Martin and, 160; traded to Yankees, 15, 45, 46, 62; and uniforms, 138, 344

Borbon, Pedro, 99, 106, 211–212; in World Series, 244–245, 275, 276, 301, 302, (in lineup) 240, 273, 299

Bosman, Dick, 180

Boston Bees, 25

Boston Braves, Babe Ruth with, 52

Boston Globe, 84, 159, 270

Boston Red Sox, 10, 68–69, 117, 123, 152; attendance at games, 18; as bad-luck team, 41–42, 43–44, 71, 72–73, 158–159; and color barrier, 85–86, 87; fans' expectations, 38–39, 47, 91–92, 172–173, 180–181, 212, 213, 215, 227; outfield problem, 40, 41, 44; in pennant race, (lose) 269, (win) 6, 17, 91, 129–130, 159, 209; in play-offs, 170, 176–181, 189–197 passim, 203–209 passim, 247; position in AL, 68, 78, 92, 97, 109, 128, 140, 149, (takes lead) 89, 93–95, 141; spring training, 45–46; winning streaks, 5, 78–82, 116, 133; in World Series, 47, 229–238, 240–252, 253, 256–282, 284–337, (defeated) 6, 14, 269, 331–333, 335–337, (pre-Series) 218–221, 225, (Series lineups) 229, 240, 257, 273, 284, 299, 321–322, (win) 237, 312; Yastrzemski signs with, represents, 4, 22 (*see also* Yastrzemski, Carl "Yaz"); Yawkey as owner, *see* Yawkey, Tom

Brennaman, Marty, 209

Brett, George, 48–50, 112, 152

Brett, Jack, 48–50, 111, 112, 152

Brett, Ken, 152, 185, 195, 212

Brett, Mrs. Jack (Ethel), 152, 156

Brett, Robin, 112

Brock, Lou, 102, 117, 118, 235

Brooke, Edward W., 73

Brooklyn Dodgers, 24, 25, 70, 189

Buckner, Bill, 137

Burleson, Rick "The Rooster," 14, 45, 46, 80, 85, 129, 151, 336; in play-offs, 180, 193, 194, 203–204, 206, 208; in World Series, 232, 236,

Burleson, Rick (*continued*)
  243–249 passim, 263, 264,
  274–276, 280, 283, 286, 296,
  301–303, 309–311, 323–328
  passim, (in lineup) 229, 240, 257,
  273, 284, 299, 322
Burrell, Louis, 28
Burrell, Stanley "Hammer," 28–29,
  154–156
Burroughs, Jeff, 110
Burton, Jim, 91, 173; in World Series,
  261, 329–330, (in lineup) 257, 322
Busby, Steve, 118
Bush, Joe, 237
Bushrod Park, 27, 28, 142

California Angels, 11, 40, 46, 80–81,
  112, 162, 269; position in AL, 68,
  97, 109, 128, 140, 149, 160; trades
  and acquisitions, 85, 161; weak
  hitting, 78–79, 151
Campanella, Roy, 33, 134
Campaneris, Bert "Campy," 78, 117,
  118, 161–162; in play-offs, 177,
  178, 180–181, 190
Candelaria, John, 198; in play-offs,
  202, 205, 207, 237, 271
Carbo, Bernie "The Clown," 43, 46, 81,
  82, 85, 268; Anderson and, 37–38,
  44–45, 140–141, 221–222; as
  throw-in, 212; in World Series, 249,
  261, 266–269, 302–303, 323–325,
  336, (home run) 306–307, 314, 321,
  (in left field) 308–309, (in lineup)
  240, 257, 298, 299, 321; and
  Yawkey, 41, 138, 222
Carew, Rod, 103, 111, 117, 120
Carlson, Dr. Kenneth, 201
Carlton, Steve, 260
Carroll, Clay "Hawk," 64, 105–106; in
  World Series, 229, 236, 261–262,
  301, 328, (in lineup) 229, 257, 273,
  299, 322
Carroll, Tom, 106
Carter, Gary, 77
Casey Stengel Park, 23, 24, 45
Castro, Fidel, 71–73, 226, 283
Cey, Ron, 117
Chalk, Dave, 161
Chambliss, Chris, 15, 71, 129
Chance, Frank, 11
Chaney, Darrel, 273, 299, 308

Chesser, Clyde, 33, 36, 41–43
Chicago Cubs, 11, 75, 79, 119, 159;
  position in NL, 67, 96, 108, 127,
  139, 148
Chicago White Sox, 18, 46, 62, 89–90,
  111, 119, 240; Dick Allen with, 21,
  159; position in AL, 68, 97, 109,
  128, 140, 149
Cincinnati Bengals, 249
Cincinnati Reds, 11, 22, 37–38, 46,
  61, 73–78, 103; in all-star game
  (1975), 117; Anderson as manager,
  see Anderson, George "Sparky";
  baseball inaugurated by, 59; as "Big
  Red Machine," 60, 65, (videotaped)
  218–219; leadoff hitters, 141;
  outfielders, 40, 183; in pennant
  race, 154, (win) 38, 53; in play-offs,
  182, 183–186, 189–195 passim,
  202–213 passim, 279, 325; position
  in NL, 67, 96, 104, 108, 127, 139,
  148; salaries, 36, 64; winning
  streaks, 107, 118, 137, 140; in
  World Series, 225, 229–237,
  239–282, 284–291, 294–330,
  (defeated) 214, (pre-Series)
  221–224, (Series lineups) 229, 240,
  257, 273, 284, 299, 321–322, (win)
  331–333, 337
Clemente, Roberto, 103, 182, 310
Cleveland Indians, 9, 18, 91–92, 135,
  147; Frank Robinson as manager,
  45, 61–62; Opening Day game
  (1975), 340; position in AL, 68, 78,
  97, 109, 128, 140, 149, 158; in
  World Series (1954), 246, 280
Cleveland, Reggie, 43, 45, 94, 129,
  261; in play-offs, 188, 189; in World
  Series, 257, 269, 281–282, 285–286,
  329–330, (in lineup) 257, 284, 322
Clyde, David, 110
Cobb, Ty, 84, 103, 195, 254–255, 315
Colburn, Jim, 95
Coleman, Jerry, 201
Coleman, Joe, 205
Colosi, Nick, 231
Conant, David, 312, 316
Concepcion, Dave, 64–65, 117, 118; in
  play-offs, 184, 190, 191–193, 202,
  207; in World Series, 232–236
  passim, 242, 244, 248–249, 258,
  260, 266–267, 276, 308, 312,

Concepcion, Dave (*continued*) 323–324, 327–329, (in lineup) 229, 240, 257, 273, 284, 299, 321

Conigliaro, Tony "Tony C.," 44, 85, 87, 135, 173, 256; home runs, 4, 39, 78; injured, 5–6, 94, (makes comeback) 7, 16, 45, 46, 68; retires, 158

Connelly, Gwen, 36

Connie Mack Stadium, 107

Connor, Bull, 86

Cooper, Cecil, 46, 85, 91, 336; in play-offs, 176, 180, 193, 196, 203, 208–209; in World Series, 230–231, 236, 241–243, 249, 258–259, 263, 298, 300–301, 328–329, (in lineup) 229, 240, 257, 299, 322

Corbett, Brad, 121

Cosell, Howard, 201

County Stadium, 94, 116

Coyle, Harry, 314–315, 316, 317

Cramer, Doc, 9

Creamer, Bob, 169

Cronin, Joe, 9, 216

Crosley Field, 35, 254

Crowley, Terry, 60, 152, 195, 273, 299, 308

Cy Young Awards, 8, 10, 59, 116, 341

Darcy, Pat, 76, 105–107; in World Series, 261, 262, 309, 311, 312–314, 316, (in lineup) 257, 299

Dark, Alvin, 29, 128, 155–156, 161–163, 227; Finley fires, 283; in play-offs, 170–172, 174–175, 178–181, 193, 196, 199, 204

Dedeaux, Rod, 162, 163, 200–201, 242, 253–254, 264, 314; at USC, 24, 79, 81, 152

Demery, Larry, 186

Dent, Bucky, 120

designated hitter introduced, 8, 19

Detroit Tigers, 71; Martin as manager, 109, (fired) 18; position in AL, 68, 78, 97, 109, 128, 140, 149, 158; v. Red Sox, 69, 82–84, 133–134, 159; spring training, 145

Dickey, Bill, 33

DiMaggio, Joe, 3, 145, 201, 216–217, 254; in old-timers' game, 97, 131, 134

Dobson, Pat, 15

Doby, Larry, 246

Dodger Stadium, 66

Doerr, Bobby, 216

Doubleday, Abner, 104

Doyle, Denny, 85, 129, 133–134, 158, 173; in play-offs, 176, 191–192, 194, 203–206, 209; traded, 293; in World Series, 232, 234–235, 241–243, 248, 263, 274, 276–277, 284–286, 300, 307–308, 311, 323–328 passim, (in lineup) 229, 240, 257, 273, 284, 299, 321

Drago, Dick (Richard A.), 158, 218, 292; in play-offs, 195–196, 207, 208–209; traded, 293; in World Series, 246, 247–249, 251, 267, 268, 307, 309–311, (in lineup) 240, 299

Driessen, Dan, 65, 299, 308, 322, 329

Dukakis, Michael, 225, 335, 336

Durocher, Leo, 11

Eastwick, Rawlins "Rawly" Jackson III, 66, 106, 107, 328; in play-offs, 195, 197, 207; in World Series, 249, 262–263, 277, 279–280, 288, 301–307, 309, (in lineup) 240, 257, 273, 284, 299

Ebbets Field, 25

Ellis, Dock, 116, 117, 212

Enberg, Dick, 160, 161, 162, 163

Esposito, Tony "Tony O.," 4

Evans, Dwight "Dewey," 45, 81, 82, 85, 151, 312; in play-offs, 179, 180; in World Series, 234, 242, 244, 258, 262, 266, 269, 275–276, 285–287, 302, 308–311, 321, 325, 327, 328, 336, (in lineup) 229, 240, 257, 273, 284, 299, 322

Everett, Albert and Carl, 146

Evers, Johnny, 11

farm system, 138

Fashion 70 magazine, 31

Feeney, Chub, 286, 342, 344

Feller, Sherm, 303

Fenway Park, 14, 170, 195, 223, 319; built (1912), 5; home runs at, 78, 93, 190; left-field wall (Green Monster), 6, 224, 229, 233, 249, 303, 323; NAACP pickets, 86; Opening Day at, 4, 68–69; shadows at, 315, 316

Ferguson, Joe, 137
Ferriss, Dave, 315
Figueroa, Ed, 81, 270
Fingers, Rollie "Buzzard," 123, 156, 163–164, 344; in play-offs, 193–194, 196
Finley, Charles O., 7, 29, 40–41, 123, 154–155, 170, 171, 343; and Dark, 29, 193, 199, (fires) 283; hated, 8–9, 15, 28, 121, 156; at play-offs, 197, 204
Fisk, Carlton "Pudge," 43, 79, 91, 92–93, 129, 213–214; injuries, 41–42, 44, 45, 85, 150, 158; in play-offs, 177, 178, 193, 194, 196, 204, 208; Rookie of the Year, Gold Glove, 214; in World Series, 232, 234, 236, 241–244, 248, 258–269, 275, 277–278, 285–286, 292, 306, 307, 309–315, 323–324, 326–330, (home run) 316–318, (in lineup) 229, 240, 257, 273, 284, 299, 321
Flood, Curt, 20–21, 22, 27, 76, 142, 144; and *Flood* v. *Kuhn*, 21
Flynt, Larry, 144
Foli, Tim, 77
Ford, Whitey, 15, 26, 130, 134, 135
Foster, George, 52–55, 61, 77, 101, 152–154; acquired by Reds, 52–53, 74–75, 102, 104; in play-offs, 189–190, 192, 193, 197, 202, 205, 207; in World Series, 229–234, 241, 248–249, 261–262, 275–276, 286, 290, 301, 308, 312, 316, 323, 327, (in lineup) 229, 240, 257, 273, 284, 299, 321
Foxx, Jimmie, 9, 216
Frederiksen, Rev. Victor, 36

Game of the Week (TV show), 145
Garner, Phil "Yosemite Sam," 177, 178, 191
Garrity, Judge W. Arthur Jr., 86–87, 92, 251
Garvey, Steve, 14, 61, 65, 117, 118, 137–138, 255
Gehrig, Lou, 11
Gerard, Lou, 314–315, 317
Geronimo, Cesar, 64, 65; in play-offs, 185–186, 192, 194, 195, 202, 205, 207, 211; in World Series, 234, 249, 260, 263–266, 276–278, 280–281,

301, 305, 312, 323, 325, 331–332, (in lineup) 229, 240, 257, 273, 284, 299, 322
Giamatti, Bart and Tony, 313, 316
"Gold Dust Twins," 47, 215
Gold Glove Award, 33, 40, 53, 130, 173, 214
Goldwater, Barry, 37, 187
Gómez, Lefty, 3, 15
Gooden, Dan, 145
Gooden, Dwight, 145–146, 344
Gooden, Ucleese, 146
Gossage, Rich, 119
Grapefruit League, 42, 46
Green, Dick, 234
Green, Pumpsie, 86
Griffey, Buddy, 210–211, 213
Griffey family, 278–279
Griffey, Ken, 53, 64, 77, 102, 141, 213; in play-offs, 184–185, 190, 192, 194–195, 202, 205, 207, 209–211; in World Series, 230, 234–236, 244–245, 248–249, 258, 261, 265, 274, 276, 278–279, 284, 300–301, 309–311, 323–324, 327–330, (in lineup) 229, 240, 257, 273, 284, 299, 321
Griffey, Ken Jr., 141–142, 209, 278–279, 329, 344
Griffin, Doug, 45, 85, 284, 286
Griffith, Clark, 9
Groh, Heinie, 201
Grote, Jerry, 97
Grove, Lefty, 100
Guidry, Ron, 130
Gullett, Don, 64, 99–100, 105–106; in play-offs, 183–186, 189; in World Series, 223–224, 230, 233–236, 282, 284–288, 311, 318, 322–325, (in lineup) 229, 284, 322

Hall of Fame, 25, 103, 247, 322, 326
Harper, Tommy, 181, 195–196
Harrington, John, 17
Harris, Franco, 39
Hartnett, Gabby, 33
Hassler, Andy, 79, 80, 81
Hearst, Patty, 70
Hebner, Richie, 184, 191, 202, 204, 211
Henderson, Bobbie, 27–28, 338–339
Henderson, Rickey, 27–28, 142–143, 338–339, 344

Henderson, Tyrone, 143
Herman, Billy, 134
Hernandez, Ramon, 209–210, 211
Herzog, Whitey, 128
Hicks, Louise Day, 86
Hoffa, Jimmy, 70
Hoffberger, Jerold, 121, 123
Holt, Jim, 180, 208
Holtzman, Ken "Jew," 78, 85, 156,
    163–164, 171–172; in play-offs,
    176–177, 180, 199, 203–204
Hooper, Harry, 312
Hornsby, Rogers, 3, 4, 52
Houston Astros, 11, 18, 88–89, 105,
    147, 212; position in NL, 67, 96,
    108, 127, 139, 148
Howard, Elston, 62
Hoyt, Waite, 15
Hubbell, Carl, 97
Hughson, Tex, 315
Hunter, James Augustus "Catfish," 7,
    156, 344; in all-star game (1975),
    119, 120; contract negotiations, 9,
    10–17, 19, (Finley and) 8, 170;
    leaves Oakland, 8, 128, 174; wins Cy
    Young Award (1974), 8, 10; with
    Yankees, 11, 14–17, 45, 46, 71,
    89–90, 93, 132, (Lee v.) 44, 129, 221
Hustler magazine, 144

Jack Murphy Stadium, 62
Jackson, Reggie, 84, 155, 159, 161,
    163, 171, 178, 344; in all-star
    game, 117; in play-offs, 174,
    179–180, 188–189, 191, 194,
    206–207; in World Series, 285, 286
Jenkins, Ferguson, 110
Jimmy the Greek, 170, 290
Johnson, Alex, 62
Johnson, Darrell "DJ," 43, 84, 214, 216,
    219–221, 227; criticized, 43, 292,
    294, 298, (fired) 293; in play-offs,
    173, 194, 195, 208; tactics, 81, 91,
    129, 197, 213; in World Series, 223,
    235–236, 247, 261–268 passim,
    277–278, 281–282, 286–287,
    300–305, 309, 312, 327–330, (and
    postgame analysis) 288, 335–336
Johnson, Walter, 226–227
Jones, Randy, 62, 100–104, 120,
    146–147, 153, 154, 223
Jones, Sam, 237

Kaat, Jim, 85, 119
Kaline, Al, 83, 91, 145
Kansas City Royals, 46, 48, 71, 82,
    111–112, 152, 156, 251; bid for
    Catfish Hunter, 12; manager fired,
    128, 171; position in AL, 68, 97,
    109, 128, 140, 149, 159; winning
    streak, 154
Kiley, John, 317
Killebrew, Harmon, 71, 111
Kingman, Dave, 55, 97
King, Nellie, 182–183, 184, 212
Kirby, Clay, 105, 106, 311
Kirkpatrick, Ed, 202
Kison, Bruce, 195
Kissinger, Henry, 241, 245, 246, 248
Koosman, Jerry, 101
Koufax, Sandy, 11, 60, 100, 105, 165,
    286
Kroc, Ray, 16
Kuhn, Bowie, 9, 19, 200, 245, 270,
    286, 342, 344; *Flood* v. *Kuhn*,
    20–21; reelected, 121–123
Kuzava, Bob, 26

Landis, Kenesaw Mountain, 123, 340
Landry, George, 270
Larsen, Don, 317
Larson, Dick, Scott, and Todd, 151
Lasorda, Tommy, 138, 201
Lau, Charlie, 48–50, 152
Lazzeri, Tony, 11
Lee, Andrew, 44
Lee, Bill "Big Bill," 79
Lee, Bill "Old Bill," 186–187,
    294–295
Lee, Bill "Spaceman," 42, 69–71,
    78–81, 87, 92–93, 95, 186–187,
    222; Catfish Hunter faces, 44, 129,
    221; Dedeaux and, 79, 152, 253;
    Johnson (DJ) and, 219, 220–221,
    268, 292, 294; injuries, 158, 172; in
    play-off, 179; traded, 293, (trade
    refused) 40–41; in World Series,
    223, 225, 237, 239–247, 250–252,
    259, 267–268, 281–282, 294, 311,
    314, 322–327, (in lineup) 240, 322,
    (pre- and postgame remarks) 270,
    289–290, 335, 336–337, (Tiant
    replaces) 294–295
Lee, Leron, 42
Lee, Mrs. Bill (Mary Lou), 44

Lewis, Duffy, 312, 316

Lindblad, Paul, 156, 162–163, 180, 204

Little League, 3, 11, 84, 187; all-star team, 146; World Series, 146

Lolich, Mickey, 69, 145

Lonborg, Jim, 315

Lopes, Davey, 137

Los Angeles Dodgers, 6, 10–11, 21, 46, 75–76, 100, 105, 165; in all-star game (1975), 117; bid for Catfish Hunter, 14; Garvey and, 137–138; O'Malley as owner, 120–122; in play-offs, 182, 325; position in NL, 67, 96, 104, 107, 108, 127, 139, 148; win NL pennant, 34, 43, 59–60, 64, 65; in World Series, 71, 174

Los Angeles Times, 69, 200

Louisville Colonels, 227

Lucchesi, Frank, 128

Luzinski, Greg, 159

Lyle, Sparky, 15, 130, 135, 165

Lynn, Fred, 44, 87, 94–95, 129, 172, 186, 245, 312, 336; in all-star game (1975), 118–119, 120; Dedeaux and, 24, 81, 253; as hitter, 43, 45, 81–85, 92, 134, 151, 158; in play-offs, 177, 193, 196, 204, 208; Rice and ("Gold Dust Twins"), 47, 215; in World Series, 236, 241, 244, 258–259, 261, 264–265, 274–276, 279–280, 296, 298–299, 307–308, 313, 324, 328–330, 333, (injured) 300, 301, 302, (in lineup) 229, 240, 257, 273, 284, 299, 322

Mackanin, Pete, 77

Mack, Connie, 11

MacPhail, Lee, 327

Maddox, Elliott, 15, 71

Maddox, Lester, 86

Madlock, Bill, 118, 119–120

Mantle, Mickey, 51, 135, 145, 146; in all-star games (1955 and 1975), 115, 116–117; drinking problem, 122, 157; in old-timers' game, 131, 134; Stengel and, 26, 37, 201

Marcum, Footsie, 9

Marichal, Juan, 232

Maris, Roger, 81

Marshall, Mike, 59, 60, 105, 137, 138

Martin, Billy, 78–79, 118–119, 197, 201; as ballplayer, 25, 26, 109, 344; manages Detroit, 109, (fired) 18; manages Oakland, fired, 344; manages Texas Rangers, 24–25, 26–27, 109–111, 122, (fired) 128, 131; manages Yankees, 131–136, 158, 160

Martin, Ned, 208–209, 336

Mason, Jim, 51

Matlack, Jon, 120

Matthews, Gary, 62

Mauch, Gene, 197

Maxvill, Dal, 284

Mayberry, John, 111–112

May, Lee, 45, 71, 140

May, Rudy, 130, 136

Mays, Carl, 227, 237, 315

Mays, Willie, 51–52, 62, 97, 280, 312

Mazeroski, Bill, 103, 304

McCarthy, Joe, 11

McCarthy, Tommy, 16

McCovey, Willie, 52, 140

McDonald's, 16

McEnaney, Will, 78, 106; in World Series, 236, 262, 303–305, 307, 330–331, (in lineup) 229, 240, 257, 299, 322

McGovern, George, 71–73

McGraw, John, 11, 25

McGwire, Mark "Tree," 151, 344

McHale, John, 88–89, 164–166, 342

McKeon, Jack, 128, 171

McNair, Boob, 9

McNally, Dave, 77, 88–89, 164; and Messersmith-McNally decision, 19, 165–166, 342–343, 344

McRae, Hal, 38, 48, 111, 120

Medich, Doc, 15, 93, 212

Messersmith, Andy, 6–7, 14, 59, 120, 138, 298; and Messersmith-McNally decision, 19–20, 165–166, 342–343, 344

Meyer, Danny, 69

MGM Grand, 30, 36

Miller, Marvin, 16, 17, 164–165, 342

Miller, Rick, 46, 82, 85, 129; in World Series lineup, 273, 299, 311, 321

Milwaukee Braves, 3, 18, 46, 115

Milwaukee Brewers, 64, 68, 71, 81, 104, 111–112, 121, 240; in all-star game (1975), 115–116; position in

Milwaukee Brewers (*continued*)
AL, 68, 97, 109, 116, 128, 140, 149,
(leads) 78, 94; winning streak, 91, 95
Milwaukee Millers, 25
Milwaukee Sentinel, 122
Minnesota Twins, 18, 46, 81, 109,
117; drop Tiant, 227; position in
AL, 68, 97, 109, 128, 140, 149
Monge, Sid, 163
Montgomery, Bob, 91, 150, 321, 330
Montreal Expos, 18, 76, 77, 105, 152,
293; McHale and, 88–89, 164–165,
342; position in NL, 67, 96, 108,
127, 139, 148
Moore, Monte, 179, 180, 194
Morales, Jose, 77
Moret, Rogelio, 85, 158, 194, 195,
218, 292; traded, 293; in World
Series, 265, 301, 303, 327–328, (in
lineup) 257, 299, 322
Morgan, Joe, 35, 75, 142, 154; in
all-star game (1975), 117, 118; as
hitter, 64–65, 76, 77, 218–219; joins
Reds, 36, 60; MVP, 189; in play-offs,
182, 185, 190, 195, 197, 202, 207,
211–212; in World Series, 231–233,
241–243, 251, 258–263, 265, 274,
278, 280–281, 285, 290, 301, 310,
317–325 passim, 328–330, (in
lineup) 229, 240, 257, 273, 284,
299, 321
Morgan, Tom, 62
Morton, Rogers, 286
Moseby, Lloyd, 142
Munson, Thurman, 15, 117, 132–133,
134, 136, 212; as hitter, 71, 90, 93,
129, 135
Murcer, Bobby, 51, 62, 118, 134
Murray, Jim, 200
Murtaugh, Danny, 195, 197–198, 207,
212
Muser, Tony, 94
Musial, Stan, 11, 81, 115, 116, 117, 210
MVPs (Most Valuable Players): AL, 21,
110, 116, 159, 214; NL, 33, 64, 143,
189, 214; World Series, 301, 306

NAACP (National Association for the
Advancement of Colored People),
86; team named for, 142
National League (NL): in all-star game
(1975), 116, 118, 119, (lineup)

117, (wins) 120; Championship
Series, 189, 205; East and West, 46,
152, 159, (standings) 67, 96, 108,
127, 139, 148; introduces
AstroTurf, 19; MVPs, 33, 64, 143,
189, 214; traditional first game, 59;
World Series losses, 11. *See also
entries for teams belonging to*
Negro Leagues, 19, 70, 85
Nettles, Graig, 15, 117, 129
Newcombe, Don, 97
New York Cubans, 69
New York Giants, 11, 25, 246
New York Mets, 11, 25, 55, 62, 101,
159, 220; Old-Timers' Day, 97–99;
position in NL, 67, 96, 108, 127,
139, 148; win play-offs (1973), 189
New York Post, 133
New York Yankees, 61–62, 80, 89–90,
98, 132; in all-star game (1975),
117; Catfish Hunter with, *see*
Hunter, James Augustus "Catfish";
defeated, 25, 122, 129–130, 304;
longevity of, 11; managers, (Martin)
131–136, 158, 160, (Stengel) 11,
25–26, 109, 145, 169, 221, (Stengel
fired) 15; position in AL, 68, 78,
91–94, 96, 109, 128, 140, 149,
(leads) 44, 46; Steinbrenner as
owner, 9, 15, 121, 131; trades by,
40, 51–52, 123, 212; and World
Series, 15, 25–26, 109, 214,
(defeated) 304
Niekro, Phil "Knucksie," 99
night games, first, 59; World Series, 8
Nixon, Richard, 9, 72
Nolan, Gary, 63, 64, 75, 77–78, 103,
105, 106; in play-offs, 198, 202,
205; in World Series, 256, 258,
260–262, 294, 299–300, (in lineup)
257, 299
Nolan, Ray, 299
Norman, Fredie, 63, 105, 106; in
play-offs, 189, 190–192, 193, 194,
197; in World Series, 273–276, 294,
300, (in lineup) 273, 299
Norris, Mike, 163
North, Billy, 171; in play-offs,
176–178, 180, 196, 208

Oakland Athletics, 34, 39, 44, 46, 71,
78, 159, 161–162; in all-star game

Oakland Athletics (*continued*)
(1975), 117, 119; attendance at
games, 18, 40, 121, 155, 174; Catfish
Hunter leaves, 8–11, 128, 174; Finley
and, 7–9 (*see also* Finley, Charles O.);
Martin as manager, 344; in play-offs,
170–172, 176–181, 184, 189–194
passim, 203–204, 208–209, 247,
260; position in AL, 68, 97, 109, 128,
140, 149, 154; win World Series,
10–11, 43, 71, 307, 344
Oakland Oaks, 25
Oakland Raiders, 39, 143
O'Connell, Dick, 41, 43, 206;
acquisitions by, 12–14, 15–16, 95,
227, 328
Odom, Blue Moon, 78
old-timers' game, 97–98, 131, 134
Oliver, Al "Scoop," 101; in play-offs,
185–186, 189–190, 192, 202,
204–205, 211–212
O'Malley, Walter, 120–121, 122, 342
O'Neil, Albert "Dapper," 86, 92, 323,
335
Orlando, Vince, 13
Orta, Jorge, 90

Palmer, Jim, 158, 170, 341
Parc Jarry, 76
Parker, Dave "Cobra," 40, 101,
102–103; in play-offs, 183–184,
191, 195, 202, 207, 211
Parnell, Mel, 221
Paul, Gabe, 169
Perez, Eduardo, 141
Perez, Tony "Mayor of Riverfront," 36,
60, 64–65, 103, 120, 141, 308; in
Hall of Fame, 326; in play-offs,
183, 185, 190, 197, 202, 271; Red
Sox view, 218–219; in World Series,
231–233, 236, 243, 247, 258–261,
263, 271–272, 276–277, 280,
283–287, 301, 312, 323, 326–330,
(in lineup) 229, 240, 257, 273, 284,
299, 321
Peterson, Bill, 142
Petrocelli, Americo "Rico," 4–5, 14,
43, 45, 78, 80, 85, 93–94, 129,
159, 173; in play-offs, 191, 193,
196; in World Series, 232, 236, 244,
259–267 passim, 285, 288,
300–301, 308, 313, 323–324, 328,

(errorless game) 336, (in lineup)
229, 240, 257, 273, 284, 299, 322
Pettis, Gary, 142
Philadelphia Athletics, 11
Philadelphia Phillies, 46, 79, 101,
106, 115, 159; Little Rock
franchise, 22; position in NL, 67,
96, 108, 127, 139, 148; trades, 20,
66, 75–76, 260
pinch-hitting, 305; early in game,
65–66
Piniella, Lou, 15, 129
Pink Floyd concert (Milwaukee), 94, 95
Pinson, Vada, 183
Pittsburgh Pirates, 22, 40, 46, 80,
101, 102–103, 116, 159;
attendance at games, 18, 39; in
play-offs, 181–186, 189–198
passim, 202, 204–207, 210–213,
279; position in NL, 67, 96, 108,
127, 139, 148, 152; win World
Series, 182, 197, 198, 304
Pittsburgh Steelers, 39, 161
Plummer, Bill, 103
Plummer, Robin, 333
Pole, Dick (Richard H.), 94, 218, 284,
286–287
Pony League, 187
Powell, Boog, 45, 61–62, 135
Powles, George, 142
Prince, Bob "Gunner," 103, 182, 184,
185–186, 190, 192, 194, 195; fired,
212

Quinlan, Karen Anne, 70

racism, 21, 22, 75–76, 85–87, 92, 146
Randolph, Willie, 207, 211–212
Reese, Pee Wee, 134
relief pitching, Sparky Anderson and,
104–107
Remy, Jerry, 85, 162
reserve clause, 20, 165
Rettenmund, Merv, 60–61, 152; in
play-offs, 195, 205; in World Series,
265, 325, (in lineup) 240, 257, 322
Reuss, Jerry, 117, 118; in play-offs,
181–183, 184–185, 209
Rhodes, James, 225
Rice, Jim, 43, 45, 102, 129–130, 134,
158–159, 336; Lynn and ("Gold
Dust Twins"), 47, 215; in outfield,

Rice, Jim (*continued*)
40, 44, 46, 81–82, 312; wins
double- and triple-A Triple Crown,
87; in World Series, 256–257, 296
Rice, Mrs. Jim (Jeannie), 87
Richardson, Bobby, 154
Rickey, Branch, 85–86, 154–155, 234,
340
Riverfront Stadium, 74, 254
Rivers, Mickey, 80
Rizzuto, Phil, 132, 201
Robertson, Mildred, 9
Roberts, Robin, 115
Robinson, Brooks, 111, 166, 310
Robinson, Frank, 27, 98, 137, 142, 183;
as manager, 45, 61–62, 340–341
Robinson, Jackie, vii, 19, 21, 26, 70,
85–86, 146, 340–341
Robinson, Mrs. Jackie (Rachel), 341
Robinson, Wilbert, 25
Rooker, Jim, 189, 190, 193
Rookie of the Year, 33
Rose, Fawn, 73–74, 333–334
Rose, Mrs. Pete (Karolyn), 333–334
Rosen, Al, 246
Rose, Pete, 35, 36, 53, 64–65, 73–75,
100–102, 141, 286, 333; in all-star
game (1975), 117, 118, 120; Foster
compared to, 153–154; hits by
(record), 254–255; in play-offs, 185,
190, 192, 195, 202, 205, 211, 325;
Red Sox view, 218–219; represents
Reds, 22, 60, (moves to Philadelphia)
76; in World Series, 230–237 passim,
241, 243, 254–255, 258, 260–265,
274, 276, 278, 281, 285, 290,
299–301, 308–310, 313, 318–320,
323–331 passim, (in lineup) 229,
240, 257, 273, 284, 299, 321
Rose, Petey, 141, 255, 334
Ross, Gary, 161, 173
Rudi, Joe, 40–41, 102, 117, 123, 159,
344; injuries, 173–174, 178; in
play-offs, 179, 191, 194, 196, 206
Ruhle, Vernon, 159
Russell, Bill, 137
Ruth, George Herman "Babe," 7, 69,
145, 174, 340; Aaron ties record of,
239; wins World Series, 237, 312;
with Yankees, 11, 25, (returns to
Boston) 52
Ryan, Nolan, 98

salaries, 9, 11–12, 14–16, 36, 38, 64,
131, 214
San Diego Padres, 46, 62–63, 89,
100–101, 103, 105, 146, 269; and
Catfish Hunter, 11, 16; manager,
219; position in NL, 67, 96, 108,
127, 139, 148
San Francisco Giants, 52, 53, 62, 95,
107, 344; attendance at games, 18,
121; position in NL, 67, 96, 108,
127, 139, 148
Sanguillen, Manny, 101, 103; in
play-offs, 185, 190, 192, 194, 202,
207, 211
Schaap, Dick, 301
Schmidt, Mike, 107, 159
Schoendist, Red, 197
Scott, George "Boomer," 86, 94,
111–112, 116, 120, 163
Seaver, Tom, 79, 118, 119, 205
Segui, Diego, 44, 218, 284, 287
Seitz, Peter, 19, 342–343
Selig, Bud, 115–116
Sewell, Rip, 3, 80, 326, 327
Shea Stadium, 89, 97, 106, 129, 143
Sheffield, Casey and Gary, 146
Shepard, Larry "Shep," 63, 106
Short, Bob, 122
Simmons, Ted, 165
Singleton, Ken, 45
slavery as analogy, 19–20
Smith, Hal, 303–304
Smith, Reggie, 38, 86, 260
Smith, Sherry, 312
Snider, Duke, 26
Southern League championship, 38
Speaker, Tris, 312
Sporting News, 95; Executive of the
Year, 328; Manager of the Year,
293; Player of the Year, 87,
159
Sport magazine, 301
Sports Illustrated, 25, 95, 169
spring training, 26–27, 39–42, 45–46
Stanley, Fred, 132
Stanton, Leroy, 161
Stargell, Willie, 22, 40, 100, 101,
102–103, 140, 145, 212; in play-
offs, 185, 189–192, 202, 207, 211
Steinbrenner, George, 15, 121,
130–132, 343; suspended, 9
Stello, Dick, 248

Stengel, Casey, 11, 23–24, 33, 37, 68–70, 79–80, 214–215, 220, 221, 337; as ballplayer, 145, 200, 236; and Billy Martin, 25–26, 109–110, 131, 135, 344; birthday celebration, 145; fired (as manager), 15, 304; in Hall of Fame, 25; illness, 157, 160, 162–163, (death and funeral) 166, 169, 200–201; at Mets Old-Timers' Day, 97–98; quoted, 25, 153, 154; in World Series, 25–26, 109, 145, 236

Stengel Field. *See* Casey Stengel Park

Stengel, Mrs. Casey (Edna), 98, 110

Stennett, Rennie, 103, 212; in play-offs, 190, 192, 202

Stephenson, Joe, 152

Stewart, Dave, 142

St. Louis Browns, 9

St. Louis Cardinals, 11, 46, 100, 159, 212, 350; in all-star game (1975), 117; position in NL, 67, 96, 108, 127, 139, 148; trades, 9, 38, 52, 75, 95, 260, (Flood) 20, 21; in World Series, 6, 21, 284

Stoneham, Horace, 20

Stowe, Bernie, 141

Sullivan, Haywood "Sully," 10

Sutton, Don, 59, 60, 118

Swann, Lynn, 172

Swoboda, Ron, 98

Tampa Tribune, 145

Tanana, Frank, 85

Taveras, Frankie, 184–186, 202, 211

Tebbetts, Birdie, 214

Tekulve, Kent, 193, 194

Tenace, Gene, 117, 120, 171; in play-offs, 176, 179, 194, 208

Terry, Ralph, 304

Texas Rangers, 12, 81, 121, 147; Martin as manager, 24–25, 26–27, 109–111, 122, (fired) 128, 131; position in AL, 68, 97, 109, 128, 140, 149

Thomasson, Hank, 142–143

Thompson, Bobby, 312

Tiant, Louis "El Tiante" Jr., 71–73, 78, 85, 149–151, 173, 177, 225–228, 247, 329; back and shoulder problems, illness, 41, 129, 151, 158, 227, 295; as gambler, 219, 273; in play-off, 170, 171–172, 176,

178–181; "vintage" performances, 69, 92–93; in World Series, 218, 268–269, 272–274, 276–282, 283, 294, 298, 300–302, 332, (game one) 221, 223, 228, 229–238, 242, 267, (in lineup) 229, 273, 299

Tiant, Louis Sr., 69–70, 72, 149–151, 186, 237–238, 299

Tiant, Mrs. Luis Jr. (Maria) and children, 149, 226, 329

Tiger Stadium, 18

Time magazine, 123

Tinker, Joe, 11

Todd, Jim, 180, 193, 204

Tolan, Bobby, 63, 165

Toledo Mud Hens, 25

Torre, Joe, 41–42, 97

Torres, Hector, 103

Torrez, Mike, 45

Triple Crown winners, 3, 6, 49

Turner, Ted, 147, 318, 343

Twitchell, Wayne, 101

uniforms, 5, 22, 61–62, 75–76, 89, 137–138, 344

Veterans Stadium, 107

Vietnam War, 70, 71, 73

Virdon, Bill, 130, 132–133, 135

Vukovich, John, 64, 65–66

Wagner, Honus, 103

Walberg, Rube, 9

Walker, Johnny, 158

Wallace, George, 86

Washington, Claudell, 40, 102, 119, 163, 171; in play-offs, 176–178, 180, 184, 191, 194

Washington Senators, 9, 122, 283

Watson, Bob, 88

Weaver, Earl, 11, 158, 198

Weiss, George, 25, 26

Wertz, Vic, 280

White, Roy, 15, 71

Wilhelmina Agency, 31, 144

Wilkerson, Mrs. Tommie, 28

Williams, Billy, 71, 159–160, 171; in play-offs, 178, 179, 196, 208

Williams, Dick, 4, 5, 112

Williams, Ted, 7, 13, 26, 61, 100, 162, 270; advice from, 4, 5, 305; hits by, 326, 327; wins Triple

Williams, Ted (*continued*)
 Crown, 3, 6; Yastrzemski compared
 to, 82, 217–218
Williams, Walt "No Neck," 62, 93
Willoughby, Jim (James A.), 95, 129,
 158, 173, 218; in World Series, 261,
 262, 266–267, 328, (in lineup) 257,
 284, 322
Wills, Maury, 201
Wilson, Don, 161
Winfield, Dave, 63, 142
Wise, Rick (Richard C.), 38, 43, 45,
 69, 93, 158, 218; in play-offs, 199,
 203, 206–207, 209, 214; in World
 Series, 237, 256, 259–260,
 311–312, 316, (in lineup) 257, 299
Woods, Jim, 209
Wood, Smoky Joe, 315
World Series, 171; *1916*, 312; *1918*,
 237; *1923*, 200, 236; *1946*, 14,
 215; *1952*, 25–26; *1953*, 109;
 1954, 246, 280; *1960*, 197, 304;
 1961, 214; *1967*, 6, 269; *1968*,
 284; *1970*, 77, 214, 307; *1970s*, 11;
 1971, 182, 197, 198; *1972*, 143,
 307; *1974*, 6–7, 14, 43, 71, 174;
 1975 pre-Series workouts,
 218–224; *1981*, 344; *1986*, 47;
 MVP, 301, 306; night games, 8;
 Stengel in, 25–26, 109, 145, 236;
 Yogi Berra in, 97. *See also entries
 for teams*
Wrigley Field, 106, 305
Wrigley, Phil, 20
Wynn, Jim, 117, 137

Yankee Stadium, 14, 17, 89, 139
Yastrzemski, Carl Sr., 186, 206,
 298

Yastrzemski, Carl "Yaz" Jr., 22, 26, 43,
 45–47, 85, 87, 186; ailments and
 injuries, 41, 158, 173, 176; and
 all-star games, 119, 275; batting
 average, 71; booed, 91, 92, 206;
 compared to Ted Williams, 82,
 216–217; at first base, 40, 308; Gold
 Glove Award, 173; hits by, 78, 129,
 130, 134, 177, (Rice outhits) 102; in
 play-offs, 176–177, 179, 180, 188,
 190, 192–194, 204, 206–207; as
 rookie, 3–5, 82–83; signing bonus,
 214; wins Triple Crown, 6, 49; in
 World Series, 233–235, 242, 244,
 248, 250, 261, 263, 267, 269–270,
 276, 281, 285, 299–300, 302,
 306–307, 309, 311, 323–324, 326,
 330–332, (in lineup) 229, 240, 257,
 273, 284, 299, 321, (moved to first
 base) 308, (postgame remarks) 336
Yastrzemski, Mrs. Carl Jr. (Carol),
 298, 299
Yastrzemski, Mrs. Carl Sr. (Hattie),
 206, 297–298, 299, 330
Yawkey, Tom, 19, 26, 138, 298; and
 all-star games, 119; and black
 players, 85–86; illness of, 17, 206,
 216; and pennant hopes, 17, 41, 95,
 199, 331–332; and salary
 arbitration, 9–10, 12–14, 15–17,
 38; and Yastrzemski, 4, 216–217
Yount, Robin, 94, 112

Zimmer, Don, 84, 134, 293; in play-
 offs, 177, 204, 214–215, 219–221,
 223; in World Series, 235, 241–242,
 262–263, 282, 307–309, 313, 326
Zisk, Richie, 182–183, 184, 189, 191,
 202, 207, 211